THE INSPECTOR GENERAL HANDBOOK

Fraud, Waste, Abuse, and Other Constitutional

"Enemies, Foreign and Domestic"

JOSEPH E. SCHMITZ

Inspector General of the Department of Defense,
2002-2005

"Whenever you inspectors general root out fraud,
waste, or abuse, you increase the confidence of the
American People in their government."

President George W. Bush, on the occasion of the 25th
Anniversary of the Inspector General Act of 1978

CENTER FOR SECURITY POLICY PRESS | Washington, DC

ISBN 978-0-578-00436-5

Library of Congress Control Number
LCTN 2013908696

CENTER FOR SECURITY POLICY PRESS, WASHINGTON, DC

THE CENTER FOR SECURITY POLICY
1901 Pennsylvania Avenue, Suite 201 Washington, DC 20006
Phone: (202) 835-9077
Email: info@securefreedom.org
For more information, please see securefreedom.org

Book design by DAVID REABOI

PRAISE FOR THE INSPECTOR GENERAL HANDBOOK

"Important reading for every inspector general."

–DONALD RUMSFELD
Secretary of Defense of the United States,
1975-1977 and 2001-2006

"Nobody knows the history, traditions, and functions of an Inspector General better than Joe Schmitz. *The Inspector General Handbook* is a practical guide for anyone working within an IG office who wants to serve in a constitutionally sound role as part of the leadership team. The IG in any organization should detect organizational performance problems early, and should enable rapid responses so that systemic problems can be addressed before they spread further or cause irreversible damage. This first-ever *IG Handbook* sheds light on an area of American government that is often misunderstood, frequently maligned, and yet indispensable to the functioning of our republic. This book is a 'must read' for all government leaders and for every lawyer who needs to know by what authority and for what purposes an Inspector General serves 'We the People' of these United States."

–JOHN ASHCROFT
former U.S. Senator and Attorney General
of the United States, 2001-2005

"The office of Inspector General can seem highly problematic, located within each executive department but reporting not only to the head of the department but also to Congress and, through Congress, to the public. Schmitz carefully examines the nature of the institution, and demystifies it while at the same time promoting respect for it. *The Inspector General Handbook* is a work of lasting value."

–MICHAEL B. MUKASEY
Attorney General of the United States, 2007-2009,
and U.S. District Judge for the Southern
District of New York, 1988- 2006

"Joe Schmitz' *Handbook* delivers a previously missing link in the understanding of post-9/11 law enforcement professionals who take an oath to support and defend the Constitution of the United States against all enemies, foreign and domestic. Of all public sector professionals, Inspectors General should be transparent; the American People ought never to wonder why an IG does what he or she does. And with Joe's *Inspector General Handbook*, that transparency is now achieved."

–LOUIS J. FREEH
Director, Federal Bureau of Investigation, 1993-2001

"The publication of this book fulfills a need that has existed for several years if not decades... Joe Schmitz has performed a singular service in writing this book... This book serves as a wonderful textbook for those who are selected to serve as an Inspector General. It also provides a source of understanding for those who rely on the efforts of Inspectors General to maintain the standards of integrity in both public and private service."

–LT GEN. RICHARD G. TREFRY, US Army (ret.)
Inspector General of the US Army, 1977-1983

"An Inspector General's mandate is to assure the integrity and efficiency of the governmental department within his charge. His duties range from the investigation of waste and fraud to the assurance that government agencies are operating within the scope of their authority. This requires the highest degree of integrity and independence, as exemplified by Joseph Schmitz's four years of service as IG for the Department of Defense. His book contains case studies illustrating the broad range of problems with which he had to deal during his tour of duty."

–JAMES L. BUCKLEY
former US Senator and US Circuit Judge for the DC Circuit, 1985-1996

"*The Inspector General Handbook* is excellently written from an insider point of view to teach about one of the most important organizational elements in any Federal Agency. Joe Schmitz never tires from teaching citizens and government personnel about the Inspectors General role in our Federal Government."

–FRANCIS "GENE" REARDON
Auditor General of the Army (1992-2003) and
Deputy Inspector General of the Department of Defense for Audit

"For everyone who does evil hates the light, and does not come to the light, that his deeds may not be exposed."

—Unattributed quote over the entrance door to the Office of the Inspector General of the Department of Defense, 2002-2005

DEDICATION

To our American "First Things," including those defining principles that underlie the Declaration of Independence, the Constitution, and the In-spector General Act of 1978.

CREDITS

The author would like to acknowledge and to thank Professor Paul Goldstein of Stanford Law School, who inspired the writing of this handbook by pointing out that, "We read every day in the newspaper about IG reports and testimony, but most of us haven't the faintest idea of what an Inspector General is" (or words to that effect). The author would also like to acknowledge the invaluable assistance of Gregg Bauer in editing the manuscript for this handbook. Finally, the author would like to acknowledge the patience and support of the author's wife of 35 years, Mollie, and of our eight children—Philip James, Joseph William, Nicholas Michael, Thomas Witbeck, Mollie Elizabeth, Patrick Carl, Katherine Theresa, and Matthias Kenneth—each of whom over the years has sacrificed personally one way or another for the production and publication of this handbook.

NOTE: The views expressed in this book are those of its author, and do not necessarily reflect those of the Department of Defense Office of Inspector General, an "independent and objective unit" within the Department of Defense (Inspector General Act of 1978 as amended, Section 2), or those of the United States of America. See Department of Defense Directive 5230.09, "Clearance of DoD Information for Public Release," August 22, 2008, Enclosure 2, Para. 3 ("The Inspector General of the Department of Defense, as an independent and objective office in the Department of Defense, is exempt from the policy review provisions of this Directive.")

http://www.dtic.mil/whs/directives/corres/pdf/523009p.pdf

CONTENTS

FOREWORD

The publication of this book fulfills a need that has existed for several years if not decades. The passage of the Inspector General Act of 1978, and the expanded concept of Inspector General in the various departments and agencies of the government as required by law, exerts an ongoing necessity for the book.

Within the Department of Defense each of the military services had long established positions and organizations of Inspectors General. As a matter of interest, there was no Inspector General at the Department of Defense level until the 1982 Amendment to the Inspector General Act of 1978 created the position.

The services objected to the establishment of such a position for a variety of reasons which resulted in the formation of a study that examined in detail the inspection, audit, and investigative establishments of each of the services. This study was called the Boutée Study. Dave Boutée was an official of Mobil Oil who was made available by that corporation for the purpose of determining how the Inspector, Investigation, and Audit functions of the services were organized and operated. This study remains today the most effective detail that delineates the Inspector General Organizations and functions in the Department of Defense.

Today when a citizen mentions the Inspector General institution, one immediately thinks of General Von Steuben and Valley Forge. This is not altogether a bad way of thinking, because the principal role of Inspector General is to be a teacher. Von Steuben filled that role superbly and probably this is his enduring legacy. In Lafayette Park, across the street from the White House, facing up Connecticut Avenue there is a statue of Von Steuben. On the plaque the tribute to him ends as follows: "He gave military training and discipline to the citizen soldiers who achieved the independence of the United States."

Sections 3039 and 5088 of Title 10, United States Code, spell out in law the functions of the service Inspectors General and the service auditors. In the case of the Army the law is brief and clear — "There is an Inspector General and he will determine and report on the economy and efficiency of the Army. He will also determine and report on the morale, discipline and esprit de corps of the Army."

When the IG Act of 1978 was being considered, the intent of its supporters in Congress was to pursue cases of fraud, waste, and abuse. So — instead of becoming teachers, the inspectors became cops. And so did the auditors! Notwithstanding this legislative history, it is interesting to note that every audit published by any audit agency usually has a statement to the effect that, "This audit was conducted according to generally accepted audit standards." This begs the question: What exactly are "generally accepted audit standards"?

Joe Schmitz has performed a singular service in writing this book, *The Inspector General Handbook: Fraud, Waste, Abuse, and Other Constitutional 'Enemies Foreign and Domestic'*. One is reminded of the warning of President John Adams in 1798, "Our Constitution was made only for a religious and moral people. It is wholly inadequate for the government of any other." The experience of the author as a member of the professional military, as a practicing lawyer in civilian life after his active duty service, and as the Department of Defense Inspector General for almost four years, provides a unique perspective to teach and train military and civilian leaders, inspectors, auditors and investigators to understand better their duties and responsibilities, whether in civilian or military endeavors, through better knowledge and understanding of the following:

* The "Accountability clause" of the Constitution of the United States, and why all public servants must take an oath to support and defend that Constitution;

* The differences between and among the military and civilian Inspectors General;

* Various provisions of the Constitution associated with endeavors by auditors, inspectors, and investigators that re-

quire decisions every day that implicate the statutory oath of office each of those officers has sworn (or affirmed); and

* The professional ethic that is the epitome of public service, requiring "the satisfaction of a social need" in the words of Professor Samuel Huntington.

This book serves as a wonderful textbook for those who are selected to serve as an Inspector General. It also provides a source of understanding for those who rely on the efforts of Inspectors General to maintain the standards of integrity in both public and private service. There is more to being an Inspector General than being "meaner than a junk yard dog," the term sometimes used by congressional and other supporters of the Inspector General Act of 1978.

It is well to remember that the two principal roles of any Inspector General are to be, first of all, the confidant of the commander (or, in civilian parlance, the agency head); and, second, to be the best teacher in any organization. Those who successfully fulfill these roles become by experience and discipline the best leaders in any military and/or civilian endeavor.

Richard G. Trefry
LTG, US Army Ret.

INTRODUCTION

Every American Inspector General takes an oath of office, whether "in the civil service or uniformed services," to "support and defend the Constitution of the United States against all enemies, foreign and domestic."[1] Inspectors General have the opportunity to live this oath every day, whether it be by supporting the "due process of law"[2] in the course of an investigation, or by supporting through inspections, evaluations, audits, or oversight activities, the constitutional mandate that, "a regular Statement and Account of the Receipts and Expenditures of all public Money shall be published from time to time."[3]

This book reflects my experiences as the former head of DoD's Office of Inspector General – generally considered the most expansive Inspector General organization in the world – from 2002 to 2005. The book is designed not only for teaching and training professionals assigned to Offices of Inspectors General throughout the federal government, but also for the benefit of government and corporate leaders who will need, sooner or later, to deal intelligently with an Inspector General. It is also a primer for students of American government who routinely ask themselves, whenever they hear or read about an Inspector General investigation, inspection, or report: "What in the world is an Inspector General?"

In plain English, this book explains by what authority and for what purpose an Inspector General does what he or she does on behalf of "We the People."[4]

Appendices further provide ready reference to the legal authorities upon and through which Inspectors General perform their duties. These include the Declaration of Independence, the Constitution, the Inspector General Act of 1978, as amended, the "Quality Standards for Federal Offices of Inspector General" published by the

President's Council of Integrity & Efficiency (PCIE), and the Inspector General Reform Act of 2008.

Someone once suggested that the Inspector General of the Department of Defense should develop an "IG Creed" along the lines of the traditional "Soldiers Creed," which begins and ends with, "I am an American Soldier."[5] Although never adopted as official policy, here is my best effort to define that creed, and in so doing, answer the question, "What in the world is an Inspector General?":

> I am an Inspector General in the United States Department of Defense, serving as an independent extension of the eyes, ears, and conscience of my commander.
>
> I am a paradigm of integrity, efficiency, accountability, and intelligent risk-taking.
>
> Dogged in the pursuit of the truth, I neither dictate to others in authority nor turn a blind eye.
>
> I show in myself a good example of virtue, honor, patriotism, and subordination.
>
> I am vigilant in inspecting the conduct of those placed under me, guarding against and suppressing all dissolute and immoral practices, including but not limited to fraud, waste, and abuse of authority, as I support and defend the Constitution of the United States against all enemies, foreign and domestic. So help me God.
>
> I am an Inspector General in the United States Department of Defense.

The case studies discussed in this book, which are mostly based on published reports, explore how IG professionals within DoD's Office of Inspector General subscribed to this creed, wittingly or unwittingly, when confronting some of the most vexing accountability challenges facing the Department of Defense and America in recent history.

Joseph E. Schmitz

Endnotes

---

[1] 5 U.S.C. § 3331.

[2] U.S. Const., Amend. V.

[3] U.S. Const., Art. I, § 9.

[4] U.S. Const., Preamble.

[5] United States Army, "The Soldiers Creed"
http://www.west-point.org/academy/malo-wa/inspirations/Creed.pdf

> "I am an American Soldier. I am a warrior and a member of a team. I serve the people of the United States of America and live the Army values. *I will always place the mission first. I will never accept defeat. I will never quit. I will never leave a fallen comrade.* I am disciplined, physically and mentally tough, trained and proficient in my warrior tasks and drills. I always maintain my arms, my equipment and myself. I am an expert and I am a professional. I stand ready to deploy, engage and destroy the enemies of the United States of America in close combat. I am a guardian of freedom and the American way of life. I am an American soldier.")

cf. United States Navy, "Sailors Creed"
http://www.history.navy.mil/library/online/creed.htm

> "I am a United States Sailor. I will support and defend the Constitution of the United States of America and I will obey the orders of those appointed over me. I represent the fighting spirit of the Navy and all who have gone before me to defend freedom and democracy around the world. I proudly serve my country's Navy combat team with Honor, Courage and Commitment. I am committed to excellence and the fair treatment of all."

cf. United States Air Force, "The Airman's Creed"

http://www.af.mil/shared/media/document/afd-070418-013.pdf

"I am an American Airman. I am a Warrior. I have answered my Nation's call. I am an American Airman. My mission is to Fly, Fight, and Win. I am faithful to a Proud Heritage, A Tradition of Honor, And a Legacy of Valor. I am an American Airman. Guardian of Freedom and Justice, My Nation's Sword and Shield, Its Sentry and Avenger. I defend my Country with my Life. I am an American Airman. Wingman, Leader, Warrior. I will never leave an Airman behind, I will never falter, And I will not fail."

PART A.

WHAT IS AN INSPECTOR GENERAL?

In order to understand what an Inspector General is, one must first understand that there are two kinds of Inspectors General: military and civilian. Military Inspectors General typically focus on "discipline, efficiency, economy, morale, training, and readiness."[1] On the other hand, the 2003 "Quality Standards for Federal Offices of Inspector General" published by the President's Council of Integrity & Efficiency outline the "fraud, waste, and abuse"-focused statutory mission of each civilian Office of Inspector General (OIG):

> OIGs have responsibility to report on current performance and accountability and to foster good program management to ensure effective government operations. The Inspector General Act of 1978 (IG Act), as amended, created the OIGs to:
>
> **1.** Conduct, supervise, and coordinate audits and investigations relating to the programs and operations of their agencies;
>
> **2.** Review existing and proposed legislation and regulations to make recommendations concerning the impact of such legislation and regulations on economy and efficiency or the prevention and detection of fraud and abuse;
>
> **3.** Provide leadership for activities designed to promote economy, efficiency, and effectiveness, and to promote ef-

forts to reduce fraud, waste, and abuse in the programs and operations of their agencies;

4. Coordinate relationships between the agency and other Federal agencies, State and local government agencies, and non-government agencies to promote economy and efficiency, to prevent and detect fraud and abuse, or to identify and prosecute participants engaged in fraud or abuse;

5. Inform their agency heads and Congress of problems in their agencies' programs and operations and the necessity for and progress of corrective actions; and

6. Report to the Attorney General whenever the Inspector General has reasonable grounds to believe there has been a violation of Federal criminal law.

In addition to audits and investigations referenced in item 1 above, OIGs may conduct, supervise, and coordinate inspections, evaluations, and other reviews related to the programs and operations of their agencies.[2]

Military Inspectors General share these same "fraud, waste, and abuse" missions with their civilian namesakes in at least two ways: First, they too are often called upon to "conduct, supervise, and coordinate inspections, evaluation, and other reviews related to the programs and operations of their agencies"[3]; and, second, uniformed military Inspectors General are subject to "policy direction" of the civilian Inspector General of the Department of Defense, who as "the principal adviser to the Secretary of Defense for matters relating to the prevention and detection of fraud, waste, and abuse in the programs and operations of the Department [may] request assistance as needed from other audit, inspection, and investigative units of the Department of Defense (including military departments)."[4] The military and civilian IG missions thus overlap, as demonstrated by the case studies in this book.[5]

According to the official biography for the Inspector General of the Department of Defense as of September 2005, "The statutorily 'independent and objective' Office of Inspector General employs approximately 1,300 civilian and military officers and employees, and provides oversight for another 60-80,000, primarily auditors, inspectors, and investigators, with an annual budget of more than $200 million. It includes as subcomponents the Defense Criminal Investigative Service (DCIS) and the Defense Financial Auditing Service (DFS). Based on post-Enron independence standards, the Inspector General is the only DoD Officer qualified to issue opinions on the financial statements of the DoD, the annual budget for which exceeds $500 billion. As the sole DoD representative on the President's Council on Integrity & Efficiency (PCIE) and, by law, 'the principal adviser to the Secretary of Defense for matters relating to the prevention of fraud, waste, and abuse in the programs and operations of the Department,' the Inspector General chairs the Defense Council on Integrity & Efficiency (DCIE), the members of which include component heads of the Audit, Inspection, and Investigative units of the military departments, and the Inspectors General of the other DoD agencies and major components."

Here is how the Department of Defense Office of Inspector General was organized in 2005, [6]demonstrating graphically how the DoD Office of Inspector General was designed to satisfy the Inspector General's statutory duty, among other duties, to "give particular regard to the activities of the internal audit, inspection, and investigative units of the military departments with a view toward avoiding duplication and insuring effective coordination and cooperation"[7]:

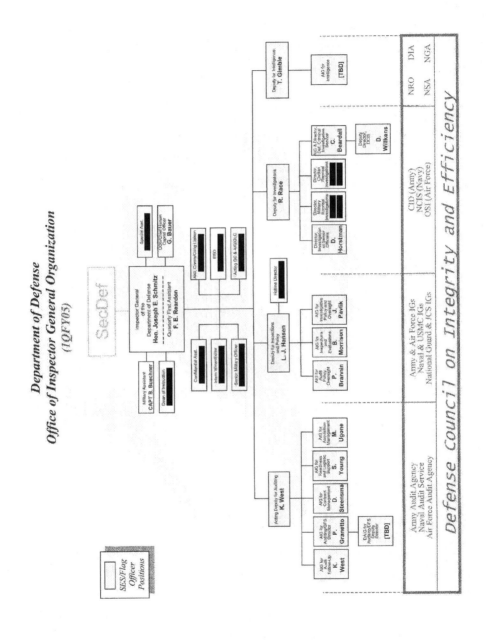

Department of Defense
Office of Inspector General Organization
(1QFY05)

SES/Flag Officer Positions

SecDef

Inspector General of the Department of Defense
Hon. Joseph E. Schmitz
Quarterly First Assistant
F. E. Reardon

Special Asst.

COS/Chief Human Capital Officer
G. Bauer

Military Assistant
CAPT B. Buechner

Dean of Instruction

Confidential Asst.

Intern Whistleblower

Senior Military Officer

AIG: Criminal/Cong Liaison

EEO

Acting DIG & AIG/OLC

Hotline Director

Acting Deputy for Auditing
K. West

Deputy for Inspections and Policy
L. J. Hansen

Deputy for Investigations
R. Race

Deputy for Intelligence
T. Gimble

AIG for Audit Follow-Up
K. West

AIG for Auditing/QIPS Director
K. B. Granetto

D/AIG for Auditing/QIPS Deputy Director
[TBD]

AIG for Contract Management
D. Steensma

AIG for Readiness and Logistic Support
S. Young

AIG for Acquisition Management
M. Ugone

AIG for Audit Policy Oversight
P. Brannin

AIG for Inspections and Evaluations
B. Morrison

AIG for Investigations Policy and Oversight
Pavlik

Director Investigations of all Senior Officials
D. Horstman

Director Military Personnel Investigations

Director Civilian Personnel Investigations

NCIS & Director, Def. Criminal Investigative Service
C. Beardall

Deputy Director DCIS
D. Wilkens

AIG for Intelligence
[TBD]

Army Audit Agency
Naval Audit Service
Air Force Audit Agency

Army & Air Force IGs
Naval & USMC IGs
National Guard & JCS IGs

CID (Army)
NCIS (Navy)
OSI (Air Force)

NRO   DIA
NSA   NGA

Defense Council on Integrity and Efficiency

[Source: http://www.dodig.mil/IGInformation/IGPolicy/Superpolicy12-27Print.pdf (last accessed August 29, 2010); consistent with Office of Inspector General policy, the names of junior employees have been redacted out of respect for privacy; Captain Bart Buechner, USNR, and Gregg Bauer, both consented to their respective names being included.]

---

[1] United States Department of the Army, Office of The Inspector General (OTIG) (http://wwwpublic.ignet.army.mil/IG_systems.htm) (last accessed August 30, 2010).

[2] President's Council on Integrity & Efficiency, "Quality Standards for Federal Offices of Inspector General," pp. 4-5 (October 2003) (footnotes omitted) (http://www.ignet.gov/pande/standards/igstds.pdf) (last accessed August 30, 2010); *see* United States Army, "Inspector General Systems" ("The mission of the [Office of The Inspector General] and [U.S. Army Inspector General Agency] is to inquire into, and periodically report on the discipline, efficiency, economy, morale, training, and readiness throughout the Army, to the Secretary of the Army and the Chief of Staff, Army.") (last accessed August 30, 2010); United States Air Force, Biography of The Inspector General (http://www.af.mil/information/bios/bio.asp?bioID=6956) (last accessed August 30, 2010) ("The Inspector General reports to the Secretary and Chief of Staff of the Air Force on matters concerning Air Force effectiveness, efficiency, and the military discipline of active duty, Air Force Reserve and Air National Guard forces."); United States Navy, "About the Naval IG" (http://www.ig.navy.mil/About_NAVINSGEN/Mission.htm) (last accessed August 30, 2010) ("Guiding Principles: To support the Department of the Navy in maintaining the highest level of integrity and public confidence we will: . . . Emphasize integrity, ethics, efficiency, discipline and readiness -- afloat and ashore."); United States Marine Corps, "Inspector General of the Marine Corps" (http://hqinetoo1.hqmc.usmc.mil/ig/) (last accessed August 30, 2010) ("Inspector General of the Marine Corps . . . mission is to promote Marine Corps combat readiness, integrity, efficiency, effectiveness, and credibility through impartial and independent inspections, assessments, inquiries, and investigations.").

[3] PCIE, "Quality Standards for Federal Offices of Inspector General," *supra*, p. 5; *see, e.g.,* United States Air Force, Biography of The Inspector Gen-

eral, *supra* ("The Inspector General provides inspection policy, and oversees the inspection and evaluation system for all Air Force nuclear and conventional forces; oversees counterintelligence operations and chairs the Air Force Intelligence Oversight Panel; investigates fraud, waste and abuse; oversees criminal investigations; and provides oversight of complaints resolution programs. He also performs any other duties directed by the Secretary or the Chief of Staff. The Inspector General is responsible for two field operating agencies: the Air Force Inspection Agency and the Air Force Office of Special Investigations.").

[4] Inspector General Act of 1978, as amended, § 8(c)(1)&(8).

[5] *Compare* Lieutenant Colonel Stephen Rusiecki, "Washington and von Steuben: Defining the Role of the Inspector General," The Journal of Public Inquiry, p. 35 (Fall/Winter 2003) (http://www.ignet.gov/randp/fw03jpi.pdf) (last accessed August 30, 2010), *with* Joseph E. Schmitz, "The Enduring Legacy of Inspector General von Steuben," The Journal of Public Inquiry, p. 23 (Fall/Winter 2002) (http://www.ignet.gov/randp/fw02text.pdf) (last accessed August 30, 2010).

[6] http://www.dodig.mil/IGInformation/IGPolicy/Superpolicy12-27Print.pdf

[7] Inspector General Act of 1978, as amended, § 8(c)(9).

CHAPTER 1. TRADITIONAL ROLES OF AN AMERICAN INSPECTOR GENERAL: THE OTHER FOUNDING FATHER

"He gave military training and discipline to the citizen soldiers who achieved the independence of the United States."

United States Congress, "Proceedings Upon the Unveiling of the Statue of Baron von Steuben, Major General and Inspector General in the Continental Army During the Revolutionary War" (1912)

Inspectors General, whether civilian or military, serve by tradition as an extension of their respective Commander's Conscience, guarding a Revolutionary War legacy of integrity, training and discipline; preventing and detecting fraud, waste, and abuses of power; and ensuring constitutional accountability ultimately to "We the People of the United States."[1] Leaders in both government and business, who may in their professional capacities need to interact with an Inspector General, should strive to become familiar with both the Inspector General's function and historical legacy.

According to tradition as well as to modern Army doctrine, an Inspector General serves as "an extension of the eyes, ears, and conscience of the Commander."[2] This tradition is closely associated with the traditional "teach & train" role of American military inspectors general. The U.S. Military Academy Inspector General website explains that an Inspector General must *"teach and train* at every opportunity."[3] This "teach & train" role is pounded into every student of the Army Inspector General School. General George Washington delegated this role to the first effective American Inspector General, Baron Frederick Wilhelm von Steuben.[4]

According to one 20th Century Army historian, "the military services of two men, and of two men alone, can be regarded as indispensable to the achievement of American Independence. These two men were Washington and Steuben... Washington was the indispensable commander. Steuben was his indispensable staff officer."[5]

The Steuben Monument graces Lafayette Park across from the White House in Washington, DC, along with monuments to Generals Lafayette, Rochambeau, and Kosciuszko. All four "testify to the gratitude of the American people to those from France, from Poland, and from Prussia who aided them in their struggle for national independence and existence."[6] Steuben's monument proclaims an artful, albeit understated, synopsis of Inspector General von Steuben's role in the birth of our nation: "He gave military training and discipline to the citizen soldiers who achieved the independence of the United States." These words bespeak not only our history, but also our present and future "first things" -- principles that define who we are.

In 1942, British author C.S. Lewis outlined what he called the Principle of First and Second Things: "You can't get second things by putting them first," Lewis wrote, "You can get second things only by putting first things first."[7] Another contemporary expert explained the principle of first and second things more bluntly, using the most basic of all "second things" to make the point: "The society that believes in nothing worth surviving for -- beyond mere survival -- will not survive."[8]

Inspector General von Steuben stood for -- and still stands for -- principles worth dying for. While "Training and Discipline" *per se* may not be "first things" for most Americans, Steuben also stood for public accountability, a "first things" American principle codified into Article I of the U.S. Constitution, which mandates that, "a regular Statement and Account of the Receipts and Expenditures of all public Money shall be published from time to time."[9] The U.S. Congress codified this, along with the principles of "Integrity & Efficiency," into the Inspector General Act of 1978. This is the statutory foundation for the Inspector General System, of which Steuben is the founding father.

Benjamin Franklin recruited Baron von Steuben in 1777 from the latter's post-Prussian Army position as "Hofmarschall" (Lord Chamberlain) of a small Hohenzollern principality in what is now Southern Germany. The Steuben family motto, *Sub Tutela Altissimi*

Semper[10] (translated, Under the Protection of the Almighty Always), might have foreshadowed the legacy of this German-American patriot: "integrity, knowledge, and loyalty to conscience."[11]

Ever since the Revolutionary War, America's military Inspector General has served as *an independent extension of the eyes, ears, and conscience of the Commander.*[12] Today, all Inspectors General in the Department of Defense, including the uniformed services, serve this role; as such, the military Inspector General is a paradigm of military leadership—the only issue is whether he or she is a good paradigm.

Today's Army Inspector General is the modern day personification of the enduring legacy of General von Steuben. The first lesson plan of the Army Inspector General School is devoted to General von Steuben and the entire three-week course is permeated with the "Von Steuben Model." Von Steuben is the role model for every one of the 239 principal Army Inspectors General. This is a veritable "IG-Network" of senior officers serving full time in assistance, inspection, non-criminal investigation, and "teach & train" functions at every major command around the world.

Modern day military Inspectors General serve in a variety of uniforms: the 239 principal Army IGs mentioned above; 150 senior Air Force IGs and an additional 2,000 counterintelligence and criminal investigative professionals report to the Air Force Inspector General; the Navy and Marine Corps together deploy more than 70 IGs in similar functions. All three service Inspectors General are three-star flag and general officers; the Marine Corps IG has two-stars. By statute, however, "No member of the Armed Forces, active or reserve, shall be appointed Inspector General of the Department of Defense."[13] This Senate-confirmed civilian officer is responsible for approximately 1,300 professional auditors, inspectors, and investigators, including 30 uniformed military officers.

Steuben is also a role model for the 69 Presidentially-appointed civilian Inspectors General throughout the federal agencies, roughly half of whom are Senate-confirmed. The Inspector General Reform Act of 2008 amended the Inspector General Act of 1978 to create the Council of the Inspectors General on Integrity and Efficiency (CIGIE), combining what were formerly known as the President's Council on Integrity and Efficiency (PCIE) and the Executive Council on Integrity and Efficiency (ECIE).[14] According to the CIGIE *Progress*

Report to the President for FY 2008, this community of, "more than 12,300 employees and 69 OIGs conducted audits, inspections, evaluations, and investigations, which resulted in:

* $14.2 billion in potential savings from audit recommendations;

* $4.4 billion in potential savings from investigative receivables and recoveries;

* 6,647 indictments and criminal informations;

* 6,866 successful prosecutions;

* 1,206 successful civil actions;

* 4,986 suspensions or debarments;

* 5,712 personnel actions;

* 337,916 hotline complaints processed;

* 6,935 audit, inspection, and evaluation reports issued; and

* 32,143 investigations closed.[15]

In addition to the Federal CIGIE community, a robust nongovernmental "Association of Inspectors General" caters to a multitude of "Inspectors General at all levels of government [who] are entrusted with fostering and promoting accountability and integrity in government."[16]

General von Steuben is best known for military training, discipline, and accountability. But he was also a man of integrity, and he had a deep aversion to fraud and waste: "Prolonged study of his official correspondence and other military papers shows them to be models of veracity and scientific precision."[17] As a result, this historical paradigm of military leadership has also become a role model for civilian IGs.

According to the official history of the Army Inspectors General, "Steuben, beginning work as an advisor to [General George] Washington, proclaimed the money department 'a mere farce,' and said that paying quartermaster agents a commission according to what they spent was a prescription for waste."[18]

"Although Maj. Gen. Friedrich W. A. von Steuben was preceded briefly by three Inspectors General, he is credited with establishing the high standards desired by Washington—integrity, knowledge, and loyalty to conscience—that have been the measure of the inspection system ever since."[19]

Von Steuben served Prince Joseph Wilhelm von Hohenzollern-Hechingen for 13 years before being recruited by Benjamin Franklin. According to Henning-Hubertus Baron von Steuben, the current head of the Von Steuben Family in Germany, those years serving the Prince "were the most difficult times of his life," and profoundly impacted his attitudes.[20] The modern day Baron explained, "Because the Prince was a spendthrift, Steuben tried everything financially to save the principality. . . . This experience shaped his understanding of honesty, probity, efficiency and truthfulness. These principles he later brought to the American Army, above all to his training of its military commanders."[21]

Inspector General von Steuben wrote "invariable rules for the order and discipline of the troops,"[22] into a military drill manual approved by Congress in March 29, 1779. In this manual he admonished that "the commanding officer of a regiment must preserve the strictest discipline and order in his corps, obliging every officer to a strict performance of his duty, without relaxing in the smallest point; punishing impartially the faults that are committed, without distinction of rank or service."[23]

Training

Inspector General von Steuben's most well known legacy, "Military Instruction," is enshrined on his monument in Lafayette Park. Upon arrival at Valley Forge in 1778, he confronted an American Army in disarray. His first task was to train General Washington's own guard.

Having proved his value as a military trainer to Washington, Steuben's acumen for training was soon applied to the entire army. According to the U.S. Army's official history of the Inspectors General, "Steuben shocked American officers by personally teaching men the manual of arms and drill, but his success helped to convince them. . . .

With Washington's support, Steuben set out to involve officers in training, making the subordinate inspectors—a body of officers drilled by Steuben—his agents."[24]

Steuben's success as a drillmaster was ambitiously adapted to the immediate task at hand, unconventionally pragmatic, and so impressive that, "Even stodgy, conservative [Continental Army General Horatio] Gates approved wholeheartedly. 'Considering the few Moments that is left us for this necessary Work,' he told Steuben, 'I should rather recommend the Discipline of the Leggs, than the Firelocks, or the hands; the preservation of Order at all Times is essentially necessary. It leads to Victory, it Secures Retreat, it saves a Country'."[25]

According to President William Howard Taft, "The effect of Steuben's instruction in the American Army teaches us a lesson that is well for us all to keep in mind, and that is that no people, however warlike in spirit and ambition, in natural courage and self-confidence, can be made at once, by uniforms and guns, a military force. Until they learn drill and discipline, they are a mob, and the theory that they can be made an army overnight has cost this Nation billions of dollars and thousands of lives."[26]

Discipline

According to the 1902 Proceedings in Congress, "[General von Steuben] made the patriotic army a disciplined and effective force—the drilled corps that ultimately won the war for freedom. He worked incessantly to do this under the greatest difficulties and the credit for it is all his own."[27] When the Pentagon commissioned its "Soldier-Signers of the Constitution Corridor" in 1986, the following signage accompanied the central oil painting of Washington at Valley Forge, surrounded by his mounted staff and tattered soldiers:

> During the coming months they would suffer from shortages of food and clothing, and from the cold, but under the tutelage of Washington and Major General Frederick Steuben would gain the professional training necessary to become the equal of the British and Hessians in open battle.

Parallel with his emphasis on training and drilling the troops, General von Steuben maintained that his inspectors "must depart from purely military inspection and must also examine financial accounts."[28] Steuben described what he encountered on arrival at Valley Forge in 1778, and how he established a system to eliminate wasteful losses of muskets, bayonets, and other Revolutionary War "accouterments":

> General Knox assured me that, previous to the establishment of my department, there never was a campaign in which the military magazines did not furnish from five thousand to eight thousand muskets to replace those which were lost . . . . The loss of bayonets was still greater. The American soldier, never having used this arm, had no faith in it, and never used it but to roast his beefsteak, and indeed often left it at home. This is not astonishing when it is considered that the majority of the States engaged their soldiers for from six to nine months. Each man who went away took his musket with him, and his successor received another from the public store. No captain kept a book. Accounts were never furnished nor required. As our army is, thank God, little subject to desertion, I venture to say that during an entire campaign there have not been twenty muskets lost since my system came into force. It was the same with the pouches and other accouterments, and I do not believe that I exaggerate when I state that my arrangements have saved the United States at least eight hundred thousand French livres a year.[29]

The state of affairs upon his arrival at Valley Forge, according to a Congressional publication, indicated "[t]here were 5,000 muskets more on paper than were required, yet many soldiers were without them. Steuben's first task was, therefore, to inaugurate a system of control over the needs and supply of arms, and, in course of time, he succeeded in carrying this control to such perfection that, on his last inspection before he left the Army, there were but three muskets missing, and even those were accounted for."[30]

The Constitution ratified by Congress after the successful conclusion of the Revolutionary War still requires that "a regular Statement and Account of the Receipts and Expenditure of all public Money shall be published from time to time."[31] This requirement of public accountability is consistent with the subsequently enacted checks on abuses of power by the national government enacted in the Bill of Rights. As explained in the 1789 Preamble to that Bill of Rights, the first ten Amendments were designed "to prevent misconstructions or abuse of its power."[32] As codified in the final article of the Bill of Rights, now known as the Tenth Amendment, the purpose of the Bill of Rights was to prevent abuses of "powers... delegated to the United States by the Constitution."[33]

Congress subsequently codified these same constitutional principles—200 years after confirming Baron von Steuben as George Washington's Inspector General—in the Inspector General Act of 1978, which created "independent and objective units" in most major federal agencies "to provide leadership and coordination and recommend policies for activities designed (A) to promote economy, efficiency, and effectiveness in the administration of; and (B) to prevent and detect fraud and abuse."[34]

Steuben's Revolutionary War legacy is exemplified in the following divisions within the modern Army Inspector General system:

Assistance Division: conducts, oversees, or assigns the responsibility for investigations and inquiries into misconduct of non-senior Army officials (Army personnel in the grade of COL/GM 15 and below) in response to allegations of impropriety, issues of systems deficiency, complaints, grievances, and matters of concern or requests for assistance received from, or presented by, soldiers, family members, retirees, former soldiers, Department of the Army (DA) Civilians, or other individuals concerned with the activities of the Army.

Inspections Division: inspect, teach, assess, report, and follow up matters affecting mission performance and the discipline, efficiency, economy, morale, training and readiness throughout the Army.

Investigations Division: conduct investigations concerning allegations made against Active and Reserve Component general officers and SES civilians and other ranks as directed.

Intelligence Oversight Division: conduct inspections and non-criminal investigations of Army sensitive activities which include Special Access Programs and other activities as prescribed in AR 380-381.[35]

The Naval, Marine Corps, and Air Force Inspectors General have slightly different albeit similar roles and organizations.[36] Each of the three military service Inspectors General identify "independence" as a guiding principle:

[Army] IGs operate within an environment consisting of the commander, the commander's soldiers, family members, DA civilian employees, retirees, and other civilians needing assistance with an Army matter and the IG system. They must be sufficiently independent so that those requesting IG assistance will continue to do so, even when the complainant feels that the commander may be the problem. Therefore, IGs must maintain a clear distinction between being an extension of the commander and their sworn duty to serve as fair and impartial fact finders and problem solvers. Commanders must also understand this clear distinction for their IGs to be effective.[37]

[Naval IG] Policy]:] All inquiries into matters affecting the readiness, integrity, discipline, and efficiency of the [Department of the Navy] shall be conducted in an independent and professional manner, without command influence, pressure, or fear of reprisal from any level within [the Department of the Navy].[38]

[The Marine Corps IG official] mission is to promote Marine Corps combat readiness, integrity, efficiency, effectiveness, and credibility through impartial and independent inspections, assessments, inquiries, and investigations.[39]

All [Air Force] IGs must maintain a clear distinction between being an extension of the commander and their sworn duty to serve as fair, impartial and objective fact-finders and problem solvers. They must be sufficiently independent so that those complainants requesting IG help will continue to do so, even when they feel that the commander may be the problem. Commanders must support this clear distinction for their IGs to be effective.[40]

Especially in military organizations, the principle of independence so fundamental to any Office of Inspector General,[41] must be tethered to the Commander for whose eyes, ears, and conscience the IG serves as an extension. This tethered independence, which is discussed more fully later in this book, is fully consistent with the Inspector General Act's requirement that an Inspector General report both to the head of his or her establishment and to the Congress, in that order.[42]

CASE STUDY: LIBERTY DAY PROJECT

Among the duties of the Deputy Senior Inspector (aka Inspector General) of the Naval Reserve Intelligence Command (NRIC), the position in which the author of this book served until being nominated to be the Inspector General of the Department of Defense, are periodic "Intelligence Oversight" inspections of 13 Reserve Intelligence Areas across the country. During Intelligence Oversight inspections, starting in October 1999, as NRIC Inspector General I routinely conducted *ad hoc* training that would address questions about not only what the Intelligence Oversight laws prohibit but, more fundamentally, why those laws allow naval reserve intelligence professionals -- and other federal officials -- to "collect, retain or disseminate information concerning United States persons only in accordance with procedures established by the head of the agency concerned and approved by the Attorney General."[43]

Answers to the "why" questions about Intelligence Oversight laws often turned on the Bill of Rights, and led to admonitions to remember that naval reserve officers serve as officers of a national government that by design is limited in power. Many of the abuses of power that led to the modern Intelligence Oversight laws are reminiscent of the abuses enumerated in the Declaration of Independence.

That is why, even today, state officers serving in our national guard units, at least while serving as state officer, retain state "police powers" unless proscribed; the opposite presumption applies for the Army, Naval, and Air Forces reserve units, which by constitutional design have no police powers except those that have been "delegated" to the national government in the Constitution itself. The final article of the Bill of Rights reminds us, "The Powers not delegated to the United States by the Constitution, nor prohibited by it to the States, are reserved to the States respectively, or to the People."[44]

On account of my experience teaching and training naval reserve intelligence professionals about the Intelligence Oversight laws, I regularly carried around with me a pocket-sized compilation of both the Declaration of Independence and the United States Constitution. At one point, I started buying in bulk the Cato Institute pocket-sized compilation, for $1 each, and giving them away to naval reserve intelligence professionals who showed an interest in learning about the Declaration of Independence and the Constitution.

Shortly after my Senate confirmation as Inspector General of the Department of Defense, I asked my new Office of Inspector General staff to price out a pocket–sized version of an official DoD electronic compilation that the Secretary of Defense had approved while I was waiting for Senate confirmation (which as of the drafting of this book was still posted at http://www.defenselink.mil/pubs/liberty.pdf). I provided the DoD Office of Inspector General staff with the $1 Cato Institute version as an example of what I had in mind.

The first price estimate for the DoD OIG to contract out an official pocket-sized version of the official DoD electronic compilation (already posted on the DoD website) came in at $12 a piece. Needless to say, I did not authorize such a blatantly excessive cost, which would have been a waste of public funds. I did, however, persist in researching precisely why the OIG staff would have been given such an outrageous price – reminiscent of the proverbial $200 toilet seat.

In the end, with a little coaching, the DoD OIG staff found a government printing contractor who could produce the pocket-sized booklet, emblazoned with the official seal of the Department of Defense on the front as well as the 800 number for the DoD Inspector General "Hotline" on the last page, for about 75 cents per "Liberty Day" booklet.

For my entire tenure as Inspector General, I utilized the pocket-sized Liberty Day booklet as an Inspector General "teach and train" handout -- in lieu of the traditional military command "challenge coin." The final page of the booklet was an "Inspector General Reference Guide," which explains the modern Inspector General's statutory duties in the context of the traditional role of an American Inspector General. It also promoted the "chain of command" as the primary avenue to report apparent violations of ethical standards and/or the law. Only if an impediment prevents utilizing the chain of command should one report allegations to the Inspector General.

Following is the text of the official Department of Defense announcement of the Liberty Day project:

U.S. Department of Defense
Office of the Assistant Secretary of Defense (Public Affairs)

News Release

On the Web:
http://www.defense.gov/Releases/Release.aspx?ReleaseID=3275
Media contact: +1 (703) 697-5131/697-5132

Public contact:
http://www.defense.gov/landing/comment.aspx
or +1 (703) 428-0711 +1

IMMEDIATE RELEASE

No. 133-02
March 19, 2002

SECRETARY OF DEFENSE RUMSFELD HONORS LIBERTY DAY

To recognize Liberty Day, Secretary of Defense Donald H. Rumsfeld today issued a compilation of key U.S. documents -- the Declaration of Independence and the Constitution -- for use by servicemembers and employees of the Department of Defense. This collection also includes excerpts from significant legislation calling for exemplary conduct by all military leaders and avoidance of fraud, waste and abuse of authority within the Department.

In his statement, Rumsfeld indicated the document is to encourage all who serve in the Department of Defense to examine these words "which together form the basis for our freedom and prosperity."

The Secretary expressed his hope this compilation will serve as a constant reminder of the sacred oath required by Congress for every individual elected or appointed to office in the civil or uniformed services:

"that I will support and defend the Constitution of the United States against all enemies, foreign and domestic; that I will bear true faith and allegiance to the same; that I take this obligation freely, without any mental reservation or purpose of evasion; and that I will well and faithfully discharge the duties of the office on which I am about to enter. So help me God."

Rumsfeld's Liberty Day proclamation and the combined Declaration of Independence/U.S. Constitution document are on the worldwide web at http://www.defenselink.mil/pubs/liberty.pdf.

The U.S. Congress designated March 16 as Liberty Day, the birthday of James Madison, fourth president of the United States. According to the October 2000 Congressional Joint Resolution, Madison was the major author of the Virginia Plan, "model and the basis for that United States Constitution that emerged from the Constitutional Convention in 1787."

1   What are the essential differences between the military and civilian Inspectors General? In what ways are they similar?

2   By what authority would any Inspector General authorize the expenditure of public money to purchase pocket-sized compilations of the Declaration of Independence and the Constitution?

3   By what authority and for what purpose would a whistleblower ever bypass the "chain-of-command" and report alleged waste, fraud, or abuse, directly to the Inspector General?

---

[1] U.S. Constitution, Preamble.

[2] Army Regulation 20-1, Inspector General Activities and Procedures 5 (Department of the Army, 2002); Army Inspector General Website, "THE IG AND THE COMMANDER RELATIONSHIP" ("IGs serve as extensions of their commander in the following three ways: [1] IGs extend the commander's eyes and ears[; 2] IGs extend the commander's voice[; and 3] IGs extend the conscience of the commander.") (http://wwwpublic.ignet.army.mil/IG_systems.htm) (last accessed August 30, 2010).

[3] Office of the Inspector General, United States Military Academy, "Inspector General Mission Essential Task List (METL)" (emphasis in original) (http://www.usma.edu/ig/metl/default.htm) (last accessed August 30, 2010).

[4] See Army Inspector General Website, "History of the U.S. Army Inspector General" (http://wwwpublic.ignet.army.mil/History_of_the_IG.htm) (last accessed August 30, 2010); Joseph Whitehorne, "Von Steuben's Legacy," The Inspectors General of the United States Army, 1903-1939, at 4 (Office of the Inspector General & Center of Military History, United States Army, 1998); Lieutenant Colonel Stephen M. Rusiecki, "Washington and von Steuben: Defining the Role of the Inspector General," The Journal of Public Inquiry, p. 35 (Fall/Winter 2003) (http://www.ignet.gov/randp/fwo3jpi.pdf) (last accessed August 30, 2010; Joseph Schmitz, "The Enduring Legacy of Inspector General von Steuben," The Journal of Public Inquiry, p. 23 (Fall/Winter 2002) (http://www.ignet.gov/randp/fwo2text.pdf) (last accessed August 30, 2010).

[5] John Palmer, General von Steuben 1 (Yale University Press, 1937).

[6] William Howard Taft, "Address of the President of the United States," reprinted in *Proceedings Upon the Unveiling of the Statue of Baron von Steuben, Major General and Inspector General in the Continental Army During the Revolutionary War* 49 (Joint Committee on Printing, 1912).

[7] C.S. Lewis, "Time and Tide," *reprinted in* GOD IN THE DOCK (1942) ("You can't get second things by putting them first; you can get second things only by putting first things first. . . . Civilizations have pursued a host of

different values in the past: God's Will, honour, virtues, empire, ritual, glory, mysticism, knowledge. The first and most practical question for ours is to raise the question, to care about the *summum bonum*, to have something to live for and to die for, lest we die.").

[8] Peter Kreeft, A Refutation of Moral Relativism: Interviews With An Absolutist 133 (1999).

[9] U.S. Const. art. I, sec. 9.

[10] Henning-Hubertus Baron von Steuben, *Chronik der Familie von Steuben* 4 (1998).

[11] Joseph Whitehorne, "Von Steuben's Legacy," The Inspectors General of the United States Army, 1903-1939, at 4 (Office of the Inspector General & Center of Military History, United States Army, 1998).

[12] Army Regulation 20-1, *Inspector General Activities and Procedures* 5 (Department of the Army, 2002).

[13] Inspector General Act of 1978, as amended, Section 8.

[14] See Homepage, Council of the Inspectors General on Integrity and Efficiency (www.ignet.gov) (last accessed August 30, 2010.

[15] CIGIE, "A Progress Report to the President: Fiscal Year 2008" (http://www.ignet.gov/randp/fy08apr.pdf) (last accessed August 30, 2010).

[16] Association of Inspectors General, Principles and Standards for Officers of Inspector General 3 (May 2001) (http://www.inspectorsgeneral.org) (last accessed August 30, 2010).

[17] Palmer, General von Steuben, *supra*, at 5.

[18] David Clary and Joseph Whitehorne, *The Inspectors General of the United States Army, 1777-1903*, 37 (U.S. Government Printing Office, 1987).

[19] Whitehorne, "Von Steuben's Legacy," *The Inspectors General, 1903-1939, supra*, at 4.

[20] Henning-Hubertus Baron von Steuben, *Chronik der Familie von Steuben, supra*, at 73.

[21] Henning von Steuben, Translated E-mail to Joseph E. Schmitz, December 1, 2002.

[22] "In Congress, 29th March, 1779," reprinted in Baron von Steuben's *Revolutionary War Drill Manual: A Facsimile Reprint of the 1794 Edition* A2 (New York, Dover Publications, 1985).

[23] Frederick William Baron von Steuben, *Revolutionary War Drill Manual: A Facsimile Reprint of the 1794 Edition, supra*, at 128.

[24] Clary and Whitehorne, *The Inspectors General, 1777-1903, supra*, at 40.

[25] Horatio Gates to Steuben, March 25, 1778, in Edith von Zemenszky, ed., *The Papers of General Friedrich von Steuben, 1777-1794*, Microfilm, 7 reels, Millwood, NY, 1976-94, 1:77, quoted in Paul Lockhart, *The Drillmaster of Valley Forge: The Baron de Steuben and the Making of the American Army*, pp. 109-10 (2008).

[26] *Proceedings Upon the Unveiling of the Statue of Baron von Steuben, supra,* at 50.

[27] United States Congress, "Proceedings in Congress Relating to Baron Steuben," July 1, 1902, reprinted in *Proceedings Upon the Unveiling of the Statue of Baron von Steuben, supra*, at 154.

[28] Clary and Whitehorne, *The Inspectors General, 1777-1903, supra*, at 37.

[29] Friedrich Kapp, *The Life of Frederick William von Steuben, Major General in the Revolutionary Army* 117 (New York, Mason Brothers, 1859) (quoting "Steuben, MS. Papers, vol. xi.").

[30] "Address of Hon. Richard Bartholdt" ("Author of the Steuben Statue Legislation"), reprinted in *Proceedings Upon the Unveiling of the Statue of Baron von Steuben, supra*, at 22-23.

[31] U.S. Constitution, Article I, Section 9.

[32] Bill of Rights, Preamble.

[33] U.S. Constitution, Amendment X.

[34] Inspector General Act of 1978, as amended, Section 2.

[35] United States Army, "The U.S. Army Inspector General Agency" (http://wwwpublic.ignet.army.mil/IG_systems.htm) (last accessed August 30, 2010).

[36] *See* "About the Naval IG"
http://www.ig.navy.mil/About_NAVINSGEN/About_NAVINSGEN.htm
("The Office of the Naval Inspector General is located at the Washington
Navy Yard and is comprised of the following offices and divisions: . . . Investigations & Assistance[;] Inspections/Command Climate/Area Visits[;]
Intelligence Oversight/ Security[;] Installations/Environment/OSH[;] Audit[;] Legal[; and] Medical and Dental."); United States Marine Corps, "Inspector General of the Marine Corps" (http://hqinet001.hqmc.usmc.mil/ig/)
(last accessed August 30, 2010); United States Air Force, Air Force Instruction (AFI) 90-301, "Inspector General Complaints Resolution," August 23,
2011, incorporating Change 1 of June 6, 2012
http://www.af.mil/shared/media/document/AFD-120228-072.pdf

[37] United States Army, Office of the Inspector General, "Welcome"
http://wwwpublic.ignet.army.mil/Welc.htm

[38] SECNAV INSTRUCTION 5430.57G, "Mission and Functions of the
Naval Inspector General," ¶5, Dec.29, 2005
http://doni.daps.dla.mil/Directives/05000%20General%20Management%2
0Security%20and%20Safety%20Services/05-
400%20Organization%20and%20Functional%20Support%20Services/543
0.57G.pdf (last accessed August 30, 2010).

[39] United States Marine Corps, "Inspector General of the Marine Corps"
(http://hqinet001.hqmc.usmc.mil/ig/) (last accessed August 30, 2010).

[40] AFI 90-301, "Inspector General Complaints Resolution," ¶1.2.3, August
23, 2011 (http://www.af.mil/shared/media/document/AFD-120228-072.pdf)
(last accessed November 25, 2012).

[41] *See* PCIE, "Quality Standards for Federal Offices of Inspector General,"
supra, p. 6 ("*Independence* is a critical element of objectivity. Without independence, both in fact and in appearance, objectivity is impaired.").

[42] *See* Inspector General Act of 1978, as amended, § 5 ("Semiannual Reports"); *see generally* Lieutenant Colonel Stephen M. Rusiecki, "Washington
and von Steuben: Defining the Role of the Inspector General," The Journal
of Public Inquiry, p. 35 (Fall/Winter 2003)
(http://www.ignet.gov/randp/fw03jpi.pdf) (last accessed August 30, 2010).

[43] Executive Order 12333 of December 4, 1981, "United States Intelligence
Activities," ¶ 2.3.

[44] U.S. Const., Amend. X.

CHAPTER 2. INSPECTOR GENERAL ACT OF 1978: STRADDLING THE SEPARATION OF POWERS

"Whenever you inspectors general root out fraud, waste, or abuse, you increase the confidence of the American People in their government."

President George W. Bush, on the occasion of the 25th Anniversary of the Inspector General Act of 1978 (2003).

        The first thing any Senate-confirmed nominee must do, after confirmation and prior to assuming his or her office, is to swear (or affirm) the statutory oath of office. This is no mere formality, as the Constitution itself requires that, "all executive and judicial officers, both of the United States and of the several states, shall be bound by oath or affirmation, to support this Constitution."[1] In implementing this constitutional mandate, Congress has prescribed the following text for every "individual, except the President, elected or appointed to an office of honor or profit in the civil service or uniformed services":

> I, AB, do solemnly swear (or affirm) that I will support and defend the Constitution of the United States against all enemies, foreign and domestic; that I will bear true faith and allegiance to the same; that I take this obligation freely, without any mental reservation or purpose of evasion; and that I will well and faithfully discharge the duties of the office on which I am about to enter. So help me God.[2]

As every Inspector General serves in "an office of honor," all IGs take the same oath.

IG Independence

Inspector General principles require that, "The Inspector General and OIG staff must be free both in fact and appearance from personal, external, and organizational impairments to independence."[3] Such independence is inherent to the "value added" by an Inspector General within any organization.

As explained in the previous chapter, all of the uniformed military Inspectors General identify "independence" as a guiding principle. This independence principle, which is discussed throughout this book, is fully consistent with the constitutional separation-of-powers and with the Inspector General Act's duty that an Inspector General report both to the head of his or her establishment and to the Congress, in that order.[4]

Whether the head of an organization is a cabinet officer, a military commander, or a chief executive officer, the operational leader should never have to question the independence and objectivity of factual findings and recommendations by the Inspector General.

How Inspectors General Fit Within the Constitutional Separation of Powers

Most American Inspectors General serving in the federal government, whether military or civilian, are appointed by the President as officers of the Executive Branch. To the extent an Inspector General is obligated by law to report to Congress, it is only after he or she has already reported to the head of the Executive Branch establishment to which he or she is assigned.

In order to understand how Inspectors General fit within the constitutional separation-of-powers, it is fundamental to understand that the separation-of-powers is part of the Founders' master plan to avoid abuses of power by government officials. Because Inspectors General are in the business of holding other people accountable, all Inspectors General, whether military or civilian, must be vigilant in avoiding any abuses of power within their own respective Offices, including but not limited to those "independent and objective units" of the Executive Branch establishments identified in the Inspector General Act of 1978, as amended.

The constitutional "separation-of-powers" is not mentioned by name in the Constitution. It is manifest in the structure of the Constitution itself, wherein Legislative powers and restrictions are addressed in Article I, Executive powers and restrictions are addressed in Article II, and Judicial powers and restrictions are addressed in Article III.

The Founding Fathers manifestly did not intend the constitutional separation-of-powers to be watertight. For example, the Office of the Vice President of the United States is described within in the Legislative Branch Article (Article I, Section 3). Likewise, the Judicial Branch Article (Article III) concludes with a description of a legislative power: "The Congress shall have the power to declare the punishment of treason, but no attainder of treason shall work corruption of blood, or forfeiture except during the life of the person attainted."

There is nothing inherently unconstitutional, therefore, about Congress' mandate in Section 2 of the Inspector General Act of 1978, as amended, that Inspectors General "provide a means for keeping the head of the establishment and the Congress fully and currently informed about problems and deficiencies relating to the administration of such programs and operations and the necessity for and progress of corrective action."[5]

By What Authority and For What Purpose Inspectors General Do What They Do?

Inspectors General derive their authority from the Constitution's own "Accountability Clause" in Article I, Section 9: "a regular statement and account of receipts and expenditures of all public money shall be published from time to time." This mandate, while prescribed in Article I, does not specify the subject of its passive verb, "shall be published." The Founding Fathers apparently intended this constitutional duty of accountability to straddle all three branches of our national government: Legislative (Article I); Executive (Article II); and Judicial (Article III).

Implementing legal guidance, whether through statute, regulations, directives, policy memoranda, or otherwise, is typically the way

governmental entities "flesh out" the more general mandates of constitutional and statutory law.

The Inspector General Act of 1978, as amended, contains
more than 20 such duties to be carried out by civilian Executive Branch
officials who have been confirmed by the United States Senate. Each
Inspector General Act duty is typically preceded by the words, "the
Inspector General shall." The "purpose" section of the Inspector General Act clarifies Congress' expectation that every Inspector General
identified by establishment in the Inspector General Act has a duty to
provide, "leadership and coordination [in] activities designed (A) to
promote economy, efficiency, and effectiveness in the administration
of, and (B) to prevent and detect fraud and abuse in, . . . programs and
operations" of his or her respective establishment. The statutory delin-
eation of establishments includes most cabinet departments and federal
agencies.[6]

The only mandatory operational functions of every statutory
Office of Inspector General (OIG) are, "to conduct and supervise audits and investigations relating to the programs and operations of the
establishments listed in section 12(2) [of the Inspector General Act]."[7]
In addition to these operational duties, each OIG is obligated by law:

> to provide leadership and coordination and recommend
> policies for activities designed (A) to promote economy,
> efficiency, and effectiveness in the administration of, and
> (B) to prevent and detect fraud and abuse in, such pro-
> grams and operations; and

> to provide a means for keeping the head of the establish-
> ment and the Congress fully and currently informed about
> problems and deficiencies relating to the administration
> of such programs and operations and the necessity for and
> progress of corrective action."[8]

Many of the larger establishments have additional specified
Inspector General duties tailored to the complexity of the establishment. For example, "In addition to the other duties and responsibilities specified in this Act, the Inspector General of the Department of
Defense shall—

(1) be the principal adviser to the Secretary of Defense for matters relating to the prevention and detection of fraud, waste, and abuse in the programs and operations of the Department;

(2) initiate, conduct, and supervise such audits and investigations in the Department of Defense (including the military departments) as the Inspector General considers appropriate;

(3) provide policy direction for audits and investigations relating to fraud, waste, and abuse and program effectiveness;

(4) investigate fraud, waste, and abuse uncovered as a result of other contract and internal audits, as the Inspector General considers appropriate;

(5) develop policy, monitor and evaluate program performance, and provide guidance with respect to all Department activities relating to criminal investigation programs;

(6) monitor and evaluate the adherence of Department auditors to internal audit, contract audit, and internal review principles, policies, and procedures;

(7) develop policy, evaluate program performance, and monitor actions taken by all components of the Department in response to contract audits, internal audits, internal review reports, and audits conducted by the Comptroller General of the United States;

(8) request assistance as needed from other audit, inspection, and investigative units of the Department of Defense (including military departments); and

(9) give particular regard to the activities of the internal audit, inspection, and investigative units of the military

departments with a view toward avoiding duplication and insuring effective coordination and cooperation.[9]

Between April 2002 and September 2005, the DoD OIG issued approximately 50 policy memoranda, most of which addressed the manner in which that particular Office of Inspector General carried out its statutory duties. The most ambitious of these policy memoranda was formal guidance on implementing each of the explicit statutory mandates in the Inspector General Act. The goal was to explain to the American people precisely how, each time Congress had used the words, "The Inspector General shall," the DoD OIG carries out that mandate.

Obligation to Prescribe and Promulgate Rules

In the absence of more formal rulemaking, the publication of policy memos fulfills a basic requirement of transparency and good governance. After all, if a leader is to hold his or her people accountable to standards of conduct, principles of due process (and fairness) require that those people be notified in advance of the standard to which they will be held accountable.

A practical manifestation of these due process principles arises in the context of judicial review of agency administrative action. The United States Supreme Court calls this the "simple but fundamental rule of administrative law" that "the agency must set forth clearly the grounds on which it acted":

> For "[w]e must know what a decision means before the duty becomes ours to say whether it is right or wrong." And we must rely on the rationale adopted by the agency if we are to guarantee the integrity of the administrative process. Only in that way may we "guard against the danger of sliding unconsciously from the narrow confines of law into the more spacious domain of policy." . . . This is essentially a corollary of the general rule requiring that the agency explain the policies underlying its action. A settled course of behavior embodies the agency's informed judgment that, by pursuing that course, it will carry out the policies committed to it by Congress.[10]

In 1765, Sir William Blackstone explained these enduring principles within the context of the four essential properties of all man-made law (as opposed to Divine Law and Natural Law):

> [M]unicipal or civil law [is] the rule by which particular districts, communities, and nations are governed; . . . Let us endeavour to explain its several properties, . . . first, it is a rule; not a transient sudden order from a superior to or concerning a particular person; but something permanent, uniform, and universal. . . . It is likewise 'a rule prescribed.' But farther: municipal law is 'a rule of civil conduct prescribed by the supreme power in a state.' Wherefore it is requisite to the very essence of a law, that it be made by the supreme power. Sovereignty and legislature are indeed convertible terms; one cannot subsist without the other.[11]

These are the enduring four properties of all man-made laws in the Anglo-American tradition of transparent government.[12] Inherent within this tradition is the obligation that the prescribed laws be well promulgated. In describing this obligation, Sir William Blackstone wrote that the government must promulgate its laws in the "most perspicuous manner" available, "not like [Emperor] Caligula, who . . . wrote his laws in very small character, and hung them up upon high pillars, the more effectually to ensnare the people."[13]

These basic principles of due process (and fairness) manifest themselves in American jurisprudence through, among other things, the two *ex post facto* clauses of the United States Constitution. The first *ex post facto* clause is in Article 1, Section 9, which is a general prohibition against passing laws after the fact, which Sir William Blackstone wrote was "even more unreasonable than" the law promulgation methodology of arguably the most infamous Roman despot, Emperor Caligula.[14] It wasn't enough for our Founding Fathers to say there shall be no *ex post facto* laws. They felt obligated to reemphasize that prohibition one section later, in Section 10, as applied to the States.

An IG-specific practical manifestation of these principles of transparent governance, which the author of this book implemented while serving as Inspector General of the Department of Defense, was in the context of investigating allegations against senior officials: "if it takes [the OIG] lawyers more than a week to tell [the IG] what the legal standard is, [the IG] will not hold anybody else accountable to that standard -- because that would be a Caligula-esque method of enforcing laws. . . . It's not part of the American system of transparent and accountable government."[15]

On November 7, 2003, the DoD OIG published on its website the first-ever compilation of official guidance on how each of the statutory mandates in the Inspector General is carried out. As of writing this book, that compilation (updated in December 2004) is still posted on the website.[16] It is first and perhaps the only such compilation thus far to be completed.

CASE STUDY: UNRESOLVED HONOR SCANDAL AND THE STATUTORY DUTY OF EXEMPLARY CONDUCT

Featured prominently in the Introduction to the Department of Defense Liberty Day booklet described in Chapter One is John Adams' 1775 "Exemplary Conduct" leadership standard, reenacted by Congress in 1997 as a tool to combat "dissolute and immoral practices" within the military. The 1997 reenactment is codified separately for each of the military departments, but for all practical purposes is verbatim from the 1775 Naval original (tailored, of course, to the Army and the Air Force):

> ART. 1. The Commanders of all ships and vessels belonging to the THIRTEEN UNITED COLONIES, are strictly required to shew in themselves a good example of honor and virtue to their officers and men, and to be very vigilant in inspecting the behaviour of all such as are under them, and to discountenance and suppress all dissolute, immoral and disorderly practices; and also, such as are contrary to the rules of discipline and obedience, and to correct those who are guilty of the same according to the usage of the sea.[17]

During the 2001 DoD Transition Team interview, the head of the Transition Team said to the Inspector General candidate, "The bad news is that the position has been vacant for two years and the office is in the midst of a nationally publicized honor scandal. The good news," he continued, "is that by the time your get confirmed by the Senate, the GAO will have come in and will tell you where all the dead bodies are buried."[18]

In the end, the bad news got worse and the good news never happened.

This nationally publicized honor scandal was laid out by Senator Charles Grassley (R-IA) in a May 21, 2001, letter to Defense Secretary Donald Rumsfeld, in which the Senator announced, "I am writing to inform you that I am conducting an oversight investigation of allegations that 12 to 15 officials in the Inspector General's (IG) office *tampered with audit materials* to alter the outcome of a Peer Review required by law. This is a major integrity violation" as a result of which, according to Senator Grassley, "The IG's office has lost its accreditation as a government audit authority."[19]

The press coverage of the honor scandal only addressed its most obvious manifestations: "a dozen IG auditors were involved in doctoring audit working papers so they could improve their performance in a peer review."[20] The Associate Press reported that the DoD Office of Inspector General, which "investigates fraud and abuse inside the Pentagon is getting a poor grade after it was caught cheating on a review of its own performance."[21]

As if the press accounts were not bad enough, what became clear within days of the new IG swearing his oath of office was that the scandal went much deeper. What also became clear, as a lesson learned, was that the head of an independent agency, even an acting head, cannot simply recuse himself, as the Acting Inspector General had, from addressing a scandal that goes to the heart and soul of the organization, simply because the allegations involve the acting agency head.[22]

Shortly after Senate confirmation, the new DoD IG soon learned that the "live body" left "in command" after the Acting Inspector General had recused himself was not even an officer of the "independent and objective" Office of Inspector General: he was a senior lawyer in the Office of the General Counsel of the Department of Defense who had been detailed to the Office of Inspector General pursuant to a 20-year-old Memorandum of Understanding (which governed the relationship between the DoD OIG and its lawyers). At the time, this apparent violation of Inspector General independence principles, which require that, "The Inspector General and OIG staff must be free both in fact and appearance from personal, external, and organizational impairments to independence,"[23] was the only such known arrangement in the federal government.

When the new Inspector General asked "his" new senior lawyer who had made the decision not to refer the nationally publicized honor scandal to criminal investigators, the lawyer replied, "I did." When the IG then asked why the lawyer had not referred the matter to criminal investigators, the lawyer replied, "Because there was no *mens rea*" (*i.e.*, no evil intent).[24]

The Inspector General Act mandates that it is the Inspector General who "shall report expeditiously to the Attorney General whenever the Inspector General has reasonable grounds to believe there has been a violation of Federal criminal law."[25] The Office of Inspector General had not had a Senate-confirmed Inspector General for three years. In fact, for more than 50% of its existence within the Department of Defense, this statutorily "independent and objective unit" was missing a Senate-confirmed leader — and it showed.

The new Inspector General's next question to the senior lawyer was rhetorical: "I might accept that answer for the re-creation of working papers, but for the backdating?" As background, the scandal involved both the re-creation of corrected audit working papers, and the backdating of those corrected working papers as if they had been the originals. To the senior lawyer's credit, he acknowledged the error in judgment. "In retrospect," the lawyer admitted, "it should have been referred to criminal investigators."

What the senior lawyer did not admit, which went to a deeper leadership challenge, was that it is not the lawyer's job to decide when to refer a matter to criminal investigation. That duty in the Office of Inspector General belongs by statute to the lawyer's client (the Office of Inspector General), and the person at the helm of that organizational client had recused himself without designating another "live body" who was legally "within" the Office of Inspector General to make those types of leadership decisions, leaving a leadership vacuum and a proverbial train wreck waiting to happen.

What the senior lawyer did not know yet was that the new Inspector General was already assembling a team of professionals who could properly package an "independent and objective" referral of the OIG audit working paper scandal to criminal investigators.

Bottom-Up Review

Upon Senate confirmation, in light of the still festering honor scandal, the new Inspector General decided not to make any major organizational decisions until an outside team of inspectors conducted an assessment of the scandal along with a 90-day bottom-to-top review of the organization. To accomplish this first ever task, the new IG turned to the most experienced military Inspector General alive at the time, Lieutenant General Richard Trefry, U.S. Army (retired).

General Trefry had served as "The Inspector General" of the United States Army (aka "TIG") from 1978 to 1983. In his retirement, the General had assumed an *emeritus* status at the Army Inspector General School at Ft. Belvoir, Virginia, still teaching a course as a contractor to new Army flag officers titled, "How the Army Runs."

It was not long before General Trefry had recruited a team of experienced former Army inspectors general, including at least one other retired general officer. Conducting a top-to-bottom review of a military organization is routine work for Army inspectors general. Army doctrine allows a new commander one such inspection upon assuming command, so that the new commander has a good idea of the strengths and weaknesses of his new command. And that is precisely what General Trefry's team set about to do for the 20-year-old Department of Defense Office of Inspector General.

While components of the Office of Inspector General had undergone peer reviews before, the Office of Inspector General itself had never been "assessed" by an outside group. The experience made a lot of experienced professional auditors, inspectors, and investigators, very nervous, especially the most senior leaders.

When the Trefry team completed its 90-day assessment, the verdict was arguably mixed but clear enough: "Never before have so many outstanding professionals been so disserved by their leaders." Suffice it to say, this conclusion made some senior leaders even more nervous.

Like any good Inspector General Report, the Trefry Report included constructive recommendations for moving forward. The new DoD IG accepted most of the more than two dozen such recommendations. The one Trefry recommendation the author of this book later regretted that he had not accepted, in retrospect, was immediately to sever the 20-year-old Memorandum of Understanding with the DoD

Office of General Counsel. The new IG knew at the time that the DoD General Counsel would strenuously object, and he decided to give him a chance to show that the then existing, albeit anomalous, arrangement between the OIG and the DoD General Counsel could work.

Stonewalling the IG

The Department of Defense's institutional disinclination towards an independent DoD Inspector General manifested itself over the years in the form of a 1984 Memorandum of Understanding (MOU) between the Department of Defense General Counsel and the Inspector General. That MOU preceded a debate in Congress over IG independence by a decade.

In 1994, Senator Charles Grassley (R-IA) introduced a legislative amendment "to require Inspectors General to employ legal counsel." In his introductory floor statement, Senator Grassley explained that his amendment was prompted by "misconduct on the C-17 program" that had led to DoD "IG recommendations that disciplinary action be taken against senior officials" — including one Darlene Druyen, who had thus far avoided discipline. According to Senator Grassley, "the legal beagles put up a stonewall that stopped the inspector general cold . . . ."

Even those who opposed Senator Grassley's 1994 amendment based their opposition on the fact that all IGs at the time already could hire their own counsel:

> "I must emphasize that . . . we already have ample authority to establish our own in-house counsel; we need no statutory amendment to ensure this outcome." Inspector General of the Department of Health and Human Services (and former DoD IG) June Gibbs Brown, April 21, 1994.

> "Because Inspectors general currently have the authority to hire counsel within their own organizations should they so desire, we believe that an amendment that requires Inspectors General to do so diminishes their authority and independence rather than augmenting it. I believe the

manner in which legal services are obtained by an Inspector General should be left to the discretion of the Inspector General, who is in the best position to evaluate the needs of his or her office." DoD Deputy Inspector General Derek Vander Schaaf, May 23, 1994.

"As Inspectors General currently have the authority to hire counsel within their organizations should they so desire, the Administration believes that such an amendment would diminish their authority and independence rather than augment it." OMB Administrator Kelman, June 3, 1994.

"Right now, the IG's have complete authority to hire outside help and increase their permanent staff if they wish to do so. This is written into law. If they feel their independence is being compromised in any way, shape or form, they have the authority to hire their own independent counsel . . . ." Senator John Glenn, June 8, 1994.

"[The DoD] IG office under existing agreements, . . . can hire independent counsel if he or she so desires." Senator Strom Thurmond, June 8, 1994.

The subject of the 1984 General Counsel-IG MOU had come up during the author of this book's Senate confirmation process. This author's attitude at the time was, "If it's not broke, don't fix it." Shortly after Senate confirmation, it broke. It broke on three specific instances between the summer of 2002 and the winter of 2003.

Manifestation #1 of a Broken GC-IG MOU: The first manifestation that something was broke came to light in the late summer of 2002, and validated the Trefry Report's overall assessment of leadership failure during and after the audit working paper scandal: the new Inspector General made a command decision to forego any Senior Executive Service ("SES") annual bonuses for the appraisal year ending June 30, 2002. When the IG announced this decision, he informed the 16 SES officers serving in the DoD Office of Inspector General that he intended to base bonuses for the next year (his first full year as Inspector General) on merit principles, and to be as generous as he could be the following year, all depending upon merit principles.

Two months after announcing this decision, the Inspector General learned that the General Counsel for the Department of Defense had awarded a significant annual bonus to the senior lawyer assigned to the Office of Inspector General. This was the same lawyer who had briefed IG after Senate confirmation on the Audit Working Paper scandal, including his own self-described command decision that "because there had been no *mens rea*, there was no need to refer the incident to criminal investigators" (or words to that effect).

The 1984 MOU stipulated that, "The performance of the Assistant General Counsel shall be evaluated by the General Counsel in concurrence with the Inspector General." For the rating period ending June 30, 2002, the General Counsel did not seek the Inspector General's concurrence on his evaluation of the lawyers assigned under the MOU, so the IG formally protested the bonus award to the senior lawyer in light of his command decision to forego any SES bonuses for the year.

The General Counsel explained in reply to this protest, "I knew what you would say, so there was no need to consult" (or words to that effect).

Manifestation #2 of a Broken GC-IG MOU: Shortly thereafter, the senior lawyer assigned to the Office of Inspector General recused himself from any involvement in an ongoing investigation by the United States Office of Special Counsel into unspecified allegations that the Inspector General had mishandled the removal of the three SES officers from the Office of Inspector General. The IG promptly informed the DoD General Counsel that there was no way for the IG to have full confidence in a lawyer who had recused himself, especially when there was no way for the IG to understand the reason for the recusal. Accordingly, the IG requested that the DoD General Counsel do whatever is necessary and appropriate to ensure that the Office had a competent and non-recused senior lawyer.

Before the DoD General Counsel could effectuate even a temporary replacement, his senior lawyer assigned to the Office of Inspector General one day casually informed the IG (as they were both leaving the building) that he "had been asked to conduct some legal analysis," the result of which was that the Inspector General legally could not be in the Department of Defense "Order of Succession." The officially promulgated "Order of Succession" lists who takes over leadership of the Department in the event something happened to the Secretary of Defense.[26]

It was of no practical consequence to the IG or to anyone else within the Office of Inspector General that the Inspector General was not included in the DoD "Order of Succession." The Inspector General's direct relationship with the Secretary was spelled out in statute.[27] What did matter was that someone other than the Inspector General had tasked the senior lawyer assigned to the OIG for legal analysis about the Inspector General's legal status, and that the Inspector General only learned about it after the analysis had been completed and delivered to the outside taskor. When the senior lawyer with whom the IG should have had an attorney-client relationship of mutual trust refused even to tell the IG who had tasked him to conduct the legal research, the IG again protested his lack of confidence to the DoD General Counsel.

Although nobody ever told the IG, based on the designated "proponent" for the DoD Directive governing the "Order of Succession,"[28] the requestor of the legal analysis was most likely within the Office of General Counsel of the Department of Defense. It didn't matter, however, who it was. What mattered was that the lawyer assigned to provide legal advice to the Inspector General had refused to inform the Inspector General, when asked by the Inspector General, who had tasked the lawyer to analyze the legal status of the Inspector General.

The DoD General Counsel soon effectuated a temporary solution by replacing the senior lawyer with another lawyer from another agency within the Department of Defense, which while welcome at the time was merely a "band-aide" on an institutional problem that would soon manifest itself in the White House and on national television.

Manifestation #3 of a Broken GC-IG MOU: The third major instance of the MOU breaking down was when the IG discovered that the lawyers assigned to Office of Inspector General had advised the investigators who were conducting an investigation into alleged improprieties by Army Lieutenant General Jerry Boykin of the wrong legal standard for the rule that General Boykin had allegedly broken in the course of delivering a number of speeches about the ongoing war efforts, mostly in religious settings and mostly critical of Islam. This investigation is described and analyzed more fully in another chapter of this book.[29] Suffice to say, upon ascertaining that the investigation was being conducted based upon only half of the applicable legal standard, the Inspector General instructed that the matter be reevaluated based on the complete legal standard. The results were significantly different.[30]

In March 2004, the IG informed the General Counsel of the Department of Defense that he had lost all confidence in the senior lawyer whom the General Counsel still identified as being detailed to the Office of Inspector General. The General Counsel only response was that he, the General Counsel, had not lost confidence (even though he had ordered a temporary replacement).

Consequently, the IG insisted for the third time that the DoD General Counsel arrange to replace the senior lawyer assigned to the Office of Inspector General. When the General Counsel refused, the IG formally abrogated the 1984 MOU. The IG also initiated paperwork for the transfer of the nine lawyer positions that for two decades had been legally within the Office of General Counsel but physically within the Office of Inspector General.

Just prior to departing office, the author of this book had the honor to swear in the first-ever Inspector General-appointed General Counsel for the DoD Office of Inspector General. Three years later, Congress enacted the Inspector General Reform Act of 2008, Section Six of which provides that, "Each Inspector General shall, in accordance with applicable laws and regulations governing the civil service, obtain legal advice from a counsel either reporting directly to the Inspector General or another Inspector General."

The next eight chapters of this book explain, chapter-by-chapter, how the various duties prescribed in the Inspector General Act of 1978, as amended, are carried out through or under the oversight of the DoD Office of Inspector General. Each chapter is introduced by an excerpt from the IG Policy Memo that explains how the respective statutory duty is carried out. That Policy Memo excerpt, by design, includes the front-loaded statutory text of the respective duty.

Chapter Review Questions:

1 By what authority and for what purpose would an Inspector General NOT publish an explanation of how he or she implements the Inspector General Act of 1978, as amended?

2 What might have motivated senior officials of an Office of Inspector General to have *"tampered with audit materials to alter the outcome of a Peer Review required by law"*? *See* 18 U.S. C. § 1001(a) ("Except as otherwise provided in this section, whoever, in any matter within the jurisdiction of the executive, legislative, or judicial branch of the Government of the United States, knowingly and willfully—

> "(1) falsifies, conceals, or covers up by any trick, scheme, or device a material fact;

> "(2) makes any materially false, fictitious, or fraudulent statement or representation; or

> "(3) makes or uses any false writing or document knowing the same to contain any materially false, fictitious, or fraudulent statement or entry;

> "shall be fined under this title, imprisoned not more than 5 years . . . , or both.").

3 Why might the evidence of the above-mentioned tampering have evaded criminal investigation for more than two years? *See* 10 U.S.C. § 5947 ("All commanding officers and others in authority in the naval service are required . . . to be vigilant in inspecting the conduct of all persons who are placed under their command; to guard against and suppress all dissolute and immoral practices, and to correct, according to the laws and regulations of the Navy, all persons who are guilty of them"); 10 U.S.C. §§ 3583 & 8583 (same "vigilant in inspecting" and "correct . . . all persons who are guilty" standards for Army & Air Force respectively).

4 How should the relationship between Inspector General and General Counsel of a federal agency or military command be structured? What are key underlying assumptions in any such relationship? How does the Inspector General Reform Act of 2008 address these assumptions?

5   By what authority and for what purpose did the President issue the following Signing Statement regarding Inspector General Reform Act of 2008?[31]

Statement by the President on H.R. 928, the "Inspector General Reform Act of 2008"

Today I have signed into law H.R. 928, the "Inspector General Reform Act of 2008." The Act amends various authorities related to Federal Inspectors General.

Section 6 of the bill gives Inspectors General the right to obtain legal advice from lawyers working for an Inspector General. It is important that Inspectors General have timely and accurate legal advice. It is also important that agencies have structures through which to reach a single, final authoritative determination for the agency of what the law is. This determination is subject to the authority of the Attorney General with respect to legal questions within, and the President's authority to supervise, the executive branch and, of course, the courts in specific cases or controversies. To this end, the "rule of construction" in section 6 ensures that, within each agency, the determinations of the law remain ultimately the responsibility of the chief legal officer and the head of the agency.

Section 8 of the bill includes provisions that purport to direct or regulate the content of the President's budget submissions, including provisions that purport to direct the President to include the comments of Inspectors General with respect to those submissions. The President's budget submissions are recommendations for enactment of legislation appropriating funds. The executive branch shall construe section 8 of the bill in a manner consistent with the President's constitutional authority to recommend for congressional consideration such measures as the President shall judge necessary and expedient.

GEORGE W. BUSH
THE WHITE HOUSE, October 14, 2008.

6 By what authority and for what purpose did United States Senators issue the following "Protest" of the President's Signing Statement for Inspector General Reform Act of 2008?[32]

October 30, 2008 Thursday

LENGTH: 830 words

HEADLINE: SENATORS PROTEST PRESIDENTIAL SIGNING STATEMENT ON INSPECTOR GENERAL RE-FORM ACT

BYLINE: States News Service

DATELINE: WASHINGTON

BODY:

The following information was released by Iowa Senator Charles Grassley:

A bipartisan group of senators says the presidential signing statement accompanying the Inspector General Reform Act passed by Congress this fall needlessly challenges two important elements of the new law. The senators have called on the President to implement the law according to its text, spirit and intent so that inspectors general have access to independent legal counsel and the ability to submit budget requests that are free from inappropriate agency influence.

The text of the letter sent today by the senators to the President is below.

October 30, 2008

The Honorable George W. Bush

President of the United States

1600 Pennsylvania Avenue, N.W.

Washington, DC 20500

Dear President Bush:

On October 14, 2008, you signed the Inspector General Reform Act of 2008. As co-sponsors of the Senate version of the Act, we believe the new law will help enhance the independence and effectiveness of our nation's Inspectors General (IGs). We write to reinforce the importance of two provisions that were singled out in your signing statement that accompanied this law.

We are pleased that your signing statement acknowledges the importance of timely and accurate legal advice for IGs. Although many IGs already have independent legal counsel, others must rely on the legal advice of their agency's general counsel office advice that may lack critical independence and could reflect inherent conflicts of interest. To address this concern, Section 6 of the Act provides important protections for the independence of IGs by allowing them to obtain legal advice from a counsel either reporting directly to the Inspector General or another Inspector General. This is an arrangement that is already working well in most of the larger departments and agencies. As the rule of construction indicates, this provision does not disrupt the authority of the general counsel within an agency. It is critical, however, that an IG have access to independent legal advice, and if an IG ultimately disagrees with a legal interpretation of agency counsel, then that IG should be free to record this disagreement, and their position on the matter, in their reports and recommendations to the head of their agency and to Congress. Congress and the public deserve the right to understand an IG's independent, unbiased position with respect to potentially inappropriate or illegal conduct.

With respect to Section 8 of the Act, we are concerned that the signing statement may indicate an intention not to comply with the law. Under the new law, the President's budget submissions to Congress must include a line item detailing the President's budget request for each IG, as well as the IG's budget request. If the President's proposed budget would substantially inhibit the IG from performing the duties of the office, the President's budget submission must also include any comments from the affected IG relating to the President's proposal. Congress included Section 8 in the law to prevent the use of the budget process to inappropriately influence, marginalize, or prevent important investigations initiated by IGs.

Inspectors General within the executive branch occupy a unique position in our government. Though these IGs are executive branch officials, the laws that established the positions mandate that these IGs submit a semi-annual report to Congress detailing significant problems, abuses, and deficiencies and outlining any recommendations for corrective action. Recommendations for corrective action may include proposals for **legislative** action. **Inspector General** reports have provided factual support for modifications to our laws and have encouraged the enactment of important legal changes. Congress relies on the information in these reports and any accompanying recommendations to fulfill its constitutional responsibilities to legislate and to oversee the Executive branch. The budget information required to be submitted to Congress under Section 8 of the Act will also be critical to the performance of Congress's constitutional mandate.

We urge you to implement the entire Inspector General Reform Act of 2008 in a manner consistent with the spirit and intent of the legislation. As public servants, we have a duty to all Americans to ensure that our government operates as efficiently as possible and with the utmost integrity. Inspectors General play an important role in helping us fulfill this duty, rooting out fraud, waste, abuse, and mismanagement in the federal government. The Inspector General Reform Act of 2008 is a critical step in ensuring that Inspectors General can continue to protect taxpayer dollars in this and future administrations.

Sincerely,

Charles E. Grassley

Claire McCaskill

United States Senator

United States Senator

Joseph I. Lieberman

Susan M. Collins

United States Senator

United States Senator

cc:

The Honorable Jim Nussle

Director

Office of Management and Budget

Executive Office of the President

LOAD-DATE: October 30, 2008

---

[1] U.S. Const., Art. VI.

[2] 5 U.S.C. § 3331.

[3] President's Council on Integrity & Efficiency, "Quality Standards for Federal Office of Inspector General," p. 8 (October 2003) ("The Inspector General and OIG staff must be free both in fact and appearance from personal, external, and organizational impairments to independence. The Inspector General and OIG staff have a responsibility to maintain independence, so that opinions, conclusions, judgments, and recommendations will be impartial and will be viewed as impartial by knowledgeable third parties. The Inspector General and OIG staff should avoid situations that could lead reasonable third parties with knowledge of the relevant facts and circumstances to conclude that the OIG is not able to maintain independence in conducting its work.") (http://www.ignet.gov/pande/standards/igstds.pdf) (last accessed August 30, 2010).

[4] *See* Inspector General Act of 1978, as amended, § 5 ("Semiannual Reports"); *see generally* Lieutenant Colonel Stephen M. Rusiecki, "Washington and von Steuben: Defining the Role of the Inspector General," The Journal of Public Inquiry, p. 35 (Fall/Winter 2003) (http://www.ignet.gov/randp/fwo3jpi.pdf) (last accessed August 30, 2010).

[5] Inspector General Act of 1978, as amended, §§2(2) & 2(3).

[6] Inspector General Act of 1978, as amended, Section 2(2) ("Purpose and establishment of Offices of Inspector General; departments and agencies involved[:] In order to create independent and objective units-- (1) to conduct and supervise audits and investigations relating to the programs and operations of the establishments listed in section 11(2); (2) to provide leadership and coordination and recommend policies for activities designed (A) to promote economy, efficiency, and effectiveness in the administration of, and (B) to prevent and detect fraud and abuse in, such programs and operations").

[7] Inspector General Act of 1978, as amended, §2(1).

[8] Inspector General Act of 1978, as amended, §§2(2) & 2(3).

[9] Inspector General Act of 1978, as amended, § 8(c).

[10] Atchison, Topeka & Santa Fe Railway Co. v. Wichita Board of Trade, 412 U.S. 800, 807-08 (1973) (internal citations omitted).

[11] William Blackstone, *Commentaries On The Law Of England*, pp. 44-46 (1765-1769).

[12] *See* Joseph E. Schmitz, "Transparency and Government Accountability: Defining Principles for Inspectors General and for Americans," Remarks as delivered by the Inspector General of the Department of Defense to the Department of State International Visitor Leadership Program, Arlington, Virginia, August 2, 2005 (http://www.dodig.mil/IGInformation/Speeches/stateinternational_080205.pdf) (last accessed August 30, 2010).

[13] *Commentaries On The Law Of England*, P. 46.

[14] Ibid.

[15] Joseph E. Schmitz, "Transparency and Government Accountability: Defining Principles for Inspectors General and for Americans," *supra*.

[16] Inspector General of the Department of Defense, "Inspector General Act Implementation and Office of Inspector General Policy Guidance (Revision 2)," December 27, 2004 http://www.dodig.mil/programs/JIGP/pdfs/DoD_Joint%20IG_Designation_Letter.pdf

[17] Naval Historical Center, "Rules for the Regulation of the Navy of the United Colonies of North-America; Established for Preserving their Rights and Defending their Liberties, and for Encouraging all those who Feel for their Country, to enter into its service in that way in which they can be most Useful," November 28, 1775 (http://www.history.navy.mil/faqs/faq59-5.htm) (last accessed August 30, 2010); *see* 10 U.S.C. §§ 3583 (Army), 5947 (Navy), & 8583 (Air Force).

[18] *See* Official Website of the United States Government Accountability Office (www.gao.gov) (last access August 30, 2010).

[19] Letter from Chairman of the Senate Finance Committee Charles Grassley to Secretary of Defense Donald Rumsfeld, May 21, 2001 (emphasis in original).

[20] J. Donnelly, "IG Under Fire For Treatment Of Execs," *Defense Week*, p. 14 (September 23, 2002).

[21] Associated Press, "Pentagon auditors get poor grade in examination," USA Today (December 5, 2001) (http://www.usatoday.com/news/washington/dec01/2001-12-05-pentagon-audit.htm) (last accessed August 30, 2010).

[22] *See* S. Wheeler, "New DoD inspector general cleans house," Insight on the News (September 30, 2002) ("Sources familiar with the investigation of the falsified audit papers tell INSIGHT that Assistant IG Lieberman was involved and 'that is what led to his retirement'.") (http://findarticles.com/p/articles/mi_m1571/is_36_18/ai_92589555) (last accessed August 30, 2010).

[23] President's Council on Integrity & Efficiency, "Quality Standards for Federal Office of Inspector General," p. 8 (October 2003) ("The Inspector General and OIG staff must be free both in fact and appearance from personal, external, and organizational impairments to independence. The Inspector General and OIG staff have a responsibility to maintain independence, so that opinions, conclusions, judgments, and recommendations will be impartial and will be viewed as impartial by knowledgeable third parties. The Inspector General and OIG staff should avoid situations that could lead reasonable third parties with knowledge of the relevant facts and circumstances to conclude that the OIG is not able to maintain independence in conducting its work.") (http://www.ignet.gov/pande/standards/igstds.pdf) (last accessed August 30, 2010).

[24] *See* Encyclopedia Britannica On-Line, "Mens Rea" ("in Anglo-American law, criminal intent or evil mind. In general, the definition of a criminal offense involves not only an act or omission and its consequences but also the accompanying mental state of the actor") (http://www.britannica.com/eb/article-9052042/mens-rea) (last accessed August 30, 2010).

[25] Inspector General Act of 1978, as amended, Section 4(d) ("In carrying out the duties and responsibilities established under this Act, each Inspector General shall report expeditiously to the Attorney General whenever the Inspector General has reasonable grounds to believe there has been a violation of Federal criminal law."); *see id.*, Section 8(d) ("Notwithstanding section 4(d), the Inspector General of the Department of Defense shall expeditiously report suspected or alleged violations of chapter 47 of title 10, United States Code (Uniform Code of Military Justice), to the Secretary of the military department concerned or the Secretary of Defense.").

[26] *See* DoD Directive 3020.04, "Order of Succession Under Executive Order 13533 and the Federal Vacancies Reform Act of 1998," August 25, 2010

(http://www.dtic.mil/whs/directives/corres/pdf/302004p.pdf) (last accessed August 30, 2010).

[27] *See* Inspector General Act of 1978, as amended, Sections 3(a) and 8(c) (1) ("Each Inspector General shall report to and be under the general supervision of the head of the establishment involved, or to the extent such authority is delegated, to the officer next in rank below such head, but shall not report to, or be subject to supervision by, any other officer of such establishment. . . . In addition to the other duties and responsibilities specified in the Act, the Inspector General of the Department of Defense shall . . . be the principal adviser to the Secretary of Defense for matters relating to the prevention and detection of fraud, waste, and abuse in the programs and operations of the Department; . . . .").

[28] *See Ibid* (beneath the date of the Directive is "GC, DoD," which designates the office responsible for keeping the Directive up-to-date, *i.e.* in this instance, the Office of General Counsel of the Department of Defense).

[29] *See* Chapter 3, *infra.*

[30] *See* Department of Defense Office of the Inspector General, "Alleged Improprieties Related to Public Speaking: Lieutenant General William G. Boykin, U.S. Army, Deputy Under Secretary of Defense for Intelligence," August 5, 2004 (http://www.dodig.mil/fo/foia/ERR/h03l89967206.pdf) (last accessed August 30, 2010) (see Chapter 7, *infra*).

[31] Signing Statement is been posted at http://www.whitehouse.gov/news/releases/2008/10/20081014-7.html

[32] "Protest" of the President's Signing Statement for Inspector General Reform Act of 2008 at http://www.ignet.gov/pande/leg/signingstatementresponse.pdf

PART B.

THE DUTIES OF AN INSPECTOR GENERAL:

Case Studies in Transparent Accountability

At one of Secretary Rumsfeld's weekly staff meetings shortly after the Coalition Forces invaded Iraq, the newly confirmed and appointed Inspector General of the Department of Defense explained to the other "direct reports" at the table the "due process" involved in the investigation of DoD senior officials. Secretary Rumsfeld had already explained to all his direct reports that the issue is not whether but when you will be investigated. The topic of senior official "due process," not surprisingly, was of interest to the audience.

One thing the Inspector General assured his new colleagues was that the model of "due process" to which his office subscribed was quite different from that of the Roman Emperor Caligula, who according to Sir William Blackstone, "wrote his laws in very small character, and hung them up upon high pillars, the more effectually to ensnare the people."[1] After the meeting, Tory Clark, the Assistant Secretary of Defense for Public Affairs, pulled the Inspector General aside and said, "IG-man, I have to say, that had to be the first time anyone has uttered the name Caligula in the Secretary's conference room."

Three years later, in the same conference room, Deputy Secretary Gordon England announced that the Inspector General's "new nickname is 'Fearless Fosdick'." The Inspector General had just completed his testimony before the Senate Armed Services Committee on the Air Force Tanker Scandal (described later in this book), at the hearing for which the Inspector General had been riddled with hostile questions and accusations. At the time, the author of this book was not familiar with the 1940's era comic book character Fearless Fosdick, whom he soon learned was a parody cartoon version of the detective

Dick Tracy, famous for always being riddled with gunshots but always surviving. Here is an artistic depiction of that character:

An Inspector General can be called worse.

Part B Endnotes

---

[1] William Blackstone, *Commentaries On The Law Of England*, p. 46 (1765-1769).

CHAPTER 3. INDEPENDENT EXTENSION OF THE EYES, EARS, AND CONSCIENCE OF THE COMMANDER (AND OF CONGRESS):

Can Chaplains Be Agents of Al-Qaeda?

"All IGs extend the eyes, ears, voice, and conscience of their commanders."

Army Regulation 20-1, "Inspector General Activities and Procedures," p. 5, ¶1-6(e)(1) (U.S. Department of the Army 2010)

An Inspector General, who by American military tradition serves as an independent extension of the eyes, ears, and conscience of the commander,1 and/or who by statute is duty-bound to report "serious problems, abuses and deficiencies" to the respective agency head and to Congress,2 can assist the agency ahead and Congress in exposing enemies of the United States Constitution who might otherwise hide behind the guise of religion. In fulfilling these roles, an Inspector General can also assist military and civilian leaders, as well as the American People, in knowing better both our enemies and ourselves—in order that we can better defeat our enemies.

The November 2008 criminal conviction in Texas of the Holy Land Foundation as a front for Hamas proves that international terrorist organizations can and do disguise themselves as charitable organizations. The November 2009 Fort Hood massacre by a commissioned Army officer who as a collateral duty "served as a lay Muslim leader running Islamic services on the base in the absence of the Muslim chaplain,"3 demonstrates that international terrorist organizations can also try to disguise their agents as military chaplains and religious lay leaders.

In Order to Win Any War, We Must Know Both Our Enemies and Ourselves

"WAR WITHOUT END" was the five-inch headline of The Washington Post Outlook section in the wake of General Stanley McCrystal's June 2010 forced resignation.[4] This headline, together with the content behind it, exposes a fundamental question gnawing at many if not most Americans: "Who are we fighting and why?" That this question persists without a clear answer more than a decade after September 11, 2001, may be our downfall. The ancient Chinese military philosopher Sun Tzu admonished 2500 years ago: "One who knows neither the enemy nor himself will invariably be defeated in every engagement."[5] Americans need to focus on our own "first things," *i.e.*, defining American principles, in order to win any war, whether it be kinetic warfare in Afghanistan or information warfare in the heartland of America.

"Precisely who are our enemies?" is the question the author of this handbook repeatedly asked military leaders when visiting Afghanistan in 2004 as Inspector General of the Department of Defense. The answers to this question were mixed. Although most coalition forces could identify Al-Qaeda and the Taliban as our enemies, most were generally unclear as to why they were our enemies, other than that they were implicated in the September 11, 2001, terrorist attacks. One coalition general officer described our enemies as, "three disparate enemies: Al Qaeda; Taliban; and HIG." The latter acronym, the general explained, referred to a warlord in the region east of Kabul on the Pakistani border known as "Engineer," who "was not a cleric."

Every civilian military leader and every Soldier, Sailor, Airman, and Marine should know our enemies. In our constitutional Republic, no American citizen should ever be confused about who our enemies are—and why they are enemies. Likewise, those truths announced as "self-evident" in our Declaration of Independence should be as clearly understood by every American today as they were self-evident at the birth of our nation.

We won the Cold War because we knew our enemies—Marxist-Leninist advocates of totalitarianism—and we knew ourselves—a People deeply rooted in the "great civilized ideas" enumerated in our Declaration of Independence: "that all men are created equal, that they are endowed by their Creator with certain unalienable Rights, that among these are Life, Liberty and the pursuit of Happiness."[6] These great civilized ideas in turn are the foundation underlying our Constitution and our Bill of Rights.

The Constitution implicitly charges the Commander-in-Chief with the duty of discerning and defining our enemies. In doing so, the Commander-in-Chief ought also to remind us of our defining principles. This is why President Ronald Reagan, in the midst of the Cold War, announced to the British House of Commons—and to the world—his vision for leaving "Marxism-Leninism on the ash heap of history":

> given strong leadership, time, and a little bit of hope, the forces of good ultimately rally and triumph over evil... Here is the enduring greatness of the British contribution to mankind, the great civilized ideas: individual liberty, representative government, and the rule of law under God.[7]

Most Americans know that al-Qaeda is an enemy. But how many Americans "know" al-Qaeda, and understand why al-Qaeda is an enemy? It is not simply because al-Qaeda has declared war against us. In this regard, on February 4, 2011, the United States Court of Appeals for the 2nd Circuit affirmed a criminal conviction under the Material Support of Terrorism Act in a case captioned *United States v. Farhane*.[8] In its opinion, the Court of Appeal explained that, "Two successive administrations have indicated that the nation is at 'war' with al Qaeda."[9] The Court of Appeals also referred to the goal of "*jihad*" as being "to establish Sharia (Islamic law)."[10]

The Court of Appeals in *Farhane* also explained the "infamous fatwa (religious decree) pronouncing it the individual duty of every Muslim to kill Americans and their allies—whether civilian or military—in any country where that could be done":

Al Qaeda is the most notorious terrorist group presently pursuing jihad against the United States. In February 1998, its leaders, including Osama bin Laden and Ayman al Zawahiri, issued an infamous fatwa (religious decree) pronouncing it the individual duty of every Muslim to kill Americans and their allies—whether civilian or military—in any country where that could be done. For a detailed discussion of this fatwa and al Qaeda's terrorist activities up to 2004—including the 1998 bombings of American embassies in Kenya and Tanzania, which killed 224 people; the October 2000 bombing of the USS Cole, which took 17 lives; and the September 11, 2001 airplane attacks on the World Trade Center and the Pentagon, which killed 2,973 persons—see The National Commission on Terrorist Attacks Upon the United States, The 9/11 Commission Report (2004)."

While al-Qaeda defines its war against the United States in terms of "*jihad,*" Shari'ah defines "*jihad*" as warfare against non-Muslims, primarily in military terms, but also in economic and cultural terms. As explained in the 2010 "Team BII Report" coauthored by former CIA Director Jim Woolsey and former DIA Director Ed Soyster, among others (the author of this handbook included), titled *Shariah The Threat To America, An Exercise In Competitive Analysis,* "shariah is held by mainstream Islamic authorities—not to be confused with 'radical,' 'extremist' or 'political' elements said to operate at the fringes of Islam—to be the perfect expression of divine will and justice and thus is characterized as a 'complete way of life' (social, cultural, military, religious, and political)."[12] Moreover, "While the terrorists can and will inflict great pain on the nation, the ultimate goal of shariah-adherent Islam cannot be achieved by these groups solely through acts of terrorism, without a more subtle, well-organized component operating in tandem with them... That component takes the form of 'civilization jihad.' This form of warfare includes multi-layered cultural subversion, the co-opting of senior leaders, influence operations and propaganda and other means of insinuating shariah into Western societies. These are the sorts of techniques alluded to by Yusuf al-Qaradawi, the spiritual leader of the Muslim Brotherhood, when he told a Toledo,

Ohio Muslim Arab Youth Association convention in 1995: 'We will conquer Europe, we will conquer America! Not through the sword, but through *dawa*.'[13] Accordingly, it is not just our soldiers in Afghanistan who must face this enemy, but also those of us here at home.

In a 2007 audio message, the late al-Qaeda "chief financial officer" Mustafa Abu al-Yazid explained that, "Jihad with money is also an obligation. And here we, in the battlefield in Afghanistan, are lacking a lot of money and a weakness in operations because of lack of money, and many mujahideen are absent from Jihad because of lack or absence of money with which they cannot carry out Jihad. Even many brothers . . . who want to sacrifice themselves for the cause of Allah, we cannot prepare them because of lack of money."[14]

Yazid's call for "Jihad with money" is fully consistent with "mainstream" Shari'ah Law, which mandates that all devout Muslims donate money to eight categories of "*Zakat*," including the financing of "volunteers for jihad." As explained in the English-language translation of *Reliance of the Traveller: A Classic Manual of Islamic Sacred Law*: "It is obligatory to distribute one's zakat among eight categories of recipients," the seventh of which is, "those fighting for Allah, meaning people engaged in Islamic military operations for whom no salary has been allotted in the army roster . . . but who are volunteers for jihad without remuneration."[15]

The word "Islam" means "submission [to Allah]" in Arabic.[16] According to Shari'ah authorities, the notion of Islamic "peace" is profoundly tied to a division of the world into two halves: the world of Islam and peace—called the "*Dar al-Islam*"—and the world of the infidel, disbelief and war—called the "*Dar al-Harb*" (*e.g.*, the United States of America). Islamic "Peace" can only be achieved through universal submission to Allah, *i.e.*, through universal imposition of Shari'ah Law. Until this occurs, Shari'ah Law imposes a duty on all devout Muslims to support "volunteers to jihad" through "*Zakat*," as well as a duty called "*Taqiyya*" to deceive non-Muslims whenever such deceit will promote Islam.[17] While nobody has suggested that all Muslims support *Jihad* and all Muslims deceive non-Muslims to promote Islam, no reputable Shari'ah expert has publicly disclaimed these two legal duties. Ignoring these prescribed Shari'ah duties is tantamount to ignoring *Mein Kampf*, Adolf Hitler's treatise that was ignored by many American leaders in the 1930's—to our great detriment.

According to one modern English language student textbook on Islam, "The word Shari'ah literally means a *straight path* (45:18) or *an endless supply of water*. It is the term used to describe the rules of the lifestyle (*Deen*) ordained for us by Allah. . . . In more practical terms, the Shari'ah includes all the do's and don't of Islam."[18] Once we understand, however, that Shari'ah also includes both duties to support "volunteers to *jihad*" through "*Zakat*" donations, and to deceive non-Muslims in order to promote Islam, we will better "know the enemy" already among us—an enemy that, by its nature, is dead-set on making itself supreme over all other legal systems, including the United States Constitution.[19] Based on these indisputable tenets, Shari'ah Law is an enemy of the United States Constitution: the two are incompatible.[20]

Lessons Learned from the Holy Land Foundation Trial
and the Fort Hood Massacre

In addition to Al-Qaeda and the Taliban in Afghanistan, the November 2008 Holy Land Foundation terrorism conviction and the November 2009 Fort Hood massacre highlight the fact that the American military operating in the United States must also "defend against threats posed by external influences operating on members of our military community."[21] Of course, the "internal threats" described in the Department of Defense's January 2010, "Independent Review Related to Fort Hood," discussed below, are not unique to the "military community."

According to the January 2010 DoD Independent Review Related to Fort Hood, "On November 5, 2009, a gunman opened fire at the Soldier Readiness Center at Fort Hood, Texas. Thirteen people were killed and 43 others were wounded or injured. The initial response to the incident was prompt and effective. Two minutes and forty seconds after the initial 911 call, installation first responders arrived on the scene. One-and-a-half minutes later, the assailant was incapacitated."[22]

While the DoD Independent Review concludes that, "To protect the force, our leaders need immediate access to information pertaining to Service members indicating contacts, connections, or relationships with organizations promoting violence,"[23] the published report of the DoD Independent Review does not mention that, "The suspected Fort Hood terrorist served as a lay Muslim leader running Islamic services on the base in the absence of the Muslim chaplain," a fact that was published on the internet shortly after the Fort Hood massacre.[24]

In its defense, the DoD Independent Review admits that, "areas in our report will require further study," and that, with regard to the only "suspect" in Fort Hood massacre, Army Major Nidan Hasan, that, "Some signs were clearly missed; others ignored."[25] The Report concludes that, "Commanders are our key assets to identify and monitor internal threats. Our findings and recommendations emphasize creating clarity for our commanders with respect to identifying behaviors that may pose internal threats and sharing that information within the Department and with other agencies. . . To account for possible emerging internal threats, we encourage the Department to develop comprehensive guidance and awareness programs that include the full range of indicators for potential violence."[26] Finally, the Report recommends that, "To protect our force, our leaders need immediate access to information pertaining to Service members indicating contacts, connections, or relationships with organizations promoting violence."[27]

Apropos is emphasis on the need to identify "organizations promoting violence" in the DoD DoD Independent Review of the Fort Hood massacre, the month after that Report the Assistant Attorney General of the United States sent a letter to Members of Congress who had inquired about "the evidence and findings by the Department of Justice and the FBI which resulted in the Council on Islamic Relations (CAIR) being named as an unindicted co-conspirator of the Holy Land Foundation." In his letter, the Assistant Attorney General wrote, "trial transcripts . . . contain testimony and other evidence that was introduced in that trial which demonstrated a relationship among CAIR, individual CAIR founders, and the Palestine Committee. Evidence was also introduced that demonstrated a relationship between the Palestine Committee and HAMAS, which was designated as a terrorist organization in 1995."[28]

Commenting publicly on the November 2008 Holy Land Foundation guilty verdicts, Patrick Rowan, Assistant Attorney General for National Security, had noted, "Today's verdicts are important milestones in America's efforts against financiers of terrorism. For many years, the Holy Land Foundation used the guise of charity to raise and funnel millions of dollars to the infrastructure of the Hamas terror organization. This prosecution demonstrates our resolve to ensure that humanitarian relief efforts are not used as a mechanism to disguise and enable support for terrorist groups."[29]

CASE STUDY: CAN CHAPLAINS BE AGENTS OF AL-QAEDA?

Investigations into the connection between the Holy Land Foundation ("HLF") and terrorist organizations began long before September 11, 2001. It was not until November 24, 2008, however, after seven days of deliberation and six weeks of testimony in the United States District Court for Northern District of Texas, that the jury convicted HLF, along with five of its leaders, on charges of providing material support to Hamas. As announced by the United States Department of Justice, "The government presented evidence at trial that, as the U.S. began to scrutinize individuals and entities in the U.S. who were raising funds for terrorist groups in the mid-1990s, the HLF intentionally hid its financial support for Hamas behind the guise of charitable donations. HLF and these five defendants provided approximately $12.4 million in support to Hamas and its goal of creating an Islamic Palestinian state by eliminating the State of Israel through violent jihad."[30]

As the Holy Land Foundation terrorism investigation was proceeding in relative obscurity, beginning in March 2003, a number of United States Senators sent letters to the DoD Inspector General requesting an inquiry into the Muslim religious organizations that were vetting candidates for, and the process for selecting, Islamic military chaplains. As background to these Senate requests, on September 29, 2003, Mr. Abdurahman Alamoudi, who had played "the lead role in establishing the Muslim Chaplain Program for the Department of Defense,"[31] was arrested at London's Heathrow Airport "on his way back from Libya with $340,000 in cash given to him by Libyan President Muammar Qaddafi for jihad. The money was to be used to underwrite a plot involving two U.K.-based al Qaeda operatives intending to kill Crown Prince (now King) Abdullah of Saudi Arabia."[32] As part of a plea agreement, "Alamoudi stipulated that he had participated in a sophisticated criminal scheme involving the attainment and transmission of money from Libya to the United States and abroad. He admitted that his unlawful conduct involved: '[e]ngag[ing] in financial transactions with the Government of Libya, a country designated under Section 6(j) of the Export Administration Act of 1979 as a country supporting international terrorism'; traveling to Libya on his United States passport without first obtaining the necessary license to do so as required by federal law; lying to United States officials by falsely denying that he had traveled to Libya when questioned upon return from such visits; concealing his interests and investments in an account in Switzerland by not reporting them on his tax returns; laundering money; and conspiring with the Libyan government and dissidents of Saudi Arabia to assassinate Saudi Crown Prince Abdullah."[33] On October 15, 2004, the U.S. District Court for the Eastern District of Virginia "sentenced Alamoudi to 23 years imprisonment and three years of supervised release and imposed $20,300 in fines. The court also entered a consent order of forfeiture in which Alamoudi agreed to forfeit the '$340,000 in cash' that had already been confiscated by British authorities 'as property derived from, traceable to, or a substitute for proceeds of his offense,' and to 'further ... forfeit' an additional '$570,000, representing proceeds of his violations of conviction'."[34]

Three weeks after Alamoudi's arrest at Heathrow Airport, on October 23, 2003, the DoD Inspector General initiated an inspection/evaluation in order to fulfill his duty to report both to the Secretary of Defense and to Congress on "serious problems, abuses, and deficiencies relating to the administration of programs and operations" of the Department of Defense.[35]

The following excerpts are from the Inspector General of the Department of Defense's "Evaluation Report on the DoD Chaplain Program," Report No. 1E-2004-001, November 10, 2004.[36]

Inspector General

United States
Department *of* Defense

Inspections and Evaluations Directorate

**Evaluation Report on
the DoD Chaplain Program**

November 10, 2004
Report No. IE-2004-001

Purpose

To evaluate the efficacy of the DoD processes to:

* add new religions to the chaplain program;

* recognize and review chaplain endorsing ecclesiastical organizations;

* recruit, train, retain, and dismiss chaplains; and

* provide Military Departments and Office of the Secretary of Defense oversight of chaplain programs.

Background

Legal actions against Islamic religious organizations that provided Islamic chaplains to the Military Departments generated congressional attention concerning the credibility of the DoD accession process for military chaplains. Beginning in March 2003, Senator Charles Schumer sent a series of letters to the DoD Inspector General requesting an inquiry into the organizations vetting candidates and the process for selecting Islamic chaplains for the Military Departments. On October 14, 2003, the Principal Deputy Under Secretary of Defense for Personnel and Readiness testified before the Senate Judiciary Subcommittee on Terrorism, Technology, and Homeland Security on the officership and credentialing of military chaplains. We initiated this evaluation on October 23, 2003, to respond to Senator Schumer's request. The DoD Inspector General met with the members of the Senate Judiciary Subcommittee on Terrorism, Technology, and Homeland Security on October 28, 2003. During this meeting, the Senators expressed their concern with current Islamic chaplains and the religious organizations (ROs) that endorse them. Congressional questions raised during testimonies are addressed in Appendix B, "Congressional Concerns." For this review, we chose not to focus on any particular faith group, but, instead, considered the overall process to effectively manage the DoD chaplain program.

Religious Freedom in the United States

The First Amendment of the United States Constitution prohibits Congress from passing laws regarding the establishment of religion, or prohibiting the free exercise of religion. Consistent with the First Amendment, as a general proposition, Government agencies cannot favor one religion over another and should not interfere with or infringe upon an individual's practice of religion. However, the free exercise clause of the First Amendment may not prevent the Government from requiring or forbidding the performance of an act based on religious beliefs, e.g., payment of taxes.

DoD Practices Incorporate Constitutional Rights to Religious Freedom

Military commanders are responsible for mission accomplishment and the good order and discipline of their units. Commanders are also required to provide appropriate religious support to all authorized individuals within their command. To balance religious freedom and military necessity, DoD established policy stating that commanders should approve requests for accommodation of religious practices when the accommodation will not have an adverse impact on military readiness, unit cohesion, standards, or discipline. However, practices and rituals associated with the individual's religious beliefs and creed must not be illegal or contrary to clearly defined public policy. DoD appoints professionally qualified clergy to accommodate the free exercise of religion in the context of military service.

Exemplary Conduct Standards for Commanders and "Others in Authority" in the Military Services

Title 10 United States Code § Sections 3583, 5947, and 8583 require Army, Navy, and Air Force commanding officers and others in authority to:

*   show in themselves a good example of virtue, honor, patriotism, and subordination;

*   be vigilant in inspecting the conduct of all persons who are placed under their command;

* guard against and suppress all dissolute and immoral practices, and to correct, according to the laws and Service regulations, all persons who are guilty of them; and

* take all necessary and proper measures, under the laws, regulations, and customs of the Service to promote and safeguard the morale, the physical well-being, and the general welfare of the officers and enlisted persons under their command or charge.

The DoD Chaplain Program

DoD recruits military chaplains to provide spiritual care for all members of the Military Departments, their family members, and other authorized persons, such as military retirees and civilian employees. Religious pluralism is a fundamental concept of the program. Chaplains are expected to perform ministry for their own faith group and provide for the rights and needs of other faith groups in their areas of responsibility.

The Under Secretary of Defense for Personnel and Readiness (USD[P&R]) exercises responsibility for the chaplain program through the Deputy Under Secretary of Defense for Military Personnel Policy (DUSD[MPP]). DoD Directive (DoDD) 5120.8, "Armed Forces Chaplains Board Charter," established the Armed Forces Chaplains Board (AFCB), consisting of the Chiefs and the Deputy Chiefs of Chaplains of the Army, the Navy, and the Air Force. Among its other duties, the AFCB makes recommendations to DUSD(MPP) on religious, ethical, and moral standards for the Military Departments, and policies for the protection of religious guarantees under the First Amendment of the U.S. Constitution. The USD(P&R) is the decision authority for recommendations concerning the chaplain program.

As of November 2003, the Military Departments had almost 2,900 active duty chaplains serving approximately 2.5 million active duty and reserve members. The Army had 1,367, the Navy had 912, and the Air Force had 612 active duty chaplains. DoD has nearly 4,800 total chaplains including those in the Reserve and National Guard. The Marine Corps uses Navy chaplains for religious ministry. The majority of Military chaplains are members of five faith groups: Protestant, Roman Catholic, Orthodox, Jewish, and Muslim.

The DoD chaplain program is governed by DoDD 1304.19, "Appointment of Chaplains for the Military Services," September 18, 1993, and an October 14, 2003 policy memorandum on the same subject signed by the Principal Deputy Under Secretary of Defense for Personnel and Readiness (see Appendix C[; This directive and policy memorandum was replaced by a new DoD Directive 1304.19 and DoD Instruction 1304.28 on June 11, 2004.]). In addition, the Army, the Navy, and the Air Force each have unique regulations governing their respective chaplain program.

The focus of the DoD chaplain program is recruitment, accession, service, and dismissal of individual military chaplains. Once recruited, candidates must meet officership, professional, and religious qualifications prior to becoming a military chaplain.

Officership qualifications include the ability to obtain and hold a security clearance based on information submitted on Standard Form 86, "Questionnaire for National Security Positions." In addition, an officer must pass any citizenship requirements, physical standards for military service, and satisfy age restrictions.

Professional qualifications deal primarily with education from an accredited school. The candidate must possess a baccalaureate degree of not less than 120 hours and 72 hours of graduate education study in theology or related subjects.

Religious qualifications include an endorsement from the chaplain's RO. The applicant must be a fully qualified clergy of the faith group and must be willing to support religious pluralism.

Officership qualifications and day-to-day activities as a military chaplain, to include training, assignments, conduct, and performance are governed by DoD and Military Department regulations and controlled by the Military Departments.

DoDD 1304.19 establishes the professional qualifications for chaplain candidates. Although specific requirements differ, the accession process is similar to the processes used by other professions, like the Medical Corps and the Judge Advocate General Corps. The sources of "licensing," or the authority to practice the profession, differ significantly. Doctors and lawyers must pass state sanctioned exams. However, chaplains receive authority to provide religious services at the discretion of the endorsing agent, who verifies that the chaplain applicant has received the requisite education and religious leadership experience.

The October 14, 2003 policy memorandum modified the requirements for the RO to certify and endorse chaplain candidates. To sponsor a candidate for the chaplaincy, the RO must:

* be formed to meet a lay constituency need for a chaplain;

* hold an Internal Revenue Code (IRC) 501(c)(3) tax exemption status; and

* present a qualified candidate.

* ROs must also agree that their candidates will perform their duties in cooperation with religious ministry professionals from other religious faith groups.

The ROs submit endorsements to the AFCB. The DUSD(MPP), through the AFCB, retains responsibility for verifying that ROs and their endorsing agents continue to meet DoD requirements and are suitable for endorsing chaplain candidates.

Definitions

The following definitions were used in this evaluation:

* **Adverse Information.** Any substantiated adverse finding or conclusion from an officially documented investigation or inquiry.

* **Church.** The Internal Revenue Service (IRS) has interpreted tax laws enacted by Congress, Treasury regulations, and court decisions to identify characteristics generally attributed to churches. Accordingly, the key characteristics of a church include: distinct legal existence; recognized creed and form of worship; definite and distinct ecclesiastical government; formal code of doctrine and discipline; ordained ministers selected after completing prescribed courses of study; literature of its own; established places of worship; regular congregations; regular religious services; schools for the religious instruction of the young; and schools for the preparation of its ministers. The IRS uses

a combination of some or all of these characteristics to determine whether an organization is a church for Federal tax purposes.

* **Endorsing Agent.** An endorsing agent is the individual authorized to provide or withdraw ecclesiastical endorsements of religious ministry professionals on behalf of an RO. The endorsing agent provides written documentation that an applicant for the military chaplaincy is fully and professionally qualified and endorsed to perform all offices, functions, sacraments, ordinances, and ceremonies required of a DoD chaplain for that RO, and is capable and authorized to minister as required within a pluralistic environment.

* **Faith Group.** A general, inclusive term that might be used to refer to a religion, denomination, sect, or cult.

* **Internal Revenue Code 501(c)(3).** Churches and religious organizations, like many other charitable organizations, qualify for exemption from Federal income tax under Internal Revenue Code Section 501 (c)(3) and are generally eligible to receive tax-deductible contributions.

* **Religious Ministry Professional.** A religious ministry professional is a fully qualified member of the clergy who is endorsed to represent an RO and to conduct its religious observances or ceremonies. The professional may be an ordained minister or the equivalent for those ROs that do not require ordination.

* **Religious Organization (RO).** An entity that is organized and functions primarily to perform religious ministries to a non-military lay constituency, and has met the religious purposes test as defined by the IRS. We are using the abbreviation RO to refer to religious organizations in this report.

* **Religious Pluralism.** The DoDI 1304.28, "Guidance for the Appointment of Chaplains for the Military Departments," describes pluralistic environment as a descriptor of the military context of ministry to support directly and in-

directly the free exercise of religion by all members of the Military Services and their family members. The instruction defines it as a plurality of religious traditions existing side-by-side in the military.

Methodology - The Crystal Focus Process

Crystal Focus is an independent and objective inspection or evaluation of a key DoD-wide program or process. The Crystal Focus process provides a transparent, yet focused evaluation of DoD issues. Normally, senior leadership requests these evaluations. We seek requestor input to develop objectives and to tailor product formats to best convey our findings. Crystal Focus products highlight the most significant issues and provide timely recommendations for senior leadership action. We conduct the reviews in accordance with the criteria in the March 1993 *Quality Standards for Inspections* published by the President's Council on Integrity and Efficiency. The project team will perform follow-up on all recommendations resulting from a Crystal Focus project. Follow-ups will normally occur at 12 and 18 months after the project is completed.

Prior to publishing the report, the Crystal Focus team briefs the results, observations, and recommendations to senior officials of the DoD Office of the Inspector General (IG); DoD management; the requestor of the review, and appropriate program managers. We provide program managers with the opportunity for formal comment and include their verbatim comments in the final report. See Appendix A for an explanation of the methodology used for this report. See Appendix G for a list of organizations visited.

The team conducted interviews with senior members in the Office of the Secretary of Defense (OSD) and leaders of the Military Departments, as well as representatives from the Internal Revenue Service, Federal Bureau of Prisons, Department of Justice Office of the IG, chaplain offices of the Military Departments, and security offices of the Military Departments. The Crystal Focus methodology included a comparison of chaplain program procedures with procedures for accessioning doctors and lawyers. We identified differences in education, training, and citizenship requirements, and the need for security clearances, where applicable.

We also surveyed RO agents who endorsed applicants for the military chaplaincy. The purpose was to determine what information the agent had gathered on the endorsed applicant, and whether the agent maintained contact with the chaplain after endorsement.

Overall Assessment

The DoD chaplain program reflects the efforts of OSD and the Services to meet the spiritual needs of Service members, while balancing national security and religious freedom. In addition, DoD now requires that ROs meet IRS tax exemption requirements. DoD directives limit program participation to professionally qualified clergy who fulfill the needs of members of the Armed Forces. The chaplain program stresses religious pluralism.

The focus of program regulations and procedures is to obtain professionally qualified clergy and to verify the candidate's officership, professional, and religious qualifications. Officership qualifications for chaplains are virtually identical to the qualifications of military officers recruited for other specialties. The professional qualifications for chaplains are similar and comparable to other military professionals, such as doctors and lawyers.

However, the certification of religious qualifications is unique within the military in that the leaders of a faith group determine the religious qualifications of their clergy person. DoD relies on religious organizations and their representative agents, which are outside government purview, to determine religious qualifications.

During our review, DoD chaplain program officials made a concerted effort to update policy and incorporated many of our suggested changes. However, the DUSD(MPP) could further improve internal operating procedures of the AFCB to administer DoD policies regarding religious organizations and their agents who endorse chaplain candidates.

DoD has an established process for recognizing and reviewing ROs that endorse applicants for the chaplaincy, and military procedures for recruiting, accessing, training, retaining, and dismissing chaplains. However, we made five observations and identified opportunities to improve the overall chaplain program with five related recommendations.

Observations

The chaplain program reflects the efforts of DoD to meet the spiritual needs of Service members, while balancing national security and religious freedom. However, the DUSD(MPP) could improve the procedures for managing information on ROs and their agents who endorse chaplain candidates. The following observations were made in support of the announced objectives:

* Observation 1. DoD adds a new religion when the Military Departments recognize the needs of a lay constituency or accept a qualified chaplain who represents a new religion.

* Observation 2. The AFCB has not exercised the option of revoking the recognition of an RO that fails to meet the DoD requirements.

* Observation 3. DoDI 1304.28 does not include nonreligious criteria to disqualify either an RO or its endorsing agent.

* Observation 4. The Army and the Navy have not established procedures to withdraw or remove a chaplain's designation for cause.

* Observation 5. The DUSD(MPP) has not issued implementing instructions to clarify policy expressed in the October 14, 2003 memorandum on the "Appointment of Chaplains for Military Service."

On June 11, 2004, the DUSD(MPP) revised DoDD 1304.19 and published DoDI 1304.28 implementing instructions. The new policies require that for ROs to participate in the DoD chaplain program, the RO must:

* be tax exempt as a church under IRC 501(c)(3);

* obtain an Employer Identification Number;

* notify the AFCB immediately when changes occur in the status of the RO, or the designated endorsing agent, or if contact addresses and telephone numbers of either are changed; and

✱ provide to the AFCB annually a complete list of endorsed chaplains.

During the evaluation, we reviewed the draft directive and instruction and identified areas for improvement. The DUSD(MPP) agreed with our suggestions and incorporated the changes to the draft policy.

Review and Recognition of Religious Organizations (continued)
Observation 3

The June 11, 2004, Department of Defense Instruction (DoDI) 1304.28, "Guidance for the Appointment of Chaplains for the Military Departments," does not include nonreligious criteria to disqualify either a religious organization (RO) or its endorsing agent.

Congressional Interest

Senator Schumer stated in his request letter that two ROs with "disturbing connections to terrorism" had endorsed chaplains. In addition, the former endorsing agent of one of the ROs was indicted on Federal charges. The ROs in question remain eligible to provide candidates for the DoD chaplain program. Existing regulations do not define instances when the Armed Forces Chaplains Board (AFCB) should take action. Examples of such instances may include proven connection to terrorist groups, serious breaches of ethics, or advocating overthrow of the U.S. Government.

The DoD Inspector General met with Senators Kyl and Feinstein on October 28, 2003, concerning muslim cleric issues. During that meeting, both senators expressed their concern regarding security reviews of ROs and endorsing agents. The senators suggested that DoD or the Department of Justice should perform background investigations on ROs and their endorsing agents before vetting a chaplain.

Discussion

The DoDI 1304.28 outlines the criteria that ROs must meet in order to endorse candidates for service as military chaplains. The endorsing agents represent the ROs, not the Government. DoD does not control the endorsing agents' appointments, their qualifications, or their endorsements of chaplain candidates. Therefore, DoD should have procedures to disqualify ROs and their endorsing agents for cause in order to reassure the public and Congress that DoD is safeguarding the military against ROs and endorsing agents guilty of violating U.S. laws.

The AFCB does not have the authority to conduct formal background investigations on ROs or their endorsing agents. We consulted with officials from the DoD Office of General Counsel, Office of General Counsel, Inspector General, and the Federal Bureau of Investigation (FBI) National Joint Terrorism Task Force about performing background investigations. Based on these consultations, we determined that privacy laws prohibit disclosure of personal information without the individual's approval. Attorney General policy does not authorize non-law enforcement officials, such as the Deputy Under Secretary of Defense for Military Personnel Policy (DUSD[MPP]) or the AFCB, to routinely request and obtain information concerning ongoing investigations of non-Government organization officials and other non-DoD personnel. However, DoD can request a law enforcement type review in cases of probable cause regarding criminal activity.

Information on ROs and endorsing agents may be available from non-law enforcement sources during the background investigations of chaplain candidates. When candidates use ROs or endorsing agents as references, Defense Security Service investigators should query those references. In addition, program officials learn of indictments and convictions of ROs, their officers, and endorsing agents from the media. However, relying solely on the media is, at best, a questionable practice, given the inherent problems of accuracy, credibility, and bias.

Currently, procedures are in place to gather, evaluate, and act on adverse information. For example, DoD reviews equal employment opportunity files and publicly disclosed financial records to identify adverse information about General or Flag Officers. As another example, the Federal Bureau of Prisons requests and receives screening information from the FBI that includes a threat assessment of national and local religious endorsing organizations. This information is advisory in nature and does not constitute a formal recommendation by the FBI. It may be reasonable to establish a screening process similar to the

Federal Bureau of Prisons that routinely canvasses existing FBI databases for adverse information concerning ROs and endorsers.

This type of information would support judgments about the religious organizations and individuals endorsing DoD chaplains and reinforce the need to develop applicable nonreligious disqualifying criteria.

Although we are not advocating a specific criterion or screening procedure, we believe that the DUSD (MPP) should consider implementing a process that can identify those ROs or endorsing agents found guilty of violating U.S. law or breach of any other nonreligious criteria. Such action would exercise due diligence toward maintaining full faith and confidence in ROs and their endorsements of chaplains to the Military.

Impact

Illegal actions or breaches of non-religious criteria of ROs or their endorsing agents could affect the selection process for military chaplains. Moreover, relations with ROs and their endorsing agents that are linked to illegal actions or breaches of non-religious criteria may negatively influence public perception of the DoD chaplain program and the DoD as a whole.

Recommendations

The Deputy Under Secretary of Defense for Military Personnel Policy should:

a Establish nonreligious criteria to justify the Armed Forces Chaplains Board withdrawal or removal of a religious organization or its agent from participating in the DoD chaplain program.

* Examples of such criteria could include:

* Advocating the violent overthrow of the U.S. Government;

* Listed on a watch list as a terrorist organization;

* Conviction of a religious organization or its principal leaders in connection with terrorism;

* Conviction of endorsing agents in connection with any criminal activity; and

* Conviction of endorsing agents for acts constituting a breach of non-religious criteria as developed by the Deputy Under Secretary of Defense for Military Personnel Policy.

b Develop screening procedures for collecting existing information from Federal Bureau of Investigation databases and public sources relating to chaplains, their supporting religious organizations, and endorsers.

c Develop and impose program sanctions against those religious organizations or their agents that fail to meet the criteria developed for Recommendation a. above. Examples of sanctions include removing the religious organization from the Armed Forces Chaplains Board list of recognized endorsing organizations or disqualifying its agent from endorsing chaplains.

d Promptly refer to the DoD Inspector General any specific allegation impacting DoD leadership's "full faith and confidence" regarding adverse conduct or behavior of an RO or endorsing agent.

Management Comments and Evaluation Response

The Deputy Under Secretary of Defense for Military Personnel Policy responded to Recommendations a. and b. that were included in the draft report. The complete response is included in Appendix D.

We added language in the discussion and congressional interest paragraphs to explain the intent of the recommendations, reworded Recommendations a. and b. and added Recommendations c. and d.

We request that the Deputy Under Secretary of Defense for Military Personnel Policy address the new recommendations in a response to the final report.

Management Comments. The Acting DUSD(MPP) nonconcurred, stating that recommended actions "were legally problematic to the DoD Office of General Counsel . . . . The DoD must remain responsible for judgments about a person's bona fides to serve as an officer and a chaplain . . . . A chaplain ordinarily receives sufficient scrutiny for selection, appointment, and merit-based retention—all centering on individual merit . . . . [The] Treasury's Internal Revenue Service should remain the focal point for institutional merit."

To make the recommendation executable, the Acting DUSD(MPP) suggested that "DoDIG should report its concerns regarding frequency of review of previous tax-exemption determinations to the Treasury Inspector General and urge more frequent reviews as a means of reducing the potential for enriching coffers of those who might post harm to the Nation."

I&E Response. Management comments are not fully responsive to the recommendations. The intent of the recommendations was for DUSD(MPP) to develop a process to react to available information, not to proactively judge institutional merit. At a minimum, DoD should be able to suspend or reject endorsements from any religious organization or endorsing agent involved in terrorist or criminal actions. We do not anticipate that DoD would contemplate adverse action while an investigation of alleged wrongdoing was under way. However, the DUSD(MPP) should have a process to address congressional concerns by taking appropriate action on organizations and agents that the courts have found guilty of violating laws aimed to safeguard the safety of the United States and its citizens.

The DoDI 1304.28, "Guidance for the Appointment of Chaplains for the Military Departments," dated June 11, 2004, and the October 14, 2003 memorandum requires tax exemption status for ecclesiastical endorsing organizations. Therefore, DUSD(MPP) should ensure that the Department of Treasury's Internal Revenue Code (IRC) 501(c)(3) criteria are adequate as a standard to qualify an RO. Resolving concerns about the credibility for DoD's use of the IRC 501(c)(3) as a tax exempt requirement is the responsibility of DUSD(MPP).

We reworded Recommendations a. and b. and added Recommendations c. and d. to emphasize the need for due diligence in screening religious organizations and their endorsing agent.

Questions Raised by Senator Schumer, March 10, 2003

How do we ensure that certifying religious organizations (ROs) are "of the highest caliber, have unimpeachable reputations, and endorse religious pluralism?"

The chaplain, not the religious organization, provides ministry to the military. DoDD 1304.19 requires chaplains of the Military Departments to "facilitate ministries appropriate to the rights and needs of other faith groups in the pluralistic military environment." The Military Chiefs of Chaplains, as members of the Armed Forces Chaplains Board (AFCB), provide recommendations to the Under Secretary of Defense for Personnel and Readiness (USD[P&R]) on the "religious, ethical, and moral standards for the Military Services." As the senior clergy person for their Military Department, they are responsible for the proper implementation of DoD policy on religious pluralism. In accordance with the October 14, 2003, DoD policy memorandum on the Appointment of Chaplains for Military Departments, organizations desiring to endorse chaplains must meet the criteria for tax exemption under Internal Revenue Code (IRC) 501(c)(3). Under that section of the code, the Internal Revenue Service (IRS) maintains two basic guidelines in determining that an organization meets the religious purposes test:

* The particular religious beliefs of the organization are truly and sincerely held; and

* The practices and rituals associated with the organization's religious beliefs or creed are not illegal or contrary to clearly defined public policy.

DoD relies upon IRS verification of the information submitted by the organization to obtain tax-exempt status. This action should improve DoD controls over endorsing religious organizations. The DUSD(MPP) will also strengthen DoD controls by having the AFCB retain current, as well as adverse, information on ROs and by updating policy.

"Is it appropriate for the GSISS [Graduate School of Islamic Social Sciences] and AMAFVA [American Muslim Armed Forces and Veterans Association] to continue in their advisory capacities?"

We did not include reviews of specific endorsing organizations. Prior to October 14, 2003, DoD had few or no tools to conduct such an assessment. However, as of October 14, 2003, DoD requires new ROs recommending religious ministry professionals as chaplains to have tax-exempt status in accordance with IRC 501(c)(3). In addition, if the Principle Deputy Under Secretary of Defense for Personnel and Readiness implements the recommendations in this report, the AFCB should have additional useful information to determine whether a particular RO should be acceptable to endorse chaplains.

Questions Raised in Congressional Testimony, October 14, 2003

Existing criteria for certifying religious organizations are insufficient. What do you plan to add? (Senator Schumer)

OSD has drafted policy that implements the requirement for IRC 501(c)(3) tax-exempt status and increases the frequency of self-certification for ROs from every three years to annually. In addition, the implementation of recommendations in Observation 3 of this report will significantly improve DoD controls over endorsing ROs.

What are the details behind the 2001 delegation to Saudi Arabia sponsored by the Muslim World League? (Senator Schumer)

The matter is outside the scope of this evaluation of the DoD chaplain program.

How do you deal with defining religions and ruling certain religions unacceptable? (Senator Durbin)

DoD is committed to the protection of religious guarantees under the First Amendment to the U.S. Constitution. Specific control procedures for reviewing religious doctrine or practices could lead to public perception that DoD favored one religion over another, or may raise questions concerning guaranteed religious freedom.

Questions Raised by Senator Kyl in a Meeting with the Inspector General of the Department of Defense, October 28, 2003

Is DoD adequately reviewing endorsing agencies?

ROs and their representing agents act as endorsing agencies for military chaplains. DoD has established criteria for both religious organizations and their agents' involvement in the program. However, First Amendment religious freedoms apply, and the DoD is constrained by the lack of any direct relationship between DoD and the endorsing organizations. DoD can improve oversight of endorsing agents through operating procedures to: (1) verify compliance to DoD requirements by new and current ROs; (2) require ROs to provide their IRC 501(c)(3) data; and (3) reject all future religious endorsements issued by those organizations that no longer comply with DoD policy.

Do the current Muslim Clerics represent the current mix of Muslim Service members?

As of April 2004, the 12 Islamic DoD chaplains on active duty represented Sunni Islam. The relative representation among military members is unknown. Military members provide religious affiliation on a voluntary basis, and the Military Departments do not differentiate between the branches of Islam.

[The following excerpts are from WorldNetDaily Exclusive, "Hasan counseled Fort Hood Muslims: Alleged Army terrorist substitute chaplain for 48," November 9, 2009 (http://www.wnd.com/?pageId=115466):

The suspected Fort Hood terrorist served as a lay Muslim leader running Islamic services on the base in the absence of the Muslim chaplain, [WorldNetDaily] has learned. He also mentored at least one young convert to Islam whose parents worked at the sprawling Texas post.

Hasan's religious activities raise the specter that others may have been radicalized, investigators worry. There are nearly 50 Muslim soldiers serving on the base.

Army Maj. Nidal Malik Hasan allegedly shot 46 fellow soldiers and security guards and murdered 13 in the worst act of terrorism on U.S. soil since 9/11.
Witnesses say the devout Muslim officer jumped up on a desk and shouted, "Allahu akbar!"—Allah is greatest—before opening fire and spraying more than 100 bullets inside a crowded building where troops were preparing to deploy to Afghanistan and Iraq.

"He was preparing for a martyrdom operation," a U.S. Army intelligence official said. "There is no evidence that this was an issue of an emotional aberration. It was well planned."

Not long after Hasan transferred to the base earlier this year, he sat down with Muslim chaplain Maj. Khalid Shabazz to discuss carrying out Shabazz's "vision" at the Fort Hood chapel when Shabazz was away. Shabazz helped lead Islamic services at the base's Iron-horse Chapel, which serves 48 Muslim soldiers.

"I found him to be very pleasant," Shabazz said of Hasan.

"Muslim Mafia" co-author Paul Sperry says Hasan is just the tip of a jihadist Fifth Column operating inside the U.S. military—which is too blinded by political correctness to see the internal threat.

"If military command is too PC to protect its own troops from Islamic fanatics on its own soil, how can Americans be confident they can protect the rest of the country?" asked Sperry, also author of "Infiltration: How Muslim Spies and Subversives Have Penetrated Washington."

He says that each branch of the military operates a counterspying unit in charge of force protection.

"Why didn't the Army investigate Hasan with all the red flags waving around him?" Sperry said. "And what other radicalized soldiers—and I would include chaplains among them—are they failing to investigate now? What is the military doing to stop the next Maj. Nidal?"

1 By what authority and for what purpose would an Inspector General evaluate the bona fides of a Military Chaplain Endorsing Agency?

2 By what authority and for what purpose would an Inspector General recommend that another government official evaluate the bona fides of a Military Chaplain Endorsing Agency?

3 By what authority and for what purpose would a DoD operational leader non-concur with an Inspector General recommendation to establish nonreligious criteria to justify the Armed Forces Chaplains Board withdrawal or removal of a religious organization from participating in the DoD chaplain program when evidence indicates that a "religious organization" is either advocating the violent overthrow of the U.S. Government, listed on a watch list as a terrorist organization, or when its principal leaders have been convicted in connection with terrorism?

4 By what authority and for what purpose would the United States Department of Defense defer to the "Treasury's Internal Revenue Service" on matters implicating terrorism threats to U.S. military personnel, as it appears to have none in the Under Secretary of Defense's non-concurrence with the DoD IG's recommendation to establish nonreligious criteria to justify the Armed Forces Chaplains Board withdrawal or removal of a religious organization from participating in the DoD chaplain program?

5 Why did the January 2010 "DoD Independent Review Related to Fort Hood" not recommend deference to the "Treasury's Internal Revenue Service" on matters implicating terrorism threats to U.S. military personnel, *e.g.*, when it observed that, "Current policy requires removal of any individual or religious organization from participation in the DoD Chaplain program only if they threaten national or economic security, are indicted or convicted of an offense related to terrorism, or if they appear on the annual State Department list of Foreign

Terror Organizations. This limited authority to deny requests for designation as ecclesiastical endorsers could allow undue improper influence by individuals with a propensity toward violence," and based on this observation recommended that the Department of Defense, "Review the limitations on denying requests for recognition as ecclesiastical endorsers of chaplains."[37]

6 Under what circumstances can a chaplain be deemed an agent of Al-Qaeda (or of any other enemy of the United States Constitution)?

7 Which "live bodies" within any federal establishment are responsible for inspecting official chaplains to ensure that none are enemy agents?

8 Are the November 2008 Holy Land Foundation terrorism convictions tantamount to identification of the Holy Land Foundation and its principal leaders as enemies of the United States Constitution? What about CAIR, ISNA, and the other 200+ unindicted co-conspirators? Are those unindicted co-conspirators presumptive enemies of the United States Constitution?

9 Why does the January 2010 "DoD Independent Review Related to Fort Hood" not mention the words "Muslim" or "Islamic" (except once in a footnote reference to a 2007 FBI Law Enforcement Bulletin titled, "Countering Violent Islamic Extremism"), when the only "suspect" in the Fort Hood massacre: (a) "served as a lay Muslim leader running Islamic services on the base in the absence of the Muslim chaplain," and, according to published accounts shortly after the massacre, "jumped up on a desk and shouted, 'Allahu akbar!'—Allah is greatest—before opening fire and spraying more than 100 bullets inside a crowded building where troops were preparing to deploy to Afghanistan and Iraq"[38]?

10 Was the Fort Hood massacre "suspect," Army Major Nidal Hasan, a "violent Islamic extremist" prior to the Fort Hood massacre? If so, why didn't his commanders identify him as such, pursuant to their statutory duties: "to be vigilant in inspecting the conduct of all persons who are placed under their command"; "to guard against and suppress all dissolute and immoral practices, and to correct, according to the laws and regulations of the Army, all persons who are guilty of them"; and "to take all necessary and proper measures, under the laws, regulations, and customs of the Army, to promote and safeguard the morale, the physical well-being, and the general welfare of the officers and enlisted persons under their command or charge"? 10 U.S.C. § 3583 (discussed in Chapter Two, *supra*).

Chapter 3 Endnotes

---

[1] *See* Army Regulation 20-1, "Inspector General Activities and Procedures," p. 5, ¶1-6(e)(1), p. 57, ¶8-1, & p. 61, ¶9-2 (U.S. Department of the Army, 2010); Army Inspector General Website, "The IG And The Commander Relationship" (http://wwwpublic.ignet.army.mil/IG_systems.htm) ("IGs serve as extensions of their commander in the following three ways: [1] IGs extend the commander's eyes and ears[; 2] IGs extend the commander's voice[; and 3] IGs extend the conscience of the commander.").

[2] Inspector General Act of 1978, as amended, Section 4(a).

[3] WorldNetDaily Exclusive, "Hasan counseled Fort Hood Muslims: Alleged Army terrorist substitute chaplain for 48," November 9, 2009 (http://www.wnd.com/?pageId=115466).

[4] "WAR WITHOUT END: The battle between civilian leaders and military brass has defined America's wars, from Vietnam and the Persian Gulf to Iraq and Afghanistan. It didn't start with McChrystal—and it won't end with Patraeus," The Washington Post Outlook, p. B1, June 27, 2010.

[5] Sun Tzu, Art of War, p. 179 (trans. Ralph D. Sawyer 1994).

[6] Declaration of Independence.

[7] Ronald Reagan, "Speech to the House of Commons," June 18, 1982 (www.fordham.edu/halsall/mod/1982reagan1.html).

[8] United States v. Farhane, 634 F.3d 127 (2d Cir. 2011), cert. denied *sub nom. Sabir v. United States*, 132 S. Ct. 833 (2011).

[9] 634 F.3d at 180, n. 7 ("Two successive administrations have indicated that the nation is at 'war' with al Qaeda. See Press Release of Remarks by President Obama on Strengthening Intelligence and Aviation Security, Jan.

7, 2010 ('We are at war. We are at war against al Qaeda, a far-reaching network of violence and hatred that attacked us on 9/11, that killed nearly 3,000 innocent people, and that is plotting to strike us again. And we will do whatever it takes to defeat them.'); Eric Lichtblau, Bush Seeks to Affirm a Continuing War on Terror, N.Y. Times, Aug. 30, 2008, at A10 (quoting administration proposal that Congress 'acknowledge again and explicitly that this nation remains engaged in an armed conflict with Al Qaeda . . . and associated organizations, who have already proclaimed themselves at war with us and who are dedicated to the slaughter of Americans'). The executive locates support for its actions in Congress's September 18, 2001 Authorization for Use of Military Force, Pub. L. No. 107-40, 115 Stat.

224 (2001). See, e.g., Harold Hongju Koh, Legal Adviser, U.S. Department of State, Address to the Annual Meeting of the American Society of International Law: The Obama Administration and International Law (Mar. 25, 2010), available at http://www.state.gov/s/l/releases/remarks/139119.htm (explaining that in light of al Qaeda's 'horrific' attacks on the United States, the United States is 'in an armed conflict with al Qaeda' that is justified by both international and domestic law).").

[10] *United States v. Farhane*, 634 F.3d at 132 ("As part of that investigation, an FBI confidential informant known as 'Saeed' cultivated a relationship with Shah, in the course of which Shah was recorded speaking openly about his commitment to jihad (holy war) in order to establish Sharia (Islamic law) . . . .").

[11] *Id.*, 634 F.3d at 132, n. 4 ("See also United States v. Moussaoui, 591 F.3d 263, 273-74 (4th Cir. 2010); In re Terrorist Bombings of U.S. Embassies in East Africa, 552 F.3d 93, 103-05 (2d Cir. 2008).").

[12] R. James Woolsey, Lieutenant General Harry Edward Soyster, US Army (retired), *et al.*, SHARIAH THE THREAT TO AMERICA, AN EXERCISE IN COMPETITIVE ANALYSIS: REPORT OF TEAM BII, p. 58 (2010).

[13] *Id.*, p. 24 (footnote citation omitted).

[14] The Investigative Project on Terrorism, "Treasury: Al Qaida in 'weakest financial condition in years'," October 14, 2009 (quoting Mustafa Abu al-Yazid) (http://www.investigativeproject.org/1460/treasury-al-qaida-in-weakest-financial-condition).

[15] *Reliance of the Traveller: A Classic Manual of Islamic Sacred Law*, p. 272 (Nuh Ha Min Keller 1991 and 1994).

[16] *See* Definition of "Islam," Webster's Encyclopedic Unabridged Dictionary of the English Language, p. 1011 (1996) ("Islam[:] Ar[abic] *islām* lit., submission (to God)").

[17] *See Reliance of the Traveller*, pp. 744-46 ("r8.0 LYING").

[18] Yahiya Emerick, "What is Islamic Law?," WHAT ISLAM IS ALL ABOUT: STUDENT TEXTBOOK, p. 354 (1997).

[19] *See, e.g.*, Yahiya Emerick, "What is an Islamic State?," WHAT ISLAM IS ALL ABOUT: STUDENT TEXTBOOK, p. 381 (1997) ("The basis of the legal and political system is the Shari'ah of Allah. Its main sources are the Qur'an and Sunnah. . . . The duty of Muslim citizens is to be loyal to the Islamic State, to live as good Muslims, . . . and to answer the call of their leader if he needs them. . . . Once we become educated in the authentic system of Islam, we must try to establish it somewhere. This is our mission. . . . To repeat what has been mentioned before, the only reason Muslim countries have banished Islam from the political process is because the systems in those countries were imposed from outside."); Seyyid Qutb, MILESTONES, pp. 129, 137 (1964) ("Islam is a comprehensive concept of life and the universe with its own unique characteristics. The concept of human life in all its aspects and relationships which are derived from it is also a complete system which has its particular characteristics. . . . [W]e reject these other systems in the East as well as in the West. We reject them all, as indeed they are retrogressive and in opposition to the direction toward which Islam intends to take mankind. . . . The truth is that Islam not only changes

concepts and attitudes, but also the system and modes, laws and customs, since this change is so fundamental that no relationship can remain.").

[20] U.S. Const., Art. VI ("This Constitution, and the Laws of the United States which shall be made in Pursuance thereof, . . . shall be the supreme Law of the Land"); *see* Mark Levin, LIBERTY AND TYRANNY, 28-29 (2009) ("Islamic law, or *sharia*, dictates the most intricate aspects of daily life, from politics and finance to dating and hygiene. There is not, and never has been, support for a national construct of this sort in America.").

[21] DoD Independent Review Related to Fort Hood, "Protecting the Force: Lessons from Fort Hood," p. 2, January 2010 (http://www.defense.gov/pubs/pdfs/DOD-ProtectingTheForce-Web_Security_HR_13Jan10.pdf).

[22] DoD Independent Review Related to Fort Hood, p. 1.

[23] DoD Independent Review Related to Fort Hood, p. 7.

[24] *See* WorldNetDaily Exclusive, "Hasan counseled Fort Hood Muslims: Alleged Army terrorist substitute chaplain for 48," November 9, 2009 (http://www.wnd.com/?pageId=115466).

[25] DoD Independent Review Related to Fort Hood, pp. 2 & 7.

[26] DoD Independent Review Related to Fort Hood, p. 3.

[27] DoD Independent Review Related to Fort Hood, p. 7.

[28] Letter from Assistant Attorney General Ronald Weich to Congresswoman Sue Myrick, February 12, 2010 (http://www.investigativeproject.org/documents/misc/360.pdf).

[29] United States Department of Justice Press Release, November 24, 2008, *supra*.

[30] United States Department of Justice Press Release, "Federal Jury in Dallas Convicts Holy Land Foundation and Its Leaders for Providing Material Support to Hamas Terrorist Organization," November 24, 2008 (http://www.justice.gov/opa/pr/2008/November/08-nsd-1046.html).

[31] *Shariah The Threat to America*, p. 127.

[32] *Id.*, p. 129 (citing in a footnote Jerry Markon, "Muslim activist sentenced to 23 years for Libya contacts," *The Washington Post*, October 16, 2004 (http://www.washingtonpost.com/ac2/wp-dyn/A36718-2004Oct15?language=printer).

[33] *United States v. Alamoudi*, 452 F.3d 310, 311-12 (4th Cir. 2006).

[34] 452 F.3d at 312; *see United States v. Alamoudi*, 1:03-cr-00513 (E.D.VA 2004) (docket available through Pacer).

[35] Inspector General Act of 1978, as amended, Section 4(a); *see* DoD Inspector General Policy Memo, "Inspector General Act Implementation and Office of Inspector General Policy Guidance (Revision 2)," December 27, 2004.

[36] http://www.dodig.mil/Inspections/IE/Reports/Final_DoD%20Chaplain%20Program.pdf

[37] DoD Independent Review Related to Fort Hood, p. 14.

[38] WorldNetDaily Exclusive, "Hasan counseled Fort Hood Muslims: Alleged Army terrorist substitute chaplain for 48," November 9, 2009 (http://www.wnd.com/?pageId=115466).

CHAPTER 4. TEACH AND TRAIN IN WASHINGTON AND BAGHDAD:

The Assassination of Inspector General al-Mokhtar

Inspector General Mission Essential Task List (METL)

*Support the Superintendent and the Chain of Command; Provide **assistance** for soldiers, cadets, DA civilians, family members, and retirees; Conduct thorough **inspections** that recognize excellence and identify systemic deficiencies; Conduct **investigations** that meet the standard of thoroughness and fairness; **teach and train** at every opportunity*

United States Military Academy, Inspector General Website
http://www.usma.edu/ig/metl/default.htm

As explained in Chapter One, the traditional "teach & train" role of an American Inspector General is pounded into every student of the Army Inspector General School. General George Washington delegated this role to Major General Friedrick von Steuben, America's first effective Inspector General.

According to the U.S. Army's official history of its Inspectors General, "By the middle of March [1778], Washington had determined to let Steuben show what he could do, reserving the Inspector General's position as a reward for success."[1] Steuben began teaching and training troops, starting with Washington's own guard detail. "Training of the Commander in Chief's guard commenced on 19 March, with Steuben in charge. Steuben himself trained one squad first, then set his subinspectors, whom Washington had been appointing for several days, to drill the other squads, while he supervised. Once the squads were trained, Steuben drilled them as a company, starting each day with squad drills, and ending with company exercises."[2]

"Steuben not only offered a good example, but specifically instructed officers in how to train their own men. After the model guard company was ready, he extended his system to battalions, then brigades, and in three weeks was able to maneuver an entire division for Washington. His inspectors were his agents. The results of the training were impressive and it did not take long to persuade Washington that Steuben knew what he was doing... On 28 March he appointed Steuben Inspector General."[3]

Teaching & Training Inspector General Professionals

In June 2003, I delivered the commencement address for the Troy State University's 12th Annual University College - Ft. Myer Commencement Ceremony. The graduates were all mid-level DoD professionals, mostly uniformed officers, who had earned their masters degrees part-time while serving in the Washington D.C. area. The title of the speech was, "Domestic Enemies and Pyrrhic Victories."[4]

As the United States was launching into its second war in two years, I sought to inspire these mid-level DoD professionals to continue developing their potential, but to do so in a manner consistent with their sworn duty to support and defend the Constitution. In the end, the Troy State graduates inspired me to focus on graduate educational opportunities for the 1,300 professionals who worked in the Office of Inspector General.

A few weeks later, I addressed another Troy State graduation ceremony, this one for DoD OIG employees. A review of the program revealed that the master's degree Troy State offered was generally good but was unconnected in any meaningful way to the Office of Inspector General's statutory mission.

This discovery coincided with a related observation that the PCIE community was generally lacking in graduate educational opportunities, and the Trefry Review team's recommendation to provide better mid-level training and cross-functional educational opportunities for auditors, inspectors, and investigators throughout the Office of Inspector General.

Dr. Charles Johnson, who had earned his Doctorate in Education while assigned by the Marine Corps to Northwestern University, accepted an invitation to come aboard the DoD Office of Inspector General as an expert consultant. Within months he had, among other improvements, replaced the Troy State master's program through a competitive bid process with a much superior Georgetown University program tailored to the specific challenges of service within the Office of Inspector General.

At the same time, Dr. Johnson organized the disparate training and educational programs throughout the various components of the Office of Inspector General into a virtual "OIG University," for which he served as the first Dean. The Georgetown University's masters program soon became available to any employee of a member of the Defense Council on Integrity & Efficiency (DCIE), and the virtual "OIG University" ultimately served as a template for an initiative by the PCIE Training Committee to improve the training and educational opportunities throughout the 60 offices of inspector general represented on the PCIE. Dr. Johnson's service as Dean of OIG University was short-lived however, due to demands placed on him by the war in Iraq.

Teaching and Training Iraqi Inspectors General

In the summer of 2003, I encountered Ambassador L. Paul "Jerry" Bremer coming out of Pentagon's "River Entrance." Ambassador Bremer was about to take over as Administrator of Iraq. In the course of our brief conversation, we discussed the historical role of an Inspector General during time of war, and the potential choices of deputies within the DoD OIG available to serve as his Inspector General in Iraq.

Ambassador Bremer interviewed two DoD Deputy Inspectors General, and hired Rear Admiral Larry Poe, USNR, who soon thereafter deployed to Iraq as the first Iraq-based American Inspector General. Admiral Poe's service as Inspector General laid the groundwork for Congress ultimately to establish the position of Special Inspector General for Iraq Reconstruction (SIGIR).[5]

A few months later, Ambassador Bremer announced publicly that one of the preconditions for transferring sovereignty back to the Iraqi people was the establishment of fully functional Offices of Inspector General in each of the Iraqi ministries. At our next encounter in the Pentagon, I remarked on the Ambassador's ambitions plan, observing that, "Not every Office of Inspector General in Washington D.C. is fully functional."

I suggested that the goal the Ambassador had set for the Iraqi ministry inspectors general would be impossible to achieve unless the DoD OIG's "Dean of Instruction," Dr. Charles Johnson, deployed to Iraq in support of the Coalition Provisional Authority. I warned that even with Dr. Johnson in charge of training, however, the task would still be "almost impossible."

Just after Christmas, Dr. Johnson deployed. Five months later, he invited me to address the 31 newly-trained Iraqi inspectors general in the Baghdad Convention Center.

The location for the speech was a caucus room in the Convention Center, which itself was on the border between the "Green Zone" and the "Red Zone." A significant portion of the Convention Center was being utilized at the time by Coalition and Iraqi law enforcement entities to screen witnesses for war crimes trials.

The IG security detail was nervous about both entering and departing the Convention Center itself, and about transiting within the Convention Center to the caucus room.

Inside the caucus room, Dr. Johnson had arranged the Iraqi inspectors general into a large rectangular seating arrangement behind folding work-tables very much like the monthly meetings in Washington D.C. of the President's Council on Integrity & Efficiency (aka PCIE).

Before saying anything to the newly-training Iraqi inspectors general, I introduced myself personally to each, proceeding around the outside of the work-tables counterclockwise, shaking hands and looking each in the eyes.

When I finally sat down at the head of the rectangular arrangement of work-tables, I was at a loss for words. Many of those 31 pairs of eyes were visibly scared. I realized many of those same eyes would be lifeless within the year; I just didn't know which ones.

The message to the new Iraqi inspectors general was simple: the prospects for success as "champions of integrity" in a post-Saddam Iraq would be no more daunting than the challenges facing General George Washington and the other founding fathers of our country in the Winter of 1778. The keys to success then and now are integrity, training and discipline, moral courage, and a firm reliance on divine providence.

As usual, the questions and answers proved the most interesting part of the exercise. In response to more than one question, my message was to be courageous, expect setbacks along the way, and not lose hope. In this regard, I pledged my office's continuing support to the fledgling Iraqi inspectors general in their difficult trials to come. Up until that point, our main contribution to their training had been Dr. Johnson, for whose mentorship more than one Iraqi inspector general expressed profound gratitude.

I also extended an open invitation to visit the DoD Office of Inspector General to any Iraqi inspector general who came to Washington D.C.

About two weeks later, my Iraqi Ministry of Defense counterpart, Inspector General Layla Jassim al-Mokhtar, came to Washington D.C. Her visit, by design, coincided with the monthly meetings of both the PCIE and the DCIE.

The day after the July 12, 2005, PCIE meeting, I expressed my profound respect for al-Mokhtar's courage. At the same time, I asked her to consider carefully whether or not she would allow my staff to video tape her comments to the DCIE on the following day, especially in light of the additional risk to her life that the eventual publication of such a video recording would effectuate, whether broadcasted in Iraq or in the United States. She agreed.[6]

She also invited me to visit her Office of Inspector General in Baghdad the following month in order to help motivate her own staff to face the challenges ahead. I accepted her invitation.

Within the month, however, Inspector General al-Mokhtar's own bodyguard shot her, ostensibly by accident. She died five weeks later in a Jordanian hospital.

The following excerpts are from the official translation of Inspector General Layla Jassim al-Mokhtar's speech to the PCIE on July 12, 2004:

> As one of 31 Iraqi Inspectors General working to build an effective anti-corruption system in Iraq and working to improve the efficiency of our ministries, I believe we Iraqi Inspectors General face many of the same challenges which you, our fellow Inspectors General, face.

> Before my remarks on Inspector General issues, I want to express the gratitude of myself and all Iraqi people for the sacrifices made by the people of the United States as well as by the US and coalition military forces in bringing freedom to Iraq. It has not been easy. It will take time to develop the governmental institutions of Iraq, including the anti-corruption system. We are grateful that your respected President and the US government are committed to assisting us in finishing the job which has begun.

> For those of you who may not be familiar with the Iraqi anti-corruption system, it was established by Coalition Provisional Authority orders and consists of three inter-related entities: The Commission of Public Integrity, the Board of Supreme Audit (which previously existed) and the Inspectors General. CPA Order 57 of February 5, 2004 provided for an effective program in all Iraqi ministries with processes of review, audit, and investigation in order to improve the level of responsibility and integrity. The program additionally provided for monitoring ministry performance and for fighting fraud, waste, abuse of power,

and any other misconduct through the offices of the Inspectors General.

In the Ministry of Defense [MoD], the Inspector General structure consists of: an Inspection Directorate, Audit Directorate, Investigations Directorate, and Administrative Directorate. There is also a proposal to establish a directorate for intelligence oversight. The MoD Inspector General office started with the following staff: an Inspection Directorate of one civilian and two military, Investigation Directorate of four civilians headed by a female legal counselor, Audit Directorate of three civilians, and Administrative Directorate of four civilians headed by a female engineer. The initial activities of the IG office were to recruit highly qualified employees who could accomplish the work to be done, then to train those employees and to make the best use of their expertise. At the start of this process, recruiting a sufficient number of qualified employees was a challenge. Some reasons for this included a lack of understanding what the mission and goals of the IG system would be. The security situation, including the location of the ministry building itself, was also an issue. Assassination of a number of MoD officials and employees also presented some recruiting difficulties. Despite the challenges, we were able to hire qualified people and that process will continue until we reach our full strength.

With regard to Inspectors General in the other Iraqi ministries, they are engaged in doing their duties. They are going about their activities intended to spread and support the concepts of integrity, transparency and efficiency. These Inspectors General are doing audits, inspections, and investigations in response to information which comes to them. . . .

These Iraqi IG's have many of the same problems and issues which confront you. They work on staff and budget issues, work to educate their ministers and other government officials on the IG mission so that IG's can be used efficiently and wisely, and they work hard at their duties. I would hope that there could be a cooperative program between the US Inspectors General offices and their Iraqi counterparts for the purpose of building and maintaining an active IG system."[7]

CASE STUDY: VALLEY FORCE IN IRAQ

According to the March 11, 2008, testimony of the Inspector General of the Department of Defense before the Senate Appropriations Committee, the DoD Office of Inspector General (OIG) had, "provided the core staff for the Coalition Provisional Authority IG, and later assisted the stand-up of the SIGIR. Since 2003 the [DoD] OIG has provided 141 full or part-time personnel in support of both organizations. . . . We continue to play a key role in developing and promoting the establishment of effective oversight and security organizations in Afghanistan and Iraq. . . . In July 2007, we initiated a project to document the lessons learned during our 3-year experience in assisting in establishing and developing a viable, sustainable, effective IG system in Iraq. This project will capture the concepts, strategies, options, and practical applications establishing a Federal IG system may be appropriate in nation building missions and as an instrument to combat fraud, waste, abuse, and corruption in developing nations. The expected completion date for the lessons learned report is April 2008."[8]

The following excerpts are from the final draft report of the DoD OIG report on the "Iraqi Principled Governance Initiative." It has never been officially published.

Lessons from Iraq
Inspector General System Implementation (2003-2007)
Report Date: May 2008

PREFACE

The Coalition entered Iraq in 2003, freed the country from its oppressive dictatorship, and dismantled its corrupt governmental infrastructure. Having achieved its military goals, the coalition immediately embarked on helping Iraq develop a democratic form of government based on strict adherence to rule of law. In doing so, it was found there were significant cultural differences between western and Iraqi perceptions of corruption and the need to avoid it within government. The urgency of quickly developing a new form of government in a failed state, that itself continued under siege, and with differing terms of reference, precipitated inefficiencies in achieving timely objectives. These might have been avoided had we had the advantage of the lessons learned as discussed herein.

This report chronicles the lessons drawn from implementing a new Iraqi institution that underpins rule of law, and is a frontline fighter in the war on corruption: the US mandated (CPA-directed) federal Inspectors General system within each Ministry of Iraqi government. After more than four years, the system remains under-developed, under-resourced, and may well be unsustainable since it lacks ability to professionally train and replenish its present complement of 3,500 auditors, inspectors, investigators, and support staff. The system of 31 Iraqi IGs and their Offices throughout Iraq clearly requires substantial time and attention to achieve lasting effectiveness; and there remain wide variations among the various offices. Although the lessons discussed herein are primarily intended to contribute to future endeavors if ever needed, they might also be of benefit is assist in fully implementing a federal Inspector General system in Iraq.

EXECUTIVE SUMMARY

"It will take time to develop the governmental institutions of Iraq, including the anti-corruption systems. Open and transparent government is only a concept to us and will take time to become permanent in Iraq."

Layla Jassim al-Mokthar, Inspector General of the Iraqi Ministry of Defense, July 12, 2005, remarks to the U.S. President's Council on Integrity and Efficiency, Washington, DC

The report assesses lessons drawn from the first four years of implementing the Iraqi Inspector General system. It attempts to assess the impact on implementation "had the lessons been known beforehand." To do so, it is important to define a desired end-state that can be used as a baseline to compare what currently is, to that which should be present at desired end-state. In this report, a desired end-state is a sustainable, professional, and integrated Inspector General system that helps prevent government corruption and improves Ministry effectiveness. These criteria of a desired end-state do not lend themselves easily to quantifiable metrics, and certainly not accurate metrics in hindsight. Therefore the method of assessment employed herein is one of identifying the criteria for success and then identifying those plans, initiatives and resources required to bring the system to that end-state. The result is lessons that are more qualitative than quantitative; more inductive than deductive.

The key lessons learned so far in the course of implementing the Iraqi IG system are: 1) the need for strong and focused leadership invested in the successful development of the system as a priority; 2) the development and dissemination of an integrated strategic plan for the system (such a plan should define the desired end-state, identify avenues to converge upon it, specify the structures required to sustain it, and state the full range of resources to attain it); and 3) the requirement to develop institutional structures within with GoI to professionalize the IG system.

* **Focused Leadership.** Across the board, Coalition leadership has been good, but because of the novelty of implementing a federal IG system, changing security conditions and priorities, multiple tasking, and a measure of ignorance of the IG system within Coalition entities, the implementation of the Iraqi IG system repeatedly faltered for want of attention. Had we been able to maintain a more continuous focus, we might have averted several significant implementation obstacles and had a far more positive assessment to report herein.

* **Joint Strategic Plan.** The need for a joint strategic plan for the creation and execution of the Iraqi IG system would seem axiomatic. However, currently there is still no such agreed upon plan, nor one for implementing Iraqi Anti-Corruption systems, in total. The Iraqi IGs had adopted a jointly developed IG Campaign plan (see Appendix F), but the MNF-I AND USM-I working group has yet to recognize it. The need prevails for an integrated Anti-Corruption strategic plan in Iraq that clearly defines a sustainable end-state, the avenues to be taken in achieving it, and the resources required.

* **Government Institutional Structures.** CPA Order 57 essentially created a new profession of independent and objective government fact-finders in Iraq. Professions require internal and external structures for sustainment, coordination, and self-policing. In Iraq, there is a crucial need for 1) an institutional training gateway (Academy of Principled Government - See Appendix G) at the national level for sustainment of the oversight profession; 2) a permanent cross-agency coordination council (JACC equivalent - see Appendix I) for strategic coordination of all systems to win the war on corruption; and 3) an independent mechanism for self–policing Iraqi oversight professionals and for providing independent evaluation and advice to the GoI on appointment and dismissal of high officials within oversight institutions.

This report is intended to help develop expertise that can be applied in future oversight systems, if creation of such systems is again deemed appropriate. However, the lessons learned might also serve in completing the work in progress in Iraq. It should be remembered that the Iraqi IG system is currently incomplete. It is not currently sustainable and is vulnerable to the vagaries of both Iraqi and US level of interest. It survives now because the Iraqi Government is tentatively convinced of its potential and awaits concrete evidence of its merits within the Ministries.

SECTION 1

Introduction

1.1—BACKGROUND

General: The report assesses lessons drawn from the first four years of implementing the Iraqi Inspector General system. It attempts to assess the impact on implementation had the lessons been known beforehand. For purposes here, a desired end-state is a sustainable, professional, and coordinated/integrated Inspector General system that helps reduce and prevent government corruption and improves the effectiveness of its ministries.

A new profession of independent and objective fact-finders was essentially created within the Iraqi government by the implementation of the Iraqi Inspectors General System (IG), the Commission on Public Integrity (CPI), and the reconstituted Board of Supreme Audit (BSA). However, two of these systems (Federal IG system and CPI) were entirely new to Iraq. And arguably so was government accountability and transparency, at least in terms of what is generally held by international standard (citation?).

Implementing a new profession to execute a new process (particularly one foreign to the participants) requires sophisticated strategic planning, dedicated resources, experts to advise and mentor the system, and creation of professional structures integral to coordination and optimization of system composing the profession.

Using hindsight then, it may be useful to pose what "might have been," if we had the benefit of historical precedent. Primarily this assessment hopes to help us learn from the experiences. Though one might point to and count successes the last four years, the bottom-line is the system has yet to achieve a state where it appears sustainable. It remains vulnerable, and requires much support. It survives, because it has taken a fragile root in the Government of Iraq (GoI); who still wait for the fruits of the IG system within all its ministries to be revealed.

Purpose. The purpose of this report is to review lessons from the four-year effort to implement a federal Inspector General (IG) system in Iraq from the vantage point of IG Advisors who worked with the system. The creation of federal IG system outside the US had never been undertaken before in our history. Though a US military IG system dates back to George Washington, the US federal IG system was created by the Inspector General Act of 1978, and is now only 30-years old.

Data Resources: The report depends largely on accounts and daily records maintained by US assigned IG advisors to Iraq from the period January 2004 through early 2008. These log books and calendars identified objectives for the day/week/month, meetings attended, agendas, summary of discussions, coordination phone calls, proposals made, and other information relevant to daily activities of supporting the IG system in Iraq.

In addition to advisor journals, the DoD IG Reachback cell was established in late summer 2004 and possesses phone and e-mail records on nearly a daily basis. Besides weekly reports for most of the period, the Director of the Reachback Cell e-mail records of daily summaries and initiative support are voluminous (almost daily contacts) and compliment other hardcopy sources.

The authors also conducted a review of the literature; especially review of multiple government-generated Lessons-Learned reports from DoD and Non-DoD sources. Detailed information related to anticorruption efforts was also drawn from quarterly CPA IG (now SIGIR) reports. .

In addition, selected congressional testimony of officers working on Anti-Corruption initiatives was reviewed, coupled with a number of interviews with key officials involved in IG system implementation.

Definitions: For the purposes of this report, the definitions listed below are used:

* **Iraqi Inspectors General System (IG)** is the system of IG offices throughout the Ministries of the government of Iraq. IG offices perform audits, inspections, and investigations to reduce fraud, and increase efficiency and effectiveness of the Ministry served. IGs are appointed by the Prime Minister for 5-years, but report to and work on behalf of their respective Ministers.

* **Board of Supreme Audit (BSA)** is an independent audit body to promote economy and efficiency. BSA promulgates Iraq's auditing standards and provides quality oversight of IG audits. The President of the Board of Supreme Audit reports to the PM.

* **Commission on Public Integrity (CPI)** is the investigative law enforcement body for, among other things, allegations of corruption. It has developed a Code of Conduct to be signed by all state employees and Financial Disclosure Forms to be filed by senior public officials. CPI is tasked to promote "transparency in government" and enhance public access to government information. Under the Constitution, CPI reports to the Council of Representatives.

* **Corruption** is defined as the purposeful disobedience to the laws that prohibit graft, bribery, fraud and other forms of stealing. (Citation?)

* **Government Fraud** is defined as the deliberate act of deception in order to acquire government resources unlawfully.

* **Abuse of power** is the use of ones position or influence to violate the basic human rights of others.

* **Waste in government** refers to the inefficient, capricious, or otherwise frivolous use of government resources.

* **Oversight** is a function of those entities in government that have the ability and duty to assess, audit, investigate and inspect on behalf of the public good to ensure transparency and accountability, and reduce fraud, waste, and abuse of power.

* **Rule of Law** is the adherence, respect, and reliance on for the ethical principles that underpin good governance to include the respect for basic human rights of its citizens, the need for transparent and accountable governance, and encourages the free participation of its citizens in government accountability.

1.2—IRAQI INSPECTORS GENERAL SYSTEM

CPA Order 57—Establishment of the Iraqi Inspectors General System

On February 10, 2004, CPA Order 57 established the ministerial "independent Offices of Inspectors General (IG) to conduct investigations, audits, evaluations, inspections, and other reviews in accordance with generally accepted professional standards."[9] The purpose of placing IGs directly in the ministries was to establish standards that fit Iraqi culture and prevent corruption and mismanagement within the ministries. The IGs have two key responsibilities concerning corruption including prevention, detection, initial investigations and referral of criminal cases either to the courts or to CPI for further investigation.[10]

Collectively, the Iraqi Inspectors General constitute one of three "Pillars of Anti-Corruption." The other two pillars are the Board of Supreme Audit (BSA) and the Commission on Public Integrity (CPI). Prior to 2004, there was no history of a Federal Inspector General (IG) system in Iraq, or other countries in the Mideast.

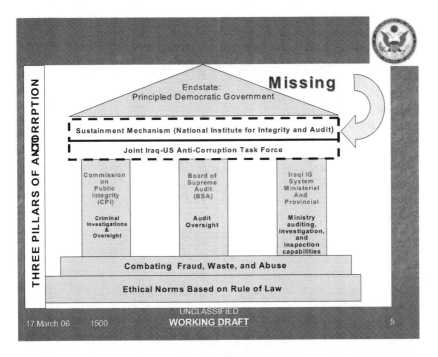

Coalition Provisional Authority (CPA) Order 57 (See Appendix D) prescribes the duties of all ministry-level Iraqi "federal" IGs. The order was in effect at the time sovereignty passed to the GoI in June of 2004. It is among those orders which remain Iraqi law." Change 1 to CPA 57 provides for an "independent budget" for all IGs. Funding in the future will be provided directly to the federal offices of inspector general from the Minister of Finance rather than from the respective Ministries. This independent funding provides a degree of financial and practical independence for the IGs.

The concept of Inspectors General as an extension of the eyes, ears and conscience of the military commander or minister appears largely a US-unique construct. At the time of introduction of the IG concept during the CPA, the basic IG organizational model suggested to GoI officials is the same functional organization seen in most USG federal-level Inspectors General. This model provides for three major functions: Inspections, Investigations, and Audit.

The text of CPA Order 57 recognized that Iraq's former regime fostered inefficiency and corruption in governmental institutions and a concerted effort is needed to restore public trust and confidence in the institutions of government.

Although not initially provided for in any official sense, the national-level Inspectors General who were appointed pursuant to the CPA orders organized an Association of Inspectors General. From among their number, these federal-level IGs select an IG to serve as the head of this association and to serve as their spokesman. This association has met monthly since introduction of the IG system to the ministries. It has served as a forum for not only the IGs, but also for representatives of the other Iraqi anti-corruption agencies to communicate and coordinate on a wide variety of issues. The head of this association at the time of this assessment is the Inspector General of the Ministry of Health. The IG association has undertaken a process of inspecting the various ministerial IG offices to promote efficiency and progress within their own ranks.

The concepts of governmental transparency and accountability are new to most Iraqis. It appears that Saddam-era Iraqi military and police experience with a "General Inspector" was experience with a position that carried the power to reward or to punish in the then-corrupt Ba'athist system. It is reported that some Iraqis viewed the establishment of a new federal GoI IG program as reimplementation of that former General Inspector system. The cultural baggage associated with the former "General Inspector" has likely provided challenges to education of Iraqis at all levels as to the positive aspects of the new IG system.

Points of Interest—CPA Order 57:

* Section 2 establishes that "The initial Inspectors General in each ministry shall be appointed...by the Administrator" and "After the assumption of full governance authority by the sovereign transitional Iraqi administration, Inspectors General shall be appointed to vacant positions by the chief executive of the transitional Iraqi administration, subject to confirmation by the majority vote of the body vested with national legislative powers."[12]

The language here is vague in its reference to the executive and legislative bodies of the transitional government, which had not yet been agreed upon. In addition, because the order specified appointments of the Inspectors General by the CPA Administrator were for a five-year term, it created both the possibility for stabilizing the GoI, but also for friction as successive Iraqi governments changed leadership at the Ministry level.

This is particularly true because Section 4 makes clear that, "An Inspector General may be removed by the relevant minister only for cause. "Cause" shall include, but shall not be limited to, malfeasance, abuse of office, and bribery."[3]

✱ Section 5, Part 18 gives the ministerial IGs the function to "Perform such other duties within the scope of their power, as defined in Section 6...as may be necessary to carry out their responsibilities under this order."

The vague nature of this clause seems to grant the IGs considerable flexibility, as their function is not narrowly defined but left deliberately broad in scope. Under Section 6, their powers are defined equally broadly.

1.3—CORRUPTION AND THE CULTURAL EFFECT

Corruption in Iraq is different than western norms, in magnitude, acceptance, and manifestations. Actually there is a difference in relative terms of reference and definitions. It is not that one side of the world knows what is right and other does not. Both know right and both know what is wrong. Yet, customs, culture, and reward practices which arose during the Saddam dictatorship continue to exert a significant effect on boundaries between acceptable and unacceptable conduct. A 2004 civil affairs military officer in Baghdad may have captured a sense of the Iraqi mentality towards corruption:

> After 35 years of living under Saddam and surviving, corruption is a survival skill. It is still a huge problem and it's institutional. Iraqis consider what we call corruption as just either the cost of doing business or the way you do business.[14]

Controlled corruption was an endemic problem under Saddam's regime. The Ba'athist party controlled all political and legal power in Iraq and thus was able to modify accountability standards and law enforcement to financially benefit those in power. This fueled an extensive corruption network ranging from the highest officers in government down to those at the lowest levels of service.[15]

Generations of corruption as a means of survival have led to the development of different cultural norms throughout Iraqi society. Contributing to the Iraqi's altered perspectives of corruption is the fact that Iraq is primarily a cash-based society where credit cards, checking accounts, and other common banking services are not available. As a result, practices that include pay-offs became not only unusually easy to make, but were reported to be routine occurrences under Saddam's rule. Rodney Bent, former Director of the Coalition Provisional Authority Office of Management and Budget from October 2003 to April 2004, commented on the differences in payment practice:

> It's a cash-based society, a government operated by cash, not by checks or financial methods. So it goes everywhere, and Saddam would foster corruption. People tended to believe that if you wanted to get something done, you needed to pay people off.[16]

Following the fall of the Ba'athist party in 2003, corruption continued. As a result, USG reconstruction and development programs directly suffered.[17] According to a joint SIGIR and DoS Inspector General report on anticorruption from July 28, 2006:

> Corruption in Iraq siphons resources from needed government services and reduces the willingness of international investors to invest in Iraq. It has been identified as a major barrier to establishing citizens' trust and confidence in their government and to improving economic growth and prosperity.[18]

Statements on Iraqi Corruption:

Prime Minister Maliki: We have inherited administrative corruption, bureaucracy, and lack of interest in citizens' needs. We admit this. However, we are continuing our efforts to put an end to such practices. The government and people should cooperate in this regard.[19]

Ambassador Bremer: "...many Iraqis are concerned about corruption. So am I. While the vast majority of Iraq's citizens are honest, we cannot forget the past. During Saddam Hussein's regime schoolyards filled with sewage while Saddam built palaces and Uday bought Ferraris. To protect the Iraqi people from this kind of corruption in the years ahead I am creating three independent, but cooperating agencies to protect the public interest."[20]

"My colleagues and I were acutely aware of the dangers of corruption. It had been institutionalized, even encouraged, under Saddam, as the Oil for Food program has shown. So we took steps to combat corruption. We established the independence of the Iraqi judiciary, appointed Inspectors General in every Iraqi ministry, revitalized an old respected Iraqi audit agency and set up a national commission to which any Iraqi can bring charges of fraud or waste. Of course these institutions alone, in a short time, cannot abolish corruption. But a start has been made."[21]

Secretary Rice: "The institutions of Saddam Hussein's government were violent and corrupt, tearing apart the ties that ordinarily bind communities together. The last two years have seen three temporary governments govern Iraq, making it extremely difficult to build national institutions even under the best of circumstances. The new government to come can finally set down real roots....To be effective, that government must bridge sects and ethnic groups. And its institutions must not become the tools of a particular sect or group."[22]

Thomas Gimble, Acting DOD IG: "Iraqi officials agree that U.S. intervention in necessary. The Commissioner on Public Integrity and the 31 ministry IGs agree that they

need a professional training mechanism that would teach
and train not only IGs, but also government officials. On
June 23, 2005, the Commissioner of Public Integrity wrote
a letter to the Ambassador, stating that:

'...fighting corruption and instilling a culture of ethics,
transparency, and accountability are critical requirements
for a democratic Iraq. [A training Institute] would further
our objectives by creating education, training, and capaci-
ty-building to personnel from CPI, the Board of Supreme
Audit (BSA), the Inspectors General (IGs) in the ministries, other Iraqi government personnel and members of
the public.'[23]

1.4—SUMMARY

This report will try to draw upon lessons from the first four-
years of implementing the Iraqi federal Inspector General system—an
initiative never before attempted outside the United States itself. It
assesses impacts on implementation in a sense from a viewpoint of
what arguably should have been a desired end-state. The sources of the
report data include a review of literature and selected interviews with
officials cited, but for the most part, data was drawn from US IG Advisor daily log journals, calendars, together with phone and electronic
records routinely exchanged between IG Advisors forward in Iraq and
the DoD IG Rear Cell Support cell. The author is responsible for conclusions drawn from the sources.

In the end, the report hopes to contribute by learning from
experiences in Iraq in order they be applied to future USG efforts to
implement oversight institutions in host countries, if so called upon to
do. Yet an operational Iraqi IG remains crucial for the furtherance of
good governance and rule of law in Iraq. Perhaps the lessons identified
here will have current value in finishing the IG system work we began
in Iraq over 4-years ago.

SECTION 2

2.1—Background

For most portions of the first four years of Iraqi IG system implementation, the system seemed largely both misunderstood and under-resourced. Although signs of increasing support are evident in 2008, the first years in particular seemed to be steps forward, then backward, then sideways, with frequent repetition of each. On the whole, the IG system remains in need of work to become fully operational and sustainable. However, at its inception, the IG system did enjoy the support of the CPA Administrator in Iraq, and that of the DoD IG in Washington. Indeed, it was Ambassador Bremer's idea to create the Iraqi system.[24]

But actually implementing an entire federal IG system in Iraq was not only difficult, it was literally unprecedented. A ministry-level Federal IG system had never been created in any government, except in the US. Yet the US federal IG system grew to maturity based on the lessons gleaned from over 200 years of Military IG system experience. CPA Coalition planners (only some of whom were US personnel) wrestled in late 2003 with defining what a federal IG system was for Iraq, and how it would be implemented in all Ministries of Iraqi government. No doctrine, no case studies, and no precedent existed to guide the planning or the implementation effort. DoD IG aided CPA with reviews of the US legislation (The IG Act of 1978) and thus helped guide the planners toward a usable model for enabling legislation for the system. Even with the Administrator's inspired direction and DoD IG's early support, CPA staff planners were not unanimous on how to implement the IG system. Some appeared to doubt whether it could be done at all. This division of opinion reportedly led to edits to the enabling legislation (CPA Order 57) that had the effect of decentralizing both the implementation and funding of the Iraqi IG offices. By doing so, the order made implementation the responsibility of each individual Iraqi ministry. This decentralization of the IG system also made the entire IG system less visible to national authorities. It indulged in the presumption that each Minister both understood the concept of the inspector general as embodied in CPA Order 57 and supported the idea of establishing an IG office within the Ministry, in the first place.

Unsurprisingly, even with the Ambassador Bremer's active support, the system launch was neither smooth nor universally enthusiastic. Although lack of attention to the IG system would become a far greater issue once CPA ended and advice and assistance responsibilities transitioned to the Embassy, it should be noted that even under CPA, the overall system had no implementation plan associated with it, no resources dedicated to it, and no designation for providing IG advisors as mentors to the newly selected IGs. Necessarily then, such progress that has occurred over the initial years was largely through initiatives sponsored and conduced by the Iraqi IGs themselves.

Over the initial years the Iraqi IG system grew to 31 offices throughout the GoI and over 3,500 personnel, primarily auditors, investigators, and inspectors. For most of the initial two years there was one US Advisor to the IGs (detailed from DoD IG). His original mission was to develop and advocate for an Iraqi Training Academy that would act as the training gateway to the Iraqi professionals serving the Anti-Corruption institutions. Once on the ground, his duties immediately broadened. Subsequently, two more individual Ministry IG advisors were added (one for Ministry of Defense-beginning in August 2004) and one for Ministry of Interior IG (beginning January 2005]).[25] Later in 2006, when Multi-National Security Transition Command-Iraq (MNSTC-I) assumed responsibility for the two security ministries (MoD and MoI), they committed even more contracted advisors to those two individual Security Ministry IG offices. As of this writing, the remaining 29 IG offices are still mentored and assisted by one US Advisor.

2.2.—HISTORICAL CONTEXT OF IG SYSTEM IMPLEMENTATION

Phase I. June 2003 - June 2004: CPA Conception/Initiation of Three Anti-Corruption Oversight Institutions (including a Federal Inspectors General System)

The concept of three interlocking government anticorruption/oversight institutions (Board of Supreme Audit (BSA), Commission on Public Integrity (CPI), and the federal IG system) developed during the summer of 2003. The announcement of plans for the IG system was not generated by the CPA staff, but was announced unilaterally by Ambassador Bremer himself to his staff in July of 2003.[26] Of the three systems, the only one for which there was precedent in Iraq was the Board of Supreme Audit. Reinstating that GAO-type institution was a comparatively straightforward matter of reconstituting it in law. The BSA headquarters in Baghdad had been damaged and some records lost, but the basic infrastructure was intact and personnel necessary to reopen the BSA were available. Even though the BSA was reconstituted by CPA Order 77 in March 2004, it was not until June that its President was appointed in writing by CPA. During the interval the favored candidate and eventual BSA President (Ihsan Kareem Ghanim al-Ghazi) filled the position on an acting basis and became an important figure within the interim Iraqi government. The CPA Senior Advisor to Ministry of Finance assigned one staff person to work with the BSA. Support to the BSA was augmented by a CPA Operations Planner (British Auditor David Kirk) who was also a close advisor to Ambassador Bremer.[27]

A newly created Commission on Public Integrity (CPI) was constituted as an independent criminal investigative body, reporting to the head of government. Its funding was mandated by law and separate from any other entity in government. The implementation plan for CPI was well conceived by US Department of Justice (DoJ) Advisors to CPA. The Iraqi staffing of CPI did not begin until June of 2004, and not reach full operation until the fall of 2004. However by May 2004, there was a 40+ person US advisory staff dedicated to supporting the CPI and its eventual programs. CPI was provided a separate budget by CPA and it also had available $11 million in funding from the INL [Bureau of International Narcotics and Law Enforcement Affairs] for startup equipment and training costs. The DOJ's International Criminal Investigative Training Assistance Program (ICITAP) provided dedicated support of CPI staff in "investigative procedures, including surveillance, physical and computer evidence, the technical aspects of investigations, and personal security.[28] At the time of appointment of first Iraqi to CPI in June 2004 (Judge Rahdi Al-Rahdi), the CPI advisory staff was well into the building process.

The federal IG system officially was established in February 2004, by CPA Order 57. It eventually grew to 31 IG offices of Inspector General operating within ministries and some other entities of government. The original IGs were appointed by Ambassador Bremer for 5-year terms, but reported and were to be funded by respective individual ministries. The IGs were tasked by Order 57 not only to do investigations, but also to perform audits, inspections, and other evaluations as well as training to improve the Ministry's efficiency and effectiveness. Though complementary in functions to two other oversight systems (CPI and BSA), the IG system as a whole was quite differently situated concerning implementation.

Other than the CPA Administrator's plan to appoint the individual Inspectors General before the end of June 2004, there was no implementation plan for creating the positions or training IGs and staffs. As noted previously, the CPA Order established decentralized funding and made establishment of IG offices the responsibility of all individual interim Ministers. There was no Development Fund for Iraq (DFI) budget provided, no INL funds, no ICITAP training planned for. What was on station for the IG system (later months of 2003 to early March 2004) was a detailed IG Advisor, Mr. Robert Dawes. Dawes was a temporary detail and worked with CPA Operations Office on behalf of the IG system. During February 2004, Dawes conducted the first two-day IG seminar training for those IGs that had been already selected and appointed. In March 2004, DoD IG sent his Dean of Instruction (Charles Johnson, PhD) to take over for Dawes. Dr. Johnson was attached to newly established CPA Inspector General office forward (CPA IG was later renamed SIGIR). Johnson became the sole Advisor to the entire Iraqi IG system across the entire federal government and its ministries. He performed this duty in Iraq for some 40 months (March 2004 to June 2007).

An early initiative of the Iraqi IGs was to form the IG Association. The model they used was the charter of the US President's Council for Integrity and Efficiency (PCIE). In the first months (March-July 2004) the association met weekly to share lessons and coordinate activities. The Association elected officials and appointed separate committees to address IG system training, legislation, and plans.

In April 2004, the US advisors to the several Iraqi anti-corruption institutions (CPI, BSA, and IG system) began a formal working group meeting on a weekly basis. The Senior Advisor for CPI was the designated chairman, and the group was denominated the Anti-

Corruption Working Group (ACWG) by its participants. From the outset, representatives of INL, USAID, Embassy Human rights and Rule of Law and others, were invited to participate in the weekly meeting, as were representatives of rule of law from other Coalition Embassies. The mission of the working group was to coordinate efforts in anti-corruption, seek efficiency and act as a conduit to raise Anti-Corruption (AC) issues within the Embassy. Although the ACWG was subject to ebbs and flows in its relative importance to AC in Iraq, it consistently provided a forum for raising system needs and issues to be addressed. The ACWG still exists today in Iraq.

It was not until June of 2004 that the final Ministry IGs were appointed. These were an IG for Ministry of Defense and IG for Baghdad Municipalities. It should be noted that with the support of SIGIR IG and others, Dr. Johnson was able to secure an allocation of Iraqi Seized Funds. Presenting the case successfully before the CPA Program Review Board (PRB), one of Ambassador Bremer's last official acts was to allocate $11 million of Iraqi seized funds to the IG system. The money was to be divided among the Ministry IG offices for start up costs, with an allocation of $3 million to go for training and as seed money for an Iraqi Academy for Principled Governance as the institution to train CPI, BSA, and IG professionals in audit, investigation, and inspection.

Phase II. July—December 2004: Anti-Corruption Transition from CPA to IRMO

At CPA inactivation on 28 June 2004, the newly created Iraq Reconstruction Management Office (IRMO) inherited the duty of overseeing anti-corruption and oversight efforts of the three new Iraqi systems. IRMO personnel were a combination of the former Chief Policy Officer (CPO) branch of CPA and CPA Ministry Advisors numbering over 300 at the time of transition from CPA to IRMO. Senior advisors to the three Iraqi oversight institutions (CPI, BSA, and IG) therefore became part of and reported to the Director, IRMO. Other important and related entities like INL, ICITAP, Embassy Human Rights and Rule of law, did not report to IRMO. While traditional embassy reporting chains typically vested an embassy economic section or political section with responsibility for anticorruption activities, particularly in the early days after CPA's inactivation there was little interface between those working in IRMO and such embassy sections on details of the Iraqi systems.

As noted, the availability of plans, financial resources, and US advisors for the three oversight institutors had always been dissimilar. The disparity became even more pronounced when the advisor to BSA departed at the time of CPA inactivation. The CPI effort alone was relatively well situated and funded. In the flood of issues before the embassy and IRMO at time sovereignty was passed to Iraq in June 2004, the lack of plans for the implementation of the IG system and the BSA became, in hindsight, keys to continuing disparities among the systems. Anti-Corruption efforts and development of the Iraqi oversight institutions, including the IG system, struggled to maintain forward motion during the balance of 2004. Among the other changes wrought by the transition form CPA to IRMO was a change in the reporting visibility of the IG and other systems.

Under CPA the advisors to BSA, CPI, and IG worked for (David Kirk) the CPA Operations and Planning Director who had daily access to the Administrator. In the IRMO structure the advisors found themselves multiple layers down the organizational structure.

An early decision by the Director of IRMO in the fall of 2004 encouraged what was called a "one-voice rule" for Iraqi Anti-Corruption (AC) program advisors. The practical impact of this action was to make the CPI Senior Advisor the single voice for efforts to develop all three Iraqi oversight systems and institutions. When David Kirk left in June 2004, there remained only one advisor (Dr. Johnson) to assist the oversight systems (IG and BSA) other than CPI. One early initiative by the Iraqi CPI in August of 2004 was to seek to absorb the IG offices under CPI control. Although this action was contrary to existing law and would materially alter the relationships among the three institutions which had been created, CPI advisory staff described the change to Director of IRMO and all Ministry advisors as a decision already made by the Iraqi government. Unfortunately this bureaucratic maneuvering by the Iraqi Commissioner of Public Integrity was apparently without authority, the Iraqi IGs successfully resisted attempts to subordinate their work to the CPI, and the effort to absorb them into CPI was not pursued within the GoI. A "one-voice" approach to this situation appeared to some observers of this transaction to place the

US advisors squarely in the role of advocating for Iraqi changes in the structure of Iraqi government outside appropriate processes for such change.

IG system interim training milestones were achieved during the fall of 2004. Some 640 Iraqi anticorruption staff members (IG offices, BSA, and CPI) were trained in Egypt during October-December in audit, investigations, and inspections. In addition the IGs, senior BSA officials and Commissioner of CPI received management training in both Egypt and England during 2004. The training was sponsored by the Iraqi IG Association. Funds to pay for the training was drawn from Iraqi seized funds allocated to the IGs by Ambassador Bremer on his last day in office.

Phase III. 2005—2006: Embassy Econ Involvement

Beginning in January 2005, two US Embassy Baghdad Chief of Mission action proposals concerning coordination and sustainability of the anti-corruption oversight institutions were staffed by the IG Advisor through the Director of IRMO. The proposals were cleared and coordinated with the then Rule of Law officer, Peter Ganser. The first proposal was for US-GoI partnership to develop the Iraqi Academy of Principled Governance. The Academy concept had been discussed among the Iraqi IGs, CPI and BSA since June of 2004. The US side had been slowed by lack of unanimity among US advisors caught up in the CPI effort to subsume the IGs into the CPI organization. The second proposal was to shift reporting for the Anti-Corruption advisors (including CPI, BSA and IGs) from the temporary IRMO organization into the more regular Embassy reporting relationship; either to Embassy Econ or Embassy Political. The rationale for that shift was not only the temporary nature of IRMO and lack of management experience in Anti-Corruption, but also as a way for the Embassy to increase the priority of its anti-corruption effort in Iraq.

The first proposal garnered immediate feedback. In late January, the Deputy Director of IRMO (MGEN Arnold Fields, USMC (Ret)) met with the IG Advisor and Judge Greg Townsend (then the Chief of Staff for the MoD Advisory team and the Advisor to the MoD IG and General Counsel) concerning the Academy Action proposal. General Fields recommended that statements of support be gained from the Iraqi IGs, the Commissioner of CPI, and from the President of BSA, to demonstrate Iraqi buy-in. The next week the IG Advisor took the Academy proposal in Arabic to each of the anticorruption institutions seeking their written statements of position on the proposed Academy.

On February 8, 2005 the Iraqi IGs met to discuss the Academy. The IGs collectively signed a Memo to Ambassador Negroponte endorsing the concept of an Iraqi national Academy of Principled Governance. The detailed IG Memo also contained their views on a governance mechanism for the Academy as well as resource estimates. CPI's response to the Academy proposal did not arrive until June 2005. CPI endorsed the need for an Academy, but suggested it be called the "CPI Training Center" and be under CPI control (rather than governed by a Board of Governors as had been recommended by the IGs). The President of BSA never responded in writing concerning the Academy. In meetings, however, he frequently stated that he saw the need for the Academy for the IG system and CPI, but did not see its value to the BSA, which had an 80-year of history of Supreme Audit functions in Iraq.

There was considerable discussion of the proposal's merit on reporting relationships for the Anti-Corruption advisors. In March of 2005, the IG Advisor began reporting directly to MajGen Arnold Fields[29] (Deputy Director, IRMO). This began a period of improved visibility of IG system needs within IRMO. During succeeding months, the proposal recommending increased Embassy control of anti-corruption also gained traction. In April, the Embassy decided that Embassy Econ Counselor would become the new Chairman of the Anti-Corruption Working Group and thus oversee anti-corruption initiatives in total. The first ACWG meeting under this arrangement occurred in May 2005. Unfortunately there was then a hiatus in meetings until a new Econ Counselor (Thomas Delare) arrived in August 2005. It was then that transition to Econ leadership truly began in earnest, and strides in coordination were immediately evident as a result of this new leadership.

In November, the Iraqi IGs proposed to Ambassador Khalilzad that the U.S. and Iraqis fight corruption jointly, through a Joint U.S.-Iraqi Anti-Corruption Task Force. There was a joint meeting of all the Iraqi anti-corruption institution heads in late November to confirm their own intent to partner with the Coalition on shared interests. Embassy Econ represented the Ambassador at that meeting. Much of the rest of 2005 was dedicated to trying to develop the USG position on its contribution when this Task Force began operations.

Also at the end of 2005, the decision was taken to pass responsibility for all aspects of development and capacity building for the two Iraqi security ministries ,those being Interior and Defense from IRMO to MNSTC-I. Military planners in MNSTCI worked with the IG Advisory about staffing needs for the two IG offices for Defense and Interior. Ultimately, a three-person IG Advisory team concept was accepted for each ministerial-level IG office. Each team was to consist of a lead GS-15 or equivalent IG Advisor and two other IG Advisors— one for IG investigations and one for Human Rights. In addition to the ministerial-level advisory teams, MNSTC-I also created four IG advisor positions to assist with development of an IG system inside the uniformed services of the Iraqi military.

In January 2006, Econ engaged the IG Advisor to help frame the strategy for the joint Iraqi-US Anti-Corruption task force and to assist with an overall Campaign Plan for building and sustaining the Iraqi IG system. By mid-February 2006, the Econ Counselor and the IG Advisor jointly briefed the DCM and Deputy Commanding General, MNF-I on a proposed joint campaign plan to bring USG and the Iraqi leadership effectively into the fight against corruption. The concept was approved, and the IG Advisor was tasked to develop the formal plan in conjunction with the Embassy sections and MNF-I planners and to brief the CoM and CG, MNFI, in the March-April 2006 timeframe.

That IG Campaign Plan was in fact jointly developed, costed, and presented to Embassy Econ by both MNF-I planner and the IG Advisor on 16 March 2006. The plan included a joint USG-GOI leadership approach to waging the war on corruption using, among other weapons, the IG system, CPI and BSA. The formal plan provided for development of the Academy of Principled Governance, for new anticorruption legislation, for provincial anti-corruption centers (including IG offices for Iraq's 18 governors), and for creation of a GoI body responsible for self-policing and performance evaluation functions in the GoI oversight systems (the Dawan) Efforts of the GoI and the coalition were to be coordinated by a Joint Anti-Corruption Council

(JACC) headed by the Iraqi Prime Minister and a suitable coalition counterpart.

To insure Iraq leadership buy-in for the Campaign plan, it was presented in Arabic to the IG Association and discussed in depth during three IG meetings in March and April of 2006. Then in a meeting of the Iraqi IG Association Embassy on 29 April 2006, all IGs signed a Memo for the Record endorsing the components and purposes of IG Campaign plan. That jointly signed Memo and Campaign plan proposal to which it related was handed over to Embassy Econ by the Iraqi IGs on that day. At that meeting, in addition to the Deputy Commissioner of CPI and members of the Iraqi Council of Representatives (CoR), many of the Senior Advisors of IRMO attended. Also attending as an honored guest of the Iraqi IGs was the US Acting DoD IG (Thomas Gimble) who at the time was visiting ISF IG offices in Iraq.

Embassy Econ next sought endorsement of the IG Campaign plan from the newly selected Iraqi Prime Minister. Unfortunately, gaining a meeting with the newly appointed PM took months to accomplish. When the meeting finally did occur, there was confusion on whether the plan was indeed jointly agreed too. The Iraqi endorsement was clear, but the Iraqi officials were left with doubt about US endorsement. The head of the Iraqi IG association was vested with responsibility to coordinate with the US Embassy to gain assurance that the plan was accepted. It appears that such assurance was not forthcoming and the IG Campaign Plan never reached formal endorsement.

The regular end-of-summer 2006 Embassy personnel rotations (particularly the trade out of Econ Counselors again precipitated the predictable lag in momentum with anti-corruption and in IG system implementation as those newly aboard became familiar with their duties.

While support for the federal IG system did not result in significant progress during the last months of 2006, MNSTC-I's commitment to Security Ministry IG offices was taking shape. Teams of Advisors were built and took vigorous hold of their mission. The net effect was to begin a professional development process for the two IG offices at MoD and MoI, as well as to build capacity within the Ministries through new transparency and accountability standards and internal controls. In addition, in the critical area of human rights and detainee operations, the two IG offices became leaders by establishing the Iraqi standards for humane treatment of detainees and by then getting to the field to out and inspect facilities and ensure the standards were being applied.

In the early fall of 2006, newly appointed Iraqi advisors to the Prime Minister (Dr. Adel Abdulla and Dr. Ali Alaq—both original CPA appointed IGs) seized the opportunity to advise the PM of the value of his IG system and its needs for developing sustainable capacities within the ministries. During October 2006, the PM directed Dr Ali to create the Joint Anti-Corruption Council (JACC) and work with the US Embassy toward implementing the IG Campaign Plan. In addition, he set aside $10 million for the Academy of Principled Governance, which was to be one of the first agenda items of the JACC.) Thus, even though the Embassy had not taken advantage of the proposed Joint IG Campaign plan, the GoI did. Through the rest of the fall and winter of 2006/2007 Embassy and Iraqi officials met to finally agree on a JACC charter that could be signed by all members.

In late 2006, a new office within the US Mission Iraq, the Office of Accountability and Transparency (OAT) was created. The original concept was to bring all advisory personnel for anti-corruption institutions under a single director who would then report to the Embassy. But from its beginnings, OAT would report to the Director of IRMO. Its first assigned advisor (James Mattil) arrived in late November.

Phase IV. 2007: Anti-Corruption Transition to OAT

Recognizing that the IG advisory effort had been chronically under-resourced from the outset, he IG Advisor recommended an IG System support plan to leadership of the new OAT. The plan to support the newly arriving IG Advisor replacement (Danny Athanasaw) was developed in concert with DoD IG and had been shared with the new IG Advisor before his deployment to Iraq. The plan recommended the IG Advisor be supported by an operations officer, a cultural advisor, 2 translators, and other IG Advisors to share the load of the 29 ministerial IG offices (minus two ISF IG offices under MNSTC-I) under OAT coordination. It was also proposed that OAT and MNSTC-I fully coordinate IG advisory guidance with the new IG Advisor so that one concerted effort for the survival, professionalization, and sustainability of the entire IG system could be maintained.

Additional support and resources for the embassy-based advisor to the 29 non-security force IGs never materialized. From the time the new IG Advisor arrived and until he departed a year later, he was essentially alone to advise his 29 Iraqi IG offices. He eventually was assigned (after 6-months) a dedicated Arabic translator. During the early months of OAT and into 2007, the GoI participated in efforts to make the Joint Anticorruption Council an operational reality. By spring, the acting OAT director made it his personal mission to work through the obstacles and in April there was finally the first meeting of all the JACC members sponsored and attended by the PM. All signed and agreed to the Charter. Within weeks of the signing, the JAAC created an Iraqi Academy Project team to develop and present a project proposal for the development of the Academy of Principled Governance. That team worked with all agencies within the GoI. OAT designated the soon to depart Dr Johnson as their representative for the Academy Project Team. A Coalition Academy Working Group, which mirrored the Iraqi project team was formed and included members of relevant Embassy departments, SIGIR, UK Embassy, US Embassy Baghdad Rule of Law coordinator, and World Bank. The two groups jointly brought together a single project proposal that was presented by the Iraqi Team Leader to the JACC formally 11 June 2007.

Both the acting OAT Director (Boots Poloquin) and the Old IG Advisor (Dr. Johnson) departed the Mission in Iraq after their extended tours were up. It is reported that the Embassy did not have a representative attend the subsequent six JACC meetings following June 2007.

Phase V. 2008: Transition of Anti-Corruption to DCM Supervision and Designation of a Senior Official to Lead

In December 2007 the US Ambassador to Iraq announced a plan which called for the dissolution of the OAT and created a special anti-corruption office reporting directly to the Deputy Chief of Mission. This new anti-corruption office would be headed by a specially selected senior and experienced individual and be tasked to integrate anti-corruption and rule of law efforts in Iraq.

A January 2008 anti-corruption conference was conducted in Iraq with both Iraqi officials and USG representatives. The Iraqi Prime Minister has called 2008 the "The Year of Anti-Corruption" in Iraq. With these developments, the time may have finally arrived when there is consensus among the GoI and the US Embassy to tackle what both label their common enemy: a culture of corruption that funds terrorism and undercuts the legitimacy of the democratic rule in Iraq.

By April the outline of a new rule of law strategic plan in anti-corruption was out for staffing. All entities had been mustered to incorporate their programs and efforts to achieve the plans eventual strategic vision, desired end-state, and action plan. The plan was due out in July 2008.

2.3—SUMMARY

Starting from nothing; with no people, no training, and no historical precedent, the Iraqi federal IG system has grown to near adolescence. It is not mature, but rather remains in the formative years. Its history is marked by ups and downs, of frustration in efforts to agree on plans, gain resources, and build capacity of the system to provide oversight to the Iraqi government.. Heroic efforts were expended by many to enable the system to survive to this point. Whether and how the system now moves down the road to become operational and sustainable are significant questions.

As of this writing (Spring 2008), there are still major challenges to the IG system in Iraq. After three attempts over 4 years there is still no institutional sustaining mechanism (Academy of Principled Governance), and no strategic plan embraced by the USG. Strong leadership is still required to complete the original vision and bring the system to fruition. As of this writing, the Iraqi IG system remains extremely vulnerable.

SECTION 3

3.1—INTRODUCTION

This section presents an assessment of the Iraqi IG implementation lessons over its initial four years. To attempt that, there is need to define (for instructional purposes) the desired end-state of an

Iraqi Inspector Generals system as a baseline to compare what currently is, to what might have been. For purposes here, a desired end-state for the Iraqi federal inspector general system is:

A sustainable, professional, and integrated Inspector General system that reduces government corruption and improves the effectiveness of its ministries.

This end-state description does easily lend itself to quantifiable metrics or statistical proof. The lessons drawn from the assessment therefore will necessarily be more qualitative than quantitative; more deductive than statistical, more reasonably predictive than irrefutable.

3.2—BACKGROUND

To begin with, it may be argued that key components of a profession were created within the Iraqi government by the implementation of the Iraqi Inspectors General System, the Commission on Public Integrity and the reconstituted Board of Supreme Audit. This implementation identified a cadre of Iraqi professionals who should be trained to perform "independent and objective" fact-finding: investigations, inspections and audits. The IG system was one of the key oversight institutions implemented to help foster a culture of accountability and transparency within each ministry of the GoI.

The notion that this professional community now exists underpins this section of the report. Institution building in a fledgling foreign democratic government like Iraq is not comparable to simple reconstruction projects. Building a profession is not like building a bridge or a water treatment plant. Institutions such as an IG system require sophisticated planning, dedicated resources, experts to advise and mentor key actors in the system, and development of professional infrastructure associated with sustaining and integrating the IG system with other systems throughout government.

3.3—ASSESSMENT CATEGORY TERMS

* **Leadership.** Leadership is the ability of an individual or group to influence, motivate, and enable others to contribute toward the effectiveness and success of a particular effort or interest.

* **Planning.** Systemic procedures used to outline and determine the best method(s) of accomplishing assigned tasks and to direct the action necessary to accomplish the assigned mission.

* **Institutional Structures.** For purpose of this report only, institutional structures are defined as the planned mechanisms that build, coordinate, and integrate the body of knowledge that defining a profession.

3.4—LEADERSHIP

General: Leadership of any initiative is key to its success, or is blamed for its failure. Leadership is a crucial a consideration in the US endeavor to create an Iraqi Federal IG system. But what does leadership normally require, beyond inspiring people to common end? One might argue strong leadership yields concrete and actionable plans, resources, delegated authorities, priority of effort, accountability, and a clear vision of the desired end-state. However with some exceptions, it not clear that the foregoing list of products has resulted from such leadership as has been applied to implementation of Iraq's IG system.

Two exceptions to the above include Ambassador Bremer himself, whose establishment of the triad of Iraqi oversight institutions (IG system, reconstituted BSA, and CPI) required foresight, commitment and perseverance. And complementing him was Joseph Schmitz, the Inspector General for DoD, who came to CPA's assistance. Even though provision of the support required an expansive view of the DoD IG lane, he committed major human resources to both Bremer's CPA IG organization and directly to the Iraqi IG system by deploying his Dean of Instruction to Iraq. That individual became the sole IG advisor and would not leave Iraq until June of 2007. Although Bremer was leading the way, that leadership did not follow-through to his staff. CPA staff work did not result in plans, resources, or vision (at least not for the IG system). Despite leadership from the top on early issues in the two instances described, translation into lasting results is still uncertain.

Without clear leadership and an accepted plan, there was insufficient guidance for the US Advisors to Iraqi oversight institutions. It was left to the individual advisors on the ground to figure out the best they could how to enable their respective system to survive and thrive. Unfortunately, this quickly led to "stovepiping" among the oversight institutions, as they competed for the meager attention and resources that existed (both on the Iraqi and USG side) for the first two years. A "zero-sum" perspective emerged on both sides. In other words, with resources being limited, whatever any one system receives is really drawn from what another 'could have had.' What could have been the three mutually supporting oversight systems working together to serve a common GoI interest often turned into individual stovepipes. One can blame individuals for such behavior, and should. But arguably the 'root cause' of such counterproductive conduct goes back availability and willingness of leaders working for overall mission success.

Lessons of Implementation Leadership:

1 Leadership in implementing a government oversight systems (AC systems), such as our effort in Iraq, requires commitment to achieving an identified end-state using associated plans and resources necessary to reach that state.

Explanation. All countries have forms of oversight. Iraq, prior to 2003, had the BSA, a court system, and a less than effective parliament system. Ministries had audit departments and often an inspections department. When we do implement oversight systems, strong leadership and commitment is necessary. There are many priorities to deal with in post-conflict environments, but we should not again underestimate the magnitude of effort and time required to build institutions. This is particularly true when a new system tends toward transformation of the culture of government business. Implementation of an oversight IG system (even a limited one) is a deliberate choice by the USG. When heading down this path, the commitment should be to leverage all our available expertise to make such systems operational and sustainable.

2 Leadership in implementation of oversight institutions is needed from the top in order to conform necessary subordinate actions to achieve the desired end-state.

Explanation. An oversight system (especially like an IG system) is usually embraced at the national level well before it becomes acceptable at lower levels of government. The benefits of oversight are reaped at the national level, but often resisted at the individual level. At least in Iraq, attempting to build consensus from the bottom-up seemed nearly impossible. It was only when the Prime Minister showed personal interest in combating corruption that the wheels of implementation began to roll.

3   Leadership is never out of style or too late. The Iraqi IG system still needs strategic leadership to become complete, professional and self-sustaining. To differing degrees, this is true of all the Iraqi Oversight institutions.

Explanation. We are not done. Rather, one might argue we have just begun to build it interlocked oversight institutions in Iraq. We may do well (as seemed to be case in 2008) to recommit leadership there, take stock of where we are and want to be, and then develop the plan and dedicate the resources to get to the desired end-state. .

4   Operational leadership authority for institution building is rightly placed upon the Chief of Mission. But success in building some oversight systems (like a pervasive Federal IG system across all entities of the host government) may require strategic leadership beyond the ordinary and the COM may be need to bring unusual or very high level US interagency solutions and expertise to bear.

Explanation. In Iraq, a pervasive oversight system like the federal IG system can be beyond the capabilities of any single US agency. Though the principles of independent and objective fact-finding aimed at improving efficiency and effectiveness is common across many offices, the execution and purposes within different ministries of government is not the same. Ministry of Health IG inspectors and Ministry of Oil IG inspectors are not the same. The hotlines they manage take vastly different complaints and allegations. The expertise required to be on the IG staff also varies by ministry functionality. A concerted effort was made by DoD IG and Department of State IG to activate the US Inspector Generals to help mentor sister IG offices in Iraq. That effort has yet to bear fruit. Without being tasked by a national directive, individual US IG offices lack the authority as well as the resources to jump into aiding a foreign IG system.

3.5—Observations Concerning Planning

General: Planning is crucial in all initiatives; but especially critical of implementing or rebuilding government oversight systems in failed states. In Iraq, since the task was implementing a federal IG system across all ministries of the host government, the requirement for solid planning was evident from early on. As indicated earlier, implementing a federal IG system had never before been attempted outside of the US. Therefore, there were no references, case studies, or doctrine to tap into to accomplish the task. That novelty does not excuse the need for a solid implementation plan; it just makes it more challenging.

Doctrine should exist for establishing or supporting rule of law programs and institutions in a post-conflict environment. That doctrine should include accountability and oversight systems that further ethical governance. US planners should possess a "how too manual" that represents the considerations and options necessary for building such institutions.

The implementation plan for an IG system needs to include scrupulous attention to the sufficiency of existing or proposed enabling legislation for the system. In Iraq, omissions from the originating order (particularly provisions concerning independence, appointment, dismissal, budget, certifications, and IG authorities) which may not be subject to change for many years, could cripple the system before it is fully operational. In Iraq changes were made to the original draft CPA order 57 during staffing. A staff dispute over accountability for the IG system led to changes in the draft Order the final language of which required each Iraqi Ministry to be individually responsible for the implementation of their IG offices, as well as for funding this new addition to their Ministry. In addition, another CPA staff dispute lead to the CPA order to state that the individual Ministers had no authority to appoint an IG, but did have authority to dismiss their IG. That authority contained a limitation that the dismissal was subject to review by the body of elected representatives (whatever that body would be called in future Iraq). The result of slight changes to Order 57 by the CPA staff turned out to be systemic minister and ministry interference with IG func-

tionality, unlawful dismissal of IGs, and 31 different IG office implementation plans, none based on knowledge of the system or its needs.
In short, those slight staff changes to the enabling legislation substantially hampered the system within the first year.

The implementation plan needs to include a strategic vision of
the desired end-state ('exit planning') and the criteria (metrics) that will
allow the USG and host nation to know when the vision has been
achieved. All identified assets need to work toward that vision as the
plan outlines. Leadership may require the USG stick to the plan, even
when the easy way out is to change it. At other times, factors that were
not known or understood during initial execution of the plan arise, and
adjustments to the plan may be necessary. Common sense prevails.
Proposed changes should be measured against a yardstick of the principles that underpin independent and objective government fact-finding.
Proposed changes which seek short-term benefit at expense of long-
term viability are seldom in the best interest of a viable system. Professionals should know the difference.

The plan for the IG system needs to estimate realistic resource requirements and then dedicate them over a period of implementation that is adequate to the task. It is seldom that the host country (typically transforming from some form of dictatorship) can simply
implement an unknown oversight mechanism "because we say so." In
Iraq, nearly all Iraqi government officials did not know what an IG was,
how it operated, or why. Some defaulted to inspection systems they
experienced under the Saddam dictatorship. We need to bring not only
plans but resources to the table. Those resources should include expert
advisors and mentors to key actors in the host nation oversight systems.

Lessons in Planning:

1 Inspector General system implementation is not possible
   without a comprehensive strategic plan that integrates it with
   other Rule of Law institutions, provides resources, sets priorities, and establishes metrics to achieve a well-defined sustainable end-state.

Explanation. After four years of implementation of Iraqi AC
systems (to include the IG system) there still no Anti-corruption System Plan for reference or to guide resources. The IGs are the only col-

lective entity to develop and present such an overall strategy to the US Mission. It was the jointly developed (MNF-I-State-GOI) and called the IG Campaign plan. The plan was integrated, strategic, addressed key institutional structures needed by all AC systems in Iraq and was costed by initiative. All 31 Iraqi IGs signed the plan and presented it in person to the US Mission on 29 April 2006. It was received, but apparently never acted upon by the USG. It is to be hoped that recent developments in 2008 change that state of affairs.

2   The plan for implementation must be managed. Resources are constantly at risk of being diverted, initiatives abandoned, priorities changed and confused, and momentum lost, unless the plan is complemented by strong leadership committed to achieving the targeted end-state.

Explanation. Even a very good plan that lacks buy-in from the top remains merely frustrated pieces of paper. The combination of a well thought out implementation plan and capable management of its execution is necessary when implementing oversight institutions. The post conflict environments are awash in shifting priorities. For building governmental institutions steady growth and strong foundation appears the best route and for the long haul.

3.6—OBSERVATIONS CONCERNING INSTITUTIONAL STRUCTURES

One way to approach the creation of oversight institutions in Iraq is to pose that they collectively represent a new profession. If one can accept that assertion, the unique body of expertise of the profession might then be "independent and objective government fact-finding" which seeks to improve effectiveness and to reduce fraud, waste, and abuses- in government." To coordinate and further that body of expertise, professionals establish physical mechanisms for the transferring the body of expertise to their members, mechanisms to grow that body of expertise through research and experimentation, and mechanisms to coordinate and integrate the profession.

In Iraq, there are at least three (3) institutional structures required for proper implementation and sustainability of the oversight institutions:

1   An Iraqi National Academy to act as a 'professional gateway' to BSA, CPI, and the IG systems and to grow the body of independent and objective fact-finding expertise in audits, investigations, and inspections;

2   a functional implementation coordination mechanism for the GoI and US (Coalition/Global partners), and;

3   an enduring functional structure for Iraqi Anti-Corruption Coordination.

In post conflict or failed state environments like Iraq or when implementing new oversight institutions, it seems there is even a greater need for these institutional structures; particularly the Academy. The term "professional gateway" requires some definition. Arguably, a "professional" is not one unless the gateway has been successfully navigated. Examples in the US include law school, medical school, military Academies (or equivalent officer gateways), seminaries and others. It is this professional gateway that a profession itself uses to not only thoroughly introduce members into the "unique body of expertise," but also to inculcate its principles, its calling to a higher good, its symbols, mottos, the meanings of its obligations.

Lessons Concerning Institutional Structures:

1   GOI and USG (and Coalition-Global partners) should partner to develop a National Iraqi Anti-Corruption Institutional Gateway (i.e., Academy of Principled Governance).

Explanation. Without a National Academy, Iraqi oversight institution may never be fully sustainable or properly professional. Iraqi IG systems (CPI, BSA and IG system) are not similar in functionality, but they all provide for government oversight and accountability and thereby serve principled governance and respect for rule of law. In other words, the institutions differ in needs, yet have in common the principles of independent and objective oversight.

What seems needed in Iraq is a true national gateway for ethical governance that integrates professional norms and specialty fact-finding training. All individuals working within AC profession should understand the profession, its calling, its unique body of expertise, it code of conduct, it service intent, its professional ethos.

Only those possessing the highest standard of government conduct should oversee and investigate government officials. If standards are not high, lawful authorities held by AC professionals are vulnerable to abuse.

2 GOI (with the US assistance) needs to create a self-policing GoI oversight structure that provides evaluations, recommendations, and the mechanism for unbiased selection and dismissal of high officials serving in its government oversight institutions.

Explanation. Without a merit-based selection and dismissal mechanism within its institutional structure, the Iraqi IG system (and all AC systems) remain subject to political manipulation and distortions. The most obvious need may relate to the selection and dismissal of its 31 Inspectors General. However, the same need exists for the top officials assigned to the CPI and the BSA. The need for self-policing, as well, is a professional norm. Unless accomplished, the system remains less than professional. The need for independent assessments of the oversight institutions was recognized by the present Prime Minister in 2007. He began using a team led by his newly appointed Anti-Corruption Coordinator (Dr. Adel Abdulla). Evaluations to date have been restricted to Iraqi IG offices. During 2007, two Iraqi IGs were relieved as a result of poor evaluations from Dr. Adel. Such a mechanism needs to be codified and planned for from the outset.

3 GOI (with US support) needs to resurrect and revamp the Joint Anti-Corruption Council (JACC) with the Prime Minister and the US Ambassador serving as co-chairmen.

Explanation. The most recent interagency and intergovernmental forum for coordination of anticorruption issues, the JACC, appears again to have fallen into disrepair. Attempts at the same type of mechanism date back as early as July 2004. Even thought the current JACC enjoyed Prime Minister endorsement in 2007, its chairman was the General Secretary for the Council of Ministers and not the PM himself. US interest in supporting the JACC after June of 2007 has not been noted.

The JACC equivalent need be institutionalized in law as a permanent government mechanism. Its first order of business is the establishment and approval of a joint AC strategy for achieving sustainable, professional, integrated and effective AC systems in Iraq, in order to win the war on corruption and improve government efficiency, transparency, accountability and effectiveness. The USG could then assign experienced advisors as support to the JACC and the conduit between the JACC and the Embassy's ACWG.

4   The Embassy needs to revamp its existing ACWG with the assignment of a suitable senior diplomat as the Chairman and a MNF-I Flag officer as Deputy Chairman, with stakeholder members from the coalition, World Bank, UN, with the heads of USAID and INL in country.

Explanation. The Embassy ACWG goes back to April 2004 when advisors to the three systems of CPI, BSA, and IG sought to create a structure for mutual support and coordination. There was at the time no official endorsement by the Embassy for the group's existence and no appointed leadership within the group itself. At the request of AC advisors, the chairmanship of the ACWG was directed to Embassy Econ in May of 2005. The ACWG has had its moments, especially under Econ Counselor Tom Delare, who made significant strides to improve AC in Iraq, using the ACWG as a platform for coordination and control. However, even that singular and superior leadership, could not influence the separate agendas of USAID, INL, and even individual stovepiped embassy advisors. Without direct linkage to senior US Mission leadership, the ACWG has largely been a forum for show and tell concerning disparate AC programs and initiatives. The new ACWG should be in direct support of the JACC and its assigned USG government advisors. The DCM should command the cooperation and support of all entities to achieve strategic aims agreed upon by the Ambassador and reflected from the JACC.

3.7—STRATEGIC TO TACTICAL - IMPLEMENTATION LESSONS

Please see Appendix D for a matrix of lessons divided 'Strategic through Tactical.' Note the interconnectivity between and among the different levels.

There are lessons drawn at the strategic (National), operational (Regional/In-Country) and tactical (Day-to-Day) implementation of the IG system. However, it is not accurate to stovepipe lessons. Lessons at the strategic level directly impact other subordinate levels.

For example, there is a contention that the at the strategic level the USG lacks doctrine, plans, even a designated Agency with the mission to be concerned with implementing an IG system. Movement from that high level to the operational level of the region, leaves little wonder that the CPA had no plans for transition of the IG system, no clear guidance on dedicated resources, and no expectation regarding the needs for experts in IG affairs to mentor Iraqi officials in future years. And then at the tactical level, it should not surprise that there was little direction; or to find parochialism among advisors as the rule and not exception, or that obstructionism within USG circles was more of a problem than winning a foreign culture to western principles of ethical governance. The enemy to IG system implementation was far too often it own weaknesses.

Strategic Lessons: Strategic lessons are largely from omissions of higher national authority to have doctrine, templates, plans, SoPs, or other guidance for implementation of a federal IG system in Iraq.

Operational Lessons: It would be a first time if the national authorities knew all, predicted all, and directed all actions concerning implementation of Iraqi oversight institutions perfectly. Professionals were assigned in Iraq to accomplish USG interests there. However, two of three oversight institutions (IG system and CPI) were started from nothing; and one (the IG system) had no history of ever being implemented outside the US. It also was often unclear to USG officials how an Iraqi Federal IG system worked or how such a system served US interests. Clear guidance to those charged with implementation of the operational plans is necessary in plans for the implementation.

Tactical Lessons: Professional Advisors assigned to the Iraqi IG system are supposed to know what they are doing. They should understand US interests. They are supposed to identify needs, communicate them, and fight for critical support and resources. They are not supposed to fail. Those providing day-to-day advice to Iraqi officials building their system are the closest to the front line and therefore have the pulse of the system they are advising. When they speak as an expert and on behalf of their system, they should be heard with credibility. There is no excuse for failing to accomplish what is a professional requirement. Building a good oversight system in a host country requires deploying the best advisors and mentors within the US government and providing the best leadership available.

3.8—SUMMARY

The key lessons learned while implementing the Iraqi IG system are:

1 the need for strong and focused US leadership invested in the full development of the system as a USG interest;

2 the development and dissemination of an integrated strategic plan for the system(s); the plan should define the desired end-state, the avenues to converge upon it, the structures required to sustain it, and the full range of resources to attain it;

3 the development of institutional structures within with GoI to professionalize, sustain, and coordinate/integrate the oversight systems. Iraq, there is need for:

    a. an institutional training gateway (Academy of Principled Government - See Appendix G) at the national level for sustainment of the oversight profession;

    b. a permanent cross-agency coordination council (JACC equivalent - see Appendix I) for strategic coordination of all systems to win the war on corruption;

    c. an independent mechanism for self–policing Iraqi oversight professionals and for providing independent evaluation and advice to the GoI on appointment and dismissal of high officials within oversight institutions.

SECTION 4

This report lists key lessons learning from the initial years implementing the Iraqi federal Inspector General system. The primary authors spent 40 months in country and therefore report from that perspective. Recitation of lessons to be taken from an effort in which authors have such an interest in the system is a major challenge. Beyond frank acknowledgment of that, and assurance that professional care and an objective approach was taken to select that which is contained herein, it is hoped that he value of the lesson identified is self-evident. The report is a stark view of the challenges that 'have not been met,' and should still to be met in Iraq. Beyond that, the lessons should instruct future efforts at planning to meet oversight needs in host countries and planning for the initiation of systems that provide oversight and advance the rule of law in SSTR missions.

For most portions of the first four years of Iraqi IG system implementation, the system seemed largely both misunderstood and under-resourced. Although signs of increasing support are evident in 2008, the first years in particular seemed to be steps forward, then backward, then sideways, with frequent repetition of each. On the whole, the IG system remains in need of work to become fully operational and sustainable.

Actually implementing an entire federal IG system in Iraq was not only difficult, it was literally unprecedented. A ministry-level Federal IG system had never been created in any government, except in the US. No doctrine, no case studies, and no precedent existed to guide the planning or the implementation effort. CPA staff planners were not unanimous on how to implement the IG system. Some appeared to doubt whether it could be done at all. This division of opinion reportedly led to edits to the enabling legislation (CPA Order 57) that had the effect of decentralizing both the implementation and funding of the Iraqi IG offices. By doing so, the order made implementation the responsibility of each individual Iraqi ministry. This decentralization of the IG system also made the entire IG system less visible to national authorities. It indulged in the presumption that each Minister both understood the concept of the inspector general as embodied in CPA Order 57 and supported the idea of establishing an IG office within the Ministry, in the first place. The net effect was that at CPA transition the IG system implementation plan associated with it, no US resources dedicated to it, and no designation for providing IG advisors as mentors to the Iraqi IG offices.

Over the initial years the Iraqi IG system grew to 31 offices throughout the GoI and over 3,500 personnel, primarily auditors, investigators, and inspectors. For most of the initial two years there was one US Advisor to the IGs (detailed from DoD IG). His original mission was to develop and advocate for an Iraqi Training Academy that would act as the training gateway to the Iraqi professionals serving the Anti-Corruption institutions. Once on the ground, his duties immediately broadened. Subsequently, two more individual Ministry IG advisors were added (one for Ministry of Defense-beginning in August 2004) and one for Ministry of Interior IG (beginning January 2005]).[30] Later in 2006, when MNSTC-I assumed responsibility for the two security ministries (MoD and MoI), they committed even more contracted advisors to those two individual Security Ministry IG offices. As of this writing, the remaining 29 IG offices are still mentored and assisted by one US Advisor.

Applicable lessons may be applied to future USG efforts to implement oversight institutions in host countries. Since an operational Iraqi IG system remains crucial to good governance and rule of law in Iraq, the description of lessons identified here may also have current value in finishing the IG system work begun in Iraq over four years ago.

The key lessons learned so far in the course of implementing the Iraqi IG system are: 1) the need for strong and focused leadership invested in the successful development of the system as a priority; 2) the development and dissemination of an integrated strategic plan for the system, (such a plan should define the desired end-state, identify avenues to converge upon it, specify the structures required to sustain it, and state the full range of resources to attain it;) and 3) the requirement to develop institutional structures within with GoI to professionalize the IG system.

* **Focused Leadership.** Across the board, Coalition leadership has been good, but because of the novelty of implementing a federal IG system, changing security conditions and priorities, multiple tasking, and a measure of ignorance of the IG system within Coalition entities, the implementation of the Iraqi IG system repeatedly faltered for want of attention. Had we been able to maintain a more continuous focus, we might have averted several significant implementation obstacles and had a far more positive assessment to report herein.

* **Joint Strategic Plan**. The need for a joint strategic plan for the creation and execution of the Iraqi IG system would seem axiomatic. However, currently there is still no such agreed upon plan, nor one for implementing Iraqi Anti-Corruption systems, in total. The Iraqi IGs had adopted a jointly developed IG Campaign plan (see Appendix F), but the MNF-I AND USM-I working group has yet to recognize it. The need prevails for an integrated Anti-Corruption strategic plan in Iraq that clearly defines a sustainable end-state, the avenues to be taken in achieving it, and the resources required.

* **Government Institutional Structures.** CPA Order 57 essentially created a new profession of independent and objective government fact-finders in Iraq. Professions require internal and external structures for sustainment, coordination, and self-policing. In Iraq, there is a crucial need for 1) an institutional training gateway (Academy of Principled Government - See Appendix G) at the national level for sustainment of the oversight profession; 2) a permanent cross-agency coordination council (JACC equivalent - see Appendix I) for strategic coordination of all systems to win the war on corruption; and 3) an independent mechanism for self–policing Iraqi oversight professionals and for providing independent evaluation and advice to the GoI on appointment and dismissal of high officials within oversight institutions.

This report is intended to help develop expertise that can be applied in future oversight systems, if creation of such systems is again deemed appropriate. However, the lessons learned might also serve in completing the work in progress in Iraq.

Chapter Review Questions:

1 By what authority and for what purpose did the DoD Inspector General detail one of his Deputy Inspectors General to the Coalition Provisional Authority in Baghdad in 2003?

2 By what authority and for what purpose did the Coalition Provisional Authority Administrator, Ambassador Paul Bremer, announce in late 2003 that among other preconditions, the establishment of an effective Office of Inspector General in every Iraqi ministry, was a precondition for the transfer of sovereignty back to the Iraqi People?

3 By what authority and for what purpose did the DoD Inspector General deploy his OIG Dean of Instruction to Baghdad in early 2004?

4 By what authority and for what purpose did the DoD Office of Inspector General NOT publish its lessons learned report (the final draft of which was extracted to build the case study above), after four years of supporting the establishment in Baghdad of a system of Inspectors General and associated anti-corruption efforts under the auspices of the "Principled Governance Initiative"?

Chapter 4 Endnotes

---

[1] David Clary and Joseph Whitehorne, "Steuben Trains the Troops," The
[2] *Ibid.* (footnote omitted).

[3] *Ibid.*, p. 39 (footnote omitted).

[4] Remarks as Prepared for Delivery by Inspector General Joseph E.
Schmitz of the Department of Defense: "Domestic Enemies and Pyrrhic
Victories," Arlington, VA, Saturday, June 7, 2003
http://web.archive.org/web/20090320204921/http://www.dodig.osd.mil/IGI
nformation/Speeches/TroyCommencement672003.pdf

[5] *See* Remarks of the Inspector General of the Department of Defense:
"Honor, Courage, Commitment -- and Class" (Retirement of Admiral Larry
L. Poe), October 24, 2003
http://web.archive.org/web/20090320204913/http://www.dodig.osd.mil/IGI
nformation/Intro_of_Iraq_MoD_IG_to_DCIE.pdf

[6] *See* Remarks as delivered by Department of Defense Inspector General
Joseph E. Schmitz to the Defense Council on Integrity and Efficiency,
"Inspector General Introduces Iraqi Counterpart To DCIE As A 'Fellow
Champion Of Integrity'," July 14, 2005
http://web.archive.org/web/20090320204913/http://www.dodig.osd.mil/IGI
nformation/Intro_of_Iraq_MoD_IG_to_DCIE.pdf

[7] Inspector General Layla Jassim al-Mokhtar's entire speech to the PCIE is
posted at
http://www.dodig.mil/IGInformation/Remarks_by_MOD_IG_Mokhtar_07
1805.pdf

[8] Hon. Claude M. Kicklighter, Inspector General of the Department of
Defense, before the Senate Appropriations Committee, "The effectiveness
of U.S. efforts to combat corruption, waste, fraud, and abuse in Iraq," pp. 2,
20-21, March 11, 2008
http://www.dodig.mil/fo/Prepared%20Statement%20-
%20IG%20DoD%20FINAL.PDF

[9] CPA Order Number 57, February 5, 2004, p. 1, retrieved online at http://web.archive.org/petabox/20040707043136/http://cpa-iraq.org/regulations/20040212_CPAORD57.pdf

[10] U.S. Department of State and the Broadcasting Board of Governors Office of Inspector General, Report Number: ISP-IQO-06-05, August 2006, p. 22.

[11] Except as it relates to the supposed flow of funding directly to the IGs, CPA Order 57 remains unchanged since its promulgation.

[12] CPA Order Number 57, February 5, 2004, p. 2, retrieved online at http://web.archive.org/petabox/20040707043136/http://cpa-iraq.org/regulations/20040212_CPAORD57.pdf

[13] *Ibid*, p. 3

[14] USIP, Association for Diplomatic Studies and Training Iraq Experience Project, Jay Bachar Interview, July 19, 2004

[15] "An Integrated Approach to Combating Corruption in Iraq," July 16, 2006, p.3

[16] USIP, Association for Diplomatic Studies and Training Iraq Experience Project, Rodney Bent Interview, September 14, 2004

[17] SIGIR, Joint Survey of the U.S Embassy-Iraq's Anticorruption Program, SIGIR 06-021, July 28, 2006, p.i

[18] SIGIR, Joint Survey of the U.S Embassy-Iraq's Anticorruption Program, SIGIR 06-021, July 28, 2006, p.i

[19] Nouri al-Maliki, interview in *Al-Iraqiya*, http://web.archive.org/petabox/20080704013117/http://www.layalina.tv/Press/PR_III.16.asp

[20] DoS, USINFO.STATE.GOV, March 25, 2004 (online at: http://merln.ndu.edu/merln/pfiraq/archive/state/2004_Mar_25-260035.pdf).

[21] The Honorable Ambassador L Paul Bremer, Ill, Committee on Government Oversight and Reform U.S House of Representatives, February 6 2007 https://house.resource.org/110/org.c-span.196561-1.pdf

[22] Condoleezza Rice, Senate Committee on Foreign Relations, October 19, 2005
http://web.archive.org/petabox/20061013213938/http://foreign.senate.gov/tes timony/2005/RiceTestimony051019.pdf

[23] Statement of Mr. Thomas F. Gimble, Acting Inspector General, DoD, before the Subcommittee on National Security, Emerging Threats, and International Relations, House Committee on Government Reform: "Iraq Reconstruction, Governance and Security Oversight, " October 18, 2005, p. 6.

[24] Admiral Poe interview statement October 2007

[25] Originally sent to help establish an Iraqi Academy of Principled Govern-ance, his mission grew to be the advisor to all 31 Iraqi IGs and to represent the IG system to Coalition leadership and Advisory Teams.

[26] Admiral Poe Interview 2007.

[27] CPA Funding Request, "PRB NO. 655 Project Name: Board of Supreme Audit—Information Systems Infrastructure & Revitalization Program," February 26, 2004. (In CPA Archive)

[28] U.S. Department of State and the Broadcasting Board of Governors Of-fice of Inspector General, Report Number: ISP-IQO-06-05, August 2006, p. 21

[29] (USMC, ret)

[30] Originally sent to help establish an Iraqi Academy of Principled Govern-ance, his mission grew to be the advisor to all 31 Iraqi IGs and to represent the IG system to Coalition leadership and Advisory Teams.

CHAPTER 5. INSPECT:

Inspecting Sex Slavery through the Fog of Moral Relativism

"The Commanders of all ships and vessels belonging to the THIRTEEN UNITED COLONIES, are strictly required to shew in themselves a good example of honor and virtue to their officers and men, and to be very vigilant in inspecting the behaviour of all such as are under them, and to discountenance and suppress all dissolute, immoral and disorderly practices; and also, such as are contrary to the rules of discipline and obedience, and to correct those who are guilty of the same according to the usage of the sea."

Continental Congress, "Rules for the Regulation of the Navy of the United Colonies of North America," Article 1 (1775)[1]

On May 31, 2002, Congressman Christopher Smith (R-NJ) and twelve other members of Congress wrote a letter to Secretary of Defense Donald Rumsfeld, requesting a "thorough, global and extensive" investigation into publicized allegations of U.S. military complicity in international sex slavery, the most heinous form of human trafficking.[2] Within days, the Commander of United States Forces Korea (USFK), four-star Army General Leon LaPorte, personally visited mein Pentagon City and asked me to address these allegations.

General LaPorte explained, "Congress expects this investigation or inspection to be joint and global. My IG in Korea is not a jointly assigned IG, and I simply do not have the authority to conduct either an investigation or an inspection that is global in scope. Likewise, The Inspector General of the Army does not have the authority to conduct a joint inspection." He therefore requested that, as the four-star equivalent civilian DoD IG, I travel to Korea to help the Commander "answer the mail" from Congress.

I responded, "The good news is that I just recently decided to stand up an Inspections capability." Up until that point, the IG office had focused on the main functional capabilities explicitly required by the Inspector General Act of 1978, as amended, namely: audits; investigations; investigative policy oversight, and audit policy oversight.[3]

"The bad news," I explained to General LaPorte, "is that it will take me about six months to staff up my new Inspections capability." I committed, however, to dispatch a team lead by the newly appointed two-star Deputy, Rear Admiral Larry Poe, USNR, to lay the initial groundwork in Korea for a personal inspection visit.

In the course of subsequent sex slavery inspections in Korea, Bosnia-Herzegovina, and Kosovo, the "lessons learned" included:

(1) Among the root causes of the recent resurgence of sex slavery, aside from the obvious profit motive of organized criminals, is a general reluctance of leaders at all levels to promulgate and enforce principle-based standards for subordinates; and

(2) Whenever leaders, especially those of us who swear to "support and defend the Constitution of the United States,"[4] become aware of humans being referred to as "just" something else (e.g., "they're just prostitutes," as discussed below), we ought never to turn a blind eye.

Before inspecting sex slavery on the ground in Korea, the DoD OIG "joint and global" inspection team met with various experts in Washington, D.C., and with international anti-trafficking advocates, including the sponsor of anti-trafficking legislation in the Russian Duma. The bill's Russian sponsor expressed little hope in the success of her proposed legislation because, as she explained through a translator, "like most Russian men, the attitude of almost all my brethren in the Duma is that, 'They're just prostitutes'." Unfortunately, the subsequent inspection validated that the Russian Duma holds no monopoly on this moral relativist attitude.

According to some Korean officials, most Russian "entertainers" on Itaewon's "Hooker Hill" and elsewhere in Korea consent to their employment status. According to the Army Military Police on the ground, however, the contracts for these Russian entertainers are involuntarily sold weekly from one establishment to another.

When one of the young U.S. Army Military Police was asked if he would like to do something about this blatant human trafficking, he unhesitatingly responded in the affirmative. He added promptly, however, that it was beyond his control. The young soldier was obviously waiting for a signal from his own chain-of-command that would empower him to combat this affront to human dignity that, to him, seemed so morally wrong.

Unbeknownst to this soldier, the top of his USFK chain of command had already sent the signal. It just hadn't made it down to his level—yet.

The next weekend, two teams of U.S. Army military police took on Itaewon's Hooker Hill, leaving 26 entertainment establishments off limits to American GIs -- and, if nothing else, sent a strong, principle-based moral message throughout the entire chain-of-command that turning a blind eye to sex slavery is not an option.

Shortly thereafter, the IG team issued a report identifying several opportunities to build on the aggressive efforts taken by the USFK leadership to combat human trafficking. In response to the IG's Phase I report, twenty-six Members of Congress, including most of those who had signed the original letter, signed a second letter to the Secretary of Defense, dated October 10, 2003, concluding with the following admonition: "Commanders and service members at all levels must understand their role in helping to eradicate the scourge of human trafficking and to avoid giving any indication that DOD turns a blind eye to this barbaric practice."

Before completing the assessment on Korea, the IG's inspection team turned its attention to the European theater where human trafficking was becoming a growing menace in Bosnia-Herzegovina and Kosovo.

In September 2003, at about the same time our office was kicking off "Phase II" of our joint and global human trafficking inspection, President Bush gave a speech to the United Nations General Assembly, in which he identified human trafficking as a "special evil." President Bush stated that the "founding documents of the United Nations and the founding documents of America . . . assert that human beings should never be reduced to objects of power or commerce, because their dignity is inherent. Both . . . recognize a moral law that stands above men and nations, which must be defended and enforced by men and nations."[5]

Four months later, as a result of our completed "Phase II" report and recommendations, the Deputy Secretary of Defense promulgated the Commander-in-Chief's "zero tolerance" policy on human trafficking, which stated:

> The responsibilities of commanders and supervisors at all levels are clear, as codified by Congress under Title 10. Those statutory provisions require commanders and others in authority 'to be vigilant inspecting the conduct of all persons who are placed under their command; to guard against and suppress all dissolute and immoral practices, and to correct . . . all persons who are guilty of them.' Efforts to combat trafficking in persons in DoD begin with the recognition that all commanding officers and other DoD officers and employees in positions of authority are expected to conduct themselves in a manner that is consistent with statutory requirements for exemplary conduct.

Concordant with these U.S. anti-trafficking efforts, the North Atlantic Treaty Organization (NATO) circulated a draft policy document on May 21, 2004 (finalized on December 2, 2004), reaffirming that human trafficking constitutes a "serious abuse of human rights, especially affecting women and children," while at the same time announcing a zero tolerance policy by NATO forces and staff.

On September 16, 2004, Secretary of Defense Rumsfeld issued a one page Memorandum on "Combating Trafficking in Persons," in which he expressed his "view on this important matter to augment the [Deputy Secretary's] January 30, 2004 memo on this subject."[6] In it,

Secretary Rumsfeld admonished that, "No leader in this department should turn a blind eye to this issue," urging commanders to "be vigilant" and "make full use of all tools available, including DoD Inspectors General and criminal investigative organizations, to combat these prohibited activities."[7]

Secretary Rumsfeld's bottom line: "I am committed to taking every step possible to combat Trafficking in Persons."[8]

In furtherance of Secretary Rumsfeld's commitment, the Department of Defense extended its "zero tolerance" policy on June 21, 2005, to contractors.[9] The new rule required "contractors to establish policy and procedures for combating trafficking in persons and to notify the contracting officer of any violations and the corrective action taken."[10]

Whatever else one might say about sex slavery in the 21st Century, the joint and global IG inspection and associated proactive measures taken by U.S. and Western leaders reaffirm the "moral truth" that human trafficking falls within those "dissolute and immoral practices" envisioned by our Continental Congress when it prescribed a leadership duty to "guard against and suppress" such practices through, *inter alia*, vigilance by leaders in "inspecting the conduct of all persons who are placed under their command."[11]

CASE STUDY: INSPECTING SEX SLAVERY

The following excerpts are from the published DoD OIG reports for Phase I and Phase II of its, "Assessment of DoD Efforts to Combat Trafficking in Persons."[12]

DEPARTMENT OF DEFENSE
OFFICE OF THE INSPECTOR GENERAL

CASE NUMBER
H03L88433128

JUL 10 2003

<u>ASSESSMENT OF DOD EFFORTS TO</u>
<u>COMBAT TRAFFICKING IN PERSONS</u>

<u>PHASE I -- UNITED STATES FORCES KOREA</u>

Prepared by Program Integrity Directorate
Office of Deputy Inspector General for Investigations

II. Background

In March 2002 Fox News broadcast a report on employment of foreign nationals in involuntary prostitution in Korea. The broadcast referred to alleged practices by owners of Korean entertainment establishments such as enticing women from Russia, the Philippines, and other countries to come to Korea to work, then withholding their passports forcing them to remain in Korea and earn their freedom to return home by practicing prostitution.

The report also suggested U.S. complicity in these scenes stemming from patronage of offending establishments by U.S. military personnel and oversight of the establishments by U.S. Military Police personnel. One segment of the report featured, among others, the following excerpt from interviews with Service members who were serving on a courtesy Patrol[13] of off-base establishments:

* In response to the question posed by the Fox reporter "So you keep these places safe? A Courtesy Patrol member replies, "Yeah, that's what we do. That's our job."

* In another excerpt, a member of the Courtesy Patrol observed: "All these bar owners buy girls at auction. These girls have to earn however much money it takes to get their passports back."

* In an earlier scene, that Service member had explained: "They [women working in bars] are told to come here to make some money. And no they don't make money. They just make enough to buy their passports back. Because the people in Russia get them a visa, passport—the whole 9 yards to work in Korea. They get off the plane and Korean nationals who work at the airport take the visa and passport away and put them in a line at the side. And they go to auction.

In a letter dated May 31, 2002, 13 members of the U.S. Congress, acting under the auspices of the Commission on Security and Cooperation in Europe ("Helsinki Commission"), requested that we investigate allegations that "U.S. military personnel, particularly those stationed in South Korea, are engaged in activities that promote and facilitate the trafficking and exploitation of women."

III. Scope

To conduct the assessment requested by Members of Congress, we made two on-site visits to various locations in Korea. During a visit conducted from December 3 to 14, 2002, we met senior USFK officials, including the Chief of Staff, Deputy Chief of Staff, Deputy Chief of Intelligence, and Provost Marshal. Additionally, we conferred with the Provost Marshal of the USFK Medical Command, personnel assigned to the Army Criminal Investigation Command, four Area Commanders, the Second Army Division Commander, and various Army camp garrison commanders. We also met with the Republic of Korea Inspector General, visited several U.S. military installations in Korea, to include Camps Casey and Bonifas and Osan Air Force Base, and conducted a site visit to the Itaewon District in Seoul (outside Yongsan Army Garrison). Finally, we met U.S. diplomatic personnel, various Republic of Korea officials, and representatives of nongovernmental organizations who were concerned with human trafficking issues.

In a second visit to USFK from March 4 to 7, 2003 we met with the U.S. Ambassador to Korea, the USFK Commander, the 2nd Infantry Division and 7th Air Force Commanders, and a number of Korean officials, to include officers of the Korean Independent Commission Against Corruption and the International Organization of Migration, the Korean Forces Inspector General, and a Korean criminal prosecutor. We again conducted site visits to the Itaewon District, Camp Casey and surrounding commercial establishments, and Osan Air Force Base.

We reviewed documents, to include policy guidance issued by various U.S. military commands throughout the USFK area, an assessment conducted by the 8th Army IG between June 14 and August 14, 2002, entitled, "Review and Assessment of Regulations, Policies, and Enforcement Practices Regarding Off Limits Establishments and Prostitution," and other relevant materials.

IV. Findings And Analysis

STANDARDS

Title 10, United States Code (U.S.C.), Sections 3583, 5947, and 8583, "Requirement of Exemplary Conduct," dated November 18, 1997

These sections establish a standard of conduct for commanding officers and others in authority in the Army (3593), Air Force (8583), and Naval Service (5947) to

(1) show in themselves a good example of virtue, honor, patriotism, and subordination;

(2) be vigilant in inspecting the conduct of all persons who are placed under their command;

(3) guard against and suppress all dissolute and immoral practices, and to correct, according to the laws and regulations of [the relevant Military Department] all persons who are guilty of them; and

(4) take all necessary and proper measures, under the laws, regulations, and customs of [the relevant Military Department] to promote and safeguard the morale, the physical well-being, and the general welfare of the officers and enlisted persons under their command or charge.

These provisions are of significance here because, in our view, they impose on commanders a responsibility to lead by example in fighting human trafficking, to be "vigilant in inspecting the conduct of all persons who are placed under their command," and to take proactive measures to discourage and punish conduct that contributes to human trafficking.

Public Law (P.L.) 106-386, Division A, 114 Stat. 1464, "Victims of Trafficking and Violence Protection Act of 2000"

The Act empowers the President and Executive Agencies to take acts to fight trafficking in persons, to include imposing economic sanctions on countries that do not act to curb trafficking, providing assistance to victims of trafficking, such as special work visas and education programs, and amends U.S. criminal laws to better define, prosecute, and punish traffickers and related offenses.

National Security Presidential Directive (NSPD)-22, "Combating Trafficking in Persons," dated December 16, 2002

NSPD-22 directs Federal agencies to "strengthen their collective efforts, capabilities, and coordination to support the policy to combat trafficking in persons." It further states: "The policy of the United States is to attack vigorously the worldwide problem of trafficking in persons, using law enforcement, diplomacy, and all other appropriate tools," and directs relevant agencies of the U.S. Government to work together to address human trafficking.

* * *

. . . . The Directive assigns the Secretary of State the lead role in implementing the Victims of trafficking and Violence Protection Act of 2000 and Task Force Initiatives.

The DoD, together with other agencies, is given the task of developing and implementing relevant training programs. The agencies must review their internal procedures, capabilities, programs, and resources necessary to implement the Directive and, within 90 days of the effective date of the Directive (December 16, 2002), promulgate plans to implement it. The Under Secretary of Defense for Policy is currently staffing the required plan.

Facts: Our assessment examined the adequacy of ongoing programs sponsored by USFK to curb Service member use of off-base establishments that may traffic in persons ("demand" side) as well as efforts to reduce the number of Korean establishments that are engaged in improper or illegal activities ("supply" side). . . .

Educational efforts:_The assessment team found tat the USFK leadership acknowledges the fact that human trafficking is a concept not necessarily tied to an individual's legal status in the country—either as local national or as guest workers in the country on a valid visa. That is, leaders with whom we spoke recognized that individuals who are subject to force, fraud, or coercion in performing a certain act—such as prostitution—are human trafficking victims. USFK teaches assigned Service members that prostitution is a violation of Korean law, and that by engaging in acts supporting prostitution, U.S. Service members may violate USFK regulations and the Uniform Code of Military Justice (UCMJ). USFK's human trafficking program is geared to the premise that if Service member involvement in off-installation prostitution is reduced (demand-side), that reduction of demand will correspondingly lead to less human trafficking and off-installation exploitation (supply–side).

USFK's human trafficking education program is a positive effort... The portion of the USFK education program that articulates prescribed standards, as reflected in the UCMJ and Service values, makes the clear point that human trafficking and illegal prostitution are incompatible with military service.[14] This portion of the USFK education program is particularly strong and should be continued. We believe that, in addition to articulating the incompatibility of prescribed military standards and military values with human trafficking, the program should also draw attention to the prescribed standards of exemplary conduct that Congress codified at 10 U.S.C. §§ 3583, 5947, and 8583, as set forth in the standards section above. These congressionally prescribed standards apply uniformly for each Service and clearly articulate every officer's and leader's responsibility with regard to human trafficking and other exploitive practices. To that end, we made the following recommendations to General LaPorte at the conclusion of our second visit:

* Bolster human trafficking situational awareness in the context of ongoing emphasis on "Core Values" and "The NCO [noncommissioned officer] Creed." Provide official "tool kit" to Service members, that includes the unclassified version of the Presidential Directive on Human trafficking[,] the requirements for exemplary conduct in Title 10, and the Trafficking Victim's Protection Act of 2000.

* Develop and deploy a "human trafficking indicators" guide for sensitizing not only Military Police and Courtesy Patrols, but each Service member.

* Emphasize individual moral decision making based on Army Core Values and "The NCO Creed" as the ultimate metric for success.

We found that USFK has embraced those recommendations. By letter dated April 4, 2003, General LaPorte advised Congressman Smith, "We renewed our emphasis on initial training for all USFK newcomers and refresher training for all personnel that highlights suspicious indicators and explains the complex inter-relationship between these issues." Additionally, by email to this office dated June 4, 2003, General LaPorte emphasized,

> Training and awareness stands as one of the pillars of our program to address prostitution and its ties to human trafficking. We will tap the various resources you mentioned as well as others to gather information that will be more informative and substantive for leaders and Service members.... Our leaders continue to make direct linkages among the topics of service, values, ethical decision-making, and prostitution and human trafficking.

* * *

Refocus Law Enforcement Efforts: Much attention was drawn to this issue because of the manner in which the member of the Courtesy Patrol who was featured on the Fox News video articulated that he was there to protect the "establishment." The statement was especially problematic because his comment gave the impression that his job was to protect what appeared to be a club using trafficked women to provide prostitution services exclusively to U.S. Service members.[15]

Notwithstanding implications in media accounts that USFK police personnel provide "protection" to predatory establishments, our assessment found that Courtesy Patrols and off-installation policing activities engaged in by U.S. Forces in Korea are focused on the protection of U.S. Service members rather than protection of any individual establishments. We did not find that uniformed U.S. Military Patrols, in any visited area, provided physical "protection" for off-installation bars. The patrols are there to provide a "Command Presence" in off-installation areas that have high concentrations of U.S. military personnel. Such a presence, whether by military law enforcement officials or other command representatives is appropriate because of the command's special responsibility for U.S. military personnel in overseas locations and because of the constant jurisdiction the UCMJ provides over Service members anywhere in the world—on or off military installations.

* * *

We found that commanders understood their authority, under USFK Regulation 190-2, "Off-Limits Areas and Establishments," to place off-installations establishments that engage in and support human trafficking, prostitution, and other exploitive practices off-limits to Service members. Notwithstanding this knowledge, we found that, for a variety of reasons, including lack of actionable information, commanders sometimes did not take the necessary steps to place establishments off-limits. At the conclusion of our second visit, we made the following recommendations that were intended to expand the use of the "off-limits" designation in order to eliminate Service member patronage of predatory establishments:

* Fully engage law enforcement and intelligence assets to collect and report indicators of human trafficking promptly to Armed Forces Disciplinary Control Board for possible off-limits show cause order.[16]

* Fully engage IG assets as a periodic and independent check on command/law enforcement efforts to identify clubs involved in human trafficking/prostitution. Designate the incumbent 8th Army IG as joint IG for USFK, allowing him to better handle joint issues. (As a matter of practice, the 8th Army IG served in a "dual-hat" capacity as the USFK IG, but was not officially designated as such.)

* Consider conducting interviews related to human trafficking through IG channels to preserve confidentiality of

sources and preclude actual or perceived whistleblower reprisal.

Again, we found that USFK leadership aggressively took action in response to those recommendations. By letter dated April 4, 2003, General LaPorte advised Congressman Smith, that USFK had established "a Korea-wide Crime Stoppers Hotline by which service members can report to the Provost Marshal any suspicious activity that relates to prostitution or human trafficking." Further, he stated that "we are publishing a USFK-wide policy that will, among other things, expressly state Courtesy Patrol (CP) reporting requirements concerning suspicious activity related to prostitution or human trafficking." As a result of those efforts, General LaPorte reported, "the Yongsan commander recently placed 26 establishments off-limits for suspicious activities relate to possible prostitution."

Further, to "Assess the effectiveness of the USFK programs," General LaPorte advised that he had "recently directed my Inspector General (IG) to conduct a 'Phase II Inspection.' The IG is now looking across the peninsula, focusing on leadership efforts, servicemember education, and the on-post and off-post environments." Subsequently, by email to this office dated June 4, 2003, General LaPorte advised, "My Inspector General haqs devoted a significant portion of his resources conducting a comprehensive inspection of our program across all five component commands and all six geographic areas." The email further emphasized,

> Military law enforcement continues to be one of the primary tools to combat this illegal activity... Leads from this [Korea-wide Crime Stoppers] Hotline and any other leads are being followed up and provided to the Armed Forces Disciplinary Control Board and aother appropriate agencies for action. We have currently designated 661 establishments as off-limits throughout Korea.

* * *

V. Conclusion

While some deficiencies existed in DoD efforts to combat human trafficking in Korea, USFK leadership has acted boldly and pro-actively to remedy these deficiencies and implement forceful and effective anti-human trafficking measures. These measures are consistent with the requirement for exemplary conduct imposed on all "commanding officers and others in authority" by title 10, U.S. Code Sections 3583, 5947, and 8583, and demonstrate a firm commitment to the "abolitionist approach to trafficking in persons" that underlies national policy set forth by NSPD-22.   In that regard, the education and training programs implemented by USFK not only provide information concerning the legal and societal implications of patronizing establishments that engage in human trafficking, but appeal to "core values" that must form the basis for moral decision making among Service members. By approaching the human trafficking issues in that manner, USFK commanders and others in authority satisfy their responsibility to "guard against and suppress all dissolute and immoral practices."

* * *

The following are selected excerpts from Department of Defense Office of Inspector General Report, "Assessment of DoD Efforts to Combat Trafficking in Persons: Phase II—Bosnia-Herzegrovina and Kosovo," Case Number H03L88433127, December 8, 2003.[17]

DEPARTMENT OF DEFENSE
OFFICE OF THE INSPECTOR GENERAL

CASE NUMBER
H03L88433128

December 8, 2003

<u>ASSESSMENT OF DOD EFFORTS TO</u>
<u>COMBAT TRAFFICKING IN PERSONS</u>

<u>PHASE II -- BOSNIA-HERZEGOVINA AND KOSOVO</u>

Prepared by the Directorate for Investigations of Senior Officials

Office of Deputy Inspector General for Investigations

.... In response to our Phase I report, 26 Members of Congress (including the original 13), signed a letter to the Secretary of Defense dated October 13, 2003 (Attachment A [to the full Inspector General Report]), concluded with the following admonition:

> Combating trafficking in human beings is an ongoing and worldwide issue. Commanders and service members at all levels must understand their role in helping to eradicate the scourge of human trafficking and to avoid giving any indication that DOD turns a blind eye to this barbaric practice.

Noting the "vast scope of the problem of trafficking in human beings" and the need to "achieve international cooperation to combat trafficking," the original Members of Congress who expressed concerns emphasized that any investigation into the issue of DoD complicity in human trafficking must be "thorough, global, and extensive." Accordingly, after completing the assessment in Korea, we turned our attention to the European theater, specifically Bosnia-Herzegovina and Kosovo, based on various indicia that human trafficking was a growing menace in those regions. In this second phase, we undertook to determine the extent to which commanding officers and other DoD officers and employees in authority were being "vigilant in inspecting the conduct of all persons who are placed under their command" (10 U.S.C. §§ 3583, 5942, 8583) and otherwise suppressing human trafficking, and whether Service members assigned to North Atlantic Treaty Organization (NATO) peacekeeping forces were engaged in any activities that promoted or facilitated the trafficking and exploitation of women.

We found negligible evidence that U.S. armed forces in the Balkans patronized prostitutes or engaged in other activities on a widespread basis that supported human trafficking. Rather we found that top U.S. military leaders in both the Stabilization Force, Bosnia-Herzegovina (SFOR), and the Kosovo Force (KFOR) implemented force protection policies that restricted contact between U.S. Service members and local establishments and effectively prohibited them from soliciting prostitutes or engaging in other activities associated with human trafficking. Further, we found that military leaders recognized the inherent dangers that human trafficking posed to good order and discipline, security, and mission accomplishment.

Those generally favorable findings with respect to U.S. Service members were tempered by the testimony of two witnesses who observed possible involvement by U.S. forces (infrequent observations of Service members patronizing local bars). Further, some representatives of non-DoD organizations, which monitored human trafficking in the Balkans, opined that U.S. Service members contributed to the human trafficking problem at some, undefined, level. Moreover, we found potential weaknesses on the part of U.S. military leadership in the Balkans in addressing human trafficking issues -- neither SFOR nor KFOR has implemented a program designed to educate Service members regarding human trafficking issues and there were no specific prohibitions on patronizing prostitutes or engaging in other activities that could directly support human trafficking. We believe those potential weaknesses warrant a general reinforcement of the U.S. approach to human trafficking in the Balkans.

We obtained testimonial evidence from embassy officials, United Nations officials and representatives from organizations that monitor human rights issues, indicating that Service members from other countries involved in NATO-led peacekeeping operations do not face the same restrictions on off-base movement imposed on U.S. Service members and were contributing to the human trafficking problem. For example, testimony indicated that Russian, Romanian, African, and Pakistani soldiers were the worst offenders with respect to human trafficking incidents in the past, including assaults of trafficked women. Accordingly, we recommend the Secretary of Defense support efforts to institute NATO policy that prohibits conduct on the part of NATO-led peacekeeping forces which could contribute to human trafficking.

With regard to DoD contractors, we found that contract employees, while considered members of the SFOR and KFOR community, are not subject to the same restrictions that are placed on U.S. Service members. For example, contractor employees are sometimes permitted to live outside U.S.-controlled military installations and, with few restrictions, to circulate in host country communities. Additionally, we determined that DoD contractors also employ many host country nationals, all of whom live in local communities and whose behavior is neither restricted nor monitored by DoD authorities. As members of SFOR and KFOR, contractor employees are forbidden from patronizing establishments designated by the United Nations or the European Union Police Mission as off-limits because of illegal prostitution and human trafficking concerns. However, we found that while some contractors make an effort to monitor their employees' activities and address employee misconduct, contractor behavior in this regard is not uniform. Not surprisingly, anecdotal evidence suggested some level of DoD contractor employee involvement in activities related to human trafficking in Bosnia-Herzegovina and Kosovo.

Based on these findings, we recommend that the Commander, United States European Command, consider the following actions:

* Continue to exercise vigilance to ensure military personnel adhere to laws and restrictions regarding activities related to human trafficking, such as prostitution. In particular, this should include regular reviews of the "Fighter Management Pass Programs" and inspections of rest and relaxation locations.[18]

* Amend General Order #1 to include provisions prohibiting engagement in all facets of prostitution and other activities related to human trafficking. These provisions should include punitive language to enable their enforcement through Article 92, UCMJ. For instance, the following subparagraph might be added to paragraph 3, "Prohibited Activities," of General Order #1: "Engaging in any activities associated with human trafficking. Such activities include obtaining the services of a prostitute, purchasing individuals for the purpose of indentured servitude or prostitution, or patronizing establishments that are suspected of involvement in human trafficking."

* Implement a training program designed to educate military personnel, contractor employees, and law enforcement personnel regarding human trafficking. Such a program should provide information on the legal, societal, and moral implications of engaging in activities that support human trafficking. In addition, law enforcement personnel should receive instruction in the provisions and application of the Military Extraterritorial Jurisdiction Act (MEJA), and es-

pecially in law enforcement measures necessary to support implementation of extraterritorial jurisdiction.

* Incorporate standard clauses in all contracts for work to be performed in Bosnia-Herzegovina and Kosovo that prohibits contractor employee involvement in activities that may support human trafficking and requires contractors to report to U.S. military authorities any information regarding involvement of their employees in such activities. Contractors should also be contractually bound to take appropriate measures to address such misconduct on the part of their employees. An example of a contract clause recently provided by this office to a contracting office is provided at Attachment B [to the full Inspector General Report]. Contracting officers should be charged to aggressively enforce such provisions.

* Implement policies to promote regular communication between U.S. military authorities, local judicial and law enforcement authorities, and the Trafficking and Prostitution Investigative Unit. Such communication would include the exchange of information regarding involvement by members of SFOR and KFOR in human trafficking related activities, and would facilitate investigations and prosecutions.

The remainder of this report provides detailed findings and conclusions of our on-the ground assessment in Bosnia-Herzegovina and Kosovo.

We believe that our assessments in Korea and the European theater, as well as our coordination with various offices in DoD, Congress, and other Federal agencies, provide the basis at this point for making recommendations for DoD-wide efforts to implement the President's "zero tolerance" policy on human trafficking.[19] As an essential first step in laying the groundwork for future efforts to eliminate DoD complicity in human trafficking, we recommend that the Secretary of Defense issue a policy statement on human trafficking that clearly and unambiguously sets forth DoD opposition to any activities that promote, support, or sanction human trafficking... Additionally, we recommend that, consistent with President Bush's address to the United Nations General Assembly on September 23, 2003, the Secretary of Defense continue efforts to implement policy that prohibits conduct on the part of NATO-led peacekeeping forces which could contribute to human trafficking.[20] In his address President Bush emphasized,

> The victims of this industry [human trafficking] also need help from members of the United Nations, and this begins with clear standards and the certainty of punishment under the laws of every country.

This office will continue to evaluate DoD efforts to combat human trafficking on a global basis as part of a regular inspection and assessment program.

II. Background

BACKGROUND ON PEACEKEEPING FORCES IN THE BALKANS

In Bosnia, a NATO-led multinational peacekeeping force, known as the Implementation Force (IFOR), began operations on December 20, 1995. IFOR consisted of approximately 65,000 uniformed personnel with the mission of establishing and maintaining a nonhostile environment. One year later NATO replaced IFOR with the Stabilization Force, Bosnia-Herzegovina (SFOR), which consisted of approximately 32,000 Service members in Bosnia-Herzegovina, approximately half that of IFOR. Over the past 6 years, SFOR forces have been reduced to approximately 12,000 Service members, divided into 3 multinational brigades. Both SFOR and its predecessor, IFOR, worked closely with the United Nations International Police Task Force (IPTF). The IPTF was replaced by the European Union Police Mission (EUPM) in January 2003.

* * *

Congressman Christopher Smith has met personally with trafficking victims. Under Attorney General John Ashcroft's leadership, the Department of Justice now treats the fight against human trafficking as a top civil rights priority. In a recent speech, the U.S. Ambassador to Moldova announced, "We often hear that trafficking is a form of slavery. That is not simply a cliché . . . . Trafficking in humans is the second most lucrative illicit business in the world after arms trafficking."[21]

One of the most comprehensive studies of human trafficking in the Balkans was published in November 2002 by Human Rights Watch (HRW), entitled "Hopes Betrayed: Trafficking of Women and Girls to Post-Conflict Bosnia and Herzegovina for Forced Prostitution" (hereinafter referred to as HRW report). The HRW report provided significant evidence that members of the IPTF engaged in human trafficking. The report stated that "Human Rights Watch investigators also found evidence that some Stabilization Force (SFOR) contractors -- civilians hired to provide logistical support for military forces based in Bosnia and Herzegovina -- engaged in trafficking-related activities." The HRW report cited evidence that "some civilian contractors employed on U.S. military SFOR bases in Bosnia and Herzegovina engaged in the purchase of women and girls."

Addressing jurisdictional issues, the HRW report stated, "Although these U.S. employees [DoD contractor personnel] enjoyed only 'functional' immunity (immunity only for acts related to their official duties), as of October 2002, not one had faced prosecution in Bosnia and Herzegovina for criminal activities related to human trafficking. Instead, when they came under suspicion, they returned to the United States almost immediately."

HRW investigators concluded that the "brisk repatriation" of U.S. personnel implicated in human trafficking "precluded Bosnian prosecutions and prevented the SFOR contractors from serving as witnesses in criminal cases against the owners of the establishments engaged in trafficking." The report then noted that "under a U.S. law passed in 2000, the U.S. government gained jurisdiction over these citizens but had not brought any prosecutions as of October 2002."[22]

HRW found that "since the end of the war in 1995, Bosnia and Herzegovina has become a major trafficking destination." Significantly for the DoD, HRW investigators concluded that, "while trafficked women and girls [in Bosnia-Herzegovina] have reported that approximately 70 percent of their clients were local citizens . . . local NGOs [nongovernmental organizations] believe that the presence of thousands of expatriate civilians and soldiers has been a significant motivating factor for traffickers to Bosnia and Herzegovina." In other words, HRW concluded that the mere presence of multinational personnel in the region financially incentivized human trafficking, giving the implication that presence of U.S. personnel contributed, at some level, to the human trafficking problem.

HRW's analysis of financial incentives represented by the U.S. presence in Bosnia-Herzegovina was supported by a report published by the United Nations Children's Fund (UNICEF), the United Nations (U.N.) Office of the High Commissioner for Human Rights, and the Organization for Security and Cooperation in Europe Office for Democratic Institutions and Human Rights. This report noted that "international clients pay higher rates and spend more money in the bars than local men," including accounting for an "estimated... 70 percent of all profits from prostitution."

* * *

BACKGROUND ON HUMAN TRAFFICKING CASES INVOLVING U.S. CONTRACTORS IN THE BALKANS

Ms. Kathryn Bolkovac was an employee of DynCorp Aerospace Technology U.K., Ltd. (DynCorp), a Department of State contractor providing personnel to serve as Police Monitors attached to the IPTF in Bosnia. In the course of her duties as a Police Monitor, Ms. Bolkovac became concerned regarding the trafficking of women and girls by organized criminal groups in Bosnia. Specifically, Ms. Bolkovac was concerned that some United Nations personnel in Bosnia were participating in human trafficking and that the police monitors and their supervisors (DynCorp employees) were facilitating, rather than combating, human rights abuses.

In July 2000, and on October 9, 2000, Ms. Bolkovac sent e-mails to multiple recipients in the United Nations and DynCorp detailing the abusive nature of human trafficking. Ms. Bolkovac also asserted that SFOR and IPTF personnel, among others, were involved in human trafficking and witness intimidation.

In April 2001 DynCorp fired Ms. Bolkovac, who subsequently alleged that her firing was in reprisal for the complaints she had made about coworkers engaged in human trafficking. Ms. Bolkovac filed suit in a U.K. Employment Tribunal for unfair dismissal.[23] Ms. Bolkovac prevailed at trial in 2003. Her case received international publicity and drew attention to issues of U.S. personnel involved in human trafficking in Bosnia and Kosovo.

A second case involved Mr. Ben Johnston, who was a helicopter mechanic employed by DynCorp under a United States Air Force contract in Bosnia.[24] In spring 2000 Mr. Johnston notified DynCorp and the U.S. Army Criminal Investigation Command (CID) that DynCorp employees were engaging in sex slavery, including the buying and selling (through purchase of passport) of underage women to use for sex and as domestic servants.[25]

According to HRW, a CID investigative report indicated that, during an interview with a CID agent, one DynCorp employee confessed to purchasing a woman from a brothel near the military base and gave a sworn statement giving details of the human trafficking operation. In addition to providing the sworn statement, the employee also "provided investigators with a pornographic videotape that appeared to document a rape" committed by a DynCorp employee involving a trafficked women. According to the HRW, it was clear from the videotape that the woman told the employee "no" prior to and during the sexual intercourse. Further, the HRW report presented verbatim testimony, taken from the CID report, of the DynCorp employee wherein he admitted having sexual intercourse with a trafficked woman after she said "no" and he admitted that "it is wrong to force yourself upon someone without their consent." However, HRW reported that CID investigators did not "properly delve into allegations that [the DynCorp employee] may have raped one of the victims on the videotape or that the women were trafficking victims. . . . Instead, the CID referred the matter to the local police for investigation." None of the contractor employees accused of trafficking-related crimes faced prosecution, according to HRW, because "local police denied to Human Rights Watch that they had authority to arrest, detain, or prosecute SFOR contractors for crimes committed in Bosnia and Herzegovina."

DynCorp fired Mr. Johnston on June 9, 2000, for bringing "discredit to the Company and the U.S. Army while working in Tuzla, Bosnia and Herzegovina." In August 2000, Mr. Johnston filed suit in federal district court in Texas for damages arising from his termination. After Ms. Bolkovac won her case at trial, DynCorp settled with Mr. Johnston.

According to publicly available testimony in Mr. Johnston's lawsuits, Bosnia police investigated DynCorp employees for human trafficking in 1999, several months prior to Mr. Johnston's and Ms. Bolkovac's complaints. The Bosnia press reported that DynCorp employees were accused of "harboring illegal immigrants and participating in organized crime activities to buy ownership (passports) of women." Reportedly, in August 1999, the Commander, Task Force Eagle, Multi-National Brigade North, located in Tuzla, Bosnia-Herzegovina, informed DynCorp of the names of the accused employees and requested the employees be removed from Bosnia within 48 hours. DynCorp complied. A few days later DynCorp reportedly fired these employees.

As a result of the Johnston case, DynCorp began requiring employees assigned overseas to sign an additional letter of agreement regarding a prohibition on human trafficking.[26] On April 24, 2002, the Subcommittee on International Operations and Human Rights, U.S. House of Representatives, held hearings on the sex slave trade in Bosnia. Mr. Johnston testified before that committee. Ms. Martina E. Vandenberg, of Human Rights Watch, provided testimony that corroborated the participation of DynCorp employees in sex slavery in Bosnia.

III. Scope

Our assessment team traveled to the SFOR Headquarters at Camp Butmir in Bosnia and to KFOR Headquarters and MNB East Headquarters, at "Film City" and Camp Bondsteel, in Kosovo in June 2003. The team was accompanied by an advisor to the U.S. Mission to the United Nations, representatives from the Center for Strategic and International Studies with a grant from the State Department, and a U.S. European Command representative. We focused our efforts on gathering information relevant to the possible involvement of DoD personnel in human trafficking and illegal prostitution and reviewing pertinent policies and procedures.

We conducted discussions with 40 officials including U.S. military commanders, members of their staffs, and representatives from various agencies and nongovernmental organizations. . . .

IV. Findings And Analysis

STANDARDS

[*See* Standards excerpts from Part I, *supra*]

FACTUAL FINDINGS

Facts Concerning Service Member Complicity in Human Trafficking

Most witnesses acknowledged the existence of a serious human trafficking problem in the Balkans that many individuals believed started, or dramatically increased, after cessation of combat operations and the influx of foreign nationals -- both contractors and NATO peacekeeping forces. However, with few exceptions, none of the witnesses we interviewed provided any first-hand observations or other evidence that U.S. Service members patronized or supported entertainment establishments that engaged in prostitution or other activities related to human trafficking...

* * *

We determined that the primary reason for the lack of involvement in off-base entertainment activities by U.S. Service members was the strict "walk out" policy adopted by U.S. military commanders, primarily for force-protection purposes. Walking out policies define the terms under which Service members may leave their bases, which are typically well secured by guards, high fences, and coiled barbed wire, for unofficial or recreational purposes. Generally, U.S. Service members were restricted to their military bases and had limited exposure to the outside economy except during official business or infrequent, controlled visits in the company of others.

For example, at Eagle Base in Tuzla, Bosnia, a key staff officer told us that military personnel are restricted to the base except when on official business (patrol). He noted that obtaining transportation (a non-tactical vehicle) required supervisor approval and a minimum of three people in the vehicle. Alcoholic beverages on the base were prohibited. BG Mason, Commander, MNB-North, told us he kept off-post restrictions strict, noting that occasionally soldiers could participate in a local sightseeing program, "A Taste of Tuzla," while in uniform. Similarly in Kosovo, U.S. Service members are prohibited from leaving Camp Bondsteel for any personal business. At Film City in Kosovo, Service members must receive permission to leave the base from their supervisor, may leave only on Sunday between 10:00 a.m. and 6:00 p.m., must stay in groups of three or more, and may visit only approved areas outside the base....

Facts Concerning U.S. Contractor Personnel

We determined that, although no DoD contract employee has been prosecuted for human trafficking-related crimes, evidence indicates that DoD contractor employees were involved in activities associated with trafficking. In the Bolkovac and Johnston cases, the evidence suggested that the problem of contractor employee participation was not an isolated one. We were told raids have been conducted on the homes of U.S. contractor employees and that women suspected of being trafficked have been found inside contract employees' homes. Employees have been fired by contractors for discipline reasons involving illegal prostitution, human trafficking, or being in off-limits establishments. In short, anecdotal evidence indicates that contract employee participation in human trafficking has been and continues to be an issue. A key factor is that DoD contractor personnel may not live on the military bases that they support and are not subject the type of walk out restrictions that are imposed on Service members.

In general, contractors do not report, nor are they required to report, allegations against their employees regarding involvement in human trafficking to U.S. military commanders (SFOR or KFOR). As a result, we found commanders were unaware of any contract employees being punished for, or accused of, human trafficking violations, except insofar as those commanders were aware of media accounts of the DynCorp cases.

The degree to which contractors monitor and act upon misconduct of their employees appears to vary greatly from contractor to contractor, and even from program manager to program manager within the same company. We identified one DoD contract program manager who proactively sought information concerning possible employee human trafficking involvement and told us that he fired several employees for illegal prostitution and human trafficking-related activities during the last year. We found that this program manager personally coordinated with local law enforcement personnel and instructed them to call him if any of his employees were found at off-limits establishments or were suspected of involvement in human trafficking. We found that not all program managers are this aggressive. Therefore, the absence of information on illegal activities of a contractor's employees does not necessarily mean such activities are not occurring.

* * *

DISCUSSION

We found negligible evidence that U.S. military personnel serving tours of duty in Bosnia-Herzegovina and Kosovo patronized prostitutes or engaged in other activities that might have the effect of supporting human trafficking on a wide-spread basis. This represents a significant difference from the situation that existed in Korea before U.S. military authorities took aggressive action to reduce Service member patronage of establishments that engaged in prostitution and to bolster law enforcement efforts to combat human trafficking. We attribute the lack of DoD complicity in human trafficking in the Balkans to three factors:

* Senior military leaders in Bosnia-Herzegovina and Kosovo appreciate the dangers that human trafficking poses to good order and discipline, security, and mission accomplishment.

* Military personnel are kept under relatively tight restrictions that prevent them from moving freely in the civilian community.

* Morale-enhancing developments such as construction of recreational facilities in Bosnia-Herzegovina and a well-organized FMPP program divert military members from prostitution and provide further incentives to avoid off-limits areas. . . .

* * *

Potential weaknesses of the U.S. military leadership's approach in Bosnia-Herzegovina and Kosovo include the lack of emphasis to all Service members on the incompatibility of prostitution and human trafficking with military core values and the absence of military legal remedies in the event soldiers do engage in activities supportive of human trafficking. Because human trafficking is approached as a force protection issue, there is no program in place to instruct military members regarding the immorality and inhumanity of human trafficking. NSPD-22 clearly mandates implementation of education programs by all Federal agencies as an important feature of the fight against human trafficking. Because there is no military standard that directly addresses patronization of prostitutes and other activities associated with human trafficking, criminal prosecution of these activities under military law is rendered more difficult.

We believe that correcting these weaknesses is consistent with the "abolitionist approach to trafficking in persons" set forth in NSPD-22, which further states, "the United States Government opposes prostitution and any related activities." The requirement to establish and enforce high standards of conduct for Service members is implicit in the obligation of military commanders to "guard against and suppress all dissolute and immoral practices," pursuant to Title 10, United States Code.

The available information regarding contractor employee involvement in activities associated with human trafficking in Bosnia and Kosovo is limited and primarily anecdotal. Even this limited information, however, suggests that DoD contractor employees may have more than a limited role in human trafficking. We were unable to gather more evidence of it precisely because there are no requirements and no procedures in place compelling contractors to gather such information regarding their employees or to report it to U.S. military authorities. DoD contractors could be compelled contractually to report misconduct of their employees and to take action to address employee misconduct. Our research revealed there are as yet no standard clauses in DoD contracts that enable the U.S. Government to standardize reporting requirements and measures to fight human trafficking among contractor employees.

With the development of legal systems in Bosnia-Herzegovina and Kosovo, and the establishment of the rule of law in those countries, local efforts to fight human trafficking have strengthened. Coordination between U.S. military leaders and local authorities in these efforts could preclude such problems as U.S. contractor employees being returned too quickly to the U.S., making them unavailable to testify in local courts. With the passage of the Military Extraterritorial Jurisdiction Act (MEJA), U.S. authorities also now have a weapon to address activities by contractor employees that contribute to human trafficking. However, U.S. law enforcement personnel will be less effective in implementing anti-human trafficking measures unless they receive training on the MEJA, coordinate with prosecutors in the U.S. who will try MEJA cases, and coordinate with local authorities in Bosnia-Herzegovina and Kosovo to enhance evidence gathering efforts.

However, DoD efforts to combat human trafficking do not depend solely on the ability to pursue criminal prosecution against civilian offenders. Investigators, inspectors, and auditors operating in DoD Inspector General organizations are not constrained by the criminal prosecutorial mandate and may properly examine the behavior of DoD contract employees. Those who violate conduct standards imposed by contract may be subject to administrative sanctions, while contractors who fail to enforce standards of conduct in their work force may face severe contractual remedies.

V. Conclusions

a With rare exception, U.S. military personnel do not engage in activities that support or sanction human trafficking in Bosnia-Herzegovina or Kosovo. Force protection restrictions effectively eliminate the possibility of involvement in such activities.

b Service members do not receive training to ensure they are aware of and sensitive to the widespread problem of human trafficking in the Balkans, and its relationship to their peacekeeping mission.

c Contractor employees are more likely than military personnel to be involved in illegal prostitution and human trafficking activities. DoD contracts do not in all cases impose the "zero tolerance" policy on contract employee behavior that is mandated by NSPD-22.

d Service members from some of the other countries that participate in the NATO peacekeeping mission are more likely to engage in activities that support human trafficking.

VI. Recommendations

As set forth in the Introduction and Summary section of this report, we believe our assessments in Korea and the Balkans over the past year provide a basis to recommend not only that the Commander, EUCOM, undertake those specific actions we have enumerated, but also that the Secretary of Defense establish a DoD policy on human trafficking that encourages commanders at all levels to: (1) educate Service members on human trafficking issues, (2) increase law enforcement efforts as needed to place offending entertainment establishments off-limits, (3) incorporate anti-human trafficking provisions in overseas contracts, and (4) examine human trafficking matters as part of established IG inspection activities.

We further recommend that the Secretary of Defense continue ongoing efforts through the North Atlantic Council of NATO to implement policy that prohibits conduct on the part of NATO-led peacekeeping forces which could contribute to human trafficking.

Chapter Review Questions:

1 By what authority and for what purpose would an IG inspect sex slavery?

2 Why did the U.S. Forces Korea Commander ask the IG of the Department of Defense, instead of the three-star Army IG, to address the allegations of complicity between Korean-based U.S. military personnel and international sex slavery?

3 Under what circumstances should a military commander (or a corporate Chief Executive Officer) call in an independent IG professional—as opposed to his own legal or compliance staff—to assess how the "tone at the top" is trickling down to the lowest levels?

4 Are human traffickers "enemies" of the U.S. Constitution? If so, why?

5 By what authority and for what purpose does Congress require all those "elected or appointed to an office of honor or profit in the civil service or uniformed services" to take an oath of office to "support and defend the Constitution of the United States against all enemies, foreign and domestic; ... So help me God"?[27]

6 Under what circumstances should an individual who is NOT "elected or appointed to an office of honor or profit in the civil service or uniformed services," such as an enlisted service member or a contractor, be required to take an oath of office to "support and defend the Constitution of the United States against all enemies, foreign and domestic"[28]?

7 During the course of the DoD IG's Human Trafficking Inspection, union lawyers representing contractors in Korea reportedly claimed that the new restrictions being imposed by the Commander, at the recommendation of the IG, could not legally be imposed upon contractors. What possible justification could there be for exempting DoD contractor personnel from the Secretary of Defense's "Zero Tolerance" policy on human trafficking?

---

[1] Recodified in 1997 for the Army, Naval Services, & Air Force at 10 U.S.C. §§ 3583, 5947, & 8583 respectively.

[2] Congressman Smith at the time was the Co-Chairman of the Commission on Security and Cooperation in Europe. His congressional co-signers were: George Voinovich; Frank Wolf; Dennis Kucinich; Steny Hoyer; Tom Lantos; Robert Aderholt; Joe Pitts; Melissa Hart; Mike Pence; Marcy Kaptur; Cynthia McKinney; and Diane Watson.

[3] *See* Inspector General Act of 1978, as amended, §3(d) ("Each Inspector General shall, in accordance with applicable laws and regulations governing the civil service—(1) appoint an Assistant Inspector General for Auditing who shall have the responsibility for supervising the performance of auditing activities relating to such programs and operations of the establishment, and (2) appoint an Assistant Inspector General for Investigations who shall have the responsibility for supervising the performance of investigative activities relating to such programs and operations."); *id.*, § 8(c)(5)&(7) ("In addition to the other duties and responsibilities specified in this Act, the Inspector General of the Department of Defense shall . . . (5) develop policy, monitor and evaluate program performance, and provide guidance with respect to all Department activities relating to criminal investigation programs; [and] (7) develop policy, evaluate program performance, and monitor actions taken by all components of the Department in response to contract audits, internal audits, internal review reports, and audits conducted by the Comptroller General of the United States.").

[4] 5 U.S.C. § 3331 ("An individual . . . elected or appointed to an office of honor or profit in the civil service or uniformed services, shall take the following oath: 'I, AB, do solemnly swear (or affirm) that I will support and defend the Constitution of the United States against all enemies, foreign and domestic; that I will bear true faith and allegiance to the same; that I take this obligation freely, without any mental reservation or purpose of

evasion; and that I will well and faithfully discharge the duties of the office on which I am about to enter. So help me God.'").

[5] George W. Bush, President of the United States of America, Address to the United Nations General Assembly, September 23, 2003 (http://www.un.org/webcast/ga/58/statements/usaeng030923.htm).

[6] Donald Rumsfeld, Secretary of Defense, Memorandum to Service Secretaries, etc., September 19, 2003, attached to Inspector General of the Department of Defense Testimony before the House Committee on Armed Services and the Commission on Security and Cooperation in Europe on "Implementing the Department of Defense 'Zero Tolerance' Policy with regard to Trafficking in Humans," September 21, 2004 (http://www.dodig.osd.mil/fo/JES_TIP_Testimony_092104.pdf).

[7] *Ibid.*

[8] *Ibid.*

[9] Defense Federal Acquisition Regulation Supplement; Combating Trafficking in Persons, 70 Fed. Reg. 35,603 (2005) (to be codified at 48 C.F.R. pts. 212, 225, and 252) (proposed with request for comments June 21, 2005).

[10] *Id.*

[11] 10 U.S.C. § 5947 (statutory Exemplary Conduct leadership standard), *supra.*

[12] "Assessment of DoD Efforts to Combat Trafficking in Persons: Phase I—United States Forces Korea," Case Number H03L88433127, July 10, 2003. ttp://www.dodig.mil/fo/Foia/H03L88433128PhaseI.PDF

[13] Within USFK, Courtesy Patrols consist of noncommissioned officers from individual company-sized units detailed to patrol off-post locations to ensure the safety and proper comportment of soldiers assigned to their units while off-duty.

[14] Each Branch of Service has its own self-prescribed values. For the Navy and Marine Corps its is "Honor, Courage, and Commitment"; for the Air

Force, "Integrity First, Service Before Self, and Excellence in All We Do"; and the Army has "Loyalty, Duty, Respect, Selfless-Service, Honor, Integrity, and Personal Courage."

[15] Neither Fox News nor USFK were able to identify the Service members serving on Courtesy Patrol who made comments during the Fox News video. There have been no reports of either reprisal or disciplinary action being taken against Service members as a result their appearances in the Fox News report. However, based on our conversations with other Service Members, we believe the Service member was repeating a generally held perception that many of the women who work in off-installation bars were exploited by debt-bondage, illegal confiscation of identity papers, and threats of physical violence. We found this perception to be corroborated by an abundance of articles on human trafficking and information from the United Nations and the Department of State's Office to Monitor and Combat Trafficking in Persons, as well statements by Korean government authorities and local non-governmental organizations which focus on aiding off-installation victims.

[16] The Armed Forces Disciplinary Control Board is the commander's tool for identifying and placing civilian establishments off-limits to Service members. According to a memorandum dated September 10, 2003, from the Chief of Staff, USFK, an investigation will be conducted "when credible evidence is presented" that the establishments "support, harbor, or in anyway sanction prostitution... Businesses may be placed 'Off Limits' to USFK personnel due to these illegal activities."

[17] The following are selected excerpts from Department of Defense Office of Inspector General Report, "Assessment of DoD Efforts to Combat Trafficking in Persons: Phase II—Bosnia-Herzegrovina and Kosovo," Case Number H03L88433127, December 8, 2003.
http://www.hrw.org/reports/2002/bosnia/ig.pdf

[18] As discussed in greater detail below, the Fighter Management Pass Programs offer Service members stationed in the Balkans an opportunity to travel on pass to three alternative locations in Europe for rest and relation.

[19] *See* National Security Presidential Directive (NSPD)-22, Combating Trafficking in Persons," of December 16, 2002, which is further described in the "Standards" section of this report. That Directive states, "The United States hereby adopts a 'zero tolerance' policy regarding United States government employees and contractor personnel representing the United States abroad who engage in trafficking in persons."

[20] We understand that the Office of the Under Secretary of Defense for Policy is already working with the North Atlantic Council of NATO to adopt standards of conduct for NATO-led forces.

[21] Ambassador Pamela Hyde Smith's remarks at the NATO Euro-Atlantic Partnership Council Meeting of July 24, 2003, in Brussels (as delivered).

[22] In November 2000, the Military Extraterritorial Jurisdiction Act of 2000, Public Law 106-523, was enacted. This Act was designed to close some of the jurisdictional loopholes that, in some instances, had rendered U.S. citizens essentially immune from prosecution for crimes committed overseas. The scope of the Act, however, is limited to "certain members of the Armed Forces and . . . persons employed by or accompanying the Armed Forces outside the United States."

[23] Ms. Bolkovac brought suit under the (U.K.) Public Interest Disclosure Act of 1998.

[24] Air Force contract number F34061-97-D0422.

[25] Because of the possibility of retaliation by DynCorp employees and the Serbian mafia, CID placed Mr. Johnston and his wife in protective custody.

[26] The letter of agreement also required DynCorp employees to notify DynCorp management of any employee engaging in human trafficking. The letter, however, did not include any indication that DynCorp would protect, and not reprise against, such whistleblowers. See, for example, 10 U.S.C. 2409, which states, "An employee of a contractor may not be discharged, demoted, or otherwise discriminated against as a reprisal for disclosing . . . information relating to a substantial violation of law related to a contract . . . ." DynCorp also indicated to this Office that it has placed 234

business establishments in Bosnia off-limits to all its employees, and that it has instructed the IPTF to inform DynCorp of any employee who visited the off-limits establishment.

[27] 5 U.S.C. §3331.

[28] Ibid.

CHAPTER 6. INVESTIGATE FRAUD, WASTE & ABUSE:

The Air Force Tanker Scandal

The Conventions of a number of the States having, at the time of adopting the Constitution, expressed a desire, in order to prevent misconstruction or abuse of its powers, that further declaratory and restrictive clauses should be added, and as extending the ground of public confidence in the Government will best insure the beneficent ends of its institution...

* * *

No person shall be held to answer for a capital, or otherwise infamous crime, unless on a presentment or indictment of a grand jury,... nor be deprived of life, liberty, or property, without due process of law...

U.S. Constitution, Preamble to Bill of Rights and Amendment V

The $23.5 billion Air Force Tanker lease proposal had been designed to "generate $2.3 billion in profit for Boeing,"[1] but instead resulted in the imprisonment of both the Chief Financial Officer of Boeing and the Chief Procurement Officer of the United States Air Force. It has been described as "the Pentagon's biggest procurement scandal since the late 1980s."[2]

Unraveling the Air Force Tanker scandal started with a distraught call from Senator John McCain's staff. A senior Air Force procurement officer, Darlene Druyen, had refused to identify the Wall Street expert who had recommended that the Air Force lease as opposed to buy a new fleet of aerial refueling aircraft to replace the Air Force's aging fleet of KC-135 tanker aircraft. According to Senator McCain's staff, the Air Force procurement officer claimed that she could not disclose the identity of the Wall Street expert on account of a non-disclosure agreement. Senator McCain's staff sensed deceit, and therefore requested an investigation.

As Darlene Druyen was not senior to the three-star Air Force Inspector General, Senator McCain's allegation of dishonesty was referred to the Air Force IG. The resultant Report of Investigation addressed a number of issues ancillary to the allegation of deceit, but did not answer the central question: Had Darlene Druyen lied to Senator McCain's staff?

The working papers appended to the Air Force IG Report made it abundantly clear that Darlene Druyen had lied to Senator McCain's staff. Based on supporting documentation, it was apparent that there was no non-disclosure agreement with the Wall Street expert, either in writing or otherwise. Senator McCain's staff was right.

When our office forwarded the Air Force IG's Report of Investigation to Senator McCain, I insisted on clarifying in the cover letter that notwithstanding all the other findings of the Air Force IG, Darlene Druyen should have been more forthright with the Senator's staff.

Subsequently, the Secretary of the Air Force called me into his office, and in the presence of the Air Force Chief of Staff, suggested that I could be sued for slander for writing such things about Darlene Druyen. Of course, I was just carrying out my statutory duty by calling it as I saw it, and being rightfully concerned about basic candor towards Congress.

On October 6, 2003, the Chairman of the National Legal and Policy Center, whose mantra is "promoting ethics in public life," sent me a letter captioned, "Allegations of Misconduct regarding the Boeing Lease Proposal." In the letter, the Chairman raised a number of "fact questions and ethical concerns" relating to Darlene Druyun's daughter Heather, whom "Boeing employed . . . while Ms. Druyun was negotiating on the Air Force's behalf on a multi-billion dollar procurement proposal from which Boeing stood to benefit."[3]

What ensued was a complex series of interlocking audits, leadership reviews, and investigations that led to two criminal convictions and the exposure of a flawed $23.5 billion effort by the Air Force to procure replacement tankers sole-source from Boeing.

On June 7, 2005, the Senate Armed Services Committee held a hearing, "To receive testimony on the Department of Defense Inspector General's Management Accountability Review of the Boeing KC-767A Tanker Program." A number of Senators asked tough questions about how I had carried out my statutory obligation of independence. Senator Carl Levin (D-MI), in particular, read a statement accusing me of violating my statutory duty of independence by consulting with White House lawyers on how best to conform with a redaction protocol agreed to by the Committee Chairman, Senator McCain, and the White House.

To be sure, conformity with a redaction protocol agreement between the Committee Chairman, Senator McCain, and the White House was a test of Inspector General independence. Some of my senior staff had suggested that I simply ignore the protocol, which I considered a legally binding agreement. At the same time, lawyers from the DoD Office of General Counsel were suggesting that redactions should be reviewed by them to ensure compliance with the White House protocol. In the end we chose carefully to steer through two "legal shoals": potential compromises to IG independence from the White House Counsel's Office on one side; and from the DoD General Counsel on the other side. From my perspective "at the helm," the redacted work product my office submitted to Congress had not run aground of either shoal.

Early on, according to the New York Times, "The Air Force took strong issue with Mr. Schmitz's conclusions and said it 'non-concurs emphatically' with nearly all of his recommendations."[4] In the end, the Air Force's senior acquisition official and the Chief Financial Officer of Boeing both went to prison, and Congress cancelled the deal.

CASE STUDY: THE AIR FORCE TANKER SCANDAL

The following are excerpts from the November 16, 2004, Plea
Agreement of Michael Sears, CFO of the Boeing Corp., which followed
the April 21, 2004, Plea Agreement and the July 7, 2004, Supplemental
Plea Agreement of Air Force Acquisition Officer Darlene Druyen, in
the U.S. District Court for the Eastern District of Virginia.

IN THE UNITED STATES DISTRICT COURT FOR THE

EASTERN DISTRICT OF VIRGINIA

Alexandria Division

UNITED STATES OF AMERICA   )
)
)   Criminal No. 04-310-A
        v.   )
)
MICHAEL M. SEARS   )
)
              Defendant.   )

STATEMENT OF FACTS

I. Background.

The defendant, Michael M. Sears, was from May 2000 until November 2003 the Chief Financial Officer of the Boeing Company ("Boeing"). In March 2002 he also became a member of the Office of the Chairman which consisted of four senior executives of the Boeing Company. He was also a member of the Boeing Strategy and Executive Councils. The defendant joined Boeing in August 1997 following the merger of Boeing and McDonnel Douglas where defendant had been employed since 1969.

Darleen A. Druyun, was from 1993 until her retirement in November, 2002, the Principal Deputy Assistant Secretary of the Air Force for Acquisition and Management. In that Senior Executive Service position, she supervised, directed and oversaw the management of the Air Force acquisition program. In addition, she provided advice on acquisition matters to the Assistant Secretary of the Air Force for Acquisitions, the Chief of Staff of the Air Force, and the Secretary of the Air Force. Prior to Druyun's service as the Principal Deputy Assistant Secretary of the Air Force for Acquisition and Management, she had a lengthy government career that included various positions in the Air Force, the Office of Management and Budget and the National Aeronautical and Space Administration.

Druyun's daughter was employed by Boeing in their student development program in St. Louis, Missouri, having been hired by Boeing in November 2000. Prior to her daughter's hiring, Druyun had contacted defendant and asked for his assistance in obtaining employment for her daughter.[1] Defendant contacted other executives at Boeing in an effort to obtain a position for Druyun's daughter.

In 2002, Druyun was overseeing the Air Force negotiations with Boeing to lease 100 Boeing KC 767A tanker aircraft. These tanker aircraft were to be extensively modified versions of Boeing's 767 commercial aircraft, and were to have as their primary mission air refueling of other military aircraft. The total value of the contract was projected to be in the range of $20 billion. Druyun participated personally and substantially as a government official through decisions, approvals, disapprovals, recommendations and the rendering of advice in connection with the negotiation of this lease agreement with Boeing. In the summer and fall of 2002, Druyun was also involved in negotiations with Boeing in her position as Chairperson of the NATO Airborne Early Warning and Control Program Management Board of Directors. This involved the restructuring of the NATO AWACS program, and the addition of $100 million in funds. The defendant did not personally participate in any of the negotiations with the Air Force in connection with any of these matters.

---

[1] Druyun had previously contacted the defendant in 2000 regarding possible employment for the boyfriend of her daughter. The boyfriend was subsequently hired and began employment at Boeing in September 2000.

II. Discussions Concerning Druyun's Employment With Boeing.

During the summer of 2002, Druyun had reached the decision that she would retire from the Air Force later that year. She did not publicly announce her decision to retire, but did notify her immediate supervisor, the Assistant Secretary of the Air Force for Acquisition, of her decision to retire on or about August 20, 2002. It was Druyun's intention, in the late summer of 2002, to seek employment in the defense industry following her retirement.

On August 13, 2002, Druyun traveled to Chicago to meet at Boeing's World Headquarters with various senior executives of Boeing, including the defendant. At some point during her visit that day, Druyun told the defendant that she was thinking of retiring later that year. The defendant told Druyun that he would like to talk to her at the appropriate time about post-government employment. Druyun advised defendant that she could not talk to defendant about her post-government employment until she completed work on certain Air Force/Boeing matters.

On September 3, 2002 , Druyun's daughter sent to the defendant an unsolicited encrypted E-mail over the Boeing Company intranet. Druyun's daughter did not personally know the defendant but was aware that her mother, Druyun, had known and had professional dealings with the defendant for a number of years. The subject line of the E-mail read "Please do not forward... RE: Darleen Druyun." In the E-mail, she advised the defendant that her mother would be retiring from the Air Force. The E-mail stated that Druyun had filed her separation papers with her JAG, but had not publically announced her decision to retire. It further stated that Druyun was interviewing with Lockheed Martin. The daughter encouraged the defendant to recruit Druyun for a position at Boeing and stated that Druyun was "officially available."   The defendant responded to the E-mail as follows:

-3-

The following are selected excerpts from the prepared testimony of the Inspector General of the Department of Defense before the Senate Armed Services Committee on the "Management Accountability Review of the Boeing KC-767A Tanker Program," June 6, 2005.[5]

INSPECTOR GENERAL
DEPARTMENT OF DEFENSE
400 ARMY NAVY DRIVE
ARLINGTON, VIRGINIA 22202-4704

HEARING TO RECEIVE TESTIMONY ON THE DEPARTMENT OF DEFENSE INSPECTOR GENERAL'S MANAGEMENT ACCOUNTABILITY REVIEW OF THE BOEING KC-767A TANKER PROGRAM

Oral Testimony of the Honorable Joseph E. Schmitz, Inspector General of the Department of Defense before the Senate Committee on Armed Services, Washington, DC, Tuesday, June 7, 2005.

Thank you Mr. Chairman, Senator Levin, Senator McCain, Senator Collins and Senator Thune:

I appreciate the opportunity to appear this morning and to answer your questions regarding our recent "Management Accountability Review of the KC-767A Tanker Program." As the publicly releasable version of the report has already been submitted and speaks for itself, I would ask that it be admitted as part of the Record. This morning I would like to introduce the Report's primary author, Deputy IG Mr. Thomas Gimble, and very briefly review the Report's genesis, its scope and methodology, and its bottom-line results. Of course, Mr. Gimble and I are prepared to answer your questions.

On December 2, 2003, Mr. Chairman, you sent a letter to the Deputy Secretary of Defense in which you suggested that I conduct an independent assessment that would "examine the actions of all members of the Department of Defense and the Department of the Air Force, both military and civilian, top to bottom, who participated in structuring and negotiating the proposed tanker lease contract" for the KC-767A Tanker Program.

Subsequently, on November 19, 2004, you and two other Members of this Committee, Senators Levin and McCain, sent another letter, this time addressed to the Secretary of Defense, reiterating that I should conduct "an assessment of accountability" along the same lines of your prior letter, and requesting that my assessment determine "what happened, who was accountable, and what actions must be taken to prevent this situation from happening again."

To accomplish this objective, our independent review team analyzed selected e-mails and memoranda from the Department of Defense, the Air Force, and the Boeing Company, and interviewed 88 individuals from the Departments of Defense and Air Force who had been involved in the Boeing KC-767A Tanker Program – to determine what happened and who was accountable during the structuring and negotiating of the proposed lease contract for the Boeing KC-767A Tanker Program.

Our review team did not interview White House officials, Members of Congress, or officials of the Boeing Company because the objective of the review focused on the accountability of members of the Office of the Secretary of Defense and of the Air Force who were involved in the Boeing KC-767A Tanker Program.

What Happened?

Although Boeing had submitted a proposal in February 2001 to the Chief of Staff of the Air Force to convert 36 Boeing 767 commercial aircraft into tanker aircraft, it was not until after September 11, 2001, that Air Force officials began meeting with Boeing Company executives to enter into an agreement to lease 100 Boeing KC-767A tanker aircraft. The proposed lease agreement generally had support of White House officials, Members of Congress, senior officials of both the Department of Defense and the Air Force, and the Boeing Company. At that time, that is, before and immediately after September 11, 2001, the Air Force had neither identified nor funded an urgent requirement for the replacement of its existing fleet of tankers.

The Department of Defense Appropriations Act for FY 2002, enacted January 10, 2002, included Section 8159, titled "Multi-Year Aircraft Lease Pilot Program," which authorized the Air Force to make payments on a multi-year pilot program "to lease not more than a total of 100 Boeing 767 aircraft" and provided that the "term of any individual lease agreement . . . shall not exceed 10 years." Without conducting an Analysis of Alternatives, the Air Force used the provisions of Section 8159 to justify an informal acquisition strategy, the focus and goal of which was expeditiously to lease 100 KC-767A tanker aircraft from Boeing through a business trust.

By not following established acquisition procedures contained in DoD Directives, the DoD and Air force officials identified in our report neither applied best business practices nor adhered to prudent acquisition procedures, and failed to comply with five statutory provisions relating to: commercial items; testing [two statutes]; cost-plus-a-percentage-of-cost system of contracting; and leases to satisfy warfighter needs.

Who Was Accountable?

Our report identifies the DoD and Air Force officials who were responsible for failing to ensure the prescribed acquisition rules and procedures were properly followed. In summary, a number of senior DoD and Air Force officials acted as if Section 8159 of the FY2002 Appropriations Act had waived various legal requirements -- statutory checks and balances -- that it had not. Moreover, as our executive summary concludes, "The system of management internal controls was either not in place or not effective because the existing acquisitions procedures were not followed in the proposed lease of the Boeing KC767A tanker aircraft."

What Actions Must be Taken to Prevent This Situation from Happening Again?

- The Department must change the cultural environment in its acquisition community to ensure that the proper internal control environment is reestablished and followed for major weapon-system acquisitions.

- The Secretary of Defense should reemphasize the need to conduct an Analysis of Alternatives for all major systems before major milestone decision points.

- DoD 5000 series guidance should emphasize that leasing is merely a method for financing the acquisition of a program, and that leased programs should be treated the same as any other acquisition programs of like cost.

- Finally, the DoD 5000 series guidance should require, at a minimum, that the decision to enter into a contract to lease a major system must be subject to the results of a Defense Acquisition Board or a System Acquisition Review Council review, as applicable.

This concludes my oral statement. Mr. Gimble and I would be happy to answer any questions you may have.

For the entire (albeit redacted) 257-page Department of Defense Office of Inspector General Report, "Management Accountability Review of the Boeing KC-767A Tanker Program," May 13, 2005, see http://www.dodig.osd.mil/fo/Foia/tanker.htm

Chapter Review Questions:

1 By what authority and for what purpose might:

    a An Air Force procurement officer withhold from a senior Senator on the Senate Armed Services Committee the identify of a Wall Street expert who had recommended that the Air Force lease as opposed to buy a new fleet of aerial refueling aircraft?

    b The IG redact from his report to Congress the names of senior White House and Senate officials pursuant to an agreement between and among a Committee Chairman, an individual member that Committee, and the White House?

2 At the June 2005 Senate Armed Services Committee hearing on the Inspector General's "Management Accountability Review of the Boeing KC-767A Tanker Program," Ranking Member Senator Carl Levin (D-MI) "called the report 'totally inadequate',"[6] while Senator John McCain (R-AZ) remarked, "I'd like to say a word about [the Inspector General of the Department of Defense], who I think has steadfastly done an outstanding job, not only on this occasion, but on other occasions. I appreciate the courage he has shown."

    a Was it appropriate for an Inspector General to consult directly with the Office of the Counselor to the President, without going through the General Counsel of the Department of Defense, in order to ensure compliance with a redaction protocol agreement between the Senate Armed Services Committee Chairman, Senator McCain, and the White House?

b What alternatives could the Department of Defense Inspector General have pursued instead of complying with a redaction protocol agreement between the Senate Armed Services Committee Chairman, Senator McCain, and the White House?

---

[1] Jeffrey St. Clair, "Onward and Downward: Book Cooking at Boeing," July 26, 2003 (http://www.counterpunch.org/stclair07262003.html).

[2] Andrea Shalal-Esa, Reuters, "Pentagon Acquisition Needs Cultural Change: Some lower-level U.S. Air Force and Pentagon officials do not yet fully recognize the need to overhaul defense procurement to make it more transparent and avoid problems of the past, the U.S. military's top internal watchdog said on Thursday," September 3, 2005 (http://www.corpwatch.org/article.php?id=12597).

[3] Letter from Chairman of National Legal and Policy Center to Inspector General of the Department of Defense, October 6, 2003 (http://www.nlpc.org/view.asp?action=viewArticle&aid=46).

[4] R. Oppel, "Pentagon Says Changes Are Needed in Boeing Jet Deal," *New York Times*, April 10, 2004 (http://query.nytimes.com/gst/fullpage.html?res=9A05E3D81338F933A25757 C0A9629C8B63).

[5] The following are selected excerpts from the prepared testimony of the Inspector General of the Department of Defense before the Senate Armed Services Committee on the "Management Accountability Review of the Boeing KC-767A Tanker Program," June 6, 2005: http://www.dodig.mil/fo/Hrng_KC767A_6-7-2005_v5.pdf

[6] M. Allen, "Details on Boeing Deal Sought: Senators Raise Questions About White House Involvement," The Washington Post, June 8, 2005 (http://www.washingtonpost.com/wp-dyn/content/article/2005/06/07/AR2005060701751.html).

CHAPTER 7. NON-CRIMINAL INVESTIGATIONS:

"A Guy Named Satan" and "Fast & Furious"

It is the policy of this Office of Inspector General that any person whose professional reputation is directly impacted by an audit, inspection, investigation, or oversight activity of this Office be afforded the 'essential constitutional promises' of procedural due process in a manner transparently consistent with [the United States Constitution, as explained by the United States Supreme Court in Hamdi v. Rumsfeld, 124 S. Ct. 2633 (2004)].

IG Policy Memo, "Due Process in the Activities of the Office of the Inspector General," August 20, 2004

In the aftermath of the terrorist attacks on September 11, 2001, U.S. Army Lieutenant General Jerry Boykin delivered a number of speeches about the ongoing war efforts, mostly in religious settings, such as churches. Some of his speeches were delivered in uniform, and many of his speeches were critical of Islam.[1] At the time, General Boykin was the senior uniformed military leader in the Office of the Undersecretary of Defense for Intelligence.

Eleven years later, in the aftermath of the terrorist attack against Americans in Benghazi, Libya, on September 11, 2012 (and substantively unrelated to either of these terrorist attacks), the Inspector General of the Department of Justice ("DOJ") released a report titled,

"A review of ATF's Operation Fast and Furious and Related Matters."
This IG Report involved, "Numerous firearms bought by straw purchasers [that] were later recovered by law enforcement officials at crime scenes in Mexico and the United States. One such recovery occurred in connection with the tragic shooting death of a federal law enforcement agent, U.S. Customs and Border Protection Agent Brian Terry . . . on December 14, 2010, as he tried to arrest persons believed to be illegally entering the United States."

The DOJ "Fast and Furious" IG Report, like the DoD IG report on General Boykin, exemplifies the IG role in investigating non-criminal allegations against senior government officials. Both IG Reports are included as case studies in this chapter.

According to the DoD IG's final report on General Boykin, which is posted on the internet and excerpted below, General Boykin's speeches "followed a standard pattern, exemplified below":

> After telling the story of Esther—a biblical figure who, according to LTG Boykin, became queen of Persia and was told she had been "raised up for such a time as this" to save her people (the Jews in Persia), LTG Boykin analogized the story to the election of President Bush who, he said, had been placed in the presidency by God "for such a time as this" (referring to the war on terrorism).

> After showing slides of the terrorist attacks of September 11, 2001, on the New York World Trade Center and the Pentagon, LTG Boykin commented, "we watched in disbelief as radical Muslims in other parts of the world danced and rejoiced in our misery."

> LTG Boykin then asked his audience, "why do they [radical Muslims] hate us?" He answered his question by stating that the United States' cultural heritage is Judeo-Christian and "[they hate us] because we support Israel and we will never abandon Israel."

While showing slides of Osama bin Laden, Saddam Hussein, and Kim Jong Il, LTG Boykin asked his audience if each of these individuals is "the enemy." He answered his own question in the negative, stating the true enemy is a spiritual one: "the principalities of darkness"; "a guy named Satan."[2]

LTG Boykin told his audience the United States is in a spiritual battle and that he was recruiting a spiritual army. He asked the audience to pray "for me, my soldiers, our leaders."

LTG Boykin then showed slides of Service members in the Special Forces and various weapons systems used by military forces in Afghanistan and Iraq. He noted how some of the Service members were lightly armed, mounted on horseback, and did not appear formidable. He discussed certain devises used by Service members as depicted in slides (personal digital assistants and laser target designators, enabling them to request and direct fire from supporting aircraft onto enemy positions and equipment). He noted these devices rendered Service members capable of defeating large forces, pointing out that these Service members could "reach back" to a greater power to defeat the enemy. He analogized this to a Christian's ability to "reach back" to a greater power through prayer.

In several of his presentations, LTG Boykin described personal experiences in operations in Iran, Somalia, and Grenada, and explained how his faith helped him to overcome difficulties he encountered during those operations.[3]

During the course of the Inspector General investigation into these speeches, lawyers assigned to the Office of Inspector General advised the investigators that a rule forbad senior DoD officials from giving speeches in religious settings. That rule, according to the lawyers, provided that, "Community relations activities shall not support, or appear to support, any event that provides a selective benefit to any individual, group, or organization, including any religious or sectarian organization..."[4]

Of course, the investigators had soon substantiated the allegations of wrongdoing based on the "rule" provided by the lawyers. There was only one problem -- the second part of the same religious setting speech rule provided an exception: "When DoD support is provided to one non-Federal entity, the DoD Component commands or organizations providing such support must be able and willing to provide similar support to comparable events sponsored by non-Federal entities."[5]

At about the same time the investigators were substantiating General Boykin's violation of the first half of the legal standard, the President of the United States was announcing on national television that he would reserve judgment on General Boykin until the DoD Inspector General completed his investigation.

The author was very familiar with the religious settings rule, having recently reviewed its precise text in preparation for a speech at a Georgetown University function. It soon became apparent that investigators had neglected to ascertain whether or not General Boykin ever declined an invitation to present his speech based upon the denomination of the inviting church. I therefore instructed that the matter be reevaluated based on the complete legal standard.

As a result, the conclusions of the investigation were significantly different. The OIG revised the findings associated with the religious setting speech rule, but stood by its conclusions regarding General Boykin's "failures to properly clear his speeches, issue disclaimers, and report travel reimbursements."[6]

The final report of investigation explained that "we did not determine whether the substance of LTG Boykin's faith-based statements constituted an appropriate topic for a speech by a senior DoD official, compromised his fitness for performing his assigned special operations or intelligence duties, or reflected on his ability to exercise sound judgment." The *by what authority and for what purpose* reasoning for this action is contained in the following three bullets:

* First, we believe freedom of expression considerations under the First Amendment to the U.S. Constitution apply in this case.

* Second, in the context of the substance of his statements, we believe LTG Boykin's fitness for duty and judgment are subjective issues for consideration solely by appropriate management officials, exercising independent and unfettered discretion, rather than for investigation by an inspector general.

* Finally, we believe our approach in this matter is consistent with the "Quality Standards for Investigations," issued by the President's Council on Integrity and Efficiency (PCIE) in December 2003, which emphasizes that investigative reports "should include a clear and concise statement of the applicable law, rule, or regulation that was allegedly violated or that formed the basis for the investigation." The PCIE standards further provide that investigators are expected to make "sound, objective assessments and observations," and avoid "personal opinions."[7]

CASE STUDY 7A: INVESTIGATE SENIOR OFFICIALS: "A GUY NAMED SATAN"

The following are selected excerpts from the Department of Defense Office of Inspector General Report, "Alleged Improprieties Relating to Public Speaking: Lieutenant General William G. Boykin, U.S. Army, Deputy Under Secretary of Defense for Intelligence," Case Number H03L89967206, August 5, 2004.[8]

DEPARTMENT OF DEFENSE
OFFICE OF THE INSPECTOR GENERAL

CASE NUMBER
H03L89967206

DATE
AUGUST 5, 2004

ALLEGED IMPROPRIETIES RELATED TO PUBLIC SPEAKING:
LIEUTENANT GENERAL WILLIAM G. BOYKIN, U.S. ARMY
DEPUTY UNDER SECRETARY OF DEFENSE FOR INTELLIGENCE

Prepared by Directorate for Investigations of Senior Officials
Office of the Deputy Inspector General for Investigations

Alleged Improprieties Related To Public Speaking:
Lieutenant General William G. Boykin, U.S. Army Deputy Under
Secretary Of Defense For Intelligence

I. Introduction And Summary

We initiated the investigation to address allegations that Lieutenant General (LTG) William G. Boykin, U.S. Army, Deputy Under Secretary of Defense (Intelligence and Warfighting Support), violated DoD regulations that pertain to speaking in a personal capacity when he made presentations to religious and other faith-based groups over the past 2 years.

After conducting an initial review of the matter, we also examined allegations that LTG Boykin violated standards concerning the wearing of the military uniform, use of Government resources and subordinates' official time, use of official travel, and receipt of payments from private sources in connection with his speaking activities. The investigation was prompted by concerns over LTG Boykin's speaking activities that were expressed by public officials and media reports in October 2003. Those concerns focused on the nature of LTG Boykin's comments, some of which were perceived by outside observers as derogatory to the Islamic faith or otherwise "inflammatory."

We found that LTG Boykin spoke at 23 religious-oriented events since January 2002, and that, with few exceptions, he appeared in uniform at those events (summary provided in Attachment 1 to this report). The events consisted of religious or "patriotic worship" services held at Christian churches in a variety of locations (13 such events), meetings of men's fellowship groups with Christian orientation (6 events), nondenominational prayer breakfasts held on military installations and sponsored by members of the military chaplaincy (3 events), and a community prayer breakfast hosted by a city mayor (1 event). LTG Boykin traveled to some speaking locations in connection with Government-funded travel for unrelated official purposes, while his travel expenses for other appearances were privately funded. With the exception of the three breakfasts sponsored by the military chaplaincy, LTG Boykin's speaking activities were sponsored by non-Federal entities and were governed by standards that apply to speeches given while acting in a personal capacity and not in connection with official duties.

We concluded that LTG Boykin's speaking activities violated applicable DoD regulations because: (1) he failed to clear the content of his speeches with appropriate DoD security and public affairs personnel;[9] (2) he failed to issue the required disclaimer on several occasions;[10]2 and (3) he failed to report his receipt of one travel payment from a non-Government source on his 2002 Public Financial Disclosure Report. However, we found that the preponderance of the evidence supported LTG Boykin's assertions that he made good faith efforts to consult regularly with legal advisors regarding his personal speaking activities. We recommend that management officials charged with taking action based on this report consider that factual finding in assessing the seriousness of the substantiated regulatory violations.

We did not substantiate misconduct on the part of LTG Boykin with respect to other aspects of his speaking activities. We concluded that LTG Boykin's wearing of the uniform in the situations at issue in this investigation did not violate pertinent DoD and Army regulations and determined that his Government-funded travel, which combined official business with personal speaking activities, complied with DoD travel requirements. Further, we concluded that the occasional use of other Government resources for his speaking activities (e.g., Government communication equipment, computers, copying machines) complied with the JER, which permits limited, incidental use of Government property for personal reasons. Finally, we determined that LTG Boykin did not accept honoraria or other compensation for his speaking activities (other than reimbursement of travel expenses).[11]

By letter dated March 17, 2004, we offered LTG Boykin an opportunity to comment on the initial results of our investigation. In his undated response, which we received on April 23, 2004, LTG Boykin disagreed with our conclusions with regard to the allegations we substantiated and strongly argued that his speaking activities complied with DoD regulations.

Further, he emphasized that he regularly sought counsel from legal/ethics advisors concerning the propriety of his speaking activities and that he followed that counsel without exception.[12]

After carefully considering LTG Boykin's response, re-evaluating the evidence, and conducting additional fieldwork, we revised our conclusions regarding: (1) uniform wear and (2) use of Government-funded travel, where we initially substantiated regulatory violations.

However, we stand by our conclusions regarding LTG Boykin's failures to properly clear his speeches, issue disclaimers, and report travel reimbursements.

With respect to our conclusion that he failed to properly clear his speeches, LTG Boykin stated that much of the DoD material he used in speeches at religious-oriented events had previously been cleared by public affairs personnel for release at other events, and that most of the information he used was already in the public domain or was available for public access. We were unable to verify LTG Boykin's assertions regarding prior clearance of material and note that prior clearance of material for presentation to one audience does not automatically convey clearance for subsequent presentations. Further, although DoD regulations permit DoD employees to use official DoD information that is already in the public domain when acting in a private capacity, the content of LTG Boykin's speeches, particularly their focus on military matters and national security issues, his appearance in uniform, and his introduction by official position support the conclusion that his speeches should have been cleared.

LTG Boykin also argued "it was never my intent to knowingly violate the JER with respect to disclaimers." He emphasized that he made clear to audiences that he "was speaking from my own point of view" and noted that none of the legal advisors with whom he consulted "raised disclaimers as an issue." Notwithstanding those arguments, we stand by our conclusion that LTG Boykin improperly failed to observe the JER disclaimer requirement on a number of occasions. In our view, the central theme of LTG Boykin's speeches concerned the fight against terrorism, arguably an ongoing DoD program, and should have been prefaced with a disclaimer that explicitly stated "the views presented are those of the speaker ... and do not necessarily represent the views of DoD." Although LTG Boykin sometimes characterized his comments as "my personal views" or "this is me speaking," his appearance in uniform, his introduction by rank/position, and his use of military visual aids required a more explicit statement to disassociate his views from DoD policy.

We recommend that the Acting Secretary of the Army take appropriate corrective action with respect to LTG Boykin, considering the mitigating factors that are discussed in this report.

This report sets forth our findings and conclusions based on a preponderance of the evidence.

II. Background

Since July 23, 2003, LTG Boykin has been assigned as the Deputy Under Secretary of Defense (Intelligence and Warfighting Support), Office of the Secretary of Defense, reporting to the Under Secretary of Defense for Intelligence. From March 2000 to July 2003, LTG Boykin served as the Commanding General, U.S. Army John F. Kennedy Special Warfare Center and School (SWC), Fort Bragg, North Carolina. From April 1998 to March 2000, LTG Boykin served as Commanding General, U.S. Army Special Forces Command, at Fort Bragg.

As Commanding General, SWC, LTG Boykin's duties included training, educating, and developing doctrine for all Army Special Operations Forces, and to "serve as the Branch/Functional proponent for all Special Forces, Civil Affairs, and Psychological Operations, both Active and Reserve Component." He was the Army's Executive Agent for security assistance training and proponent for Special Operations Forces simulation (war gaming). He reported directly to Commanding General, Headquarters, U.S. Army Special Operations Command (Commander, USASOC).

As Deputy Under Secretary of Defense (Intelligence and Warfighting Support), LTG Boykin is responsible for coordinating the activities of all DoD intelligence activities and for the resourcing and training of DoD intelligence assets. He advises the Secretary of Defense on intelligence policy and operations. His other duties include overseeing development and acquisition of new technology for the intelligence community, overseeing the collection and coordination of intelligence on non-U.S. persons outside the United States, and coordinating with other Government agencies (including Congress) and foreign countries on intelligence issues.

On October 15, 2003, NBC's "Nightly News with Tom Brokaw," reported that a "highly decorated general [LTG Boykin] who is one of the leaders of a secretive new Pentagon unit formed to coordinate intelligence on terrorists and help hunt down Osama bin Laden, Saddam Hussein and other high-profile targets has a history of outspoken and divisive views on religion -- Islam in particular."

In a letter to the Secretary of Defense dated October 17,2003, the Chairman and Ranking Member of the Senate Armed Services Committee, requested that we review the remarks attributed to LTG Boykin to determine whether LTG Boykin's behavior was "inappropriate."

III. Scope

During our review of the matter, we did not determine whether the substance of LTG Boykin's faith-based statements constituted an appropriate topic for a speech by a senior DoD official, compromised his fitness for performing his assigned special operations or intelligence duties, or reflected on his ability to exercise sound judgment. We took this action for three reasons.

* First, we believe freedom of expression considerations under the First Amendment to the U.S. Constitution apply in this case.

* Second, in the context of the substance of his statements, we believe LTG Boykin's fitness for duty and judgment are subjective issues for consideration solely by appropriate management officials, exercising independent and unfettered discretion, rather than for investigation by an inspector general.

* Finally, we believe our approach in this matter is consistent with the "Quality Standards for Investigations," issued by the President's Council on Integrity and Efficiency (PCIE) in December 2003, which emphasizes that investigative reports "should include a clear and concise statement of the applicable law, rule, or regulation that was allegedly violated or that formed the basis for an investigation."

The PCIE standards further provide that investigators are expected to make "sound, objective assessments and observations," and avoid "personal opinions."

Accordingly, this investigation obtained evidence needed to evaluate LTG Boykin's speaking activities against well established DoD standards that apply to speaking activities undertaken by DoD personnel in their personal capacities, irrespective of their rank or position, as well as other ethical issues described above.

We conducted over 40 interviews, including interviews of LTG Boykin, members of his staff at SWC, clergymen who sponsored his speaking engagements, and others familiar with matters at issue. In addition, we reviewed the six available video and audio recordings of LTG Boykin's speaking engagements in religious environments, LTG Boykin's travel and finance documents, and other relevant documents, such as financial disclosure forms, material advertising LTG Boykin's appearances, and itineraries.

* * *

V. Other Matters

As described above, LTG Boykin's argument that his personal speaking activities complied with applicable regulations was based, in significant part, on ethics advice that he said he, or members of his staff, received from various sources in the Special Operations Judge Advocate community. Although LTG Boykin's assertions regarding the receipt of legal advice were corroborated by members of his staff, the judge advocates who were in a position to render such advice had limited recollection of doing so.

We interviewed eight judge advocates who were in a position to give LTG Boykin ethics advice during his tenure as Commander, Special Forces, and Commander, SWC, including those whom LTG Boykin identified. With few exceptions (a recommendation not to wear the uniform to a speaking engagement in 1999, use of military aircraft, advice concerning receipt of travel benefits, and approval for travel to Daytona, Florida), none of those advisors could recall specifics of any other advice given to LTG Boykin or his staff with respect to his personal speaking activities. Moreover, we found no written record of ethics consultations with regard to the speaking activities that are the subject of this investigation. Accordingly, we could not verify the nature of the communications between LTG Boykin and ethics advisors—in particular, whether LTG Boykin "made full disclosure of all relevant circumstances," as required by Section 2635.107(b) of the JER, and whether resultant feedback demonstrated full awareness of those circumstances.

In our view, the regulatory violations identified during this investigation may have been avoided had ethics information been communicated in more comprehensive, preferably written, fashion. Accordingly, we are encouraged by an "Information Paper" issued by the Department of the Army Standards of Conduct Office on June 3, 2004, which provided the following "guidance regarding teaching, speaking, and writing related to official duties:"[13]27

> All requests for speaking, writing and teaching for topics, subjects and experiences that are related to official duties shall be reviewed by an Ethics Counselor. In order to render an effective ethics opinion, Counselors are encouraged to obtain all of the relevant information, e.g., complete description of the subject matter, theme, setting, nature of experience(s), characters, and military information (weapons, ordnance, aircraft, vessels, operations, tactics/strategy). Whether the writing or presentation contain classified material. Whether the presentation or writing will be illustrated, or contain pictures, maps or drawings, and the source of the documents. Finally, whether the writing or presentation has been passed through the Public Affairs Officer.

We recommend that the Acting Secretary of the Army continue to emphasize the requirement for full disclosure of relevant information when seeking ethics opinions and the need to properly address and document legal advice provided by command legal advisors to commanders.

VI. Conclusions

a   LTG Boykin violated DoD Regulations pertaining to release of official information by failing to clear his speeches with proper DoD authority.

b LTG Boykin violated the JER by failing to preface his remarks with a disclaimer.

c LTG Boykin did not violate applicable regulations by wearing his military uniform when making speeches sponsored by religious-oriented organizations.

d LTG Boykin complied with the JFTR when conducting personal speaking activities during Government-funded travel.

e LTG Boykin did not misuse Government property or subordinates in connection with his personal speaking activities.

f LTG Boykin failed to report travel reimbursement exceeding $260 from one non-Federal entity on his 2002 Public Financial Disclosure Report.

g LTG Boykin did not improperly accept honoraria or other compensation from non-Federal entities.

VII. Recommendations

We recommend that the Acting Secretary of the Army take appropriate corrective action with respect to LTG Boykin, considering the mitigating factors that are discussed in this report.

Additionally, as discussed on the "Others Matters" section of this report, we recommend that the Acting Secretary of the Army continue to emphasize the requirement for full disclosure of relevant information when seeking ethics opinions and the need to properly address and document legal advice provided by command legal advisors to commanders.

We recommend that LTG Boykin confer with his DoD ethics advisor to determine whether he should file an amended Public Financial Disclosure Report for 2003 to report receipt of travel reimbursement from outside sources in 2003.

The following are selected excerpts from the Department of Justice Inspector General's September 20, 2012, Testimony before the House Committee on Oversight and Government Reform.[14]

U.S. Department of Justice
Office of the Inspector General

A Review of ATF's Operation Fast and Furious and Related Matters

(REDACTED)

Office of the Inspector General
Oversight and Review Division
September 2012
Re-issued November 2012
(Some previously redacted material unredacted)

Good morning Mr. Chairman, Ranking Member Cummings, and Members of the Committee,

I appreciate having the opportunity to appear before you today to testify about the findings of my Office's report into ATF's Operation Fast and Furious and related matters, a report that details a pattern of serious failures in both ATF's and the U.S. Attorney's Office's handling of the investigations and the Department of Justice's response to Congressional inquiries about those flawed operations. This is my first opportunity to testify before the Congress since I was sworn in as the Department of Justice's Inspector General just five months ago.

During the confirmation process, I made a commitment to the Congress and the American people that I would continue the strong tradition of the Office of the Inspector General for independence, nonpartisanship, impartiality, and fairness. Those are the standards that I and the Office of the Inspector General applied in conducting the review of Operation Fast and Furious and related matters, and in preparing this report. As in all our work, we abided by one bedrock principle—to follow the facts and the evidence wherever they lead.

Methodology

As the report indicates, we reviewed over 100,000 documents and interviewed over 130 witnesses, many on multiple occasions. We decided what documents to request, and what interviews to conduct. The witnesses we interviewed served at all levels of the Department, ranging from the current and former Attorneys General, to the line agents serving in the field offices in Phoenix and Tucson, Arizona. Very few witnesses refused our request to be interviewed, and we have noted those instances in our report. The Justice Department provided us with access to the documents we requested, including post-February 4 material concerning the Department's representations to Congress.

We operated with complete and total independence in our search for the truth, and the decision about what to cover in this report and the conclusions that we reached were made by me and my Office, and by no one else.

I am pleased that we have been able to put forward to the Congress and the American people a full and complete recitation of the facts that we found, and the conclusions that we reached, with minimal redactions by the Department to our report. The Administration made no redactions for Executive Privilege, even though our report evaluates in detail and reaches conclusions about the Department's post-February 4 actions in responding to Congress. Additionally, at our request, the Department has agreed to seek court authorization to un-redact as much of the wiretap information as possible (consistent with privacy and ongoing law enforcement interests). If the court agrees to the Department's request, we will shortly issue a revised version of the report with this material unredacted.

Let me now turn to the substantive findings in our report.

Background

On October 31, 2009, special agents working in the Phoenix office of the Bureau of Alcohol, Tobacco, Firearms and Explosives (ATF) received information from a local gun store about the recent purchases of multiple AK47 style rifles by four individuals. Agents began investigating the purchases and soon came to believe that the individuals were so-called "straw purchasers" involved in a large-scale gun trafficking organization responsible for buying guns for transport to violent Mexican drug trafficking organizations. This investigation was later named "Operation Fast and Furious."

By the time ATF and the U.S. Attorney's Office for the District of Arizona (U.S. Attorney's Office) publicly announced the indictment in the case on January 25, 2011, ATF agents had identified more than 40 subjects believed to be connected to a trafficking conspiracy responsible for purchasing over 2,000 firearms for approximately $1.5 million in cash. The vast majority of the firearms purchased by Operation Fast and Furious subjects were AK-47 style rifles and FN Herstal 5.7 caliber pistols. During the course of the investigation, ATF agents seized only about 100 of the firearms purchased, the result of a strategy jointly pursued by ATF and the U.S. Attorney's Office that deferred taking overt enforcement action against the individual straw purchasers while seeking to build a case against the leaders of the organization.

Numerous firearms bought by straw purchasers were later recovered by law enforcement officials at crime scenes in Mexico and the United States. One such recovery occurred in connection with the tragic shooting death of a federal law enforcement agent, U.S. Customs and Border Protection Agent Brian Terry. On January 16, 2010, one of the straw purchasers, Jaime Avila, purchased three AK-47 style rifles from a Phoenix-area gun store. ATF agents learned about that purchase 3 days later and, consistent with the investigative strategy in the case, made no effort to locate Avila or seize the rifles even though ATF had identified Avila as a suspect in November 2009. Two of the three rifles purchased by Avila on January 16 were recovered 11 months later at the scene of the murder of Agent Terry, who was shot and killed on December 14, 2010, as he tried to arrest persons believed to be illegally entering the United States.

The next day, and in response to Agent Terry's murder, ATF agents arrested Avila. Several weeks later, on January 19, 2011, the U.S. Attorney's Office indicted 20 Operation Fast and Furious straw purchasers and gun traffickers. As of September 1, 2012, 14 defendants, including Avila, have entered guilty pleas to one or more counts of the indictment.

The flaws in Operation Fast and Furious became widely publicized as a result of the willingness of a few ATF agents to publicly report what they knew about it, and the conduct of the investigation became the subject of a Congressional inquiry. On January 27, 2011, Senator Charles E. Grassley wrote to ATF Acting Director Kenneth Melson that the Senate Judiciary Committee had received allegations that ATF had "sanctioned the sale of hundreds of assault weapons to suspected straw purchasers," who then transported the firearms throughout the southwest border area and into Mexico. On February 4, 2011, the Department of Justice (Department) responded in writing by denying the allegations and asserting that "ATF makes every effort to interdict weapons that have been purchased illegally and prevent their transportation to Mexico." However, after examining how Operation Fast and Furious and other ATF firearms trafficking investigations were conducted, the Department withdrew the February 4 letter on December 2, 2011, because it contained "inaccuracies."

Also on January 27, 2011, Senator Grassley's staff brought the allegations of one ATF agent to the attention of the Office of the Inspector General (OIG). We interviewed the agent and began a preliminary inquiry into the matter. On February 28, 2011, Attorney General Eric Holder requested the OIG to conduct a review of Operation Fast and Furious, and we agreed to conduct the review.

During the course of our review we received information about other ATF firearms trafficking investigations that raised questions about how those investigations were conducted. Our investigation included a review of one of them, Operation Wide Receiver, which was conducted by the Tucson office of ATF's Phoenix Field Division with the assistance of the U.S. Attorney's Office in 2006 and 2007, but which was later prosecuted by the Department's Criminal Division.

Findings

* ATF and the U.S. Attorney's Office Share Equal Responsibility for the Strategic and Operational Failures in Operations Wide Receiver and Fast and Furious

* The Failure to Adequately Consider Public Safety and the Lack of Sufficient Controls

We concluded that both Operation Wide Receiver and Operation Fast and Furious were seriously flawed and supervised irresponsibly by ATF's Phoenix Field Division and the U.S. Attorney's Office, most significantly in their failure to adequately consider the risk to the public safety in the United States and Mexico. Both investigations sought to identify the higher reaches of firearms trafficking networks by deferring any overt law enforcement action against the individual straw purchasers—such as making arrests or seizing firearms—even when there was sufficient evidence to do so. The risk to public safety was immediately evident in both investigations. Almost from the outset of each case, ATF agents learned that the purchases were financed by violent Mexican drug trafficking organizations and that the firearms were destined for Mexico.

Yet, in Operation Fast and Furious, we found that no one responsible for the case at either the ATF Phoenix Field Division or the U.S. Attorney's Office raised a serious question or concern about the government not taking earlier measures to disrupt a trafficking operation that continued to purchase firearms with impunity for many months. We also did not find persuasive evidence that any supervisor in Phoenix, at either the U.S. Attorney's Office or ATF, raised serious questions or concerns about the risk to public safety posed by the continuing firearms purchases or by the delay in arresting individuals who were engaging in the trafficking. This failure reflected a significant lack of oversight and urgency by both ATF and the U.S. Attorney's Office, and a disregard by both for the safety of individuals in the United States and Mexico.

In addition to the sheer volume of firearms purchasing activity in both investigations, the challenges agents faced in conducting surveillance should have called into question the wisdom of a longer-term approach whose success was dependent on being able to observe how the firearms were crossing into Mexico and to know what happened to them once they got there. We believe the limitations and the ineffectiveness of the surveillance should have prompted ATF and U.S. Attorney's Office personnel responsible for conducting and supervising the case to assess whether they could responsibly conduct investigations as large and ambitious as Operations Wide Receiver and Fast and Furious.

The Inappropriate Use of Cooperating Federal Firearms Licensees to Advance the Investigations

Agents in Operation Wide Receiver and Operation Fast and Furious used the substantial cooperation of Federal Firearms Licensees (FFL) to advance the investigations. The relationships with the FFLs in these two investigations created at least the appearance that ATF agents approved or encouraged sales of firearms that they knew were unlawful and that they did not intend to seize. In Operation Wide Receiver, agents clearly sanctioned the unlawful sale of firearms because the FFL was a paid ATF informant; in Operation Fast and Furious, we found that agents emphasized to the cooperating FFLs the value of their cooperation and sought additional cooperation that could be satisfied only by completing sales, at least giving the impression to these FFLs that ATF wanted the sales to continue. We also believe that, while there may be circumstances where the government can appropriately seek the cooperation of an FFL, there is a potential conflict between the ATF's regulatory and criminal law enforcement functions with respect to FFLs when the ATF seeks their ongoing and extensive assistance in an investigation.

Issues Regarding Coordination with Other Law Enforcement Agencies in Operation Fast and Furious

In Operation Fast and Furious, ATF missed an early opportunity to advance the investigation when it failed to exploit information provided by the DEA in December 2009 that may have led to the identification of a significant individual connected to its investigation. Among other things, ATF failed to conduct a potentially important surveillance because it did not have enough agents available to staff a surveillance operation due to the approaching holidays. ATF would later learn that this individual was a subject of an unrelated joint FBI-DEA investigation. We also found instances where ATF resisted efforts by ICE to conduct independent or coordinated investigations even though ATF had insufficient resources to handle such a large case and ICE has primary jurisdiction over export violations involving munitions and firearms.

Former Attorney General Mukasey Was Not Made Aware That ATF Had Allowed Guns to "Walk" in Operation Wide Receiver or Any Other Investigation

Former Attorney General Mukasey became Attorney General after investigative activity in Operation Wide Receiver was concluded. We found no evidence that he was informed that ATF, in connection with Operation Wide Receiver, was allowing or had allowed firearms to "walk." We found that Mukasey was briefed on ATF's attempts to use controlled deliveries—a law enforcement technique that witnesses told us differs significantly from "walking" in that it involves the delivery of contraband under surveillance or other control by law enforcement agents, with arrests and interdictions at the point of transfer—in a different ATF firearms trafficking investigation involving a lead subject named Fidel Hernandez. While the briefing paper mentioned that ATF's attempts to conduct controlled deliveries had been unsuccessful, we found no basis to conclude that this briefing put Mukasey on notice of Operation Wide Receiver or of "walking" as a tactic employed in ATF investigations.

The Wiretap Applications Submitted to the Department's Criminal Division in Operation Wide Receiver and Operation Fast and Furious Contained "Red Flags" Regarding the Conduct of the Investigations

We reviewed all 14 wiretap affidavits in both Operation Wide Receiver and Operation Fast and Furious and concluded that the affidavits in both cases included information that would have caused a prosecutor who was focused on the question of investigative tactics, particularly one who was already sensitive to the issue of gun walking, to have questions about ATF's conduct of the investigations. However, during our review we found no evidence that any of the 5 Deputy Assistant Attorneys General (DAAG) who reviewed the 14 wiretap applications in connection with Operations Wide Receiver and Fast and Furious identified any issues or raised any concerns about the information contained in the applications. In light of the explicit statutory assignment of responsibility for authorizing wiretap applications, we were concerned by the statements of the three DAAGs we interviewed that they did not regularly review wiretap applications, instead relying on summary memoranda they received. Our report recommends that DAAGs should be required to conduct a review of wiretap applications and affidavits that is sufficient to enable them to form a personal judgment that the application meets the statutory criteria.

We further found that given DAAG Weinstein's discovery in March and April 2010 of "gun walking" issues in Operation Wide Receiver, coupled with the information he learned about Operation Fast and Furious in April and May 2010, his review of the first cover memorandum to the wiretap application and affidavit that he received in Operation Fast and Furious in May 2010 should have caused him to read the affidavit and ask questions about the operational details of Operation Fast and Furious.

ATF Headquarters' Failure to Provide Meaningful Oversight in Operation Fast and Furious

We found that Operation Fast and Furious received little or no supervision by ATF Headquarters, despite its connection to a dangerous narcotics cartel in Mexico, the serious risk it created to public safety in the United States and Mexico, and its potential impact on the country's relationship with Mexico. Sufficient information was available to ATF's senior leadership, up to and including Acting Director Melson, about the investigative tactics used and the corresponding risk to public safety, yet ATF leadership repeatedly failed to act in a timely fashion on this information. Further, ATF senior officials ignored warnings about gun walking from their own employees. We determined that, by the first months of 2010, ATF Headquarters' deference to the Phoenix Field Division imperiled the agency's obligation to protect the public. We concluded that ATF's senior leadership should have recognized that its agents were failing to take adequate enforcement action as straw purchasing activity continued at an alarming pace, and should have instituted measures to promptly conclude the case, even if over the objections of its Phoenix Field Division or the U.S. Attorney's Office. We also determined that ATF's senior leadership failed to seek timely closure of the investigation, even after its Deputy Director recognized the need to conclude the investigative phase and asked for an "exit strategy." We found that Deputy Director Hoover and Acting Director Melson did not review the exit strategy until 2011, after the Fast and Furious investigation was publicly announced on January 25, 2011. We concluded that the "exit strategy" that Deputy Director Hoover asked for was never implemented and that the first arrest did not occur until December, immediately after Agent Terry's murder.

The Failure by the Department's and ATF's Senior Leadership to Sufficiently Inquire About Operation Fast and Furious After Agent Terry's Shooting

Senior leadership at both the Department and ATF did little in the immediate aftermath of Agent Terry's shooting to try to learn how two weapons that had been purchased 11 months earlier by a previously-identified subject of Operation Fast and Furious ended up at the murder scene. While ATF Acting Director Melson and ATF Acting Deputy Director Hoover promptly requested information after learning of the connection, and promptly notified the Office of the Deputy Attorney General about the information, they failed to initiate a review of the matter. Similarly, when stories appeared on the Internet alleging that ATF had allowed firearms to "walk" to Mexico and that one of the firearms may have been linked to the death of a federal law enforcement officer, Acting Director Melson expressed concern about

ATF employees leaking information and forwarded the matter to ATF Internal Affairs for investigation after being assured by four or five supervisors that the allegation on the Internet was false.

We further concluded that although Attorney General Holder was notified immediately of Agent Terry's shooting and death, he was not told about the connection between the firearms found at the scene of the shooting and Operation Fast and Furious. We determined that Attorney General Holder did not learn of that fact until sometime in 2011, after he received Sen. Grassley's January 27 letter. Senior Department officials were aware of this significant and troubling information by December 17, 2010, but did not believe the information was sufficiently important to alert the Attorney General about it or to make any further inquiry regarding this development. We concluded that an aggressive response to the information was required, including prompt notification of the Attorney General and appropriate inquiry of ATF and the U.S. Attorney's Office. However, we found that senior Department officials who were aware of the information took no action whatsoever.

Had the Department's senior leadership taken immediate action after learning that weapons found at the scene of a federal law enforcement agent's murder were linked to a straw purchaser in an ATF firearms trafficking investigation, the Department likely would have gathered information about Operation Fast and Furious well before it received the inquiry from Sen. Grassley about the very same issue in late January 2011. The Department, however, did not do so.

Attorney General Holder Was Not Made Aware of the Potential Flaws in Operation Fast and Furious Until February 2011

We found no evidence that Attorney General Holder was informed about Operation Fast and Furious, or learned about the tactics employed by ATF in the investigation, prior to January 31, 2011. We found it troubling that a case of this magnitude, and one that affected Mexico so significantly was not directly briefed to the Attorney General. We would expect such information to come to the Attorney General through the Office of the Deputy Attorney General. However, we found that neither ATF nor the U.S. Attorney's Office sufficiently advised the Office of the Deputy Attorney General about the investigation itself or of any operational concerns regarding the investigation.

The Failures in the Department's Responses to Congressional Inquiries

We concluded, as did the Department, that its February 4, 2011, response letter to Senator Grassley contained inaccuracies, particularly its assertion that ATF "makes every effort to interdict weapons that have been purchased illegally and prevent their transportation to Mexico." However, we also found that, by March or April 2011, senior Department officials knew or should have known that ATF had not made "every effort to interdict weapons that [had] been purchased illegally and prevent their transportation to Mexico," either in Operation Fast and Furious or other firearms trafficking investigations and therefore the February 4 letter contained inaccuracies.

The Department's February 4 Letter Contained Inaccuracies Due to a Significantly Flawed Drafting Process

We found that a poorly executed information gathering and drafting process, as well as questionable judgments by Department officials, contributed to the Department's inclusion of inaccurate information in its February 4 response letter to Senator Grassley. In preparing this letter, Department officials relied on information provided by senior component officials that was not accurate, primarily from U.S. Attorney Burke, ATF Acting Director Melson, and ATF Deputy Director Hoover. These officials failed to exercise appropriate oversight of the investigation, and to some extent were themselves receiving incorrect or incomplete information from their subordinates about it. These deficiencies contributed substantially to the provision of inaccurate information to Department officials who were responsible for responding to Congressional inquiries.

We further concluded that the Department officials who had a role in drafting the February 4 letter should have done more to inform themselves about the allegations in Sen. Grassley's letter and should not have relied solely on the assurances of senior officials at ATF and the U.S. Attorney's Office that the allegations were false. While the Department should be able to rely on the representations of its senior component officials in responding to Congressional inquiries, we do not believe that the gravity of the allegation in this instance was met with an equally serious effort by the Department to determine whether ATF and the U.S. Attorney's Office had allowed the sale of hundreds of weapons to straw purchasers. This was particularly the case here because the Department knew that hundreds of assault weapons had indeed been sold to straw purchasers during Operation Fast and Furious and that two of those firearms had in fact been found at the scene of Agent Terry's murder. Under these circumstances, we believe that the Department should have independently assessed the facts surrounding the related allegations by Sen. Grassley in late January 2011, rather than relying on ATF's and the U.S. Attorney's Office's assurances that they were baseless.

The Failure by AAG Breuer and DAAG Weinstein to Draw a Connection Between the Allegations in Senator Grassley's Letters and Their Knowledge of Operation Wide Receiver

We also found that a critical deficiency in the Department's knowledge of relevant information resulted from the failure by AAG Breuer and DAAG Weinstein to draw a connection between the allegations in Sen. Grassley's letters and their knowledge of Operation Wide Receiver, an investigation in which ATF employed similarly flawed tactics. At the Department, Breuer, Weinstein, and a few other Criminal Division attorneys knew about Operation Wide Receiver. Additionally, Weinstein knew about Operation Fast and Furious from his discussions with a senior ATF official in April and May 2010 and his review and authorization of three wiretap applications in May and June 2010. Weinstein also was directly and substantially involved in drafting the Department's February 4 response letter to Sen. Grassley.

Breuer testified before Congress on November 1, 2011, that he made mistakes by not telling senior Department leadership about the problems with Operation Wide Receiver when he learned of them in April 2010, and by failing to draw a connection between those problems and the allegations concerning the conduct of Operation Fast and Furious in January and February 2011. We agree with this assessment. Weinstein, by contrast, told the OIG that Operation Wide Receiver "had not come to mind as being possibly relevant to this response" because he believed Sen. Grassley's allegations were limited to Operation Fast and Furious.

The Department Knew or Should Have Known by the Date of its May 2 Letter that it could Not Reaffirm the Accuracy of the Entire February 4 Letter

We found that the Department's statement—"It remains our understanding that ATF's Operation Fast and Furious did not knowingly permit straw buyers to take guns into Mexico"—in its May 2 letter responding to another inquiry from Sen. Grassley reasonably could have been understood by Congress and the public as at least a partial reaffirmation of the Department's February 4 letter. However, we determined that senior Department officials knew or should have known by that date that, while ATF may not have allowed straw purchasers to buy firearms so that they themselves could take the guns to Mexico, ATF had in many instances allowed straw purchasers to buy firearms knowing that a third party would be transporting them to Mexico. Thus, we concluded that the May 2 letter was true only in the most literal sense.

We further concluded that, by the date of its May 2 response letter, senior Department officials responsible for drafting the letter also knew or should have known that ATF had not made "every effort to interdict weapons purchased illegally and prevent their transportation to Mexico," either in Operation Fast and Furious or other firearms trafficking investigations, and that the Department's February 4 letter contained inaccuracies and could no longer be defended in its entirety.

Indeed, we noted that the Department, in its first four responses to Congressional questions following its February 4 letter, appropriately made no substantive comments about the investigation in light of the additional information it had learned and its referral of the matter to the OIG in February. Given that senior Department officials' confidence in the accuracy of the February 4 letter was decreasing rather than increasing as their internal review progressed, we found it troubling that the Department's subsequent May 2 letter to Sen. Grassley included a substantive statement—albeit a qualified one—regarding the Fast and Furious investigation that could have been read to reaffirm the prior questioned letter. We believe that the Department should have continued to refrain from making substantive statements about both the February 4 letter and the Fast and Furious investigation, as it did in its four prior letters to Congress, or state that there were significant concerns about the accuracy of the February 4 letter and that Department officials would not respond to further inquiries until they determined the actual facts.

Similarly, we found that the Department should not have provided testimony on June 15 before the House Committee on Oversight and Governmental Reform in a manner that created ambiguity and uncertainty regarding whether the Department was still defending its February 4 and May 2 letters.

Conclusion

Our review of Operation Fast and Furious and related matters revealed a series of misguided strategies, tactics, errors in judgment, and management failures that permeated ATF Headquarters and the Phoenix Field Division, as well as the U.S. Attorney's Office for the District of Arizona and at the Headquarters of the Department of Justice. In this report, we described deficiencies in two operations conducted in ATF's Phoenix Field Division between 2006 and 2010— Operation Wide Receiver and Operation Fast and Furious. In the course of our review we identified individuals ranging from line agents and prosecutors in Phoenix and Tucson to senior ATF officials in Washington, D.C., who bore a share of responsibility for ATF's knowing failure in both these operations to interdict firearms illegally destined for Mexico, and for pursuing this risky strategy without adequately taking into account the significant danger to public safety that it created. We also found failures by Department officials related to these matters, including failing to respond accurately to a Congressional inquiry about them.

Based on our findings, we made six recommendations designed to increase the Department's involvement in and oversight of ATF operations, improve coordination among the Department's law enforcement components, and enhance the Department's wiretap application review and authorization process. The OIG intends to closely monitor the Department's progress in implementing these recommendations.

Finally, we recommend that the Department review the conduct and performance of the Department personnel as described in this report and determine whether discipline or other administrative action with regard to each of them is appropriate.

Chapter Review Questions:

1   Under what circumstances, by what authority, and for what purpose might a command legal advisor not document his or her legal advice to the commander?

2   When an Inspector General must review "legal advice provided by command legal advisors to commanders" in order to conduct an investigation, under what circumstances, if any, can the attorney-client privilege be invoked to withhold information from the Inspector General?

3   In the context of an Inspector General review of "legal advice provided by command legal advisors to commanders," to whom does the attorney-client privilege belong, and who has the authority to waive it?

4   Is there a mechanism whereby the subject of an Inspector General investigation can disclose privileged attorney-client communications to an Inspector General without waiving the attorney-client privilege?

1 *See generally* K. Rhem, "Inspector General to Investigate General's Comments," American Forces Press Service, October 21, 2003 (http://www.defenselink.mil/news/newsarticle.aspx?id=28279).

2 *Cf.* Ephesians 6:12 ("For our struggle is not with flesh and blood but with the principalities, with the powers, with the world rulers of this present darkness, with the evil spirits in the heavens.").

3 Department of Defense Office of the Inspector General, "Alleged Improprieties Related to Public Speaking: Lieutenant general William G. Boykin, U.S. Army, Deputy Under Secretary of Defense for Intelligence," pp. 8-9, August 5, 2004 (http://www.dodig.osd.mil/fo/foia/ERR/h03l89967206.pdf).

4 Department of Defense Directive 5410.18, "Public Affairs Community Relations Policy," Paragraph 4.2.9, November 20, 2001.

5 *Ibid.*

6 Department of Defense Office of the Inspector General, "Alleged Improprieties Related to Public Speaking: Lieutenant general William G. Boykin, U.S. Army, Deputy Under Secretary of Defense for Intelligence," at 2.

7 *Id.*, p. 4.

8 "Alleged Improprieties Relating to Public Speaking: Lieutenant General William G. Boykin, U.S. Army, Deputy Under Secretary of Defense for Intelligence," Case Number H03L89967206, August 5, 2004. http://www.dodig.mil/fo/Foia/ERR/h03l89967206.pdf

9 DoD Directive 5230.9, "Clearance ofDoD Information for Public Release," and Army Regulation (AR) 360-1, "The Army Public Affairs Program," impose restrictions on public release of "official DoD information," Official DoD information is defined, in part, as information that "was ac-

quired by DoD employees as part of their official duties or because of their official status within the Department"

[10] Pursuant to DoD 5500.7-R, "Joint Ethics Regulation (JER)," a disclaimer, when required, "shall expressly state that the views presented are those of the speaker . . . and do not necessarily represent the views of DoD."

[11] For reasons set forth in the "Scope" section of this report, we did not critique the content of LTG Boykin's speeches.

[12] While the following paragraphs provide what we believe is a reasonable synopsis of responses provided by LTG Boykin, we recognize that any attempt to summarize risks oversimplification and omission. Accordingly, we incorporated comments by LTG Boykin throughout this report where appropriate and provided copies of his response to the Acting Secretary of the Army together with this report.

[13] As described throughout this report, LTO Boykin's speeches to religious-oriented groups were a personal activity, not part of his official duties. However, the substance of his speeches related to his official duties, and the circumstances of their presentation (in military uniform, introduction by rank/position) created a perceived association with his official duties.

[14] The following are selected excerpts from the Department of Justice Inspector General's September 20, 2012, Testimony before the House Committee on Oversight and Government Reform. http://www.justice.gov/oig/testimony/t1220.pdf; the entire IG Report, albeit redacted, titled "A Review of ATF's Operation Fast and Furious and Related Matters," September 19, 2012, is posted at http://www.justice.gov/oig/reports/2012/s1209.pdf

CHAPTER 8. AUDIT:

Reporting to the American People on How Their Government Spends Their Money

[A] regular statement and account of receipts and expenditures of all public money shall be published from time to time.

U.S. Constitution, Article I, Section 9.

Most public sector audits, whether or not conducted by an Office of Inspector General, satisfy in one way or another the constitutional imperative that, "a regular statement and account of receipts and expenditures of all public money shall be published from time to time."[1] The Inspector General Act of 1978, as amended, requires that, "Each Inspector General shall . . . appoint an Assistant Inspector General for Auditing who shall have the responsibility for supervising the performance of auditing activities relating to programs and operations of the establishment."[2] The professional standards for those auditing activities are promulgated by the United States General Accountability Office, in what is referred to as the "Yellow Book."[3]

As explained by the Comptroller General of the United States in the Introduction to the Yellow Book:

> The principles of transparency and accountability for the use of public resources are key to our nation's governing processes. Government officials and recipients of federal moneys are responsible for carrying out public functions

efficiently, economically, effectively, ethically, and equitably, while achieving desired program objectives. High-quality auditing is essential for government accountability to the public and transparency regarding linking resources to related program results.[4]

In the aftermath of the Enron accounting scandal of 2001,[5] and the ensuing enactment by Congress of the Sarbanes Oxley Act of 2002,[6] the Government Accountability Office prescribed two overarching independence principles for all public sector audit organizations:

> (1) audit organizations must not provide nonaudit services that involve performing management functions or making management decisions and

> (2) audit organizations must not audit their own work or provide nonaudit services in situations in which the non-audit services are significant or material to the subject matter of the audits.[7]

The following case study illustrates how these independence principles enable auditors to shed light better for the American People to see how their government is spending their money—pursuant to our Constitution's mandate in Article I, Section 9, that "a regular statement and account of receipts and expenditures of all public money shall be published from time to time."

On April 15, 2010, the Inspectors General of the Department of Defense and of the Department of State both appeared before the Senate Committee on Homeland Security and Governmental Affairs, Subcommittee on Contracting Oversight, to report on their joint audit of "Contracts for Afghan National Police Training." The DoD Inspector General testified that:

> Oversight of U.S. contingency operations in Southwest Asia is a top priority of the DoD IG. As the principal oversight agency for accountability within the Department of Defense, the DoD IG is committed to providing effective and meaningful oversight in Southwest Asia. Our priority is to assist DoD and the Congress in identifying and deterring waste, fraud, and abuse of taxpayer monies;

and, most importantly, ensuring the brave men and women serving in Southwest Asia are as well equipped and led as possible. We will continue to coordinate and integrate our efforts within the oversight community to minimize duplication and ensure oversight coverage is as comprehensive and effective as possible.[8]

Finally, a key distinction between the public sector audit and inspection functions, both sometimes conducted side-by-side within the same Office of Inspector General, is the applicability of Yellow Book professional standards to the former, and a separate set of professional standards and traditions to the latter. The two functions are bound together by a common overarching purpose, "to assure that [government] resources are used efficiently and effectively and that [government] actions comply with laws and regulations."[9] In constitutional parlance, both auditors and inspectors carry out a duty to account—independently and objectively—to their stakeholders and ultimately to the American People on how their government is spending their money.

CASE STUDY: TRAINING AND MENTORING OF AFGHAN NATIONAL POLICE

The following are selected Excerpts from "DOD Obligations and Expenditures of Funds Provided to the Department of State for the Training and Mentoring of the Afghan National Police," Department of State Report No. MERO-A-10-06, Department of Defense Report No. D-2010-042, February 9, 2010.[10]

Department of State Report No. MERO-A-10-06
Department of Defense Report No. D-2010-042   February 9, 2010

United States Department of State
and the Broadcasting Board of Governors
Office of Inspector General

Department of Defense
Office of Inspector General

DOD Obligations and Expenditures of Funds Provided to the Department of State for the Training and Mentoring of the Afghan National Police

Results in Brief: DOD Obligations and Expenditures of Funds Provided to the Department of State for the Training and Mentoring of the Afghan National Police

What We Did

We conducted this audit in response to a congressional request. Our objective was to review the status of Afghanistan Security Forces funds that DOD provided to the Department of State (DOS) for the training of the Afghan National Police (ANP), the contract management activities, and the ability of the ANP training program to address the security needs for Afghanistan.

What We Found

The DOS Civilian Police Program contract does not meet DOD's needs in developing the ANP to provide security in countering the growing insurgency in Afghanistan. The DOS and DOD agreed to have DOD assume contractual responsibility for the primary ANP training program, which includes Regional Training Centers, basic ANP training, mentoring within the Afghan Ministry of Interior, and the DOD police mentor teams embedded in ANP units in districts throughout Afghanistan. The DOS internal controls were ineffective. We identified internal control weaknesses in the DOS contract oversight for the ANP training program. DOS did not:

* maintain adequate oversight of Government-furnished property,

* maintain contract files as required by the Federal Acquisition Regulation,

* always match goods to receiving reports, or

* follow internal control procedures requiring in-country contracting officer's representatives to review contractor invoices to determine if the costs were allowable, allocable, or reasonable prior to payment and validate deliverables.

We were unable to determine if DOS expended Afghanistan Security Forces funds provided by DOD in accordance with Congressional intent.

We also identified $80 million in potential monetary benefits. In addition, DOS and DOD have not provided enough resources to adequately train members of the Afghan Women's Police Corps.

What We Recommend

The Commanding General, Combined Security Transition Command-Afghanistan, should:

* clearly define the requirements for the ANP training program and establish contractor performance standards that will meet those requirements and

* direct the contracting officer for the new DOD contract to assign sufficient contracting officer's representative staff and implement effective contractor oversight procedures.

The Assistant Secretary of State for the Bureau of International Narcotics and Law Enforcement Affairs should request audit support from the Defense Contract Audit Agency and request refunds of any costs that the Defense Contract Audit Agency determines to be unallowable, unallocable, or unreasonable.

The Commanding General, Combined Security Transition Command-Afghanistan, in coordination with the Assistant Secretary of State for the Bureau of International Narcotics and Law Enforcement Affairs, should increase the resources devoted to developing the Afghan Women's Police Corps.

The Assistant Secretary of State for the Bureau of Resource Management and Chief Financial Officer should:

* determine the status of the Afghanistan Security Forces funds provided by DOD;

* return any funds in excess of the amounts identified as appropriate disbursements and, at a minimum, return $80 million; and

✳ make appropriate corrections to the annual financial statements and communicate any errors found to DOD.

The Under Secretary of Defense (Comptroller)/Chief Financial Officer should make appropriate corrections to the annual financial statements and request refunds from DOS.

The Director, Defense Contract Audit Agency, should review public vouchers submitted under task orders 4305 and 5375 and conduct an audit of the ANP training program.

Management Comments and Our Response

The Deputy Commanding General, Combined Security Transition Command-Afghanistan responding for the Commanding General, provided comments that were responsive to draft Recommendations A.1.-2., B.1., and B.3.a.-b. However the comments were nonresponsive to draft Recommendations B.3.c.-d.; therefore, we request comments to the final report.

The Acting Assistant Secretary of State for the Bureau of International Narcotics and Law Enforcement Affairs comments were nonresponsive. The Acting Assistant Secretary stated that he had requested assistance from the Defense Contract Audit Agency in 2007, and audit work started in March 2009. However, we determined that no audit work has been done and we requested an action plan and timeframe for engaging Defense Contract Audit Agency audit support.

The Assistant Director, Defense Contract Audit Agency, comments were responsive.

We learned subsequent to the draft audit report that the Combined Security Transition Command-Afghanistan would retain control of the Women's Police Corps training program.

Therefore, we redirected the recommendation to increase resources devoted to developing the Afghan Women's Police Corps to the Combined Security Transition Command-Afghanistan.

The Assistant Secretary of State for the Bureau of Resource Management and Chief Financial Officer did not provide comments to the draft report; therefore, we request comments in response to the revised recommendations in the final report.

The Under Secretary of Defense (Comptroller)/Chief Financial Officer comments were responsive to the draft recommendation. We request comments in response to the final report.

* * *

Please provide comments by March 9, 2010.

* * *

INTRODUCTION

Objectives

We conducted this audit in response to a congressional request. Our objective was to review the status of Afghanistan Security Forces (ASF) funds that the DOD provided to the Department of State (DOS) for the training of the Afghan National Police (ANP).

Specifically, we reviewed the contract, task orders, statements of work, and related modifications to ensure that they complied with Federal regulations and met the needs of the DOD. We also reviewed contractor invoices to determine whether the claimed costs were allowable, allocable, and reasonable. See Appendix A for a discussion of the scope and methodology and prior coverage, and see Appendix B for the congressional request.

Background

In 2005, the Combined Security Transition Command-Afghanistan (CSTC-A) officially assumed the lead role on behalf of the U.S. Government in the reformation of the ANP. CSTC-A is under the control of the United States Central Command (CENTCOM).

Under CSTC-A's operational control is Task Force Phoenix, responsible for training, mentoring, and advising the Afghan National Army and the ANP. The International Police Coordination Board was formed in 2007 in an effort to improve international coordination of ANP training. The U.S., the United Nations, and the European Union agreed with the Afghan government to introduce common standards to coordinate the efforts of all countries contributing to reforming the

Ministry of Interior (MOI) and the ANP. The MOI controls the ANP. The goal is to develop the Afghan security forces to protect the local population and provide a stable rule of law.

CSTC-A's role is to plan, program, and implement structural, organizational, institutional, and management reforms of the Afghanistan National Security Forces (ANSFs). Mission success for CSTC-A is defined as fielding an ANSF, which includes the ANP, that is professional, literate, ethnically diverse, tactically competent, and capable of providing security throughout Afghanistan. The purpose of these ANSFs is to develop a stable Afghanistan, strengthen the rule of law, and deter and defeat terrorism within Afghanistan's borders. According to the Council on Foreign Relations,

> Senior U.S. military officials have said America's exit strategy is tied to Afghanistan's ability to provide its own security. The North Atlantic Treaty Organization and coalition partners have embraced the concept that improving the capability of Afghan forces is the quickest way to exit."[11]

During the spring of 2007, the Joint Coordination and Monitoring Board[12] approved increasing the ANP staffing levels to 82,000. As of March 15, 2009, more than 80,000 positions, 96 percent of their authorized staffing levels, have been filled. The MOI expects to fill the remaining 2,000 positions by December 2009.

The ANP consists of the following different police organizations:

* Uniformed Police,

* Border Police,

* Civil Order Police,

* Counter Narcotics Police,

* Criminal Investigation Police, and

* Counter Terrorism Police.

The Uniformed Police are the single largest police element with more than 40,000 positions. They are responsible for general law enforcement, public safety, and internal security throughout the provinces and districts of Afghanistan. The Afghan Border Police, with an authorized strength of 17,000, are responsible for patrolling Afghanistan's borders, conducting counter-smuggling operations, and managing immigration.

The Civil Order Police are responsible for responding to civil disturbances in large urban areas and patrolling in high-threat areas. In addition, the Civil Order Police also temporarily replace entire Uniformed Police districts while they attend Focused District Development training. Focused District Development is the framework for implementing the ANP training program. It is used to organize the training of the police force that will serve each district and evaluate their effectiveness.

The other three ANP organizations are smaller and have more specialized missions. The Counter Narcotics Police are responsible for the elimination of the production and trafficking of illicit drugs. The Criminal Investigation Division Police investigate a wide range of criminal offenses. The Counter Terrorism Police are responsible for conducting counter-insurgency operations.

Presidential Decision Directive 71, "Strengthening Criminal Justice Systems in Support of Peace Operations," February 24, 2000, directed DOS to establish a new program that would train civilian police for international peacekeeping missions around the world. In response to this directive, the DOS Office of Acquisition Management awarded the Civilian Police Program (CIVPOL) contract in February 2004.

According to the CIVPOL contract (contract number S-LMAQM-04-C-0030), the contractor is responsible for:

* providing a cadre of up to 2,000 experienced law enforcement personnel available to serve in civilian peacekeeping missions overseas;

* providing pre-deployment and deployment support; including contract program management, uniforms, and equipment;

* arranging transportation for basic, in-service, and special-ized training programs developed by the Government for the cadre of law enforcement personnel;

* maintaining a database for U.S. contributions to a particu-lar international organization and creating additional data-bases, as required, to manage records relating to the cadre of law enforcement personnel; and

* providing procurement services for equipment for foreign police and construction services to support foreign police.

DOS issued two contract task orders under the CIVPOL con-tract to support the ANP training program. These two task orders di-rected the contractor to provide personnel and life support for the ANP training program including:

* qualified international civilian police advisors,

* life support services,

* security services, and

* communication support services.

These two task orders are valued in excess of $1 billion and expire on January 31, 2010.

Prior to FY 2005, international donors financed the bulk of the Afghan budget through the Law and Order Trust Fund for Afghan-istan, administered by the United Nations Development Program. The U.S. contribution to that fund was $20 million in FY 2004, $40 million in FY 2005, and $9.5 million in FY 2006. In addition to police salaries, trust fund contributions pay for nonlethal equipment, facilities, re-cruitment, training, and institutional development.

Since FY 2005, the U.S. has appropriated approximately $15.3 billion for the DOD managed Afghanistan Security Forces Fund. Since FY 2006, DOD transferred $1.04 billion of these funds to the DOS Bureau of International Narcotics and Law Enforcement Affairs (INL) to support the ANP Training Program.

Since 2006, DOS and DOD have implemented three Memoranda of Agreement (MOAs) regarding the oversight of the ANP Training Program. Under these MOAs, DOS accepted responsibility for procuring services related to the ANP Training Program, managing and reporting on the ASF funds transferred from DOD, and overseeing the contract and ensuring quality contractor performance.

DOS agreed to perform the following specific tasks:

* receive funds from DOD and execute the program within those funding limits;

* continue to implement the program and oversee the contracts to provide adequate ANP training to meet the requirements identified by CSTC-A and coordinated with DOS;

* designate one or more in-country contracting officer's representatives (I-CORs) to provide direct contractor oversight and quality assurance to the contracting officer's representative (COR);

* administer funds in accordance with applicable laws and regulations and keep complete records of the use of funds and track items and services through delivery to trainees;

* ensure the Chief of Mission and CSTC-A Commander are fully informed of all activities and operations, including results of monitoring and reporting; and

* report to the DOD Financial Officer that the funds were expended for the purposes for which they were provided and return excess funds to DOD upon conclusion of its (DOS) responsibilities.

Review of Internal Controls

DOS Office of Inspector General Audit Manual, chapter 8, April 2009, outlines guidance from the Office of Management and Budget Circular A-123, "Management's Responsibility for Internal Control," which defines management's responsibility for internal controls in Federal agencies. The Office of Management and Budget Circular A-123 provides guidance to Federal managers on improving the accountability and effectiveness of Federal programs and operations by establishing, assessing, correcting, and reporting on internal controls. It also requires a strengthened process for conducting management's assessment of the effectiveness of internal controls over financial reporting based on widely recognized internal control standards. We identified internal control weaknesses for DOS. DOS did not have the following internal controls for contract administration and oversight:

* INL did not conduct management assessment visits, and

* COR and I-CORs did not always match goods to receiving reports, maintain adequate oversight of Government-furnished property, or maintain complete contract files.

Implementing recommendations in Findings B and C will improve INL contract and administration procedures. We will provide a copy of this report to the senior official responsible for internal controls in INL.

Finding A. National Strategy

The DOS CIVPOL contract does not meet DOD's needs in developing the ANP to provide security in countering the growing insurgency in Afghanistan because the current contract arrangement does not allow DOD to make rapid changes in ANP training as the security situation in Afghanistan changes. As a result, the ANP lacks the necessary skills to combat the growing violence in Afghanistan and to provide a more stable and secure environment for Afghanistan citizens.

Security Situation

DOD entered into an agreement with DOS to provide funding on an existing contract for civilian police advisors to train and mentor ANP in 2006. At that time, the security situation in Afghanistan was more stable and suitable for a civilian police force whose sole mission is to enforce the rule of law. This contributed to the decision to use the existing CIVPOL contract with the contractor to train, mentor, and equip elements of the Afghanistan MOI, which includes the ANP. Since that time, the security situation in Afghanistan has changed significantly as the insurgency has grown, and according to a CSTC-A senior official, the current CIVPOL contract no longer meets DOD needs. The ANP must now focus not only on enforcing laws among the general public, but also on combating a growing insurgency.

ANP average monthly death rates for officers, non-commissioned officers, and patrolmen have steadily increased in the last 4 years, from 24 in 2006 to 123 in 2009. As the insurgency threats escalate, the need for additional ANP personnel with enhanced combat skills increases. This results in a requirement for increased training capacity and more police mentor teams to develop the new ANP forces. In addition, as the insurgent tactics evolve, the ANP members need to learn additional skills to protect themselves and preserve security for the citizens of Afghanistan.

The Afghanistan MOI personnel that we interviewed stated that the contractor has made progress in training ANP. However, many challenges impede the progress, such as low literacy rates, deceptive recruiting tactics, desertions, and corruption among ANP.

According to CSTC-A Training Command personnel, in June 2009, the Joint Coordination and Monitoring Board agreed to increase the number of ANP forces from 86,800 to 96,800. The Chief of Mission stated that despite excellent coordination between the U.S. Embassy and CSTC-A, the lack of a single, unified chain of command has sometimes created confusion and unnecessary delays in enhancing the program.

According to CSTC-A senior officials, to effectively train and mentor the new ANP officers and soldiers, DOD needs the flexibility to rapidly respond to the security environment and be able to direct the contractor to construct new training facilities to accommodate the increases in ANP forces, develop a new security-focused curriculum, and mentor ANP members in combat tactics. Under the current contract arrangement, DOD must coordinate any changes through INL, which causes delays in implementation.

For example, the current MOA between DOS and DOD states that DOD must provide updated training requirements 120 days in advance; however, according to INL personnel the process actually requires 6 months to implement.

According to the contractor security reports, during 2006, hostile activities were primarily in the south and southeast portions of Afghanistan, and travel was unrestricted in most of the country. In 2007, hostile activities spread west and north, attacks on nonmilitary targets increased, civilian death tolls rose, and travel restrictions became common in the south and east. Hostile incidents spread north in 2008. Kabul was encircled, hostilities targeting non-government organizations and international aid groups increased, supply and aid convoys were frequent targets, and deaths among coalition forces and civilians were at their highest. Additionally, ANP deaths have also increased each year. See Figure 1 below.

Because of these increases in violence and the rising death rates among ANP, CSTC-A leadership stated that they feel the existing

Figure 1. Average Monthly Afghan National Police Deaths

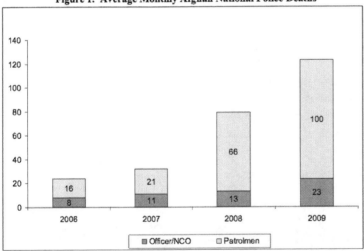

Note: Averages are based on monthly casualty statistics provided by the Afghanistan Ministry of Interior.

curriculum is not the best method for developing the ANP to achieve the emerging national strategy in Afghanistan. Instead, CSTC-A stated they believe the focus of ANP training should be enhanced to include more counterinsurgency and tactical skills training. This more resembles military training than civilian police force training. In March 2009, the President announced a comprehensive new strategy for Afghanistan, which included the emphasis on training and increasing the size of Afghan security forces.

Base Contract

The current CIVPOL contract is ambiguous and because DOS is the contracting agency DOD cannot direct the contracted advisors and mentors and Afghan trainers as needs change.

According to a CSTC-A senior official, DOD must communicate changing requirements through INL and wait for changes to be implemented. The contract task orders simply require the contractor to provide personnel, life support, and communications. The current task orders do not provide any specific information regarding what type of training is required or any measurement of acceptability.

Additionally, the current contract does not include any measurement of contractor performance. Therefore, a new contract has been proposed. The proposed contract, which DOD will manage, should clearly specify training requirements. Additionally, the proposed contract and task orders should clearly state that the contractor must fulfill these specified training requirements.

Memorandum of Agreement

INL and INL/Narcotics Affairs Section-Kabul (NAS-K) administer the CIVPOL contract in coordination with overall direction from CSTC-A. The current MOA between DOS and DOD states that the Commander, CSTC-A, determines overall program requirements for developing the ANP, executes the program, and allocates funds; however, DOD does not have authority to direct the CIVPOL contract. This lack of contractual authority has restricted the ability of CSTC-A to rapidly modify ANP training to respond to the rising insurgency.

Contract Requirements

CSTC-A develops the DOD requirements memoranda for INL; however, the program requirements documents do not stipulate how the ANP are to be trained or the desired outcome.

The requirements memoranda we reviewed for December 2008 and January 2009 request that INL maintain current levels of support at the DOS-operated Regional Training Centers (RTCs) and provincial and sustainment sites throughout Afghanistan.

The memoranda also specify the number of mentors and the short-term continuation of the program of instruction development. CSTC-A requested that the training capacity be expanded at two RTCs and an increase in intelligence mentors. Additionally, CSTC-A requested in-processing teams at the RTCs with the capability to deploy to sustainment sites and support Mobile Training Teams and provide Trauma Assistance Personnel Training. CSTC-A also requested further clarification and justification for the Women's Police Corps, INL Flight Support (Air Wing), and the Family Response Unit. Although DOD requirements memoranda include the levels of mentor support to accomplish ANP training, they do not provide any specifics regarding how ANP are to be trained.

CSTC-A uses capabilities milestones as a method to describe ANP progress in achieving a level of self-sustaining readiness. The capability milestones are:

* **Capabilities Milestone 1:** Police element is fully capable of conducting law enforcement operations un-aided (without mentors), has at least 85 percent of equipment and personnel, and is self-sustaining;

* **Capabilities Milestone 2:** Police element is capable of conducting law enforcement; has 70-84 percent of equipment and personnel, still requires mentor support, but is not self-sustaining;

* **Capabilities Milestone 3:** Police element has presence in its geographic location, is partially capable of conducting law enforcement with coalition support, and has 50-69 percent of equipment and personnel; and

* **Capabilities Milestone 4:** Police element is formed, but incapable of conducting law enforcement operations, and has less than 50 percent of equipment and/or personnel.

Of 64 districts that CSTC-A evaluated as of August 2009, 11 met Capabilities Milestone 1; 21 met Capabilities Milestone 2; 27 met Capabilities Milestone 3; and 5 remained at Capabilities Milestone 4. These districts did not achieve CSTC-A capabilities milestone projections, which were that ANP should reach Capabilities Milestone 2 by 2009.

Contract Action Delays

According to CSTC-A leadership, the INL contracting process is slow and cumbersome, which hampers the ability of DOD and the ANP to quickly respond to the rapidly changing security environment in Afghanistan. CSTC-A leadership stated that using DOS as the contracting agency is no longer the most efficient method to address the changing security environment in Afghanistan. In 2006, when the security environment in Afghanistan was more stable, DOD decided to use the existing CIVPOL contract to implement the ANP training program. However, the current operating environment requires a different approach, and the ANP training program that is in place does not provide the ANP with the necessary skills to successfully fight the insurgency, and therefore, hampers the ability of DOD to fulfill its role in the emerging national strategy.

Although both organizations, DOS and CSTC-A, have similar long-term goals for the ANP, DOS is focused on training the police to be an effective civilian police force after security in Afghanistan has stabilized. DOD is focused on survival and tactical training of ANP to counter the growing insurgency. CSTC-A officials stated that they believe that if DOD has contractual authority, and is not required to coordinate program changes through another agency, program requirements can be implemented faster. In an ever changing environment, efficiency is necessary in order to rapidly respond to the current, more volatile security situation. The training that CSTC-A will assume will be based on survivability and tactical maneuvering, while INL will continue training the ANP in traditional community policing tactics.

Proposed Contract Changes

The Chief of Mission and Commander, International Security Assistance Forces, recommended the transfer of responsibility for implementation of basic Afghan police training and field mentoring to DOD. Specifically, they recommended that CSTC-A assume contractual responsibility for the primary ANP training program, which includes RTCs, basic ANP training, mentoring within the MOI, and CSTC-A's police mentor teams embedded in ANP units in districts throughout Afghanistan.

Currently, ANP training is conducted by Afghan experienced police forces with oversight by the contractor's mentors and advisors. Although the need for the ANP to increase its capability to effectively respond to the increased insurgent activity is critical for the security of Afghanistan, the need to develop a competent and effective civilian police force remains. The Embassy's country team and CSTC-A agree that INL should revert to its traditional police training role to support development of civilian police through training in advanced leadership, criminal investigation, and professional development.

Dividing the ANP training and mentoring responsibilities between DOD (for basic training) and INL (for advanced training) should result in a stronger, more effective ANP force. This will provide the citizens of Afghanistan with an ANP force that is capable of adapting to and surviving the changing security threats and is capable of performing advanced civilian police duties.

Management Actions

During our fieldwork in Afghanistan, we learned of a joint proposal between DOS and DOD for DOD to assume responsibility for the basic ANP training and field mentoring and INL to retain responsibility for advanced ANP training. To assist the transition from INL-Kabul to CSTC-A and ensure improved communication between the two organizations, we issued a memorandum to DOS and DOD recommending that they form a transition oversight committee to manage the transition of Government property, logistics, contracting, information technology, curriculum, resource management, and programs of instruction. For details, see Appendix D for the memorandum and Appendix E for management comments on the memorandum.

Recommendations, Management Comments, and Our Response

A. We recommend the Commanding General, Combined Security Transition Command-Afghanistan:

1 Clearly define the requirements for the Afghan National Police training program.

2 Establish contractor performance standards that will meet DOD's requirements for training and mentoring the Afghan National Police.

Combined Security Transition Command-Afghanistan Comments: The Deputy Commanding General, responding for the Commanding General, agreed and the comments included a detailed description of the requirements for the Afghan National Police training program. The Deputy Commanding General also included the goals of the Afghan Police Training program to simultaneously reform and expand the Afghan National Police; provide resources to train and reform police and execute the force generation of new police; increase recruiting, improve retention, and reduce attrition; and improve leadership and dismiss corrupt police officials. The Deputy Commanding General stated that he has developed performance standards, with input from contract bidders, to include measures of performance, and that measures of effectiveness are being incorporated into the Quality Assurance Surveillance Plan.

Our Response: The Deputy Commanding General, CSTC-A, comments were responsive, and the actions meet the intent of the recommendations.

Finding B. Contractor Oversight

DOS contracting officials and CORs did not conduct adequate surveillance for two task orders in excess of $1 billion. Specifically, the COR and I-CORs did not:

* maintain adequate oversight of Government-furnished property,

* maintain contract files as required by the Federal Acquisition Regulation (FAR), or

* always match goods to receiving reports.

These conditions occurred because contracting officials did not adequately staff I-CORs for ANP task orders and did not prepare a Quality Assurance Surveillance Plan (QASP) for one of the two ANP task orders. As a result, DOS personnel provided no assurance to the contracting officer that the Government received all of the goods and services procured by the contractor or that DOS received the best value when contracting for services. In addition, the COR inappropriately approved contractor invoices for payment, as discussed in Finding C.

Contracting Officer's Representative Assignment

Minimal Government oversight of the ANP task orders increased the risk of fraud and waste of Government funds. The COR is responsible for overseeing contractor performance and determining whether the contractor accomplishes the technical and financial aspects of the contract. The COR and I-CORs are responsible for monitoring and inspecting the contractor's progress and performance, receiving deliverables, approving invoices, notifying the contracting officer of deficiencies, performing property administrator duties for Government-furnished property, performing acceptance tests of goods and services, and maintaining contract files.

COR and I-COR Assignment

Prior to our site visit to Afghanistan, we requested that Afghanistan, Iraq, and Jordan Support (AIJS) officials and the contracting officer provide a list of I-CORs serving in Afghanistan and their dates of service since the contracting officer did not assign an administrative contracting officer. The contracting officer provided an abbreviated list of CORs and I-CORs and stated that the COR could provide information about service in Afghanistan; however, the COR was unable to provide that information. According to the COR and I-CORs, I-CORs are frequently rotated in and out of Afghanistan but no record was maintained by the contracting officer to document dates of service in Afghanistan.

In addition, the contracting officer provided delegation letters for I-CORs that included assignments of authority for personnel that the COR, I-CORs, and contracting officer could not identify as working as an I-COR further demonstrating the lack of control over COR and I-COR staffing. The contracting officer should immediately terminate the delegation of I-COR authority of all inactive or reassigned I-CORs to provide an accurate count of existing I-CORs. Without terminating inactive I-CORs, the contracting officer maintains a roster of I-CORs that misrepresents the number available to oversee the contractor and includes personnel who should not have the authority to represent the contracting officer. The contracting officer issued one COR and seven I-COR delegation letters[13] to monitor the ANP task orders. Of the seven active I-COR delegations, one does not work on ANP task orders, two cannot monitor task order S-LMAQM-08-F-5375 (task order 5375), one works only half of the year, three were located in the U.S., and only three were located in Afghanistan. Only one I-COR possessed authority to oversee task order 5375 prior to June 2009 despite nearly $325 million obligated prior to June.

The contracting officer should be able to identify the assignments and locations of CORs and I-CORs assigned to task orders, terminate assignments of individuals no longer working on ANP task orders, and increase the number of I-CORs to adequately perform contract surveillance.

Civilian Police Program Master Contract

The contracting officer assigned one COR and five I-CORs to perform oversight of seven task order contracts valued at $1.6 billion. These task orders are executed under three indefinite-delivery, indefinite-quantity master contracts awarded to three different contractors. Each task order contract supports different disciplines under the CIVPOL master contract with two task orders, S-LMAQM-05-F-4305 (task order 4305) and task order 5375, executing the ANP program. Examples of the programs executed by the task orders include the ANP, Poppy Eradication, Corrections Sector Support, and Justice Sector Support. Each program has its own statement of work (SOW) with the

ANP program possessing 18 different SOWs that state the requirements of the program. The COR and I-COR responsibilities for all seven task orders were the same as outlined in their delegation letters. These duties included preparing purchase requests, defining project requirements, performing inspections, accepting work for the Government, resolving technical issues, reporting costs not appropriately charged to the contract, validating all vendor invoices, and maintaining an inventory of Government-furnished property.

ANP Task Orders

On August 15, 2005, the contracting officer for INL awarded task order 4305 for the ANP. However, due to the size and complexity of the contract, contract oversight was grossly understaffed with one COR prior to July 2006 despite obligating more than $232 million. During 2006, the contracting officer delegated administrative authority to one COR and two I-CORs, however, during our site visit, we were unable to find any evidence of surveillance by the two I-CORs. By the beginning of 2008 nearly $675 million was obligated without any evidence of an I-COR functioning in Afghanistan. From February 2008 to July 2009, the ANP contract was increased by another $598 million and task order 5375, as well as multiple SOWs, was added to the contract. In 2008, another I-COR was assigned authority to the ANP task orders followed by four more I-CORs as late as June 2009. In addition, these I-CORs were assigned to five other Civilian Police Program task orders. The ANP and Civilian Police Program task orders have a total value of $1.6 billion.

Despite the increased number of I-CORs assigned to the ANP task orders, only three I-CORs were in Afghanistan during our site visit while two I-CORs and the COR were stateside at headquarters. The in-country designation attached to the I-COR is misleading because the majority of I-CORs do not perform their functions in Afghanistan. To adequately fulfill the various roles and responsibilities required of the COR and I-COR, more CORs and I-CORs are required in Afghanistan to perform contractor oversight. For example, performing product and service inspection, accepting work on behalf of the Government, and maintaining inventory lists of Government-furnished property require a physical presence at the place of performance.

According to the I-CORs, they do not have enough staff to sufficiently monitor contractor performance. Due to the number of task orders under the I-CORs purview, the I-CORs stated they can only spend approximately 20 percent of their time on task orders 4305 and 5375. According to the I-CORs, most of that time is spent reviewing contractor purchase order requests and receipt of items in excess of $3,000. Therefore, the I-CORs did not have time to perform other required tasks, such as performing quality assurance and overseeing Government-furnished property as required by their letters of delegation.

According to INL officials, they are billeted for 7 I-CORs however, they have not reached their maximum capacity. To ensure adequate COR and I-COR staffing, the contracting officer should reassess the staffing needs of the ANP task orders and designate the appropriate number of CORs and I-CORs. In addition, the contracting officer should ensure that I-CORs perform their functions in Afghanistan as designated by their "in-country" status.

Quality Assurance Surveillance Plan

DOS contracting and INL program officials did not develop a QASP for task order 4305.

A QASP describes the procedures the Government will use to ensure that the actual performance of a contractor meets the requirements of the SOW. According to FAR Subpart 46.4, "Government Contract Quality Assurance," March 2005, a QASP should be developed in conjunction with the performance work statement. FAR Subpart 46.4 also states that the QASP should include a description of all work requiring surveillance, location of inspections, and the method for accepting the goods or services.

Task order 5375 included a QASP but the QASP was never updated to include requirements established in ten SOWs after it was implemented. Because the QASP was not updated with the additional SOWs, the QASP did not include all requirements in task order 5375. In addition, the QASP specifically identifies four functional areas requiring surveillance including food services, equipment accountability, security, and advisor appointment. For each functional area, a quality assurance evaluator was supposed to establish a surveillance program outlining the frequency and methods for observing or monitoring services. However, the I-CORs in Afghanistan acknowledged that a surveillance program was never created to oversee the four functional areas. As a result, contract surveillance may not be conducted consistently among a rotational staff of

I-CORs.

A defined QASP created prior to the start of contract performance and updated with additional requirements can eliminate gaps in contract surveillance and ensure that goods and services provided by contractors are in accordance with the terms of the contract.

Without a proper QASP, contracting officials have no standards for determining whether goods or services provided by contractors comply with contractual requirements. ANP contracting officials should develop a QASP to go along with the SOW for each task order before contract performance begins.

Government-Furnished Property

Neither DOS nor the contractor maintained a current inventory list of Government furnished property. During our site visits to three ANP training facilities, we were unable to locate over half of the items of a random sample of property generated by the contractor. The FAR 52.245-1, "Government Property," requires a contractor to create and maintain an inventory listing of all Government-furnished and contractor-acquired property in its possession. The inventory must be complete, current, and auditable.

Furthermore, the FAR requires the maintenance of specific data, such as product description, manufacturer, model number, unique item identifier (for example, serial number), and unit acquisition cost.

Procurement Information Bulletin 2007-21, "Contractor Held Government Property Requirements," June 27, 2007, specifies responsibilities for the property administrator, including managing all Government-furnished property and contractor-acquired property under the contract. These responsibilities include determining whether property should be provided to the contractor; determining the method of and providing directions on the disposition of property; ensuring contractor compliance with contract requirements for property, including conducting all required inventories; and properly identifying all relevant contracts for all relevant property involved. The delegation of authority for the property administrator provides additional specifics, including monitoring the contractor's management of and quarterly and annual reporting on Government-furnished and contractor-acquired property, ensuring that the contractor conducts all required inventories, and reviewing inventory lists and reports maintained by the contractor to verify that they contain the basic information required by the FAR. This authority was delegated to the COR and the ICORs assigned to task orders 4305 and 5375.

During site visits to three ANP training facilities, we verified only 34 items from a random sample of 123 items from three strata (vehicles, sensitive items [weapons], and electronics). We selected the sample from the contractor's property management system the day before the first inventory check. We considered the items verified if the ANP site coordinators could identify the location of the Government-furnished property or provide supporting documentation to substantiate the item's existence.

During our site visit to the Kandahar training center, we were unable to locate nine sensitive items including pistols, rifles, and scopes at the training site provided on the inventory list. The site coordinator stated that the property assignments for sensitive items were maintained at the contractor's headquarters in Kabul. At the contractor's headquarters in Kabul, we located or viewed documentation showing that the weapons were signed out by contractor personnel. However, only two other items of the remaining 89 non-sensitive items could be located. The site coordinator stated that the list was inaccurate and out of date but the list was generated by the contractor's logistics coordinator the evening prior to the site visit.

During our site visits to Kandahar, Bamyan, and Herat; the contractors stated that CORs and I-CORs did not conduct regular site visits and never conducted an inventory of Government-furnished property. After a natural disaster occurred at the Kandahar ANP facility that destroyed substantial amounts of Government-furnished property, I-CORs never performed an inventory to assess the extent of destroyed property. As a result, lost, damaged, and destroyed items remained on the property book until August 2009 when the contractor initiated the process with the I-CORs of removing these items from the Government-furnished property list.

Inaccurate inventories resulted from minimal oversight of Government-furnished property and indicate a deficiency in the internal controls of both the contractor and INL.

I-CORs should have visited Kandahar regularly and discovered the destroyed equipment and required the contractor to report missing or destroyed equipment immediately, consistent with the requirements in the SOW. The need for complete and accurate accounting for Government-furnished property held by the contractor is critical, as the ANP task orders were scheduled to terminate in January 2010, resulting in contractor held, Government-owned property to be returned to the Government. Without accurate inventory lists, the I-COR has no means of determining whether all Government-owned property has been properly accounted for.

Contract Files

I-CORs did not maintain the necessary documentation that is required in contract files.

The DOS Foreign Affairs Handbook (FAH) states that CORs are expected to maintain a file documenting significant actions and containing copies of trip reports, correspondence, and reports of deliverables received under the contract. The purpose of the file is to provide easy access to technical information and work progress and to ease transition to a new COR. The FAH lists items to be maintained in the files, including the complete procurement request package, the solicitation, the technical and cost proposals submitted by the contractor, the contract and all modifications, progress reports, correspondence and telephone synopses to and from the contractor, documentation of the acceptability or unacceptability of deliverables, documentation of site visits, and copies of invoices.

During our review of the I-COR contract files for task orders 4305 and 5375, we were unable to locate SOWs, copies of invoices, correspondence with the contractor, documentation of acceptability of goods and services, and documentation of site visit results. The I-CORs stated that they maintain COR files on their individual office computer or personal e-mail files; however, we were not shown any evidence other than some correspondence with the contractor. These files on individual computers are not accessible to other I-CORs.

COR files were particularly important in the field, where I-CORs were rotated frequently and were entitled to 2 months each year away from post for rest and relaxation purposes. Rapidly changing SOWs accompanied with escalating contract costs place a premium on oversight and smooth transition among a constant rotation of I-CORs. However, because the COR files are not readily available to others and may not be complete, incoming or acting I-CORs may not have the information and institutional knowledge they need to properly administer and monitor the contract.

Reviewing Contractor Invoices

CIVPOL contracting officers and their CORs did not review 100 percent of contractor bills to ensure the billings always corresponded to the actual goods and services received.

See Finding C for a detailed discussion on the review of contractor bills.

Recommendations, Management Comments, and Our Response

B.1. We recommend the Assistant Secretary of State for the Bureau of International Narcotics and Law Enforcement Affairs and the Commanding General, Combined Security Transition Command-Afghanistan, ensure that the contracting officer for the Civilian Police Program contract perform a complete inventory of Government-furnished property under task orders 4305 and 5375 and reconcile the inventory count to the Government-furnished property book maintained by the contractor.

Assistant Secretary of State for the Bureau of International Narcotics and Law Enforcement Affairs Comments: The Acting Assistant Secretary of State, INL, generally agreed, stating that INL takes seriously the need to account for Government-purchased property and that INL has completed an inventory of property for the CIVPOL task orders.

Our Response: The Acting Assistant Secretary of State's comments were responsive, and the actions meet the intent of the recommendation.

Combined Security Transition Command-Afghanistan Comments: The Deputy Commanding General, responding for the Commanding General, agreed and stated that CSTC-A formed a working group with INL, Counter-Narcoterrorism Technology Program Office, and the Defense Contract Management Agency (DCMA) that led to the successful exchange of critical information and data necessary for contract transition among agencies. The Deputy Commanding General also stated that INL and the contractor conducted an inventory of more than 91,000 pieces of property to ensure an easy transition of property from INL to CSTC-A.

Our Response: The Deputy Commanding General's comments were responsive, and the actions meet the intent of the recommendation.

B.2. We recommend the Assistant Secretary of State for the Bureau of International Narcotics and Law Enforcement Affairs:

a. Ensure that the contracting officer for the Civilian Police Program contract strengthens existing internal controls over contract administration, oversight, and financial reporting to comply with Foreign Affairs Handbook requirements.

Assistant Secretary of State for the Bureau of International Narcotics and Law Enforcement Affairs Comments: The Acting Assistant Secretary of State, INL, generally agreed and stated that INL currently has four I-CORs at post and is preparing three I-CORs for deployment. In addition, the Acting Assistant Secretary said that INL is expanding the number of I-CORs at post from seven to eleven within the next several months to enhance the contract oversight capability. The Acting Assistant Secretary added that INL plans to publish ICOR operating procedures and guidelines to standardize their duties.

Our Response: The Acting Assistant Secretary of State's comments were responsive. We believe that increasing the number of I-CORs and publishing the I-COR operating procedures and guidelines will result in improved control over contract administration, oversight, and financial reporting to comply with the FAH.

b. Ensure that the contracting officer for the Civilian Police Program contract establishes and maintains contracting files that are complete and easily accessible in accordance with the contracting officer delegation letters and the Foreign Affairs Handbook.

Assistant Secretary of State for the Bureau of International Narcotics and Law Enforcement Affairs Comments: The Acting Assistant Secretary of State, INL, generally agreed and stated that the COR retains complete contract files in Washington D.C. where the COR is located. The Acting Assistant Secretary also stated that INL intends to provide I-CORs with electronic accessibility to contract files, including a SharePoint site for correspondence.

Our Response: The Acting Assistant Secretary of State for the Bureau of International Narcotics and Law Enforcement Affairs comments were partially responsive. I-CORs are required to maintain contract files as delegated by their letters of assignment and the FAH. Contract files need to be readily available to I-CORs in the field so they can respond accurately and rapidly.

Electronic accessibility of contract files and a SharePoint site for correspondence is an acceptable method of maintaining contract files; however, INL did not provide a description of the timeframe to implement an electronic file sharing system. We request that the Assistant Secretary of State for the Bureau of International Narcotics and Law Enforcement Affairs provide additional comments in response to the final report that specify a completion date for establishing an electronic file sharing system.

B.3. We recommend the Commanding General, Combined Security Transition Command-Afghanistan, direct the contracting officer for the new DOD-managed ANP training program to:

a. Designate an administrative contracting officer in Afghanistan to implement immediate changes and conduct contractor oversight.

Combined Security Transition Command-Afghanistan Comments: The Deputy Commanding General, responding for the Commanding General agreed, stating that CSTC-A will implement numerous oversight measures after the contract transitions to CSTC-A. The Deputy Commanding General stated that the Assistant Commanding General-Police Development will provide contract management oversight.

Contract management responsibilities will include providing a lead COR and 20 in country quality assurance representatives. Additionally, the Deputy Commanding General stated that CSTC-A established military contract oversight for all advisors and trainers at three levels—ministerial systems, institutional advisors/trainers, and regional and fielded forces.

Our Response: The Deputy Commanding General's comments were responsive, and the actions meet the intent of the recommendation.

b. Designate a full-time property administrator to oversee all Government furnished property for contracts supporting the Afghan National Police Program.

Combined Security Transition Command-Afghanistan Comments: The Deputy Commanding General, responding for the Commanding General, agreed, stating that the DCMA will provide property management oversight. In addition, the Deputy Commanding General stated that DCMA will review the awarded contractor's property management system.

Our Response: The Deputy Commanding General's comments were responsive, and the actions meet the intent of the recommendation.

c. Develop a Quality Assurance Surveillance Plan that addresses high-risk areas of the Afghan National Police training contract.

Combined Security Transition Command-Afghanistan Comments: The Deputy Commanding General, responding for the Commanding General, agreed and provided a flowchart of contract responsibility and an organizational structure of the DCMA contract management and oversight process. The Deputy Commanding General stated that the flowchart and organizational structures provide a top-level view of contract management responsibilities for the ANP training program.

Our Response: The Deputy Commanding General's comments were not responsive. The Deputy Commanding General's comments did not indicate that CSTC-A was going to develop a QASP. According to FAR subpart 46.4, a QASP should be developed in conjunction with the performance work statement. Accordingly, we request that the Commanding General provide additional comments in response to the final report that provide greater detail regarding the timing and drafting of a QASP.

   d. Establish and maintain contracting files that are complete and easily accessible in accordance with the delegation letters and the Defense Federal Acquisition Regulation Supplement.

Combined Security Transition Command-Afghanistan Comments: The Deputy Commanding General, responding for the Commanding General, agreed and provided a flowchart and an organizational structure of contract responsibility of the DCMA contract management and oversight process. The Deputy Commanding General stated that the organizational structures and flowcharts provide a top-level view of contract management responsibilities for the ANP training program.

Our Response: The Deputy Commanding General's comments were not responsive. The Deputy Commanding General stated that contract management responsibilities will include providing a lead COR and 20 in-country quality assurance representatives. He did not state whether CORs would maintain individual contract files for each contract or task order assigned as required by Defense Federal Acquisition Regulation Supplement 201.602-2, "Procedures, Guidance, and Information." Additionally, the Deputy Commanding General did not state that CSTC-A would maintain the contract documents in an electronic file sharing system, such as the Electronic Document Access system, as required by Defense Federal Acquisition Regulation Supplement 204.2, "Procedures, Guidance, and Information," to provide all COR and in-country quality assurance representatives valuable contract information. We request that the Commanding General provide additional comments in response to the final report that provide details on the establishment and maintenance of contracting files.

     e. Evaluate and assign the appropriate number of in-country contracting officer's representatives to oversee the Afghan National Police program.

     Combined Security Transition Command-Afghanistan Comments: The Deputy Commanding General, responding for the Commanding General, agreed, stating CSTC-A will implement numerous oversight measures after the contract transitions to CSTC-A. The Deputy Commanding General stated that the Assistant Commanding General-Police Development will provide contract management oversight.

     Contract management responsibilities will include providing a lead COR and 20 in country quality assurance representatives. Additionally, the Deputy Commanding General stated that a combined 184 COR and technical officer representatives will report to the lead COR who will oversee all levels of the program. The Deputy Commanding General concluded that military commanders will replace contractors at each training facility to conduct contract oversight, as INL currently does.

     Our Response: The Commanding General's comments were responsive, and the actions meet the intent of the recommendation.

Finding C. Contractor Invoice Review

     DOS personnel could not ensure that funds allocated by the DOD for the ANP program were expended to meet DOD requirements in accordance with the MOA between the DOS and DOD. This occurred because DOS did not follow internal control procedures that established that I-CORs were to review contractor invoices to determine if the costs were allowable, allocable, or reasonable prior to payment and validate deliverables. As a result, DOS officials paid the contractor for goods and services that may not have been allowable or reasonable under two of the task orders supporting the ANP contract.

Criteria

The FAH, DOD Regulation 7000.14-R, "DOD Financial Management Regulation," (FMR), and FAR address the topics of reviewing invoices to ensure that costs are allowable, allocable, and reasonable, and of reviewing contractor payments. Specifically, the FAH states that contractors must periodically submit invoices to request payment.

The FMR provides details on contractor entitlement to payment on invoices and the associated documentation requirements. In addition, the FAR states that expenses billed to the Government are limited to costs that are allowable,[14] allocable,[15]F and reasonable.[16]

The Defense Contract Audit Agency (DCAA) Contract Audit Manual 7640.1, "Defense Contract Audit Manual," prescribes auditing policies and procedures and furnishes guidance in auditing techniques for personnel engaged in the performance of the DCAA mission.[17]7

Review of Contractor Invoices

INL AIJS personnel did not conduct sufficient invoice reviews as required by their delegation letters. These invoice reviews are necessary to determine whether the contractor was entitled to payment for submitted invoices, or prepare and maintain the supporting documents necessary to show contractor entitlement to payment. Specifically, as discussed in Finding B, an I-COR confirmed that no QASP existed and management assessment visits did not occur. Therefore, I-CORs did not conduct site visits to accept or validate delivery of invoiced goods and services; unless the items were sensitive or of a high-dollar value, such as night-vision goggles or armored vehicles. Instead, the I-CORs relied on the contractor to accept delivery of inventory and maintain the supporting documentation to show that goods were received or services were performed.

I-CORs did not use standardized procedures to review, deny, or approve contractor-submitted purchase order requests. In addition, the COR inappropriately approved contractor invoices without assurance that the Government received what it paid for.

Supporting Documentation

An I-COR stated that I-CORs were rarely provided and did not maintain copies of contractor invoices. Instead, an I-COR stated that supporting documentation and invoices were provided to and maintained by AIJS in Washington, D.C., even though they were not accessible to I-CORs. Without invoices, I-CORs did not know what goods were procured and could not accept delivery or review inventory. According to the FAH, volume 14, handbook 2, "Contracting Officer's Representative," the COR must maintain a copy of all invoices and vouchers and a payment register, indicating the balance of funds remaining. Furthermore, without these necessary documents, we could not determine if invoices approved for payment by the COR were allowable, allocable, or reasonable within the contract scope. DOS plans to implement a web-based tool that will provide I-CORs access to all contract documentation maintained by AIJS in Washington, D.C.

The FAH, volume 14, handbook 2, also states that contractors must periodically submit vouchers or invoices. The COR should review the vouchers or invoices to determine the validity of the costs claimed and relate total expenditures to the progress of the contract.

This is particularly important under cost-reimbursement contracts, where a COR can gain evidence of performance problems through examining the contractor's vouchers.

However, vouchers alone do not provide sufficient information for tracking financial progress. Therefore, the Government is entitled to ask the contractor for information that is necessary to understand whether the charges billed are allowable, allocable, and reasonable—the basic tests that the contractor's costs must pass to be reimbursed. If it appears from charges billed that the contractor may be spending more than is reasonably necessary for certain parts of the work, the COR should contact the contractor for additional explanation or substantiation for those costs.

Acceptance of Goods and Services

The COR and the I-CORs did not have evidence to support that invoiced goods and services were actually received for the ANP task orders we reviewed because, according to an I-COR, I-CORs did not normally accept delivery of inventory or services; therefore, I-CORs did not prepare and could not maintain receiving reports. The I-COR delegation letters require them to perform inspections and reviews and accept contractor work. We believe that the CSTC-A plan to adequately staff the contract oversight function, as discussed in the management comments on Recommendation B.3.e, will improve the acceptance of goods and services for the ANP training program.

Prior to August 2009, the contractor self procured, self accepted, and invoiced an unlimited number of purchase requests, each of which totaled $3,000 or less. According to I-CORs, until June 2009, I-CORs did not even review contractor purchase requests below the $3,000 threshold unless the supply was sensitive, such as night-vision goggles.

An I-COR also stated that I-CORs were generally unaware of the items ordered by contractors, and that I-CORs did not have any way to verify if the ordered item was delivered. The I-COR even acknowledged that it was possible that the Government was being invoiced for equipment that could not be verified as ever having been received.

The FAH, volume 14, handbook 2, states that once acceptance[18] is accomplished, the contractor is excused from further performance and can no longer be held responsible for unsatisfactory effort. According to I-CORs, the contractor was responsible for self-acceptance of goods and services other than sensitive goods and high-dollar value goods, such as up-armored vehicles. Without checks and balances over the procuring, receiving, and invoicing process, the contractor could potentially invoice the Government for goods and services never received or that were unsatisfactory.

Purchase Order Requests

According to an I-COR, I-CORs did not use standardized procedures to review, deny, or approve contractor-submitted purchase order requests. Specifically, the contractor's Logistic Supervisor stated that the contractor had an established property management system, which the contractor used to procure property, register property, and track in country distributions. According to the contractor's Procurement Manager, the contractor used the property management system to submit purchase order requests and the associated supporting documentation for review by the I-CORs. None of the three I-CORs located in Afghanistan during our site visit were able to use the contractor's property management system to deny or approve contractor purchase order requests.

Of the three, only one I-COR even had access to the contractor's property management system; however it was "view only access," and the I-COR was never trained on the system. Therefore, the I-CORs completed the review and denial or approval process of purchase order requests outside the contractor's property management system through e-mail. Not using the contractor's property management system increased the possibility that the same purchase request(s) could be submitted and approved multiple times. We believe that the CSTC-A plan to provide property management oversight and to adequately staff the contract oversight function and, as discussed in the management comments on Recommendation B.3.e, will improve the purchase order review process for the ANP training program.

Invoice Review Process

DOS personnel did not conduct sufficient invoice reviews to determine whether the contractor was entitled to payment for submitted invoices. Specifically, AIJS personnel were responsible for completing a high-level invoice review, which consisted of verifying 10 basic items, such as the vendor name, invoice number, and contract number. Even though this review was in accordance with the Prompt Payment Act,[19] the process did not address whether contractor invoice costs were allowable, allocable, or reasonable.

According to a financial management advisor, financial management advisors did not perform reviews for invoices of less than $3,000. The financial management advisors performed invoice reviews only on invoices of more than $3,000, and therefore, did not determine whether the contractor invoice costs were allowable, allocable, or reasonable prior to payment.

Both the contracting officer and the COR responsible for approving the contractor invoices recognized that the invoice reviews were not sufficient to determine whether invoice costs were allowable, allocable, or reasonable prior to payment. The contracting officer signed modification 17 to contract S-LMAQM-04-C-0030, which stated that all invoices were to be treated as provisional and subject to subsequent reviews, audits, and appropriate adjustments. Furthermore, the COR wrote a caveat on the invoices that he signed that referenced modification 17.

AIJS also established a separate Invoice Reconciliation Team. The financial program management advisor stated that her team was reviewing 100 percent of approved invoices under contract S-LMAQM-04-C-0030. As of July 30, 2009, the Invoice Reconciliation Team had not reviewed invoices under task orders 4305 and 5375; however, the AIJS personnel emphasized that they had identified $322 million in invoices under contract S-LMAQM-04-C-0030 that were approved even though they were not allowable, allocable, or reasonable. Furthermore, the Invoice Reconciliation Team estimated that approximately 50 percent of the approved invoices had errors.

The Invoice Reconciliation Team will not review the invoices paid with ASF funds for several years. A DCAA review of the invoices and public vouchers paid with these funds will allow DOS to collect refunds during the funds' availability periods.

Billing and Payment Entitlement

The COR and I-CORs did not prepare or maintain supporting documents as evidence that the payment of invoices was in accordance with established policy. Specifically, the COR and I-CORs did not prepare or maintain receiving or inspection reports to document contractor entitlement to invoice payments because the COR and I-CORs did not accept delivery of goods and services. The COR and I-CORs also neglected to perform site visits to validate the existence or completion of goods and services. Instead, the COR accepted the contractor's invoice as proof of supply delivery or service completion.

Therefore, the contractor's approved invoice ended up serving as the Government's approval of goods or services accepted by the contractor. DCAA identified significant internal control deficiencies in the contractor's billing system.[20]

FAR 31.2, "Contracts with Commercial Organizations," August 17, 2007, states that expenses billed to the Government are limited to costs that are allowable, allocable, and reasonable. FMR volume 10, chapter 1, states that contractor invoice payments cannot be made without Government personnel determining entitlement to the payment. Further, receipt of a "proper"[21] invoice, proof of receipt, and acceptance, as well as the contract terms and conditions, determine entitlement. According to FMR, volume 10, chapter 7, "Prompt Payment Act," July 2002, a disbursing office must be provided supporting documents as evidence that the payment is proper. The supporting documents normally consist of a contract, invoices from a contractor, and a receiving report completed by the offices receiving the property or service. According to the FMR volume 10, chapter 8, "Commercial Payment Vouchers and Supporting Documents," May 2008, a contractor is entitled to payment when the contracting officer issues a contract, prepares a receiving report, and approves the invoice that a contractor submits for payment.

The Government has the right to "disallow" costs and not reimburse the contractor for costs that are unreasonable in nature or amount. The right to exercise this power should encourage the contractor to manage efficiently. When the contractor realizes that the Government is not monitoring performance or watching costs, the likelihood of unreasonable costs in invoicing will increase.

Under the MOA between DOS and DOD, DOS agreed to use the ASF funds provided by DOD to provide support for the ANP training program. The weaknesses we identified in the contractor invoice review process prevent DOS from ensuring that the funds were expended in accordance with the MOA.

Recommendations, Management Comments, and Our Response
Added, Deleted, and Renumbered Recommendations

As a result of management comments and additional audit work, we added Recommendation C.2.a. and deleted draft Recommendation C.2.c. Draft Recommendations C.2.a.-b. were renumbered as C.2.b.-c., respectively.

C.1. We recommend that the Director, Defense Contract Audit Agency:

a. Include public vouchers submitted under task orders 4305 and 5375 of the Afghanistan National Police Program indefinite-delivery, indefinite-quantity contracts as part of its review of public vouchers in accordance with the procedures identified in the Defense Contract Audit Agency Manual 7640.1, "Defense Contract Audit Manual."

Defense Contract Audit Agency Comments: The Assistant Director, DCAA, agreed, stating that DCAA should have been reviewing the billings submitted to the DOS under task orders 4305 and 5375. However, DCAA has not been provided the funding to perform the reviews of vouchers nor delegated the authority to approve interim vouchers submitted to the DOS paying office. Therefore, the Assistant Director recommended that DCAA be delegated the authority to review and authorize interim vouchers for reimbursement and be provided funding to accomplish these tasks. The Assistant Director also stated that DCAA will include the follow-on contract in its established pre-payment and post-payment sampling and review plans. As a result, DCAA will review and provisionally approve interim vouchers submitted and the progress or milestone payments.

Our Response: The Assistant Director's comments were responsive, and the actions meet the intent of this recommendation.

b. Conduct an audit of the Afghanistan National Police Program to include cost reimbursable line items.

Defense Contract Audit Agency Comments: The Assistant Director, DCAA, agreed, stating that DCAA met with DOS to explain the audit services available. On September 25, 2007, DCAA submitted a proposal to perform audit services, which was authorized on November 27, 2007, by DOS. However, on October 24, 2008, the DOS contracting officer canceled the authorization; therefore, DCAA did not perform the audits proposed. The Assistant Director also recommended that DOS engage DCAA to perform post-award audits of initial task order award proposals and subsequent task order modifications to ensure that the Government's interest is protected. However, the Assistant Director warned that because DOS did not engage DCAA to perform real-time reviews, the results of DCAA's audits will be qualified.

Our Response: The Assistant Director's comments were responsive, and the actions meet the intent of this recommendation.

* * *

Finding E. *Afghan Women's Police Corps*

The DOS and DOD ANP Program has not provided the necessary number of trained female police because the training facility lacks the capacity to train an adequate number of Women's Police Corps (WPC) members. The lack of a sufficient number of trained WPC members impairs the effectiveness of the law enforcement function in Afghanistan.

Need for Women's Police Force

Reports issued by DOS and DOD during the past three years have identified the need for an Afghan women's police force. An interagency assessment of Afghanistan's police training and readiness was conducted jointly by the DOS and DOD, which reported in November 2006, that there were only 91 low-ranking female police officers in Afghanistan—a country of approximately 28 million people. The report further stated that the number of female police needed to increase substantially because, in a Muslim society, only female police can closely interact with female suspects and respond to domestic disputes.

INL issued a report, "The Islamic Republic of Afghanistan's Criminal Justice Sector," in July 2008, reiterating that women were vastly underrepresented in Afghanistan's police force. Furthermore, the Afghan MOI has recognized the importance of training female police officers. In the summer of 2008, the MOI issued a directive to the Afghan National Police Academy, the Kabul Zonal Police Command, and the police command centers at the districts and provinces to increase the professional education of the women's police force.

Trained female police officers can effectively perform duties that, given Afghanistan's customs, are more appropriate for women to undertake than men. Examples include staffing of family response units that respond to cases of domestic violence and security tasks at airports and border crossing check points.

Afghan Culture

The Afghan WPC training program has not reached its full potential because of challenges posed by Afghanistan's culture and traditions. Afghan women have traditionally been viewed in a subordinate role.

Although the new Afghanistan constitution, enacted in 2004, advocates equal rights for men and women, in practice, women have still not achieved the equality mandated.

Some of the fundamental obstacles and challenges that must be overcome to facilitate women's induction into the ANP are:

* an overwhelming majority of the women in Afghanistan are either uneducated or illiterate;

* religious and cultural taboos regulate women's roles in society;

* women are relegated to traditional roles, such as household or kitchen duties, child rearing, and low-level secretarial work; and

* male family members, tribal leaders, and clerics dictate the roles of women in society, which are generally very restrictive and confined.

Training Capacity

The first INL-funded women's police training program was conducted at the Heart Regional Training Center in July 2007. Planning for a dedicated WPC facility began in February 2008. Following the planning and construction phases, the first WPC training class was held in Kabul in November 2008. According to INL officials, a second

WPC training facility in Jalalabad was scheduled to begin training classes in November 2009.

Both the Kabul and Jalalabad facilities are designed to train 30 women recruits over an 8-week training cycle. The Kabul WPC has trained 20 to 42 female police per class through its first four training cycles since November 2008.

While we believe that the U.S.-funded ANP program has laid the foundation for an effective women's police training program, progress made so far is not adequate. At the time of our audit only one women's training facility in Kabul was in operation, whereas there were eight training centers for male police officers in Afghanistan.

According to statistics provided by the U.S. training and mentoring contractor, 172,130 ANP have completed basic and advanced training courses and of those ANP, only 131 are women.

According to the information provided by INL, approximately $6.6 million was provided to construct and operate the WPC facilities in Kabul and Jalalabad. This amount is insignificant compared to the total funding of approximately $7 billion provided by the Government for the ANP program.

Recommendations, Management Comments, and Our Response

Redirected Recommendation

We revised draft Recommendation E.1. and E.2. to redirect the recommendations to the Commanding General, Combined Security Transition Command-Afghanistan, in coordination with the Assistant Secretary of State for the Bureau of International Narcotics and Law Enforcement Affairs and the Afghan Ministry of Interior.

E. We recommend that the Commanding General, Combined Security Transition Command-Afghanistan, in coordination with the Assistant Secretary of State for the Bureau of International Narcotics and Law Enforcement Affairs, and the Afghan Ministry of Interior establish and implement a plan within a specific timeframe that will:

1. Increase the training facility capacity for female police members and provide them training to conduct law enforcement in accordance with the requirements of the Capability Milestones discussed in Finding A.

2. Recruit an adequate number of female training instructors and mentors to staff those training centers.

Assistant Secretary of State, Bureau of International Narcotics and Law Enforcement Affairs, Comments: The Acting Assistant Secretary of State, INL, agreed that more resources should be devoted to training Afghan female police but stated that the training requirements and funding are regulated by the Combined Security Transition Command-Afghanistan.

Our Response: According to the Senior IG Advisor, Command Inspector General, Combined Security Transition Command-Afghanistan, DOD will assume responsibility for the Women's Police Corps when the new contract is established. We request that the Commanding General, Combined Security Transition Command-Afghanistan, review the redirected recommendations and provide comments in response to the final report.

Chapter Review Questions:

1   By what authority and for what purpose do Offices of Inspector General conduct audits?

2   Who promulgates professional standards for OIG audits, and what is the name of the publication in which those standards are prescribed?

3   What are the difference between and the common features of audits and inspections?

4   By what authority and for what purpose would two separate Offices of Inspector General conduct a joint audit?

Chapter 8 Endnotes

---

¹ U.S. Const., Art. I, Section 9.

² Inspector General Act of 1978, as amended, §3(d)(1).

³ *See* General Accountability Office, "Government Auditing Standards," July 2007 Edition (http://www.gao.gov/new.items/d07731g.pdf).

⁴ *Id.*, p. 1.

⁵ *See* United States House of Representatives, Committee on Energy and Commerce, Subcommittee on Oversight and Investigations, "Financial Collapse of ENRON Corporation, with Focus on ENRON's Inside and Outside Counsel," March 14, 2002 http://ftp.resource.org/gpo.gov/hearings/107h/78506.pdf William C. Powers, Jr., "Report of Investigation by the Special Investigative Committee of the Board of Directors of Enron Corp.," February 1, 2002 http://fl1.findlaw.com/news.findlaw.com/wp/docs/enron/specinvo20102rpt1.pdf

⁶ Pub.L. 107-204, 116 Stat. 745, enacted July 30, 2002.

⁷ *See* "Government Auditing Standards," July 2007 Edition, p. 41 (explaining in a footnote that, "The concepts of significance and materiality include quantitative as well as qualitative measures in relation to the subject matter of the audit."); President's Council on Integrity & Efficiency, "Qualify Standards for Federal Offices of Inspector General," aka Silver Book, p. 11 (October 2003) ("Auditors and audit organizations within OIGs have a specific independence standard required by *Government Auditing Standards*. This standard requires that, while auditors have the capability of performing a range of services for their clients, in some circumstances it is not appropriate for them to perform both audit and certain nonaudit services for the same client.") (http://www.ignet.gov/pande/standards/igstds.pdf).

[8] Hon. Gordon S. Heddell, Inspector General of the Department of Defense, "Contracts for Afghan National Police Training," April 15, 2010 http://www.dodig.mil/fo/Foia/ERR/h03l89967206.pdf

[9] Richard Leach, Auditor General of the Navy, and Vice Admiral Ronal Route, USN, Naval Inspector General, "Auditors Don't Inspect and Inspectors Don't Audit: Comparison of the Naval Audit Service and Naval Inspector General Functions," *Defense AT&L*, p. 20 (May-June 2005).

[10] "DOD Obligations and Expenditures of Funds Provided to the Department of State for the Training and Mentoring of the Afghan National Police," Department of State Report No. MERO-A-10-06, Department of Defense Report No. D-2010-042, February 9, 2010 http://www.dodig.mil/Audit/reports/fy10/10-042.pdf

[11] Greg Bruno, "Afghanistan's National Security Forces," Council on Foreign Relations Backgrounder, New York, April 16, 2009.

[12] The Joint Coordination and Monitoring Board consists of representatives from the Afghan Government and the International Community and coordinates the implementation of the Afghanistan Compact, which defines the principles of political cooperation for the period of 2006 to 2011. The Joint Coordination and Monitoring Board provides direction to address issues of coordination, implementation, and financing for the benchmarks and timelines of the Compact and reports on the implementation.

[13] According to FAR 42.202, "Assignment of Contract Administration," contracting officers may delegate contract administration authority. The delegation authorizes the appointee to perform specified tasks under an identified contract.

[14] A cost is allowable only when the cost is reasonable, allocable, and conforms to the terms of the contract (FAR 31.201-2).

[15] A cost is allocable if it is (a) incurred specifically for the contract; (b) benefits both the contract and other work, and can be distributed to the contract and other work in reasonable proportion to the benefits received; or

(c) necessary to the overall operation of the business, although a direct relationship to any particular cost objective cannot be shown (FAR 31.201-4).

[16] A cost is reasonable if, in its nature and amount, does not exceed that which would be incurred by a prudent person (FAR 31.201-3).

[17] DCAA's mission is to perform services regarding contracts and subcontracts to all DOD components responsible for procurement and contract administration.

[18] Acceptance means an authorized Government official acknowledges that goods and services received conform to contract requirements.

[19] The Prompt Payment Act ensures that Federal agencies pay vendors in a timely manner.

[20] *Report on Audit of Billing System,* Audit Report No. 03181-2009D11010001.

[21] According to FAR 52.232-25(a)(3), "Prompt Payment," October 2008, an invoice is considered proper when it contains the name and address of the contractor, invoice date, contract number, description, quantity, unit of measure, unit price, and price of goods delivered or services performed.

CHAPTER 9. INVESTIGATIVE OVERSIGHT:

Friendly-Fire Death of Corporal Patrick Tillman

In addition to the other duties and responsibilities specified in this Act, the Inspector General of the Department of Defense shall . . . initiate, conduct, and supervise such audits and investigations in the Department of Defense (including the military departments) as the Inspector General considers appropriate[,] develop policy, monitor and evaluate program performance, and provide guidance with respect to all Department activities relating to criminal investigation programs[, and] give particular regard to the activities of the internal audit, inspection, and investigative units of the military departments with a view toward avoiding duplication and insuring effective coordination and cooperation.

Inspector General Act of 1978, as amended, Section 8(c)

Who inspects the inspector? Within the Department of Defense, Congress has explicitly deemed all audits and investigations, including but not limited to the audits conducted by the military department Auditors General and the investigations conducted by the uniformed Inspectors General of each military department, subject to the supervision of the DoD Inspector General: "In addition to the other duties and responsibilities specified in this Act, the Inspector General of the Department of Defense shall . . . initiate, conduct, and supervise such audits and investigations in the Department of Defense (including the military departments) as the Inspector General considers appropriate."[1] That supervision also extends to non-criminal "command" investigations conducted by uniformed soldiers in the battlefield, such as the investigations associated with the friendly-fire death in Afghanistan of Army Corporal Patrick Tillman.

Of course, each Senate-confirmed Inspector General remains under the oversight of the various Committees of the United States Congress, including but not limited to the Senate Homeland Security and Governmental Affairs Committee, which Committee "owns the Inspector General Act" and through which Committee each Presidential nominee to an Inspector General position must be "sequentially referred" in the course of the Senate confirmation process.[2] Congress exercises its oversight of Inspectors General through its review of statutorily mandated semi-annual reports to Congress,[3] as well as through the various Committees regularly calling upon Inspectors General to testify about their audit, inspection, investigative, and oversight activities.

An article in *Rolling Stone* magazine has been credited with forcing the early retirement of General Stanley A. McChrystal, Commander of NATO's International Security Assistance Force and U.S. Forces-Afghanistan, in July 2010. That same article describes General McChrystal's role in the cover-up of famed NFL star Pat Tillman's death by friendly fire in Afghanistan:

> After Cpl. Pat Tillman, the former-NFL-star-turned-Ranger, was accidentally killed by his own troops in Afghanistan in April 2004, McChrystal took an active role in creating the impression that Tillman had died at the hands of Taliban fighters. He signed off on a falsified recommendation for a Silver Star that suggested Tillman had been killed by enemy fire. (McChrystal would later claim he didn't read the recommendation closely enough—a

strange excuse for a commander known for his laserlike attention to minute details.) A week later, McChrystal sent a memo up the chain of command, specifically warning that President Bush should avoid mentioning the cause of Tillman's death. "If the circumstances of Corporal Tillman's death become public," he wrote, it could cause "public embarrassment" for the president.[4]

Corporal Tillman was killed by friendly fire during combat operations in Afghanistan on April 24, 2004. The foreword of the 85-page DoD OIG report, "Review of Matters Related to the Death of Corporal Patrick Tillman, U.S. Army," reprinted below, provides the circumstances that precipitated this IG review:

> The course of this review, in particular the central issues, was framed through a series of requests from the Army Inspector General, Members of Congress, and the family of Corporal Patrick Tillman concerning Corporal Tillman's death by friendly fire while participating in combat operations in Afghanistan on April 22, 2004.

> Within 30 days thereafter, Corporal Tillman's death was investigated twice by Army officers under the provisions of Army Regulation 15-6, "Procedures for Investigating Officers and Boards of Officers." Because of unresolved concerns regarding the nature of Corporal Tillman's death and its aftermath, a third investigation was completed by an Army general officer in January 2005. However, by letter dated April 21, 2005, Mr. [REDACTED], father of Corporal Tillman, raise significant issues with the results of that investigation.

> By memorandum dated June 2, 2005, the Army Inspector General requested that this Office conduct an independent review of concerns expressed by Mr. [REDACTED]. After completing an initial assessment, we requested that the Army Criminal Investigation Command conduct a full investigation into the facts and circumstances of Corporal Tillman's death. Concurrently, we conducted a review of

the three investigations noted above, the adequacy of Army notifications to the Tillman family in the weeks following his death, and the basis for the posthumous award of the Silver Star.

Several Members of Congress also questioned the series of events that led to Corporal Tillman's death, subsequent investigations, the need to establish accountability in matters concerning the death and its aftermath, and the possibility of an Army cover-up. Correspondence to this Office from Senator John McCain in July 2005 and Representative Michael M. Honda in August 2005 questioned specific findings of the investigations. Correspondence from Senator Charles Grassley, Representative Zoe Lofgren, and Representatives Honda, Ike Skelton, Christopher Shays, and Dennis Kucinich in March 2006 reiterated those concerns, requested further explanations regarding Army actions taken following Corporal Tillman's death, and asked for briefings after we completed our work.

In addition, the Senate Armed Services Committee, the House Armed Services Committee, and the Subcommittee on National Security, Emerging Threats, and International Relations (House Committee on Government Reform) requested the results of our review.

This report provides the results of our review and summarizes results of the concurrent investigation by the Army Criminal Investigation Command. The full Army Criminal Investigation Command report is being issued separately. We concur with the results of that investigation. Although some of the Army activities related to Corporal Tillman's death remain classified, this report is unclassified to promote maximum utility and avoid delays that would attend a classified issuance.

CASE STUDY: FRIENDLY FIRE DEATH OF
CORP. PATRICK TILLMANN

The following are selected excerpts from 85-page Department of Defense Office of Inspector General Report, "Review of Matters Related to the Death of Corporal Patrick Tillman, U.S. Army," Report Number IPO2007E011, March 26, 2007.[5]

Inspector General
United States
Department *of* Defense

Review Of Matters Related
To The Death Of
Corporal Patrick Tillman, U.S. Army

Report Number IPO2007E001

March 26, 2007

TABLE OF CONTENTS

Review Of Matters Related To The Death Of
Corporal Patrick Tillman, U.S. Army

I. Introduction And Summary

We initiated the review to address allegations that three sequential investigations into the "friendly fire" death of Corporal (CPL) Patrick Tillman, U.S. Army, on April 22, 2004, in Afghanistan, did not meet established investigative standards and, therefore, failed to disclose relevant facts of his death or assign requisite accountability. Additionally, our review sought to determine whether those investigations, as well as the delayed notifications to CPL Tillman's family members and the posthumous award of the Silver Star based on erroneous information, were indicative of an Army effort to conceal the circumstances of CPL Tillman's death or possible misconduct by those involved.[6] In doing so, we focused our review on the following specific issues:

* Did responsible officials comply with applicable standards for investigating friendly fire deaths?

* Did responsible officials comply with applicable standards for notification of next of kin of CPL Tillman's death and related investigations?

* Did responsible officials comply with applicable standards for award of the Silver Star to CPL Tillman?

Apart from those issues, our initial assessment found that questions remained regarding the events that transpired during the course of the friendly fire incident itself, particularly with respect to conduct of the Service members involved. Because of its investigative capability and independence, we requested the Army Criminal Investigation Command (CID) to investigate the circumstances of CPL Tillman's death and the death and injuries to others in the incident. After conducting extensive investigative work, including restaging of the incident on-site, the Army CID found insufficient evidence to support any further action under the Uniform Code of Military Justice.[7] We concur with that conclusion and have provided a summary of those investigative results at Appendix A to this report. The Army CID will issue its full report separately.

Our review concluded that CPL Tillman's chain of command made critical errors in reporting CPL Tillman's death and in assigning investigative jurisdiction in the days following his death, and bears ultimate responsibility for the inaccuracies, misunderstandings, and perceptions of concealment that led to our investigation. For example, CPL Tillman's chain of command failed to timely report suspected death by friendly fire. Established Army policy required notification of death by friendly fire, which was suspected the day following the incident, up through the chain of command as well as to the Army Safety Center.[8] In turn, DoD guidance required that the Combatant Commander convene a legal investigation and authorized the cognizant Service to convene any safety investigation required by its regulations. The safety investigation required by Army regulations would have been conducted by a board of trained, experienced investigators who would have collected, processed, and retained forensic evidence, and coordinated with criminal investigative authorities if warranted. Both legal and safety investigations would have been independent of CPL Tillman's immediate chain of command and, therefore, not vulnerable to accusations that command Service members were shielded from culpability.

None of CPL Tillman's superiors complied with these requirements. Instead, after clear evidence of fratricide emerged the day following the incident, CPL Tillman's battalion commander (a lieutenant colonel three levels below the Combatant Commander), with the concurrence of his regimental commander, appointed a subordinate Army captain to investigate.

That investigation, completed in about 2 weeks, determined CPL Tillman's death was fratricide caused by leadership failures and tactical errors. Dissatisfied with the thoroughness of that investigation, CPL Tillman's regimental commander (a colonel) ordered his own executive officer (a lieutenant colonel) to conduct a second investigation. That investigation, building on the first, was completed in 9 days, confirmed death by friendly fire, and provided expanded findings on the contributing tactical errors. No independent investigator; that is, outside CPL Tillman's immediate chain of command, was appointed by appropriate authority until 6 months after CPL Tillman's death. A safety investigation was not initiated until nearly 6 months after the incident when most of the forensic evidence had been destroyed. Expertise available from the Army CID was not obtained until we initiated this review.

We concluded that the first two investigations, conducted by officers in CPL Tillman's battalion and regiment under Army Regulation (AR) 15-6, "Procedures for Investigating Officers and Boards of Officers," were tainted by the failure to preserve evidence, a lack of thoroughness, the failure to pursue logical investigative leads, and conclusions that were open to challenge based on the evidence provided. More significantly, neither investigator visited the site to visually reenact the incident, secure physical evidence, take photographs, or obtain accurate measurements. In addition, the first investigating officer, with advice from his legal advisor, withheld information concerning suspected fratricide from medical examiners who raised questions based on anomalies they discovered during the autopsy. As a result, the first two investigations lacked credibility and contributed to perceptions that Army officials were purposefully withholding key information concerning CPL Tillman's death.

In November 2004, because of lingering concerns regarding CPL Tillman's death, the Acting Secretary of the Army directed that Lieutenant General (LTG) Phillip R. Kensinger, Jr., Commander, U.S. Army Special Operations Command (Airborne) (USASOC), conduct a third investigation. LTG Kensinger appointed a subordinate, Brigadier General (BG) Gary M. Jones, Commander, U.S. Army Special Forces Command (Airborne), to conduct the investigation.

BG Jones' investigation was more thorough than the first two, included an on-site visit, and was pronounced legally sufficient by LTG Kensinger's Staff Judge Advocate in January 2005.

Subsequent review by the Army Inspector General raised concerns that caused BG Jones to conduct additional investigative work and file supplementary information.

However, weaknesses remained. Like the first two investigators, he also failed to interview some witnesses who were part of the unit that fired on CPL Tillman's position. He did not assess accountability for failures by the chain of command (including LTG Kensinger) to comply with Army policy for reporting and investigating friendly fire incidents, to coordinate with other investigative authorities, to provide timely information concerning suspected friendly fire to CPL Tillman's next of kin, and to ensure accuracy in documentation submitted in support of the Silver Star.

Notwithstanding our conclusions with respect to these three investigations, we emphasize that all investigators established the basic facts of CPL Tillman's death—that it was caused by friendly fire, that occupants of one vehicle in CPL Tillman's platoon were responsible, and that circumstances on the ground at the time caused those occupants to misidentify friendly forces as hostile. None of the investigations suggested that CPL Tillman's death was other than accidental. Our review, as well as the investigation recently completed by the Army CID, obtained no evidence contrary to those key findings.

CPL Tillman's family members were not told of the investigations and subsequent fratricide determination until 35 days after CPL Tillman's death, despite Army regulations that require next of kin be advised of additional information concerning a Service member's death as that information becomes available. Because CPL Tillman's regimental commander desired to keep information concerning the death "close hold" until investigative results were finalized, no "supplemental reports" were issued to correct initial reports that CPL Tillman's death was caused by enemy fire. Although LTG Kensinger knew friendly fire was suspected and under investigation before he served as the Army representative at CPL Tillman's memorial service on May 3, 2004, he decided to withhold notification from family members until all facts concerning the incident could be verified. Certain senior Army officials were aware of the friendly fire investigation in early May, but none took measures to ensure that family members were, at a minimum, advised that CPL Tillman's death was under review. We find no reasonable explanation for these failures to comply with Army regulations.

Finally, the citation and narrative justification submitted to support the Silver Star awarded to CPL Tillman contained inaccurate information—particularly with respect to descriptions that suggested CPL Tillman performed heroically in the face of, and was killed by, enemy fire. The two supporting valorous witness statements stamped "original signed" were attributed to two of CPL Tillman's platoon members, but were drafted by others and contained inaccurate information. The posthumous presentation of the Silver Star to CPL Tillman as if he had been killed by the enemy was ill-advised and contributed to continuing mistrust of Army representations to family members, especially since LTG Kensinger and other officials knew at the time that friendly fire was the likely cause of his death.

We recommend that the Acting Secretary of the Army take appropriate corrective action with respect to officials whom we identified as accountable for the regulatory violations and errors in judgment that are described in this review. Additionally, we recommend that the Acting Secretary initiate a review of the Silver Star award to ensure that it meets regulatory requirements. We note that the Army already has taken action to delay approval of posthumous valor awards until completion of pending investigations and has strengthened guidance concerning next of kin notifications.

This report sets forth our findings and conclusions based on a preponderance of the evidence.

II. Background

On April 22, 2004, the 2nd Platoon, A Company, 2nd Battalion, 75th Ranger Regiment was conducting operations in the vicinity of Magarah, Afghanistan. Because of difficulties caused by an inoperable tactical vehicle, and the mission to achieve an established objective by nightfall, the platoon ground assault convoy, consisting of 41 Army Rangers, 4 Afghan Military Forces (AMF) soldiers, and 12 vehicles, was split into 2 groups or "serials."[9] Serial 1 consisted of 19 Ran tr l' 'n 4 U.S. vehicles and 2 AMF vehicles, including First Lieutenant (1LT) [REDACTED] (the Platoon Leader), CPL Tillman; and 4 AMF soldiers.[10] Serial 2, commanded by Sergeant First Class (SFC) [REDACTED] (the Platoon Sergeant), consisted of 22 Rangers and two local Afghans traveling in 4 U.S. vehicles and a privately owned local vehicle (referred to as a "jinga" or "jingle" truck). The jinga truck, driven by a local Afghan, was towing a fifth (inoperable) U.S. vehicle.

After the split, Serial 1 traveled down the canyon road without incident arriving in the Vicinity of the village of Manah. Serial 2, however, did not proceed along the separate planned route because SFC [REDACTED] believed the risk of accidental injury or death to be too great given the terrain. Therefore, SFC [REDACTED] ordered Serial 2 to travel down the same canyon road that Serial 1 had taken earlier.

While traveling down the canyon road, Serial 2 came under attack from enemy mortar or rocket propelled grenades and small arms fire originating from the top of the canyon walls. Upon hearing the attack behind them, Serial 1 personnel, led by Staff Sergeant (SSG) [REDACTED] (the squad leader), dismounted their vehicles and moved on foot through a small (6-building) village to an elevated spur overlooking the canyon road below and across from the southern ridge-line. CPL Tillman, Private First Class [REDACTED] and an AMF soldier positioned themselves on the forward slope of the spur visible from and exposed to the canyon road below. 1LT [REDACTED] and Specialist (SPC) [REDACTED] (the Radio Operator), having been by handling communications devices, were positioned at the base of a building in the village some distance below and to the rear of SSG [REDACTED] and other Serial 1 personnel.

The first U.S. vehicle in Serial 2 was led by SSG [REDACTED] (the squad leader), with a driver and five other occupants. As SSG [REDACTED] and his crew moved down the canyon road, they fired their weapons in suppressive fire along the canyon walls. When SSG [REDACTED]'s vehicle exited the narrow portion of the canyon road below the spur where CPL Tillman and his team were located, occupants saw muzzle flashes coming from that position. SSG [REDACTED] and his team directed their fire toward the muzzle flashes killing both CPL Tillman and the AMF soldier. As SSG [REDACTED]'s vehicle proceeded pas the spur toward the village, the vehicle occupants continued to fire on the building in the settlement hitting 1LT [REDACTED] in the face and SPC [REDACTED] in the knee and chest with small arms fire.

A chronology of events following the incident is provided as Appendix B to this report.

III. Scope

In the course of our review, we interviewed 106 witnesses with knowledge of the matters under review, including soldiers from CPL Tillman's platoon, the chain of command of the 75th Ranger Regiment, the Commander, Joint Task Force (the operational commander over the Ranger Regiment in Afghanistan), and the former Commander, USASOC, who had administrative control of the Rangers. We also interviewed the Army officers who conducted the three command investigations of the friendly fire incident; the Army Chief of Staff; the Commander, U.S. Central Command (CENTCOM), who had overall operational control of the Rangers; and the Commander, U.S. Special Operations Command (SOCOM). To further address matters which arose during the review we also conducted 42 follow-up interviews. In addition, we reviewed each of the earlier investigations and all of the documents associated with those investigations, as well as relevant e-mail messages and internal documents within the operational and administrative chains of command of the Ranger Regiment and similar communications within the Department of the Army.

As indicated above, inconsistencies in prior testimonial accounts of the incident, the failure to preserve forensic evidence, and alleged deficiencies in the investigations ultimately led to allegations that Army officials may have been attempting to conceal misconduct on the part of Service members who were involved in the fratricide and its aftermath. In an effort to obtain maximum evidence to resolve those matters, we requested that the Army CID investigate CPL Tillman's death and the death and injuries to the other soldiers. That investigative work was undertaken concurrent with our review. A summary of results is provided at Appendix A.

A full report is being issued separately.

IV. Findings and Analysis

A. Did responsible officials comply with applicable standards for investigating friendly fire deaths?

Responsible officials failed to comply with applicable standards for investigating friendly fire deaths. Lack of timely notification from the chain of command that friendly fire was suspected delayed Army Safety Center involvement and prevented CENTCOM from convening a legal investigation. Neither of the first two investigating officers was properly appointed, visited the scene, preserved physical evidence, identified and interviewed all relevant witnesses, or resolved factual inconsistencies among witness statements. The second investigating officer drew conclusions not supported by evidence included in his report. Additionally, Ranger Regiment personnel withheld from the

Armed Forces Medical Examiner (AFME) and Army CID the fact that friendly fire was suspected.

The final investigating officer, a general officer, failed to interview all of the Rangers involved to resolve the uncertainty in the sequence of events that occurred on April 22, 2004; failed to apply relevant standards and assign accountability for the mishandling of physical evidence; failed to fully address the next of kin notification issue as a violation of applicable regulations; failed to pursue inaccuracies related to the Silver Star award, reached findings not supported by testimony, and, in fact, exacerbated the situation by sharing those findings on the Silver Star with family members, senior Army officials, and Members of Congress during official briefings; and failed to pursue misrepresentations on the part of LTG Kensinger related to the next of kin notification issue. Further, LTG Kensinger provided misleading testimony to the third investigating officer and this Office when he denied that he knew friendly fire was suspected before the memorial service for CPL Tillman.

Standards

Note: The following standards set forth requirements for reporting and investigating incidents where the suspected cause of death is friendly fire. We examined the three command investigations conducted with regard to CPL Tillman in light of those standards.

Department of Defense Instruction (DoDI) 6055.7, "Accident Investigation, Reporting, and Record Keeping," dated October 3, 2000

The Instruction applies to all DoD Components, to include the Military Departments and Combatant Commands, and sets forth DoD guidance for safety and legal investigations of accidents.[11] As to the relationship between the two types of investigations, the Instruction states at Subsection 5.2.6, "The safety investigation is the primary investigation and shall control all witnesses and evidence."

With regard to friendly fire incidents, the Instruction directs that DoD Components "shall prepare" a legal investigation report, in addition to any authorized safety investigation report, in "all suspected cases of Friendly Fire." The Instruction further directs the Heads of

DoD Components to comply with Section E4.7, "Investigating Friendly Fire Accidents," which states,

> For all accidents falling within the definition of Friendly Fire, the Combatant Commander will convene a legal investigation to determine the facts of the incident and guide further action. In consultation with the Combatant Commander, Service or other commanders may convene a safety investigation as required.

The Instruction defines "Friendly Fire" as,

> A circumstance in which a member of a U,S. or friendly military force are.mistakenly or accidentally killed or injured in action by U.S. or friendly forces actively engaged with an enemy or who are directing fire at a hostile force or what is thought to be a hostile force.

The Instruction is silent on the procedures to be used to conduct legal investigations into friendly fire incidents, but notes generally at Section 4.6 that legal investigations are to inquire into facts and circumstances as well as "to obtain and preserve all available evidence" for use in administrative actions, litigation, and claims. Further, Sections 5, "Responsibilities," and Enclosure 4, "Procedures," require that the Heads of DoD Components establish procedures implementing the Instruction, to include developing time lines for routinely updating the primary next of kin of accident fatalities regarding the status of safety and legal investigations.[12]7

DoDI 5154.30, "Armed Forces Institute of Pathology," dated March 18, 2003

Enclosure 2, "The AFME System," charges the AFME to conduct forensic investigations, to include autopsies, to determine the manner and cause of death in all cases where an active duty Service member is killed. Paragraph E2.2.6 directs that the AFME shall receive notification of the deaths of all Service members on active duty, and shall have the authority to review all pertinent information, to include investigative reports, photographs, and evidence.

Army Regulation (AR) 15-6, "Procedures for Investigating Officers and Boards of Officers," dated September 30, 1996

The Regulation establishes Army procedures for administrative investigations and boards of officers that are not specifically authorized by any other directive. The stated purpose of AR 15-6 investigations and boards is to ascertain facts, make recommendations, and report them to the appointing authority. Introductory language in the Regulation notes that investigations or boards appointed under a specific regulation or directive may apply AR 15-6 procedures, and that, in the case of conflicting provisions, the more specific regulation takes precedence over the terms of AR 15-6.

Recognizing the existence of other investigations, Subparagraph 1-4.d, "Concurrent investigations," directs appointing authorities, investigating officers, and boards

> [W]ill ensure that procedures under this regulation do not hinder or interfere with a concurrent investigation directed by higher headquarters, ... or an investigation being conducted by a criminal investigative [activity]. In cases of concurrent or subsequent investigations, coordination with the other command or agency should be made to avoid duplication of investigative effort, where possible.

With regard to specific responsibilities, Paragraph 1-5, "Function of investigations and boards," establishes the duty of the investigating officer or board to

> Ascertain and consider the evidence on all sides of each issue, thoroughly and impartially, and to make findings and recommendations that are warranted by the facts and that comply with the instructions of the appointing authority.

Subparagraph 2-1.a, "Authority to appoint," directs that only a general court-martial convening authority (GCMCA) may appoint an investigation or board for incidents resulting in the death of one or more persons. With regard to qualifications, Subparagraph 2-1.c, "Who may be appointed," requires that investigating officers and board members,

[S]hall be those persons who, in the opinion of
the appointing
authority, are best qualified for the duty by reason of their education, training, experience, length of service, and temperament, [and] [W]ill be senior to any person whose conduct or performance of duty may be investigated, or against whom adverse findings or recommendations may be made, [with limited exception].

Subparagraph 2-1.c continues, that should an investigating officer discover during the investigation that completion of the investigation requires examining the conduct or performance of duty of, or may
result in findings or recommendations adverse to, a person senior to
the investigating officer, he must report that fact to the appointing
authority. The appointing authority is then obligated to appoint a more
senior investigating officer or conduct a separate inquiry into the matters pertaining to that person.

With regard to standard of proof, findings, and recommendations, Paragraphs 3-9, "Findings," and 3-10, "Recommendations,' require
that findings be supported by the preponderance of the evidence of
record in the report, and that recommendations be consistent with
those findings.

Paragraph 3-15, "Exhibits," details the handling of evidence and
its inclusion in the investigating officer's written report. With regard to
physical objects, Subparagraph 3-15.b, "Real evidence," highlights the
importance of including clear and accurate written descriptions or depictions (such as photographs) of physical evidence in the report. The
Subparagraph further stresses, "The real evidence itself should be preserved, including chain of custody where appropriate, for use if further
proceedings are necessary." The exhibit in the report should tell where
the real evidence can be found, and after final action has been taken in
the case, the evidence should be disposed of as for provided in Army
regulation.

AR 385-40, "Accident Reporting and Records," dated November 1, 1994
The Regulation defines "accident" as "an unplanned event that
causes personal injury or illness, or property damage." Paragraph 2-2,
"Accident and incident classes," groups accidents into four classes ac-

cording to their consequences. An accident resulting in a fatality qualifies as a "Class A" accident, the most serious of the four classes.

In addressing fratricide, the Regulation notes that DoDI 6055. 7 is the primary authority for investigating and reporting friendly fire accidents. Subparagraph 2-4.q, "Fratricide," states that friendly fire accidents are "special situations" that must be reported promptly and investigated thoroughly with both a safety investigation conducted under the provisions of the Regulation and a legal investigation conducted under the provisions of the Regulation and AR 15-6.[13]

Paragraph 1-4, "Responsibilities," requires commanders at all levels to comply with the Regulation's accident reporting and investigating requirements, and specifically charges commanders of Army Major Commands to ensure that accidents are investigated and analyzed.

Paragraph 3-2, "Commander's responsibility," provides general guidance and requires the commander who first becomes aware of any Army Class A accident to immediately notify, through the chain of command, the Commander, Army Safety Center. Should a Class A accident occur in combat, Paragraph 3-5 still requires immediate notification of the Army Safety Center designated contact, unless the senior tactical commander waives notification based on his determination that the situation, conditions, and/or time does not permit normal reporting and investigation. The senior tactical commander's decision to waive normal reporting and investigating must be reported in writing along with the commander's name and rank.

Paragraph 1-8, "Collateral investigation and reports," states that the safety investigation board has priority over the legal investigation, and Paragraph 1-9, "Accident investigation board appointing authority," directs, in relevant part, that the commander having general court-martial jurisdiction over the unit responsible for the operation or personnel involved in the accident appoint the safety investigation board.

Chapter 4 details guidance for safety investigations, and, in Paragraph 4-3, "Class A andB Accident Investigations," provides for two different procedures for safety investigations of accidents: a centralized accident investigation[14] or an installation-level accident investigation.

Both centralized and installation-level investigations require the appointing authority to appoint a safety investigation board of three or more members. However, in a centralized investigation the Commander, Army Safety Center, provides to the appointing authority Safety Center personnel to serve as board members and identifies to the appointing authority any special requirements and qualifications for local board members. The Regulation empowers the Commander, Army Safety Center, to determine whether a centralized or installation-level investigation will be conducted, and directs him to make that determination "upon notification of a Class A or B accident." Finally With regard to safety investigation boards, Paragraph 4-2 requires board members to be from organizations other than the activity or unit incurring the accident and to be screened to ensure that no member has an interest in the accident that may bias the outcome of the investigation.

With regard to gathering evidence at the accident scene, Paragraph 4-5, "Accident scene preservation," provides that where the situation does not permit the scene to be preserved, Military Police or CID personnel will remove all items of evidence needed for their investigation and, whenever possible, will photograph the items before they are collected. Debris that must be moved will be stored in a secure area and guarded until released by the board president. The appointing authority will ensure that photos are taken and a sketch of the scene is made with sufficient detail and measurements to allow a scale drawing to be made. Further, all damage and ground markings incident to the accident will be identified and photographed before measurement and cleanup of the accident scene. The sketch and photographs will be provided to the president of the board as soon as possible after arrival.

AR 600-8-1, "Personal Affairs, Army Casualty Operations/Assistance/Insurance," dated October 20, 1994

The Regulation prescribes policies and tasks governing U.S. Army casualty operations. The Regulation reiterates the requirement that fatal accidents be investigated with both safety and legal investigations. Paragraph 2-12, "Casualty reporting during hostilities," states, in part, at subparagraph d:

All suspected friendly fire incidents will require an AR 15-6 investigation. A board of officers will be appointed under AR 15-6 to inquire into the suspected friendly fire incident. The board will be appointed by the commander having general court martial jurisdiction over the unit to which the casualty was assigned (or a higher authority designated by a commander authorized to make such designation) .... The board will consist of not less than three commissioned officers (field grade recommended).

AR 600-34, "Fatal Training/Operational Accident Presentations to the Next of Kin," dated January 2, 2003

The Regulation provides Army guidance on legal investigations of fatal accidents and presentations on such accidents to a soldier's next of kin. Paragraph 1-15, "The appointing/approving authorities of the [legal] investigation," mandates the appointment of investigating officers in accordance with the Regulation and AR 15-6.[15]

Paragraph 1-18, "Concept," directs legal investigations "conducted under the provisions of AR 15-6, AR 385-40, and this regulation" in "all suspected cases of friendly fire." The paragraph also states that the investigating officer in a legal investigation is "usually appointed· by the general court-martial convening authority (GCMCA) [of the unit concerned], [and] will conduct a timely and accurate [legal] investigation of the mishap." Further, the Regulation states that the Director of Army Safety initiates a safety investigation concurrent with the legal investigation, and, given the time sensitivity, safety, and readiness implications of the investigation's findings, the safety investigation process "is given primacy in access to evidence, witnesses, and the mishap scene."

Chapter 3, "[Legal] Investigations," notes that DoDI 6055.7 requires each Service to conduct both a safety and legal investigation into certain types of accidents, and that the guidance for conducting legal investigations is explained in AR 385-40, AR 27-20 [Claims], "and in the case of fatal training/operational accidents, this regulation."

AR 735-5, "Policies and Procedures for Property Accountability," dated June 10, 2002

The Regulation establishes Army policies and procedures for accounting for Army property, to include property that is damaged or destroyed. Paragraph 14-19, "Destruction of contaminated clothing and equipment," authorizes replacement of contaminated individual clothing and an adjustment to property records for contaminated organizational clothing and individual equipment destroyed by direction of medical authority. The destruction must be documented in a memorandum signed by the unit commander which names the medical officer who directed the destruction.

Joint Publication 4-06, "Joint Tactics, Techniques, and Procedures for Mortuary Affairs in Joint Operations," dated August 28, 1996

Appendix B, Subparagraph 4.a, "Personal Effects on Remains," states that when the remains of deceased personnel arrive at the unit marshaling area, staff should check the remains for personal effects and organizational equipment. The paragraph further directs,

> Remove serviceable organizational and government equipment from the remains and return serviceable equipment to the appropriate supply activity. Unserviceable equipment and all clothing are left on the remains.

USASOC Regulation 385-1, "Safety - Accident Prevention and Reporting," dated March 1, 2000

The Regulation applies to USASOC subordinate commands, to include the 75th Ranger Regiment. Subparagraph 1-5.f charges commanders to ensure that the accident investigation and reporting requirements of AR 385-40 and this regulation are accomplished. Similarly, Paragraph 3-1 charges all USASOC units to comply with the requirements of AR 385-40 and this regulation, and Paragraph 3-3 requires all Army accidents to be investigated and reported to the immediate commander whose operation, personnel, or equipment is involved, and to the USASOC Safety Office. Subparagraph 3-6.g requires major subordinate units to establish procedures to ensure a unit experiencing an accident involving a fatality immediately notifies the USASOC Emergency Operations Center.

Facts

As a preliminary matter, to understand who was responsible to report and investigate CPL Tillman's death, it is important to note that military forces are generally subject to multiple chains of command and control, with the two principal ones being the operational chain of command and the administrative chain of command. The operational chain of command exercises operational control over assigned forces. Operational control normally provides full authority to organize commands and forces and to employ those forces as the commander in operational control considers necessary to accomplish assigned missions. It does not, in and of itself, include authoritative direction for logistics or matters of administration, discipline, internal organization, or unit training.

The operational chain of command for CPL Tillman's unit -- 2nd Platoon, A Company, 2nd Battalion, 75th Ranger Regiment -- for the operation during which he was killed was

1 Headquarters, Operations Team

2 Headquarters, 75th Ranger Regiment (Forward)

3 Headquarters, Joint Task Force

4 CENTCOM

The first GCMCA in that operational chain of command was the Commander, CENTCOM.

The administrative chain of command exercises administrative control over assigned forces. Administrative control is the direction or exercise of authority over subordinate or other organizations in respect to administration and support, including discipline, personnel management, control of resources and equipment, and other matters not included in the operational missions of the subordinate or other organizations. The administrative chain of command for CPL Tillman's unit was

1 Commander, 2nd Battalion, 75th Ranger Regiment

2 Commander, 75th Ranger Regiment

3 Commander, USASOC

The first GCMCA in the administrative chain of command was the Commander, USASOC. As a further point, we note that as a command within the Department of the Army, USASOC (as well as its subordinate units such as the 75th Ranger Regiment) is subject to Department of the Army regulations and guidance.

1. Captain [REDACTED]'s Investigation

Facts

Testimony established that on the evening of April 22, 2004, after the incident that killed CPL Tillman and the AMF Soldier, and wounded 1LT [REDACTED] and SPC [REDACTED], both First Sergeant (1SG) [REDACTED], Company First Sergeant, and Captain (CPT) [REDACTED], Commander, A Company, traveled separately to join 2nd Platoon at the scene. That night PFC [REDACTED] told 1SG [REDACTED] that PFC [REDACTED] believed he was fired on by members of Serial 2. At approximately sunrise on April 23, 1SG [REDACTED] told CPT [REDACTED] that 1SG [REDACTED] suspected the incident involved fratricide.

On the morning of April 23, 2004, Lieutenant Colonel (LTC) [REDACTED], Commander, 2nd Battalion, who had been several miles away from the site on patrol with B Company, also arrived at the scene. Shortly after his arrival, LTC [REDACTED] heard individually from CPT [REDACTED], 1SG [REDACTED], and Command Sergeant Major [REDACTED], Regimental Sergeant Major (who was with Serial 2 on April 22), that each believed the incident was possible fratricide and should be investigated. LTC [REDACTED] testified that he decided to initiate an investigation and appointed as investigating officer CPT [REDACTED], Commander, Headquarters and Headquarters Company, 2nd Battalion, who was located at the battalion forward operating base (FOB). By midday on April 23, LTC [REDACTED] informed Colonel (COL) James C. Nixon, Commander, 75th Ranger Regiment, who was operating from a separate location in Afghanistan, that LTC [REDACTED] suspected fratricide and had initiated an investigation.

* * * *

2. Lieutenant Colonel [REDACTED]'s Investigation

* * * *

3. Brigadier General Jones' Investigation

* * * *

B. Did responsible officials comply with applicable standards for notification of next of kin with regard to Corporal Tillman's death and related investigations?

* * * *

C. Did responsible officials comply with applicable standards for award of the Silver Star to Corporal Tillman?

* * * *

We recommend that the Acting Secretary of the Army, the approval authority for the Silver Star, review CPL Tillman's valorous award recommendation and take appropriate action after considering an accurate analysis of the facts and circumstances leading to CPL Tillman's death by friendly fire on April 22, 2004.

We also recommend that the Acting Secretary address and take action as he deems appropriate for the failure of LTC [REDACTED], COL Nixon, and MG McChrystal, to submit an accurate Silver Star recommendation, that either recognized CPL Tillman's death by friendly fire, or alerted Acting Secretary Brownlee to the special circumstances of a pending friendly fire investigation, in advance of his considering CPL Tillman's Silver Star recommendation.

We further recommend that the Acting Secretary address and take action as he deems appropriate for LTG Kensinger's failure to alert Acting Secretary Brownlee that friendly fire was suspected.

V. CONCLUSIONS

1 COL Nixon failed to initiate, through the chain of command, timely notification to the Army Safety Center and CENTCOM of suspected friendly fire in CPL Tillman's death. As a result, neither organization could comply with its respective responsibility to assess the need for a centralized safety investigation or to convene a legal investigation.

2 CENTCOM failed to issue written implementing guidance required by DoDI 6055.7, "Accident Investigation, Reporting, and Record Keeping."

3 Each of the three AR 15-6 investigations conducted into the death of CPL Tillman was deficient, and thereby contributed to inaccuracies, misunderstandings, and perceptions of concealment. Those deficiencies included:

* CPT [REDACTED] and LTC [REDACTED] were not appointed as investigating officers by a GCMCA or at the direction of the CENTCOM Commander.

* CPT [REDACTED] and LTC [REDACTED] failed to visit the scene to visually reenact the incident, secure physical evidence, take photographs, or obtain accurate measurements.

* CPT [REDACTED] and LTC [REDACTED] failed to interview all relevant witnesses and address inconsistencies in witness testimony.

* CPT [REDACTED] failed to preserve or document real evidence.

* CPT [REDACTED] and MAJ [REDACTED], with the apparent concurrence of LTC [REDACTED], withheld from the AFME and CID the fact that friendly fire was suspected in the death of CPL Tillman, thereby impeding completion of the AFME's final autopsy report.

* LTC [REDACTED] drew conclusions not supported by evidence included in his report.

* BG Jones failed to interview all of the Rangers in Serials 1 and 2 to resolve the uncertainty in the sequence of events that occurred on April 22, 2004.

* BG Jones failed to apply relevant standards and assign accountability for the mishandling of physical evidence in the days following CPL Tillman's death.

* BG Jones failed to fully address the next of kin notification issue as a violation of applicable regulations.

* BG Jones failed to pursue inaccuracies related to the Silver Star award, reached findings not supported by testimony, and, in fact, exacerbated the situation by sharing those findings with family members, senior Army officials, and Members of Congress during official briefings.

* BG Jones failed to pursue misrepresentations on the part of LTG Kensinger related to the next of kin notification issue.

4 LTG Kensinger failed to timely appoint a safety board to investigate the fratricide incident as required by Army regulation.

5 LTG Kensinger provided misleading testimony to BG Jones and this Office when he denied that he knew friendly fire was suspected before the memorial service for CPL Tillman.

6 Responsible Army officials failed to notify the primary next of kin as soon as they reasonably suspected friendly fire.

* COL Nixon was accountable for his decision to delay notification to the primary next of kin until the completion of the friendly fire investigation.

* LTG Kensinger was also accountable as he was the commander with administrative control over the 75th Ranger Regiment, and was in a position to inform the primary next of kin prior to or immediately after CPL Tillman's memorial service but decided not to do so.

7 Responsible officials failed to comply with the Army military award regulation when they submitted a Silver Star recommendation that included inaccurate information and a misleading citation that implied CPL Tillman died by enemy fire.

* LTC [REDACTED], COL Nixon, and MG McChrystal are accountable for the inaccurate award recommendation.

* MG McChrystal and LTG Kensinger are accountable for the failure to inform the award approval authority (Acting Secretary Brownlee) of suspected friendly fire.

VI. RECOMMENDATIONS

We recommend that the Acting Secretary of the Army take appropriate corrective action with respect to the officials whom we identified as accountable for the regulatory violations and errors in judgment that are described in this review. Additionally we recommend that the Acting Secretary initiate a review of the Silver Star award to ensure that it meets regulatory requirements. We note that the Army has already taken action to delay approval of posthumous valor awards until completion of pending investigations and has strengthened guidance concerning next of kin notifications.

We recommend that the Commander, CENTCOM, issue written implementing guidance required by DoDI 6055.7.

1 By what authority and for what purpose did the Army Inspector General request that the DoD Office of Inspector General conduct an independent review of concerns expressed by Corporal Tillman's father regarding the nature of Corporal Tillman's death and its aftermath, including a third investigation completed by an Army general officer in January 2005?

2 Why do Army regulations require that investigating officers "be senior to any person whose conduct or performance of duty may be investigated, or against whom adverse findings or recommendations may be made," with limited exceptions?

3 Why did the DoD Inspector General's findings of accountability for, (a) "LTG Kensinger provid[ing] misleading testimony to BG Jones and th[e DoD Office of Inspector General] when he denied that he knew friendly fire was suspected before the memorial service for CPL Tillman," and (b) "the failure to inform the award approval authority (Acting Secretary [of the Army] Brownlee) of suspected friendly fire" only reach as far as LTG Kensinger and MG McChrystal respectively?

4 How does the "misleading testimony" of an Army Lieutenant General implicate the statutory leadership standard enacted by Congress in 1997, that:

> All commanding officers and others in authority in the Army are required - (1) to show in themselves a good example of virtue, honor, patriotism, and subordination; (2) to be vigilant in inspecting the conduct of all persons who are placed under their command; (3) to guard against and suppress all dissolute and immoral practices, and to correct, according to the laws and regulations of the Army, all persons who are guilty of them; and (4) to take all necessary and proper measures, under the laws, regulations, and customs of the Army, to promote and safeguard the morale, the physical well-being, and the gen-

eral welfare of the officers and enlisted persons under their command or charge?[16]

5 Should the civilian Secretaries of the military departments, i.e., the Secretaries of the Army, Navy, and Air Force, be held accountable to the same leadership standard enacted by Congress in 1997 for, "All commanding officers and others in authority in [each of the military departments]"? Should the Secretary of Defense be held to the same leadership standard?

6 By what authority and for what purpose would the Inspector General of the Department of Defense hold himself to the statutory leadership standard enacted by Congress for, "All commanding officers and others in authority in the Army," Navy, and Air Force respectively?

---

[1] Inspector General Act of 1978, as amended, §8(c).

[2] Sequential referral means that the nominee is vetted first by the Senate Committee with primary jurisdiction over the executive branch department or agency to which the Inspector General is to be appointed, after which the nomination is referred to the Senate Homeland Security and Governmental Affairs Committee for further vetting at the discretion of the Chairman of that Committee.

[3] *See* Inspector General Act of 1978, as amended, §5.

[4] Michael Hastings, "The Runaway General: Stanley McChrystal, Obama's top commander in Afghanistan, has seized control of the war by never taking his eye off the real enemy: The wimps in the White House," *Rolling Stone* 1108/1109, July 8-22, 2010, on newsstands Friday, June 25 (http://www.rollingstone.com/politics/news/17390/119236?RS_show_page=0).

[5] Review of Matters Related to the Death of Corporal Patrick Tillman, U.S. Army," Report Number IPO2007E011, March 26, 2007. The entire report is available in redacted form at http://www.defenselink.mil/home/pdf/Tillman_Redacted_Web_0307.pdf

[6] We initiated our review in response to a request from the Army Inspector General, who determined that an independent examination was needed after the third Army investigation failed to resolve issues raised by the Tillman family.

[7] Based on initial Army investigations, some of the Service members involved in the incident received non-judicial punishment for dereliction of duty under Article 15 of the Uniform Code of Military Justice.

[8] In 2005 the Army Safety Center was renamed the Army Combat Readiness Center.

[9] Service members involved in this incident were at the time members of the U.S. Army, 75th Ranger Regiment, and its subordinate units unless otherwise identified.

[10] ILT [REDACTED] like many other Service members involved in the friendly fire incident and its aftermath, has since been promoted. However, in this report, we will identify Service members using the rank and position that they held at the time of events at issue unless otherwise noted.

[11] A "safety" investigation is conducted to determine the cause of an accident with the sole purpose of preventing future accidents. In general, safety investigation reports are privileged and not releasable outside safety channels. A "legal" investigation is undertaken to inquire into all the facts and circumstances surrounding an accident, as well as to obtain and preserve all available evidence for use in litigation, claims, disciplinary actions, or adverse administrative actions.

[12] The phrase "primary next of kin" is defined in DoDI 1300.18, "Military Personnel Casualty Matters, Policies, and Procedures," as the unremarried surviving spouse.

[13] Army publications refer to "legal" and "safety" investigations as "collateral" and "accident" investigations, respectively.

[14] A later paragraph of the Regulation refers to the centralized investigation as a "USASC [U.S. Army Safety Center] accident investigation board."

[15] With regard to the appointment of single investigating officer versus a board of officers, we find AR 600-34 (which requires only a single investigating officer) to be controlling in this case rather than AR 600-8-1 (which requires a board of officers). AR 600-34 specifically addresses legal investigations of friendly fire cases and was published more recently than AR 600-8-1. Additionally, the most recent version of AR 600-8-1, dated April 7, 2006, gives the appointing authority the option of appointing either a single officer or a board of at least three officers to inquire into the suspected friendly fire incident.

[16] 10 U.S.C. §3583 ("Requirement of exemplary conduct"); *see* 10 U.S.C. §§ 5947 & 8583 (same leadership standard for the Naval Services and Air Force respectively); Continental Congress, "Rules for the Regulation of the Navy of the United Colonies of North America" (1775), Article 1 (www.history.navy.mil) (original 1775 version of the same leadership standard); Continental Congress, "Articles of War" (1775) (A November 1775 Amendment required not only that an officer found guilty of fraud "be *ipso facto* cashiered, and deemed unfit for further service as an officer," but also that "it be added in the punishment, that the crime, name, place of abode, and punishment of the delinquent be published in the news papers, in and about the camp, and of that colony from which the offender came, or usually resides: after which it shall be deemed scandalous in any officer to associate with him.").

CHAPTER 10. INTELLIGENCE OVERSIGHT:

Why Didn't We Know About 9/11 Beforehand?

The Conventions of a number of the States having, at the time of adopting the Constitution, expressed a desire, in order to prevent misconstruction or abuse of its powers, that further declaratory and restrictive clauses should be added, and as extending the ground of public confidence in the Government will best insure the beneficent ends of its institution...

* * *

The powers not delegated to the United States by the Constitution, nor prohibited by it to the States, are reserved to the States respectively, or to the people.

U.S. Constitution, Preamble to Bill of Rights and Amendment X

Oversight of the intelligence activities of the United States federal government is a shared responsibility of the Executive and Legislative branches of the national government.[1] These two branches, together with the Judiciary in cases and controversies within the jurisdiction of federal courts, include a number of structural checks on governmental abuses of power in the realm of intelligence activities. Inspectors General, as explained in this chapter, serve a vital role in these structural checks on abuses of governmental power.

For over three decades, Executive Order 12333, titled "United States Intelligence Activities," has been the primary regulatory instrument guiding the United States intelligence community. It directs that intelligence activities be conducted in a "responsible manner that is consistent with the Constitution and applicable law and respectful of the principles upon which the United States was founded."[2] The most recent amendments to Executive Order 12333, issued in 2008, continue to emphasize these principles:

> Timely, accurate, and insightful information about the activities, capabilities, plans, and intentions of foreign powers, organizations, and persons, and their agents, is essential to informed decisionmaking in the areas of national security, national defense, and foreign relations. Collection of such information is a priority objective and will be pursued in a vigorous, innovative, and responsible manner that is consistent with the Constitution and applicable law and respectful of the principles upon which the United States was founded.[3]

"Principles Upon Which the United States Was Founded"
(as applied to Intelligence Oversight)

In order fully to understand the concept of Intelligence Oversight, one must first understand the following foundational assumptions:

1   By constitutional design, the federal government of the United States of America is a government of limited powers, in contrast to the governments of each State within the United States, to which the Tenth Amendment acknowledges, "The powers not delegated to the United States by the Constitution, nor prohibited by it to the States, are reserved . . ."[4]; and

2   All three branches of the national government are bound by the principle of limited national government formalized in the Tenth Amendment.

The Constitution established a system of shared powers, in both a vertical direction (between the national government and the States), and horizontally within the federal government. Under Article I, "The Congress shall have Power . . . to pay the Debts and provide for the common Defense and general Welfare of the United States...; To define and punish Piracies and Felonies committed on the high Seas, and Offenses against the Law of Nations; To declare War...; To raise and support Armies,...; To provide and maintain a Navy; To make rules for the Government and Regulation of the land and naval Forces; to provide for calling forth the Militia, and for governing such Part of them as may be employed in the Service of the United States..."[5] Under Article II, "The President shall be Commander in Chief of the Army and Navy of the United States, and of the Militia of the several States, when called into the actual Service of the United States."[6]

Under the constitutional "separation of powers," if the President abuses his power as Commander in Chief, both the Legislative and the Judicial branches serve as structural "checks" on such abuses, the former through the "power of the purse," the latter through the power of judicial review.

In 1936 and then again in 1992, the United States Supreme Court provided a 10th Amendment-based test for checking abuses of power by the national government. In 1992, the Supreme Court reaffirmed its own limited judicial review role in the context of striking down the Low-Level Radioactive Waste Policy Act of 1985 as unconstitutional:

> Our task would be the same even if one could prove that federalism secured no advantages to anyone. It consists not of devising our preferred system of government, but of understanding and applying the framework set forth in the Constitution. "The question is not what power the Federal Government ought to have but what powers in fact have been given by the people." *United States v. Butler*, 297 U.S. 1, 63 (1936).[7]

Since 1992, the Supreme Court has struck down at least four efforts by Congress to exercise national power without constitutional authority:

* *New York v. United States*, 505 U.S. 144 (1992) (striking down the Low-Level Radioactive Waste Policy Act of 1985);

* *United States v. Lopez*, 514 U.S. 549 (1995) (striking down the Gun-Free School Zones Act of 1990);

* *Boerne v. Flores*, 521 U.S. 507 (1997) (striking down the Religious Freedom Restoration Act of 1993); and

* *Printz v. United States*, 521 U.S. 898 (1997) (striking down the 1993 Brady Act).

Intelligence Oversight Rules and Procedures

"U.S. person" is defined by Executive Order 12333 to mean "a United States citizen, an alien known by the intelligence agency concerned to be a permanent resident alien, an unincorporated association substantially composed of United States citizens or permanent resident aliens, or a corporation incorporated in the United States, except for a corporation directed and controlled by a foreign government or governments." Rules and procedures for the collection, retention, and dissemination of information about "U.S. persons," while addressed separately in various intelligence community regulations and directives implementing Executive Order 12333, are not exclusive to the intelligence community. For example, DoD Directive 5200.27, titled "Acquisition of Information Concerning Persons and Organizations not Affiliated with the Department of Defense," prescribes a general prohibition against, "collecting, reporting processing, or storing information on individuals or organizations not affiliated with the Department of Defense, except in those limited circumstances where such information is essential to the accomplishment of the Department of Defense missions..."[8]

Intelligence activities, by their very nature, create potential for abuses of power in the collection, retention, or dissemination of information about U.S. persons. Accordingly, the intelligence community has more detailed rules and regulations to constrain such abuses. The

Department of Defense and each of the military departments has its own version of implementing rules and procedures for Executive Order 12333's general admonition that intelligence activities be conducted in a "responsible manner that is consistent with the Constitution and applicable law and respectful of the principles upon which the United States was founded."[9] For example, the Department of Defense emphasizes that:

> All DoD intelligence and CI activities shall be carried out pursuant to the authorities and restrictions of the U.S. Constitution, applicable law, Reference (c) [Executive Order 12333], the policies and procedures authorized herein, and other relevant DoD policies authorized by Reference (b) [DoD Directive 5143.01, "Under Secretary of Defense for Intelligence," November 23, 2005]. Special emphasis shall be given to the protection of the constitutional rights and privacy of U.S. persons.[10]

In addition to its Directive on "DoD Intelligence Activities," the Department of Defense has a detailed Regulation titled, "Procedures governing the activities of DoD intelligence components that affect United States persons," which prescribes standards for the collection, retention, and dissemination of information about U.S. persons by intelligence components within the Department of Defense.[11] This Regulation includes a slightly expanded version of the definition of the term "United States Person" in Executive Order 12333:

> (1) A United States citizen;

> (2) An alien known by the DoD intelligence component concerned to be a permanent resident alien;

> (3) An unincorporated association substantially composed of United States citizens or permanent resident aliens;

> (4) A corporation incorporated in the United States, except for a corporation directed and controlled by a foreign government or governments. A corporation or corporate subsidiary incorporated abroad, even if partially or wholly

owned by a corporation incorporated in the United States, is not a United States person.[12]

The DoD Intelligence Oversight Regulation also prescribes duties of each individual DoD employee, "including contractors and persons otherwise acting at the direction of such an agency,"[13] and of all Inspectors General for identifying and reporting "questionable activities." The Regulation defines these as, "any conduct that constitutes, or is related to, an intelligence activity that may violate the law, any Executive Order or Presidential directive, including E.O. 12333, reference (a)), or applicable DoD policy, including this Regulation"[14]:

a Each employee shall report any questionable activity to the General Counsel or Inspector General for the DoD intelligence component concerned, or to the DoD General Counsel or the ATSD(IO).

b Inspectors General, as part of their inspection of DoD intelligence components, and General Counsels, as part of their oversight responsibilities shall seek to determine if such components are involved in any questionable activities. If such activities have been or are being undertaken, the matter shall be investigated . . . . If such activities have been undertaken but were not reported, the Inspector General shall also ascertain the reason for such failure and recommend appropriate corrective action.

c Inspectors General, as part of their oversight responsibilities, shall, as appropriate, ascertain whether any organization, staffs, or offices within their respective jurisdictions but not otherwise specifically identified as DoD intelligence components, are being used for foreign intelligence or counterintelligence purposes to which Part 2 of E.O. 12333, (reference (a)), applies, and, if so, shall ensure the activities of such components are in compliance with the Regulation and applicable DoD policy.

d   Inspectors General, as part of their inspection of DoD intelligence components, shall ensure that procedures exist within such components for the reporting of questionable activities, and that employees of such components are aware of their responsibilities to report such activities.[15]

While all Inspectors General are required to receive and either to investigate or to refer out for investigation, allegations of "questionable activities" involving possible abuses of power within the intelligence community, the Department of Defense has established an Intelligence Oversight Officer who is required by Directive to coordinate with the DoD Office of Inspector General.[16] That DoD Intelligence Oversight Officer is the Assistant to the Secretary of Defense for Intelligence Oversight (ATSD(IO)), and serves as, "the focal point for all contacts with the Intelligence Oversight Board of the President's Foreign Intelligence Advisory Board (since renamed the President's Intelligence Advisory Board) pursuant to [Executive Order 12863, "President's Foreign Intelligence Advisory Board," September 13, 1993, as amended by Executive Order 13070, December 15, 1997; Executive Order 13301, May 14, 2003; and Executive Order 13376, April 13, 2005], and shall perform the responsibilities assigned in DoD Directive 5148.11"[17]:

> The Assistant to the Secretary of Defense for Intelligence Oversight shall serve as the principal staff assistant and advisor to the Secretary and Deputy Secretary of Defense for the independent oversight of all intelligence, counterintelligence, and intelligence-related activities (hereafter referred to collectively as "intelligence activities") in the Department of Defense. In this capacity, the ATSD(IO) shall ensure that all intelligence activities performed by any of the DoD Components are conducted in compliance with Federal law, Executive orders, Presidential directives, and DoD Directives System issuances.[18]

The duties of the ATSD(IO) include, "Report[ing] the following to the Secretary and Deputy Secretary of Defense, and the Intelligence Oversight Board of the President's Foreign Intelligence Advisory

Board . . . at least quarterly, in coordination with the [General Counsel], DoD":

* Significant oversight activities undertaken.

* Significant DoD intelligence activities of questionable legality or propriety, the investigative action on them, and the current status until the matter is resolved.

* Matters of concern or substance arising out of inspections and investigations conducted by the ATSD(IO); the DoD GC's accounting of applications to the Foreign Intelligence Surveillance Court; and, significant items from the intelligence oversight reports submitted to the ATSD(IO) by the DoD Components.[19]

In carrying out these duties, the ATSD(IO) is authorized by the Secretary of Defense to, "Require an Inspector General or other cognizant investigative official of a DoD Component to report allegations of improprieties or illegalities of intelligence activities by, or within, a DoD Component."[20]

The ATSD(IO) and the General Counsel, DoD, shall report in a timely manner to the White House Intelligence Oversight Board all activities that come to their attention that are reasonably believed to be illegal or contrary to Executive Order or Presidential directive. They will also advise appropriate officials of the Office of the Secretary of Defense of such activities.[21]

The major DoD Components, including the military departments, have their own rules and procedures for how each carries out Intelligence Oversight activities.[22]

Posse Comitatus Act

Closely allied to Executive Order 12333 as a check against abuses of federal power is the Posse Comitatus Act. Posse Comitatus was enacted by Congress in 1878 to restrict domestic law enforcement activities of the United States military in response to abuses committed during the reconstruction period following the Civil War.[23] The Posse Comitatus Act makes it a federal crime to use, "any part of the Army or the Air Force as a posse comitatus or otherwise to execute the laws," unless "expressly authorized by the Constitution or Act of Congress":

> Whoever, except in cases and under circumstances expressly authorized by the Constitution or Act of Congress, willfully uses any part of the Army or the Air Force as a posse comitatus or otherwise to execute the laws shall be fined under this title or imprisoned not more than two years, or both.[24]

Although the statute on its face only applies to the Army, "the Air Force is covered under the law by later amendment because its origins lie within the Army... [I]t is followed by the Department of the Navy through incorporation of its proscriptions into regulations issued by the Secretary of the Navy."[25]

Consistent with this longstanding criminal prohibition by Congress, Department of Defense regulations prohibit the following forms of direct assistance to civilian law enforcement agencies unless otherwise expressly authorized by federal statute – such as, for example but not limited to, the Inspector General Act of 1978, as amended:

* Interdiction of a vehicle, vessel, aircraft, or other similar activity;

* A search or seizure;

* An arrest, apprehension, stop and frisk, or similar activity;

* Use of military personnel for surveillance or pursuit of individuals, or as undercover agents, informants, investigators, or interrogators.[26]

Because both the Posse Comitatus Act and Executive Order 12333 involve checks on abuses of power by the federal government, and because the occasions for such abuses can sometimes overlap in the context of intelligence activities, Posse Comitatus Act training is often combined with Intelligence Oversight training, especially within the intelligence community, typically during the course of a periodic Intelligence Oversight Inspection conducted by an Inspector General.

The following are selected excerpts from "Alleged Misconduct by Senior DoD Officials Concerning the Able Danger Program and Lieutenant Colonel Anthony A. Shaffer, U.S. Army Reserve," September 18, 2006.[27]

DEPARTMENT OF DEFENSE
OFFICE OF THE INSPECTOR GENERAL

REPORT OF INVESTIGATION

CASE NUMBER
H05L97905217

DATE

SEP 1 8 2006

ALLEGED MISCONDUCT BY SENIOR DOD OFFICIALS
CONCERNING THE ABLE DANGER PROGRAM AND
LIEUTENANT COLONEL ANTHONY A. SHAFFER, U.S. ARMY RESERVE

Prepared by the Office of the
Deputy Inspector General for Investigations

The course of this investigation, in particular the central issues, was framed through a series of requests from Members of Congress, the Defense Intelligence Agency (DIA), and Lieutenant Colonel (LTC) Anthony A. Shaffer, U.S. Army Reserve.

In letters to the Secretary of Defense dated October 7, 2005, and to this Office dated October 18, 2005, Representative Curt Weldon requested an explanation for the suspension of LTC Shaffer's security clearance and "a detailed report on the destruction of LTC Shaffer's documents and other files." In a floor speech on October 21, 2005, Representative Weldon alleged that DIA included Government property and classified documents in a shipment of personal effects to LTC Shaffer.

In a letter to the Secretary of Defense dated October 20, 2005, Chairman Duncan Hunter, House Armed Services Committee, requested that we "conduct an independent review of the facts and circumstances surrounding DIA' s actions to revoke LTC Shaffer's security clearance."

In a letter to this Office dated October 21, 2005, Chairman Charles E. Grassley, Senate Finance Committee, asked that we review LTC Shaffer's representations concerning Able Danger's "alleged early warnings" of the September 11, 2001 (9/11), terrorist attack and whether LTC Shaffer was "subjected to any action which constituted reprisal for disclosures related to Able Danger."

In a letter to this Office dated December 20, 2005, Senators John McCain and Joseph Lieberman requested that we investigate allegations that Able Danger identified 9/11 terrorists before the attack, DoD failed to share that information with cognizant Government agencies, and DoD closed down Able Danger prematurely, improperly destroying Able Danger records.

In a joint letter to this Office dated February 8, 2006, Representatives Peter Hoekstra and Frank R. Wolf asked that we "investigate what intelligence the Able Danger program generated regarding al Qaeda, Mohammed Atta, and other 9/11 highjackers," and whether, if generated, that intelligence was shared with the FBI. Additionally, Representatives Hoekstra and Wolf asked us to investigate alleged destruction of Able Danger intelligence and the nature of Able Danger information shared with the 9/11 Commission.

By letter dated November 1, 2005, the General Counsel, DIA, asked us to conduct all independent assessment of matters involving LTC Shaffer. Because the background and fact patterns for allegations involving Able Danger and LTC Shaffer are similar, we address them in a single report to avoid duplicative effort and to provide a single repository for the results of our investigative work.

Although many aspects of the Able Danger program remain classified, this report is unclassified to promote maximum utility and avoid delays that would attend a classified issuance. We believe the issues are fully addressed without the inclusion of classified information.

Table Of Contents

VI.   RECOMMENDATIONS

Alleged Misconduct By Senior DOD Officials Concerning
The Able Danger Program And Lieutenant Colonel
Anthony A. Shaffer, U.S. Army Reserve

I.   INTRODUCTION AND SUMMARY

We initiated the investigation to address allegations that senior DoD officials mismanaged a DoD antiterrorist program known as
"Able Danger," and that in doing so they sought to end the military and
civilian careers of a key proponent of Able Danger, Lieutenant Colonel
(LTC) Anthony A. Shaffer, a member of the U.S. Army Reserve who
also held a civilian position as a senior intelligence officer in the Defense Intelligence Agency (DIA).[28]

Allegations concerning Able Danger became public in August
2005 when media sources reported allegations, made by LTC Shaffer,
that the identities of terrorists involved in the attack of September 11,
200f *(9111)*, were discovered by Able Danger before the attack, but
DoD officials prohibited Able Danger personnel from sharing that information with law enforcement authorities. Subsequently, Members of
Congress contacted this Office requesting investigations into unfavorable actions allegedly being taken by DIA officials against LTC Shaffer
for making those allegations, as well as into the allegations themselves.
In response to those communications, we formulated the following
issues/allegations that warranted investigation and will be addressed in
this report:

Allegations involving the Able Danger program:

*   Did the Able Danger team identify Mohammed Atta and
     other 9/11 terrorists before the 9/11 attack?

*   Did DoD officials prohibit Able Danger members from
     sharing relevant terrorist information with the Federal Bu-
     reau ofInvestigation (FBI), the Central Intelligence Agency

(CIA), or other agencies which could have acted on that information?

* Did DoD officials improperly direct the destruction of Able Danger mission related data?

* Did DoD officials terminate the Able Danger program prematurely?

* Did DoD officials execute the Able Danger mission in compliance with applicable intelligence oversight guidance?

* Did DIA officials, when cleaning out LTC Shaffer's civilian office, improperly destroy *Able* Danger documents that LTC Shaffer had accumulated?[29]

* Did DIA officials improperly ship Government property and classified documents to LTC Shaffer's attorney when disposing of what they believed to be LTC Shaffer's personal property?

Allegations of reprisal against LTC Shaffer:

* Did DIA officials take action to suspend LTC Shaffer's access to classified information and revoke his security clearance in reprisal for his communications to Members of Congress or the National Commission on Terrorist Attacks Upon the United States (9/11 Commission) regarding Able Danger -- or in reprisal for his earlier communications to the DIA Inspector General (IG)?[30]

* Did DIA officials issue LTC Shaffer unfavorable (military) Officer Evaluation Reports (OERs) in reprisal for his communications with the 9/11 Commission staff regarding Able Danger?

Conclusions concerning Able Danger issues

We found that in October 1999, General (GEN) Henry H. Shelton, U.S. Army, then-Chairman of the Joint Chiefs of Staff, directed the U.S. Special Operations Command (USSOCOM) to develop a "campaign plan"; that is, an operational concept that when implemented would obtain detailed information on international terrorist organizations, identifying terrorist leaders, command and control infrastructures, and supporting institutions.

The unclassified name for the initiative to develop such a campaign plan was "Able Danger."

An "Operational Concepts Working Group" consisting of *six* to eight members was established at USSOCOM to produce the campaign plan, which called for the use of state-of-the-art information technology tools to gather information on international terrorists from Government data bases and open sources (to include the World Wide Web) with the initial focus on al Qaeda. The campaign plan was presented to GEN Shelton in January 2001. Upon presenting the campaign plan to GEN Shelton, USSOCOM's tasking was satisfied, the Able Danger mission was terminated, and the Able Danger team disbanded. Data mining and visualization tools similar to those employed by Able Danger to formulate the campaign plan were subsequently incorporated into intelligence gathering efforts at USSOCOM.

We concluded that prior to September 11, 2001, Able Danger team members did not identify Mohammed Atta or any other 9/11 hijacker. While we interviewed four witnesses who claimed to have seen a chart depicting Mohammed Atta and possibly other terrorists or "cells" involved in 9/11, we determined that their recollections were not accurate. Testimony by witnesses who claimed to have seen such a chart varied significantly from each other, and in some instances testimony obtained in reinterviews was inconsistent with testimony that witnesses provided earlier. In particular, we found inaccurate LTC Shaffer's assertions regarding the existence ofpre-9h1I information on the terrorists and his suggestion that DoD officials thwarted efforts to share Able Danger information with law enforcement authorities. In drawing this conclusion, we found particularly persuasive the sworn testimony of witnesses who disavowed statements and claims that LTC Shaffer attributed to them.

The preponderance of witness testimony indicated that recollections concerning the identification of 9/11 terrorists were linked to a single chart depicting al Qaeda cells responsible for pre-9/11 terrorist attacks, which was obtained but not produced by the Able Danger team.

That chart (Figure 1 of this report) was produced by Orion Scientific Corporation (Orion) in May 1999 and contained the names and/or photographs of 53 terrorists who had been identified and in many cases, incarcerated, before 9/11, including a Brooklyn cell, but it did not identify Mohammed Atta or any of the other 9/11 terrorists. Our review of Able Danger team records found no evidence that Able Danger team members had identified Mohammed Atta or any of the other terrorists who participated in the 9/11 attack.

With respect to allegations concerning prohibited contacts between Able Danger and law enforcement authorities, we found no evidence to corroborate LTC Shaffer's claims that Able Danger members were prohibited by DoD officials from attending meetings he allegedly arranged with the FBI. All witnesses who were in a position to know denied LTC Shaffer's claim that efforts to meet with FBI antiterrorism units were made, much less thwarted by DoD officials. One Able Danger team member alleged that he was prohibited from providing the chart at Figure 1 to the FBI by a senior USSOCOM official sometime in early 2000. However, the senior official did not recall the incident and we are persuaded that the chart would have been of minimal intelligence value to the FBI. Accordingly, any decision to prohibit transfer of the chart would not have been inappropriate under the circumstances.

We found that large quantities of data that had been collected at two locations as part of the Able Danger data mining mission were destroyed. One intelligence analyst told us that he destroyed approximately "2.5 terabytes" of Able Danger data that had been collected at the Land Information Warfare Activity (LIWA), Fort Belvoir, VA, where Able Danger activities were initially located. Additionally, an Able Danger analyst testified that a large quantity of "extraneous" data was destroyed when the Able Danger team departed its second location – a contractor facility in Garland, Texas -- and returned to USSOCOM. We found no basis to conclude that either of those destructions was improper, but rather followed established procedure and violated no regulation.

As indicated above, we concluded that the Able Danger project was appropriately terminated after it had met its objective of producing an antiterrorism campaign plan. Further, we determined that it complied with applicable intelligence oversight guidance.

With respect to allegations concerning the improper disposal of materials located in LTC Shaffer's DIA office, we found no evidence to corroborate LTC Shaffer's assertion that he came to possess a significant volume of Able Danger documents in his DIA office, rendering the allegation of their improper destruction moot. Witnesses whom LTC Shaffer identified as being aware of Able Danger documentation he purportedly stored in his DIA office did not corroborate his assertions in that regard. In particular, Able Danger team members, whom LTC Shaffer asserted had left Able Danger documentation with him for safekeeping on their travel to Washington, D.C., denied doing so. DIA employees responsible for cleaning out LTC Shaffer's office acknowledged destroying some Government documents, but none recalled seeing any documents associated with Able Danger. Accordingly, we concluded the alleged improper destruction did not occur.

We concluded that DIA officials did not improperly ship classified documents or Government property of significant value to LTC Shaffer.[31] We confirmed that DIA shipped seven boxes of personal items to LTC Shaffer's attorney. A member of congressional committee staff provided us four classified documents (six pages) that LTC Shaffer indicated were included in that shipment.[32] However, the evidence was insufficient to conclude that any classified items were in the boxes at the time that DIA officials shipped them. Additionally, LTC Shaffer provided us a Government-owned Global Positioning Satellite (GPS) unit that he said was included in the boxes that were sent to his attorney. We confirmed, by serial number, that this GPS unit had been provided to LTC Shaffer in Afghanistan by a DIA contractor employee, but we found that LTC Shaffer never returned the GPS unit to DIA. As a result, that GPS unit could not have been included by DIA employees in the boxes that were shipped to LTC Shaffer's attorney.

Conclusions concerning reprisal

We concluded that DIA officials did not reprise against LTC Shaffer, in either his civilian or military capacity, for making disclosures regarding Able Danger or, in a separate matter, for his earlier disclosures to the DIA IG regarding alleged misconduct by DIA officials. In that regard, we identified the following communications which warranted consideration during our analysis of alleged reprisal.[33]

* Communications that LTC Shaffer asserted he made to the DIA IG, as part of two investigations during the March to December 2002 period. Although our investigation found that LTC Shaffer was not the source of some of the communications, nevertheless, for purposes of this investigation, we assumed that DIA officials believed that he was the source. (The communications and investigation were not related to Able Danger.)

* Communications during a meeting with staff members of the 9/11 Commission in October 2003, while serving in Afghanistan. LTC Shaffer testified that he told the 9/11 Commission staff members that Able Danger discovered the identity of 9/11 terrorists before the attack but was prevented from sharing that information with law enforcement authorities. However, four witness also present at the meeting unanimously disputed LTC Shaffer's recollection -- testifying, under oath, that LTC Shaffer made no such claims for Able Danger at that meeting.

* Disclosures regarding Able Danger to Members of Congress beginning in February 2005 and to the media beginning in August 2005.

The overriding unfavorable action taken by DIA officials following those disclosures was the final revocation of LTC Shaffer's access to classified information in September 2005 and the revocation of his security clearance in February 2006. That revocation essentially ended LTC Shaffer's career as an intelligence officer, both at OIA and in the Army Reserve.[34]

We concluded that DIA officials would have taken action to revoke LTC Shaffer's access and clearance regardless of his disclosures to the DIA IG, the 9/11 Commission staff members, Members of Congress, or the media. We found that the action was based on misconduct by LTC Shaffer that was substantiated during an official DIA IG investigation taken together with other security-related issues that were not previously sufficient to trigger adverse security action at DIA. Of note, the final decision to revoke LTC Shaffer's access was recommended by a panel of three senior intelligence officers, one of whom was not a DoD employee. Sworn testimony from those panel members compellingly demonstrated that their recommendation regarding LTC Shaffer followed established security guidelines, was justified by circumstances, and would have occurred absent his disclosures. Moreover, our comparison of LTC Shaffer's case to those of other DIA employees who had their access or clearances revoked found no basis to conclude that DIA's actions with respect to LTC Shaffer were outside the norm or otherwise gave evidence of disparate treatment.

Finally, we concluded that an OER issued to LTC Shaffer in September 2004 would have contained the same [REDACTED] ratings had he not made protected communications to the DIA IG and the 9111Commission staff members and, therefore, was not an act of reprisal. However, we found minor procedural anomalies in the processing of LTC Shaffer's OER that warrant review by the Director, DIA.

II.   BACKGROUND

In October 1999 GEN Shelton tasked USSOCOM to develop a campaign plan to deter al Qaeda. As part of the tasking, USSOCOM was directed to employ advanced analytical information technology tools. Further, USSOCOM's campaign plan was to be integrated into an overarching interagency plan. The unclassified name for the tasking was "Able Danger." The Able Danger program was classified "Top Secret" and only personnel with a "need to know" were "read-on" to the program.

GEN Shelton testified that he had no specific recollection of term "Able Danger" or the Able Danger program, but did recall that while he was Chairman of the Joint Chiefs of Staff he was concerned about al Qaeda and the need to develop a holistic view of al Qaeda. GEN Shelton stated,

> the genesis of starting to try to collect on a worldwide basis against terrorists, 'came about as a result of me looking at all the information that was coming into the Chairman's office, and seeing that we would get -- we were just being inundated with information, and it wasn't really intelligence, but little snippets.

USSOCOM's initial goal was to identify al Qaeda's worldwide operations. GEN Peter J. Schoomaker, current Army Chief of Staff, and formerly Commander, USSOCOM, characterized Able Danger as "an effort to put together a campaign plan to address the al Qaeda terrorist network."

The Operational Concepts Working Group (OCWG) -- a term used to identify USSOCOM personnel assigned to produce the campaign plan—represented the core personnel working on Able Danger and ranged from six to eight members. Throughout the duration of Able Danger, various USSOCOM officers and civilian employees augmented the OCWG as necessary. For ease of reference in this report, we refer to the OCWG and its augmentees collectively as the "Able Danger team."

Colonel (Col) [REDACTED], U.S. Air Force, served as the Director of the Able Danger team from June 2000 to January 2001. Col [REDACTED] reported to Major General (MG) Geoffrey C. Lambert, U.S. Army, former Director, Center for Operations, Plans and Policy, USSOCOM. MG Lambert, in turn, reported directly to GEN Schoomaker on issues related to Able Danger. Captain (CAPT) (then-Commander) [REDACTED], U.S. Navy, who was assigned to the Center for Intelligence and Information Operations at USSOCOM, served as the Operations Officer for the Able Danger team from its inception until the end of October 2000. At the time, Rear Admiral (RDML) Thomas W. Steffens, U.S. Navy, was the Director, Center for Intelligence and Information Operations. By the nature of his position, RDML Steffens was involved with the Able Danger mission.

The Able Danger team focused on "identifying and exploiting vulnerabilities associated with al Qaeda's command and control infrastructure, its leadership and supporting organizations." In order to accomplish these goals, the team employed advanced analytic tools and methodologies that were available in the 1999-2000 time frame. It sought to identify linkages and patterns in large volumes of data (data mining) and display the mined data in a user-friendly fashion for intelligence analysts and operations planners (data visualization). The data that the members mined came from Government data bases supplied by various intelligence agencies and organizations as well as open source material. Open source material included information retrieved from the World Wide Web. Additionally, the team attempted to initiate a collaborative environment (chat room) for members of the intelligence community, within and outside DoD, to share information.

The Able Danger team initially arranged to utilize the Joint Warfare Analysis Center (JWAC), Dahlgren, VA, for support. JW *AC,* at that time, offered the Able Danger team an analytical tool called the Situational Influence Assessment Module (SIAM). SIAM allowed users to "construct graphic depictions of complex, cause-and-effect relationships involving uncertainty." GEN Schoomaker stated, "One of the reasons we went to JWAC is I remember telling people that JWAC-type tools would probably be useful to us because we had used them operationally in the past."

On November 22, 1999, an "Initial Planning Conference Announcement" was communicated to the various Able Danger participants. This conference was held January 10-14, 2000, at JWAC. Attendees to the conference represented a wide cross section of the intelligence community and included members of the DIA, CIA, National Reconnaissance Office, National Security Agency, National Geospatial-Intelligence Agency, and other intelligence organizations. The participants used SIAM to attempt to map out the al Qaeda network. Regarding their results, CAPT [REDACTED] testified, "with high-priced help . . . we still couldn't do it . . . it was feckless." Accordingly, other options for support to the Able Danger mission were considered.

CAPT [REDACTED] testified that during the January conference at JWAC, LTC Shaffer approached him and recommended that CAPT [REDACTED] contact Dr. [REDACTED], a civilian intelligence analyst then-working for LIWA. LIWA was a subordinate organization of the U.S. Army Intelligence and Security Command (INSCOM). Accordingly, immediately after that conference, CAPT [REDACTED] visited Dr. [REDACTED] at LIWA and she provided an overview of LIWA's capabilities, showing him various products, CAPT [REDACTED] recalled that, within 3 or 4 days of his LIWA visit, Dr. [REDACTED] provided three charts to LTC Shaffer, who, in turn, delivered them to CAPT [REDACTED] at USSOCOM headquarters in Tampa, Florida.

As discussed at Section IV. A. of this report, the three charts that were provided to CAPT [REDACTED] included two charts that were produced by Orion and one chart that was produced by LIWA. The Orion charts are depicted at Figures 1 and 2.[35] An example of the type of chart that was produced by LIWA and provided to CAPT [REDACTED] is depicted at Figure 3.[36] All three charts are examples of link analysis.

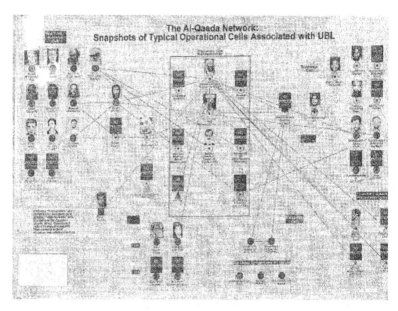

Figure 1.

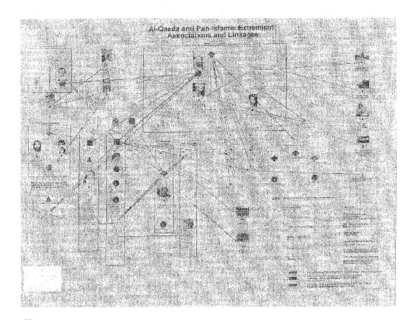

Figure 2.

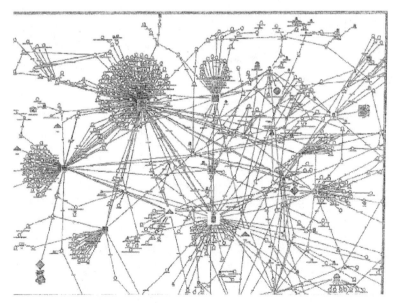

Figure 3.

Subsequent Able Danger conferences were held at JWAC during the periods January 24-27 and February 9-17, 2000. Dr. [REDACTED] and Mr. [REDACTED], formerly an active duty major in the u.s. Army assigned to LIWA as Chief, Intelligence Branch, attended the conference that was held January 24-27, 2000. During this conference CAPT [REDACTED] traveled to LIWA and met with senior officials there to pursue a cooperative association between Able Danger and LIWA.

At the February 2000 JWAC conference, Mr. [REDACTED] attended but Dr. [REDACTED] was prohibited by the LIWA commander from attending. Mr. [REDACTED] stated Dr. [REDACTED] did not attend "because they [INSCOM and LIWA leadership] were not happy with her ability to get along well with others." In a timeline prepared by CAPT [REDACTED] for this Office, an entry for February 14, 2000, provided, "Dr. [REDACTED] removed from program." Dr. [REDACTED] testified she was, thereafter, "very limited" in the support she could do for the Able Danger team and that she was "being minimized." Although we agree that Dr. [REDACTED] role in the Able Danger program itself was limited, we believe she played a significant role in the Able Danger controversy because she subsequently claimed to have seen Mohammed Atta depicted on charts she provided to CAPT [REDACTED] in January 2000. Dr. [REDACTED] also claimed that on September 25, 2001, she had a brief glimpse of a chart prepared before the 9/11 attack, which depicted terrorist activities and which she believed contained a picture of Mohammed Atta.

CAPT [REDACTED] testified that although he was disappointed with the products that had been produced at JWAC, he was very impressed by what he had seen during his two visits to LIWA as well as by the three charts that had been provided to him by Dr. [REDACTED] via LTC Shaffer. CAPT [REDACTED] thereby decided that support for the Able Danger mission should be moved from JWAC to LIWA. However, he indicated that his chain of command essentially ignored his suggestion to move Able Danger mission support to LIWA. Nonetheless, since CAPT [REDACTED] was convinced that LIWA could offer the best assistance, he worked through the command's reluctance to move operations to LIWA. He testified, "I was pretty adamant that we needed to shift. . . . So I started to hook up systems that would allow us in Tampa to have access to the data [at] LIWA."[37]

Though CAPT [REDACTED] was convinced that Able Danger should be associated with LIWA, and appeared to have been receiving some support from LIWA, *it* was not until mid-March 2000 that USSOCOM established a working relationship with LIWA. CAPT [REDACTED] testified that on March 3, 2000, GEN Schoomaker was briefed by the *Able* Danger team on their progress to date. CAPT [REDACTED] testified, "He [GEN Schoomaker] walked over and I sat there and I walked him through a lot of classified discoveries using these tools on the system linked in to [LIWA]." CAPT [REDACTED] stated that within 2 weeks of the March 3, 2000, briefing, LIWA was officially associated with the Able Danger mission. Regarding the March 3, 2000, briefing, GEN Schoomaker stated, "I know that JWAC was probably less useful than what I saw at LIWA. So it was a LIWA kind of thing that people wanted."

LIWA offered a facility with cutting-edge technology that enabled the Able Danger team to process large amounts of both Government and open source data. When the Able Danger team became associated with LIWA, Dr. James E. Heath was the Senior Intelligence and Technical Advisor for INSCOM. Dr. Heath testified that the LIWA suite of technologies included "Oracle data bases, parsers, geographic visualization, [and] relationship [constructors], [which were] essential to us from an intelligence standpoint." He characterized the use of this technology as,

> You have a lot of cool ways to visualize [data] and interact with it, and so now you have this haystack of information . . . these tools have the capability to interact with it, allow you to find needles within that haystack effectively and quickly.

In anticipation of providing extensive support to Able Danger, Mr. [REDACTED] collected approximately 2.5 terabytes of open source data that could serve as a data repository for analytical studies by Able Danger members. However, despite the advanced capability there, LIWA's direct support to Able Danger ultimately consisted primarily of a mid-March 2000 training session for some of the Able Danger intelligence analysts. Dr. [REDACTED], Mr. [REDACTED], and two intelligence analysts under Mr. [REDACTED]'s supervision provided the training support.[38]

Shortly after the March 2000 training session, Lieutenant General (LTG) Robert W. Noonan, Jr., U.S. Army, then-Commanding General, INSCOM, ordered LIWA to limit support for Able Danger to training and familiarizing team members on the LIWA tools. LTG Noonan imposed this limitation because of issues related to collecting data on United States persons that arose during a previous project at LIWA that generated significant interest at the highest levels in DoD. LIWA's decision to limit support to training, without allowing analysis of data, effectively halted meaningful progress by the Able Danger team for about 3 months (March through June 2000).

CAPT [REDACTED] testified that LIWA had not produced anything of significance for Able Danger prior to terminating its support. Other than the three charts he received from Dr. [REDACTED], he assessed the value of the intelligence that had been gained while Able Danger was associated with LIWA as "zero."

Dr. [REDACTED] corroborated CAPT [REDACTED] testimony in that regard, stating that products other than the three charts were of minimal importance to Able Danger. Dr. Heath agreed, describing the LIWA support as "the SOCOM guys come down, just like we had lots of other people come down and sit with the analysts for a week or two, get a sense for what you could do." He added that further support for Able Danger was prohibited by the INSCOM commander until specific authorization from the Office of the Secretary of Defense was received.

CAPT [REDACTED] testified that eventually Dr. [REDACTED] recommended that he move the Able Danger operation to Raytheon Company's Garland, Texas, facility, since LIWA could not support it. Dr. [REDACTED] formerly Chief Scientist, Intelligence Division, Raytheon Company, told us that Raytheon, which set up the LIWA facility in 1997, constructed a backup center at the Garland facility with capabilities that he believed were "actually better but they were at least the same" as those of LIWA. Thereafter, USSOCOM entered into a $750,000 contract with Raytheon Company to provide support to Able Danger for the period July 17 to October 17, 2000.

Dr. [REDACTED] stated that the Garland facility was organized so that Able Danger worked in a secure area separate from Raytheon Company employees, who did not get involved in Able Danger activities. He stated, "Only Special Forces or Government people could go in that room and so they may have had stuff in there, but, you know we weren't allowed to see." Dr. [REDACTED] characterized Raytheon Company's support as,

> Well we provided them the JWICS [Joint Worldwide Intelligence Communications System] lines and analyst workstations and interfaces to national collection systems and secure telephones and faxes and so on. And also provided them know-how on the processes on putting together the whole software and setting up the process for collection and analysis.

When the Able Danger team arrived at the Garland facility the members were disappointed that the capabilities they were led to believe would be in place were not.

CAPT [REDACTED] testified that though there was a computing system at the facility, "it didn't have the tools on it. The tools didn't migrate well." CAPT [REDACTED] estimated that the Garland facility was not operational for "60,65 [days]" after his arrival on July 1, 2000. Accordingly, the facility was not fully operational until about September 1, 2000. One witness testified that when .the Garland facility was finally operational the capabilities exceeded those that had been shown to the team members at LIWA.

CAPT [REDACTED] added "When the 3-month time limit expired, Gen Schoomaker gave me yet another monthto work it, because I think he was pretty happy." CAPT [REDACTED] testified that USSOCOM paid $250,000 for this additional month at the Garland facility. This extension enabled the Able Danger team to continue work at the Garland facility until mid-November 2000.

When the Garland facility became operational, Able Danger team members applied the data mining and visualization tools to data from Government data bases and the World Wide Web. Dr. [REDACTED] stated, "They got 6 years of classified data from 18 agencies in one location." With regard to open source data, Dr. [REDACTED] testified, "they started from scratch." Dr.

[REDACTED] estimated the Able Danger team members were collecting data from 10,000 Web sites each day. He said, "What we were doing is collecting data from news Web sites and terrorist's Web sites and things like that." However, we found that the Able Danger team members generally limited their searches to English language Web sites.[39]

Dr. [REDACTED] testified that sometime in September 2000, she took leave and traveled to the Garland facility in order to interview for a position there with the Raytheon Company. She was hired effective September 28, 2000, and began working at the Garland facility shortly thereafter. As a Raytheon Company employee, Dr. [REDACTED]'s association with the Able Danger mission was limited. She stated, "I was a contractor. I wasn't a Government person at that time, so there was a lot that happened that I wasn't privy to."

On October 10, 2000, GEN Schoomaker traveled to the Garland facility and was briefed on the progress of the Able Danger program. CAPT [REDACTED] characterized the briefing as What we tried to impart on him at that meeting was, "Hey, we've got the pieces in place. We've got the data sets here. We're starting to process it. We're starting to come up with vignettes that we think are warranted and we need to look at. People are looking at doing it this way. We think it's fast, we think it's robust and it's credible."[40]

Witnesses who were present at the briefing testified that GEN Schoomaker was very impressed with the technology he observed at the Garland facility. CAPT [REDACTED] testified, "Gen Schoomaker said, you know, 'you guys are too far away. This four-month prototype effort in Garland has been fun but I want you guys closer.'" MG Lambert testified that "everyone agreed with that decision [to move the analytical capabilities to USSOCOM headquarters]."

GEN Schoomaker testified he had anticipated USSOCOM having a local capacity of advanced analytical tools and data mining. He stated, "From the very beginning, these things looked [like] they had promise." GEN Schoomaker added, "It was always intended to be brought back into our spaces [at USSOCOM headquarters] so that our analysts would be able to do this every day." GEN Schoomaker provided, "It didn't make any sense for us to have it all the way in Texas. It was there because of the contractor facility."

On October 12, 2000, Col [REDACTED] sent a memorandum to the Able Danger team members in which he discussed a meeting he had that day with MG Lambert and Brigadier General (BG) James W. Parker, U.S. Army, Director, Special Operations Information Operations (SOIO), USSOCOM. Based on that meeting, Col [REDACTED] outlined "the current picture of the future." In his memorandum, Col [REDACTED] advised that the Able Danger team "will dissolve with the 15 Dec [December 15, 2000] publication of the IO [Information Operations] Campaign Plan." He added that as a follow on mission to the Able Danger team, SOIO would take "the lead in developing the SOCC [Special Operations Collaborative Center]." He added, "As you could tell, the CINC [GEN Schoomaker] was and is very happy with your accomplishments." Col [REDACTED] also wrote, "**your only concern is the IO Campaign Plan.**" (emphasis in original).

In an attachment to Col [REDACTED]'s memorandum of October 12, 2000, the vision, charter, and command relations of the SOCC were discussed. The charter provided that "the SOCC will develop and use non-traditional techniques and procedures to define areas for IO applications to obtain the initiative in combating transnational threats." It also stressed the need for "close collaboration between DOD and Other Government Agencies." In a follow-on memorandum of October 17,2000, Col [REDACTED] advised Able Danger team members of GEN Schoomakers guidance to "capture the Able Danger team capabilities and develop an IO planning cell in *USSOCOM/SOIO* around them."

In a letter dated October 23, 2000, Col [REDACTED] ordered CAPT [REDACTED] to return from the Garland facility to USSOCOM headquarters. CAPT [REDACTED] characterized this order as being "fired" and expressed his frustration that he was prohibited from continuing with data mining operations. He returned to USSOCOM headquarters on October 30, 2000, and then worked on bringing the capabilities that were at the Garland facility to USSOCOM. He continued to work this issue through May 2001.

Col [REDACTED] testified that the Able Danger team was "a hundred percent successful" in regard to being "a proof of concept for data mining and its capability to support operational planning." He added, however, in terms of the other aspects of the mission, identifying al Qaeda and analyzing its vulnerabilities, the team was only "30 percent" successful. He stated the weakness was that, "as far as we got was to identify . . . a proposed indication of the al Qaeda network. It was not validated." CoI [REDACTED] testified that additional work was required in attaining "more interagency connectivity and then the bridge, once we had developed actionable intelligence, a bridge into operational planning." Col [REDACTED] stressed the importance of interagency connectivity and highlighted that "the military targets [account for) maybe five percent of actually engaging the al Qaeda network."

MG Lambert characterized the success of the Able Danger team as "it helped ... make people realize that you can use automated tools to [discover) that very hard human networking business much more effectively and much quicker." However, MG Lambert testified "we didn't get the mission accomplished." He explained, "It ended up, the final product was just a framework, you know it was . . . just a template." He added, "But it was worth a try and there were some benefits. . . . So it was a success, it was worth the money for that, but we didn't get the mission accomplished."

Similarly, RDML Steffens was favorably impressed by the technology employed by the Able Danger team while at the Garland facility. He stated that those capabilities were "a fabulous tool." He added, "As soon as you saw it, it impressed you with the, what it could do as far as reviewing and linking information and also the visual presentations that it gave you, enabled you to see how things were connected."

CAPT [REDACTED] assessed that prior to his departure at the end of October 2000, the Able Danger team "had made very little progress." He commented that the team had collected a significant amount of data from open sources, but "still hadn't set the architecture to analyze it very well."

In summary, the history of Able Danger, from its inception in October 1999 to its termination in January 2001, demonstrated that its work product was limited to the development of a "Campaign Plan" that formed the basis for follow-on intelligence gathering efforts.[41] The first 9 months of Able Danger were characterized by "false starts" and repeat efforts to find a suitable operating environment and location. Its initial placement at the JWAC and subsequent association with LIWA achieved nothing other than a basic level of familiarization with state-of the-art analytical tools and capabilities. Essentially no significant progress on Able Danger was made until September 2000 when operations at the Garland facility began. Those operations collected data from other agencies and thousands of Web sites in order to apply analytical tools that would make connections and linkages between data points to demonstrate a strategy for attacking the al Qaeda infrastructure. Operations at Garland continued for about 2 months, sufficient to develop such a strategy; i.e., a Campaign Plan, but were then terminated.

LTC Shaffer's Involvement with Able Danger

Because of the representations that LTC Shaffer made regarding Able Danger, we sought to determine the nature of his participation in, hence knowledge of, Able Danger activities.

Based on our interviews with individuals familiar with the Able Danger mission, we determined that his participation was limited. A summary of his involvement follows:

* LTC Shaffer testified that in December 1999, while on travel in active duty status from DIA, he met with GEN Schoomaker at USSOCOM headquarters. According to LTC Shaffer, GEN Schoomaker asked LTC Shaffer to contact CAPT [REDACTED] to discuss the Able Danger mission. GEN Schoomaker testified he did not recall this meeting or ever meeting LTC Shaffer, but did not deny that the meeting may have occurred. MG Lambert and RDML Steffens, two senior USSOCOM officials closest to the Able Danger program, did not recall meeting LTC Shaffer during the *1999/2000* time period.

* LTC Shaffer was one of nearly 500 people who were "read-on" to the Able Danger program.

* LTC Shaffer attended the three Able Danger conferences at JWAC in January and February 2000.

* LTC Shaffer was responsible for putting CAPT [REDACTED] in contact with Dr. [REDACTED] at LIWA in order to determine whether LIWA could support the Able Danger mission. Subsequently, LTC Shaffer delivered three charts from Dr. [REDACTED] to CAPT [REDACTED] that demonstrated link analysis.

* LTC Shaffer told us that at the request of GEN Schoomaker he "negotiated" with the LIWA commander an arrangement between USSOCOM and LIWA for LIWA to support the Able Danger mission. However, we could not corroborate this assertion as the LIWA commander (now retired) refused our request for an interview and, as indicated above, GEN Schoomaker did not recall ever meeting LTC Shaffer.

* We found that LTC Shafter traveled to Garland on one occasion, but we found no evidence that he conducted any significant work there. LTC Shaffer told us that, during his one visit to Garland, he was engaged in "looking at the data versus what we're going to do with the data and creating the options."

* LTC Shaffer assisted Able Danger team members in receiving special authorization that enhanced their ability to access various World Wide Web sites and coordinated with DIA and other intelligence agencies to provide data bases to the Able Danger team.

Witness testimony concerning LTC Shaffer's involvement and contributions was inconsistent. CAPT [REDACTED] and Dr. [REDACTED] characterized LTC Shaffer's contributions to the Able Danger mission as significant. CAPT [REDACTED] stated that LTC Shaffer got the Able Danger team data bases, provided an analyst who came to the Garland facility, and linked CAPT [REDACTED] with LIWA. Another witness, who was a key participant on the Able Danger team, characterized LTC Shaffer's involvement on Able Danger as "basically the delivery boy," referring to LTC Shaffer's assistance in providing "classified tapes from DIA." This witness added that LTC Shaffer "wasn't part of the team as he's claimed to be. He helped us out in bringing some data down and that was about it."

III.   SCOPE

In the course of our investigation, we obtained sworn testimony from 98 witnesses with knowledge of the matters under investigation, including GEN Shelton, GEN Schoomaker, LTC Shaffer, CAPT [REDACTED], Dr. [REDACTED], members of the Able Danger team, DIA officials who were involved with Able Danger or LTC Shaffer, and contractor employees involved with the program. Because of inconsistencies in testimony and need for follow-up, we conducted re-interviews of key witnesses, including LTC Shaffer who was interviewed four times and CAPT [REDACTED], who was interviewed three times. Additionally, we examined relevant documentation.

This report is unclassified, which caused us to omit certain factual information that might be relevant, but not essential, to resolution of the issues under consideration. In our view, the issues are fully addressed with unclassified information.

As indicated above, we evaluated reprisal allegations involving LTC Shaffer from i\\io perspectives -- his status as a Service member and his status as a DIA civilian appropriated fund employee. While the guidelines for conducting such reprisal analysis vary because of the different statutes involved, we focused on the central question in any reprisal case -- would the unfavorable actions have been taken absent the employee's whistleblower activity? To give full consideration to LTC Shaffer's situation, we presumed that his perceived involvement in two DIA IG investigations in 2002; his discussions with the 9/11 Commission staff members in October 2003; and his communications regarding Able Danger with Members of Congress and the media in 2005 all constituted "protected communications" for purposes of reprisal analysis.

We then focused our analysis on the basis for unfavorable actions taken against him to determine whether those actions were justified based on factors apart from LTC Shaffer's communications.

IV.   FINDINGS AND ANALYSIS

A. Did the Able Danger team identify Mohammed Atta and other 9/11 terrorists before September 11, 2001?

Much has been reported in the media and in Congressional deliberations regarding the possibility that Able Danger identified Mohammed Atta and other terrorists associated with the attack of 9/11. That possibility was based on statements by LTC Shaffer and others who recalled seeing a chart, created before *9/11,* that allegedly contained a photograph of Mohammed Atta in connection with an al Qaeda "New York" or "Brooklyn cell" or, at a minimum, displayed his name along with the names of other suspected terrorists.

We found no charts or other documentation created before 9/11 that contained a photograph or name of Mohammed Atta and was produced or possessed by the Able Danger team. Further, we found no contemporaneous documentary evidence that such a discovery had been made by Able Danger. As a result, the resolution of this issue rests on witness testimony -- particularly the credibility and consistency of testimony by witnesses who claimed to have seen such a depiction of Mohammed Atta. We set forth the following summaries of relevant testimony to address this matter.

CAPT [REDACTED]

CAPT [REDACTED] served as the Operations Officer for the Able Danger team from its inception in October 1999 through October 2000 and was closely involved in all Able Danger activities. We interviewed him on three occasions; December 13, 2005, February 17, 2006, and May 24, 2006. During each interview he discussed a chart that allegedly contained a photograph of Mohammed Atta. At the first interview CAPT [REDACTED] was "100 percent [certain] Mohammed Atta's image was on the chart." At the second interview he acknowledged there was "a compelling amount of evidence that would make it appear that I did not see Mohammed Atta." In the third interview CAPT [REDACTED] stated, "I'm convinced that Atta was not on that chart, the chart we had."

CAPT [REDACTED] testified that within "3 or 4 days" of meeting with Dr. [REDACTED] at LIWA in January 2000, LTC Shaffer delivered three charts to him at USSOCOM headquarters.[42] After initially denying that Figure 1 was one of those charts, CAPT [REDACTED] eventually testified that Figure 1 was one of the original charts and that Figure 2 was also one of the charts. He described the third chart that was delivered to him as a "propeller chart," Figure 3 is an example of such a propeller chart, but is not the chart that was delivered to CAPT [REDACTED].

During our initial interview, CAPT [REDACTED] testified that he was certain that Mohammed Atta's photograph was on one of the three charts delivered to him in January or February 2000 which portrayed a Brooklyn cell. While he believed that photographs of other 9/11 terrorists were on the chart, he was not as certain as he was about Mohammed Atta's photograph. He testified,

> I know 100 percent Mohammed Atta's image was on the chart. I pretty well recollect that there were three [terrorists], at least three others, but I have not gone into any depth in trying to recreate the memory of who any of them were. All I know is what I originally saw on the days shortly after *9/11* and that was him.

CAPT [REDACTED] also stated that in addition to the Brooklyn cell there were four other cells depicted on the chart. He recalled the cells were "Dar es Salaam, Kenya, Tanzania, [and] Nairobi.[43]

* * *

VI. CONCLUSIONS

a   The anti-terrorist program, Able Danger, did not identify Mohammed Atta or any of the other 9/11 terrorists before the 9/11 attack.

b   Able Danger members were not prohibited from sharing intelligence information with law enforcement authorities or other agencies that could have acted on that information. In fact, Able Danger produced no actionable intelligence information.

c The destruction of Able Danger documentation at LIWA and Garland was appropriate and complied with applicable DoD regulations.

d The Able Danger program was not terminated prematurely. It concluded after it had achieved its objective and its work products were used in follow-on intelligence gathering efforts at USSOCOM.

e DoD officials executed the Able Danger program in compliance with applicable intelligence oversight guidance.

f DIA officials did not improperly destroy Able Danger documentation when cleaning out LTC Shaffer's office spaces. We concluded that LTC Shaffer did not serve as a repository for Able Danger documentation as he alleged.

g DIA officials included some Government property in the personal belongings that were shipped to LTC Shafter after they were removed from his office spaces. However, the Government property was of minimal value (pens, aged Government documents, and computer disks). DIA officials did not improperly include classified documents or the Government GPS in that shipment.

h DIA officials did not suspend LTC Shaffer's access to classified information or revoke his security clearance in reprisal for his communications regarding Able Danger. Rather, the adverse actions taken with respect to LTC Shaffer's access and security clearance followed established process and were justified apart from his protected communications.

i DIA officials did not issue LTC Shaffer an unfavorable OER for his protected communications to the 9/11 Commission. The OER would have been issued absent those protected communications.

j LTC Shaffer's OER did not properly reflect non-rated time pursuant to applicable Army regulations and he could have been issued an optional 60-day OER for service in Afghanistan. By separate correspondence we advised LTC Shaffer of his options for correcting his military record and offered our assistance if he chooses to do so.

VII.   RECOMMENDATIONS

We recommend that the Director, DIA, review procedures concerning disposition of personal belongings when abandoned by DIA employees and procedures for rendering military performance reports to ensure that Service requirements are met.

Chapter Review Questions

1 By what authority and for what purpose does the Department of Defense maintain an Intelligence Oversight Officer who is in not part of the DoD Office of Inspector General?

2 What role, if any, might the DoD's Intelligence Oversight Office have played in identifying the intelligence-related allegations that ultimately were investigated by the DoD Office of Inspector General?

3 Under what circumstances might an individual who witnesses what he thinks might be an abuse of power within the intelligence community not report his concerns either to the chain of command or to an Inspector General?

---

[1] *See* United States Central Intelligence Agency, "Intelligence Oversight," updated September 10, 2009 (https://www.cia.gov/library/publications/additional-publications/the-work-of-a-nation/intelligence-oversight/index.html).

[2] Executive Order 12333, "United States Intelligence Activities," ¶2.1, December 4, 1981.

[3] *Id.*, as amended July 30, 2008.

[4] U.S. Const., Amendment X.

[5] U.S. Const., Article I, Section 8.

[6] U.S. Const., Article II, Section 2, cl. 1.

[7] *New York v. United States*, 505 U.S. 144, 157 (1992) http://www.law.cornell.edu/supct/html/91-543.ZS.html

[8] DoD Directive 5200.27, "Acquisition of Information Concerning Persons and Organizations not Affiliated with the Department of Defense," ¶3.1, January 7, 1980 (http://www.dtic.mil/whs/directives/corres/pdf/520027p.pdf).

[9] Executive Order 12333, ¶2-1.

[10] DoD Directive 5240.1, ¶4-1, August 27, 2007 (http://www.dtic.mil/whs/directives/corres/pdf/524001p.pdf).

[11] DoD 5240.1-R, "Procedures governing the activities of DoD intelligence components that affect United States persons," December 1982 (http://atsdio.defense.gov/documents/5240.html).

[12] DoD 5240.1-R, Definitions, ¶27(a); *see id.* ¶27(b) ("A person or organization outside the United States shall be presumed not to be a United States person unless specific information to the contrary is obtained. An alien in

the United States shall be presumed not to be a United States person unless specific information to the contrary is obtained.").

[13] DoD 5240.1-R, Definitions, ¶10 ("Employee. A person employed by, assigned to, or acting for an agency within the intelligence community, including contractors and persons otherwise acting at the direction of such an agency.").

[14] DoD 5240.1-R, Procedure 15, B(1).

[15] DoD 5240.1-R, Procedure 15,

[16] DoD Directive 5148.11, "Assistant to the Secretary of Defense (Intelligence Oversight)," ¶4-14, May 21, 2004 (http://atsdio.defense.gov/documents/51481p.pdf).

[17] DoD Directive 5240.1, ¶5-3.

[18] DoD Directive 5148.11, "Assistant to the Secretary of Defense (Intelligence Oversight)," ¶4, May 21, 2004 (http://atsdio.defense.gov/documents/51481p.pdf).

[19] *Id.*, ¶4-6.

[20] *Id.*, ¶6.6.1.

[21] DoD 5240.1-R, Procedure 15, ¶3(e).

[22] *See* Army Regulation 380-10, "U.S. Army Intelligence Activities," ¶15-6, May 3, 2007 (http://www.army.mil/usapa/epubs/pdf/r381_10.pdf); Secretary of the Navy Instruction 3820.3E, "Oversight of Intelligence Activities Within the Department of the Navy," September 25, 2005 (http://www.fas.org/irp/doddir/navy/secnavinst/3820_3e.pdf); Air Force Instruction 14-104, "Oversight of Intelligence Activities," April 16, 2007 (http://www.fas.org/irp/doddir/usaf/afi14-104.pdf); *see also* Marine Corps Inspector General Program: Intelligence Oversight Guide (Marine Corps Inspector General 2009); Defense HUMINT Service, "Intelligence Law Handbook," Publication CC-0000-181-95 (September 1995).

[23] *See* Defense HUMINT Service, "Intelligence Law Handbook, ¶8.4, September 1995 ("Historical Note").

[24] 18 U.S.C. §1385.

[25] Intelligence Law Handbook, ¶8-4(e).

[26] DoD Directive 5525.5, "DoD Cooperation with Civilian Law Enforcement Officials," Enclosure 4, ¶E4.1.3, January 15, 1986 (Administrative Reissuance Incorporating Change 1, December 20, 1989) (http://www.fas.org/irp/doddir/dod/d5525_5.pdf); *see* Intelligence Law Handbook, ¶8-9.

[27] "Alleged Misconduct by Senior DoD Officials Concerning the Able Danger Program and Lieutenant Colonel Anthony A. Shaffer, U.S. Army Reserve," September 18, 2006. http://permanent.access.gpo.gov/lps83632/r_H05L97905217-PWH.pdf

[28] LTC Shaffer served in DIA as both a civilian employee and, when called to active duty, a military officer. Because the allegations cover time periods and events that relate to both his military and civilian duties, we will refer to LTC Shaffer using his military rank in this report.

[29] As discussed in this report, LTC Shaffer was placed on administrative leave from DIA and vacated his office in April 2004. His office was then cleared for occupancy by another employee.

[30] The *9/11* Commission was created by congressional legislation signed by President George W. Bush in November 2002. The Commission's mission was to prepare a full account of circumstances surrounding the September 11, 2001, terrorist attacks and report its findings to the President and Congress.

[31] We acknowledge that some Government office supplies may have been included in the shipment (e.g., commercially available pens, pencils, blank CD ROM disks), but considered that inclusion an oversight not warranting further investigation.

[32] LTC Shafter provided the four documents to congressional staff.

33 In conducting reprisal analysis, we recognize that whistleblower complaints made by civilian employees in the intelligence community are excluded from the jurisdiction of the Office of Special Counsel under Section 2302 (a)(2)(c) of Title 5, United States Code. However, it is our policy to apply Title 5 standards for all investigations into complaints of reprisal submitted by civilian appropriated fund employees.

34 Based on the revocation of his access and anticipated revocation of his clearance, LTC Shaffer was proposed for removal from his DIA civilian position in November 2005. That action was held in abeyance pending completion of this investigation. LTC Shaffer continued on paid administrative leave.

35 Photographs of Figures 1 and 2 were retrieved from a laptop computer that contained Able Danger material in a safe at USSOCOM Headquarters. We did not locate the original charts.

36 We did not locate the actual chart that had been provided to CAPT [REDACTED].

37 Dr. [REDACTED] testified that the Able Danger team did not have access to LIWA's data. Rather, she had provided CAPT [REDACTED] file transfer protocol (FTP) access that enabled *CAPT* [REDACTED] to download products that were uploaded by LIWA personnel for him.

38 Mr. [REDACTED] told us that after he was read on to Able Danger, he began accumulating large quantities of data primarily from open sources. He said that he subjected that data to LIWA analytical tools and found numerous potential al Qaeda links in the United States, However, he acknowledged that he had not vetted this preliminary work and that he did not identify any of the 9/11 terrorists or other potential targets of interest.

39 CAPT [REDACTED] told us that he performed a number of searches of Portuguese language Web sites.

40 Coincidentally, this briefing occurred 2 days before the attack on the USS COLE (DDG-67) in Aden, Yemen. CAPT [REDACTED] told us that Yemen was mentioned as a "hotspot" during the briefing, but characterized

any assertion that GEN Schoomaker failed to act on a warning of an imminent threat there as "all crap."

[41] The campaign plan itself is classified.

[42] CAPT [REDACTED] first met Dr. [REDACTED sometime between
January 10 and 14, 2000, while at JWAC for the Initial Planning Confer-
ence, On CAPT [REDACTED] 's timeline is an entry for January 23, 2000,
"LIWA provides suggestions . . . including demos." Accordingly,
we'concluded the charts were provided to CAPT [REDACTED] between
January 15 and 23, 2000.

[43] We noted that Dar es Salaam is the capitol of Tanzania, and Nairobi is
the capitol of Kenya. The U.S. Embassies in Dar es Salaam and Nairobi
were both attacked on August 7, 1998.

Chapter 11. WHISTLEBLOWER REPRISAL:

Tombstones at Arlington National Cemetery

Any employee who has authority to take, direct others to take, recommend, or approve any personnel action, shall not, with respect to such authority, take or threaten to take any action against any employee as a reprisal for making a complaint or disclosing information to an Inspector General, unless the complaint was made or the information disclosed with the knowledge that it was false or with willful disregard for its truth or falsity.

Inspector General Act of 1978, as amended, §7(c)

There are at least six types of reprisal allegations, governed by five separate but related sets of statutory standards. Moreover, within the federal government there are overlapping responsibilities for the various types of reprisal allegations. For example, while the U.S. Office of Special Counsel has primary responsibility for overseeing civilian whistleblower reprisal investigations throughout the federal government, [1] any Office of Inspector General can receive and process a civilian whistleblower reprisal allegation. Likewise, any Office of Inspector General within the Department of Defense, whether civilian or military, can process a reprisal allegation by a uniformed military Service member:

*   "If the Inspector General receiving such an allegation is an Inspector General within a military department, that Inspector General shall promptly notify the Inspector General of the Department of Defense of the allegation," 10 U.S.C. §1034(c)(3)(B), and

* "the results of the investigation shall be determined by, or approved by, the Inspector General of the Department of Defense (regardless of whether the investigation itself is conducted by the Inspector General of the Department of Defense or by an Inspector General within a military department)." 10 U.S.C. §1034(c)(3)(E).

The statutes governing reprisal allegations and associated primary proponents are as follows:

Type of Reprisal Allegation:	Primary Investigative Office(s):	Governing Law:
Civilian Whistleblower Protection (GS employees)	U.S. Office of Special Counsel	5 U.S.C. §2302
Military Whistleblower Protection	Military Dep't IGs & DoD IG	10 U.S.C. §1034
DoD Civilian Whistleblower Protection (non-GS):	DoD Inspector General	IG Act, as amended, §7
* Nonappropriated Fund employees;		10 U.S.C. §1587

Type of Reprisal Allegation:	Primary Investigative Office(s):	Governing Law:
✳ Contractor Employees		10 U.S.C. §2409
Intelligence Community Whistleblower Protection	DoD Inspector General	IG Act, as amended, §8H

Some federal agencies, such as the Department of Defense and the military departments, treat "Improper Referrals for Mental Health Evaluation" as a separate category of reprisal allegations. In this regard, the Department of Defense has promulgated DoD Directive 6490.1 and DoD Instruction 6490.4, each governing, "Mental Health Evaluations of Members of the Armed Forces." Under the DoD Directive, "The Inspector General of the Department of Defense shall: ... Conduct or oversee an investigation of an allegation submitted by the Service member or the Service member's legal guardian to an IG that the member was referred for a mental health evaluation in violation of this Directive or DoD Instruction 6490.4."[2] In any event, Title 5 of United States Code includes "a decision to order psychiatric testing or examination" among its list of ten specified "personnel actions" that could form the basis for a whistleblower reprisal allegation.[3]

The DoD IG Hotline maintains general information about each type of reprisal allegation and a sample reprisal complaint letter at: http://www.dodig.mil/hotline/reprisal_complaint.htm

For any whistleblower reprisal investigations, whether under Title 5, Title 10, or the Inspector General Act, the whistleblower (aka complainant) bears the burden of establishing the first three of the following four required "elements" for substantiating whistleblower reprisal:

> ✳ The complainant made a "disclosure of information" protected by statute (aka a "protected communication"), such as an EEO complaint or a lawful communication either to a Member of Congress or to an Inspector General;

* An official in a position to effectuate an adverse personnel action either (a) took or threatened to take an adverse personnel action, or (b) withheld or threatened to withhold a favorable personnel action[4]; and

* The official responsible for taking, withholding, or threatening the personnel action knew about the protected communication.[5]

If the complaining whistleblower establishes these first three elements by a preponderance of the evidence (*i.e.*, more likely than not), the burden shifts to the complained against official to establish – by a clear and convincing evidence standard[6] -- that:

* The personnel action would still have been taken, withheld, or threatened even if the protected communication had not been made.[7]

Civilian Whistleblower Protection (GS Employees)

Under Section 2302(b)(8) of Title 5, United States Code, it is illegal to, "take or fail to take, or threaten to take or fail to take, a personnel action with respect to any employee or applicant for employment because of—

> **(A)** any disclosure of information by an employee or applicant which the employee or applicant reasonably believes evidences—
>
> > **(i)** a violation of any law, rule, or regulation, or
> >
> > **(ii)** gross mismanagement, a gross waste of funds, an abuse of authority, or a substantial and specific danger to public health or safety, if such disclosure is not specifically prohibited by law and if such information is not specifically required by Executive order to be kept secret in the interest of national defense or the conduct of foreign affairs; or

(B) any disclosure to the Special Counsel, or to the Inspector General of an agency or another employee designated by the head of the agency to receive such disclosures, of information which the employee or applicant reasonably believes evidences—

> **(i)** a violation of any law, rule, or regulation, or

> **(ii)** gross mismanagement, a gross waste of funds, an abuse of authority, or a substantial and specific danger to public health or safety.[8]

Under Title 5, other than the provision regarding a "disclosure to the Special Counsel, or to the Inspector General of an agency or another employee designated by the head of the agency to receive such disclosures" quoted above, the identity of the recipient to whom a "protected disclosure" is made, which might qualify the discloser as a protected whistleblower, is not further specified.[9]

Military Whistleblower Protection

Under the Military Whistleblower Protection Act, "protected communications" include communications not only with Members of Congress and IGs, but also with any "member of a Department of Defense audit, inspection, investigation, or law enforcement organization" or with "any person or organization in the chain of command."[10]

The following chronology is posted on the website of the Office of the Inspector General of the Department of Defense (http://www.dodig.mil/INV/MRI/pdfs/Timeline.pdf), and is illustrative of the special interest Congress has taken in military whistleblowers, and the evolving legal standards for military whistleblower reprisals:

History of Military Whistleblower Protection Act and Statute
Prohibiting the Use of Mental Health Evaluations in Reprisal

1985 - Congresswoman Barbara Boxer introduces a bill to provide protections for military whistleblowers.

1986 - Substance of Boxer bill becomes an amendment to the FY 1987 House Defense Authorization bill. The language dies in conference between the House and Senate.

November 1987 - The Defense Acquisition Policy Panel of the House Armed Services Committee holds a hearing on the Boxer bill to protect military whistleblowers. The witnesses include whistleblowers Chief Petty Officer Michael R. Tufariello, U.S. Naval Reserve, and Major Peter C. Cole, U.S. Army National Guard, Texas. Mr. Derek Vander Schaaf, Deputy Inspector General, Department of Defense, also testifies.

1988 - Boxer's "Military Whistleblower Protection Act" (10 U.S.C. 1034) is enacted as part of the FY 1989 Defense Authorization Act. It is intended to protect military members who make disclosures of wrongdoing to Members of Congress or an IG from reprisal. It requires the DoD to investigate allegations of whistle blower reprisal from military members.

1990 - Boxer amendment to the FY 1991 Defense Authorization Act prohibits the referral of military members for mental health evaluations (MHE) in reprisal for making protected communications as defined by the 10 U.S.C. 1034. It requires the DoD to implement regulations specifying procedures for referring military members for MHEs.

1991- Congress includes an amendment to 10 U.S.C. 1034 in the FY *1992/1993* Defense Authorization Act extending protections to whistleblowers that make disclosures to auditors, criminal investigators, inspectors, and other DoD law enforcement officers.

1992 - Congress includes a Boxer provision in the FY 1993 Defense Authorization Act requiring the DoD to implement regulations governing the referral of military members for MHEs. It again prohibits referring military members for MHEs in reprisal for making communications protected under 10 U.S.C. 1034.

1994 - As part of the FY 1995 Defense Authorization Act, Congress again expands the protections afforded under 10 U.S.C. 1034. It broadens the definition of "protected communication" to include allegations of sexual harassment or discrimination. It also expands the universe of those to whom protected communications can be made, to include any person or organization designated pursuant to regulations or' administrative procedures to receive such communications, including those in the military member's chain of command.

1998 - Congress amends 10 U.S.C. 1034 to do the following: 1) give Military Department IGs the authority to receive allegations of whistleblower reprisal and conduct preliminary inquiries into such allegations; 2) require Military Department IGs to report receipt of reprisal allegations to the DoD IG within 10 days and to have their reports of preliminary inquiry and investigation reviewed and approved by the DoD IG; 3) reduce burdensome administrative requirements; and 4) insert the word "gross" before the word "mismanagement."

2002 - The Homeland Security Act transfers the assets and personnel of the U.S. Coast Guard from the Department of Transportation to the Department of Homeland Security. Therefore, references in 10 U.S.C. 1034 to the Department of Transportation are replaced with references to the Department of Homeland Security.

2004 - The FY 2005 Defense Authorization Act amends 10 U.S.C. 1034 to clarify that any individual within a Military member's chain of command can receive protected communications, as well as any person or organization designated by regulation or established procedure to receive protected communications.

2007 - The Directive which implements 10 U.S.C. 1034 is reissued. Included among the revisions to DoDD 7050.06 is the addition of the definition of "chain of command" as: the "succession of commanding officers from a superior to a subordinate through which command is exercised, but also the succession of officers, enlisted members or civilian personnel through whom administrative control is exercised, including supervision and rating of performance."[11]

Under the Military Protection Act, the whistleblower should report any allegation of a retaliatory personnel action to an Inspector General within 60 days; otherwise, the IG is not required by the statute to conduct even a preliminary inquiry:

> Neither an initial determination ["whether there is sufficient evidence to warrant an investigation of the allegation"] nor an investigation . . . is required in the case of an allegation made more than 60 days after the date on which the member becomes aware of the personnel action that is the subject of the allegation.[12]

DoD Non-GS Civilian Employee Whistleblower Protection

Section 1587 of Title 10, United States Code, which is implemented within the Department of Defense by DoD Directive 1401.03, "DoD Nonappropriated Fund Instrumentality (NAFI) Employee Whistleblower Protection," defines a NAFI employee as:

> a civilian employee who is paid from nonappropriated funds of Army and Air Force Exchange Service, Navy Exchange Service Command, Marine Corps exchanges, or any other instrumentality of the United States under the jurisdiction of the armed forces which is conducted for the comfort, pleasure, contentment, or physical or mental improvement of members of the armed forces. Such term includes a civilian employee of a support organization

within the Department of Defense or a military department, such as the Defense Finance and Accounting Service, who is paid from nonappropriated funds on account of the nature of the employee's duties.[13]

This special whistleblower protection statute stipulates that:

Any civilian employee or member of the armed forces who has authority to take, direct others to take, recommend, or approve any personnel action shall not, with respect to such authority, take or fail to take a personnel action with respect to any nonappropriated fund instrumentality employee (or any applicant for a position as such an employee) as a reprisal for—

(1) a disclosure of information by such an employee or applicant which the employee or applicant reasonably believes evidences—

> (A) a violation of any law, rule, or regulation; or

> (B) mismanagement, a gross waste of funds, an abuse of authority, or a substantial and specific danger to public health or safety;

> if such disclosure is not specifically prohibited by law and if the information is not specifically required by or pursuant to executive order to be kept secret in the interest of national defense or the conduct of foreign affairs; or

(2) a disclosure by such an employee or applicant to any civilian employee or member of the armed forces designated by law or by the Secretary of Defense to receive disclosures described in clause (1), of information which the employee or applicant reasonably believes evidences—

> (A) a violation of any law, rule, or regulation; or

> (B) mismanagement, a gross waste of funds, an abuse of authority, or a substantial and specific danger to public health or safety.[14]

DoD Directive 1401.03 assigns responsibility for investigating whistleblower reprisal allegations by NAFI employees to the DoD Inspector General: "The IG DoD shall:

5.1.1. Receive complaints of reprisal by NAFI employees, former employees, or applicants, and expeditiously determine whether there is sufficient evidence to warrant an investigation.

5.1.2. Notify the NAFI employee, former employee, or applicant, and the Director, Administration and Management (DA&M), OSD, if the IG DoD determines that an investigation will not be conducted.

5.1.3. Conduct an investigation if it has been determined that investigation of a complaint of reprisal is warranted. Upon completion of the investigation, provide the Under Secretary of Defense for Personnel and Readiness (USD(P&R)) and the DA&M with a report of findings of fact, conclusions, and recommendations.

5.1.4. Protect the confidentiality of NAFI employees, former employees, or applicants making protected disclosures unless the IG DoD determines that disclosure of the employee's, former employee's, or applicant's identity is necessary to resolve the complaint(s)."[15]

Within the Department of Defense, the heads of DoD Components, including military departments and various subordinate DoD agencies—some of whom have their own Offices of Inspector General—are required to, "Ensure that NAFI employees, former employees, or applicants making disclosures of information the employee or applicant reasonably believes evidences a violation of law, rule, or regulation; mismanagement; a gross waste of funds; an abuse of authority; or a substantial or specific danger to public health or safety; or any reprisal, are advised of their right to submit complaints directly to the IG DoD and of the procedures for doing so," and to, "Ensure that complaints of reprisal received from NAFI employees, former employees, or applicants are forwarded to the IG DoD."[16]

Defense Contractor Employee Reprisal

Section 2409 of Title 10, United States Code, establishes standards for the protection of Defense contractor employees, "from reprisal for disclosure of certain information":

(a) Prohibition of Reprisals.--(1) An employee of a contractor or subcontractor may not be discharged, demoted, or otherwise discriminated against as a reprisal for disclosing to a person or body described in paragraph (2) information that the employee reasonably believes is evidence of the following:

(A) Gross mismanagement of a Department of Defense contract or grant, a gross waste of Department funds, an abuse of authority relating to a Department contract or grant, or a violation of law, rule, or regulation related to a Department contract (including the competition for or negotiation of a contract) or grant.

(B) Gross mismanagement of a National Aeronautics and Space Administration contract or grant, a gross waste of Administration funds, an abuse of authority relating to an Administration contract or grant, or a violation of law, rule, or regulation related to an Administration contract (including the competition for or negotiation of a contract) or grant.

(C) A substantial and specific danger to public health or safety.

(2) The persons and bodies described in this paragraph are the persons and bodies as follows:

(A) A Member of Congress or a representative of a committee of Congress.

(B) An Inspector General.

(C) The Government Accountability Office.

(D) An employee of the Department of Defense or the National Aeronautics and Space Administration, as applicable, responsible for contract oversight or management.

(E) An authorized official of the Department of Justice or other law enforcement agency.

(F) A court or grand jury.

(G) A management official or other employee of the contractor or subcontractor who has the responsibility to investigate, discover, or address misconduct.

***

(b) Investigation of Complaints.—

(1) A person who believes that the person has been subjected to a reprisal prohibited by subsection (a) may submit a complaint to the Inspector General . . . .

(2) [T]he Inspector General shall make a determination . . . within 180 days after receiving the complaint [unless there is] an extension of time . . . up to [an additional] 180 days, as shall be agreed upon between the Inspector General and the person submitting the complaint. . .

The Inspector General of the Department of Defense is designated by DoD Directive to, "Receive and investigate complaints of reprisal for making disclosures protected by [Section] 2409 of title 10, United States Code."[7]

Improper Referrals for Mental Health Evaluation

According to Department of Defense Directive 6490.1, "Mental Health Evaluations of Members of the Armed Forces":

4.3.2. No person may refer a Service member for mental health evaluation as a reprisal for making or preparing a lawful communication to a Member of Congress, any appropriate authority in the chain of command of the Service member, an IG or a member of a DoD audit, inspection, investigation or law enforcement organization.
***

5.2. The Inspector General of the Department of Defense shall:

5.2.1. Conduct or oversee an investigation of an allegation submitted by the

Service member or the Service member's legal guardian to an IG that the member was referred for a mental health evaluation in violation of this Directive or DoD Instruction 6490.4 . . . .[19]

Whistleblower Misrepresentations of Material Fact

According to guidance promulgated by the DoD Office of Inspector General, "On rare occasions, you may come across an assertion by a third party that the whistleblower knew or should have known that the information provided in the initial protected communication was not true. If that is the case, you must resolve the issue of 'reasonable belief.' If you find that the complainant either made false statements or intentionally misrepresented the truth regarding the reported wrongdoing, then you may refer the matter for appropriate command action and close the reprisal investigation."[20]

Both the Inspector General Act of 1978 and the official reprisal complaint form utilized by the United States Office of Special Counsel (posted at http://www.osc.gov/documents/forms/osc11.htm) envision the possibility that intentional misrepresentation of material facts by a whistleblower could result in criminal prosecution of the whistleblower for making a false official statement. Specifically, Section 7(c) of the Inspector General Act disclaims any obligation to protect a whistleblower if, "the complaint was made or the information disclosed with the knowledge that it was false or with willful disregard for its truth or falsity."[21] Likewise, OSC Form 11 requires complainants to sign under penalty of perjury before any reprisal investigation is commenced, citing 18 U.S.C. § 1001 as the basis for criminal prosecution if the reprisal complaint includes "a false statement or concealment of a material fact."[22]

Federal Agency Compliance with Whistleblower Protection Laws

The United States Office of Special Counsel offers a training and certification program to assist federal agencies with both understanding and complying with federal whistleblower protection laws. Following is an overview of the Office of Special Counsel's certification program, as posted on its website:

The Office of Personnel Management recognizes 2302(c) certification as a "**suggested performance indicator**" for 'getting to green' on the Strategic Management of Human Capital element of the President's Management Agenda.

In 1994, Congress responded to reports of widespread ignorance in the federal workforce concerning employees' right to be free from prohibited personnel practices (PPP), especially retaliation for whistleblowing, by enacting 5 U.S.C. §2302(c). That provision charges "[t]he head of each agency" with responsibility for "ensuring (in consultation with the Office of Special Counsel) that agency employees are informed of the rights and remedies available to them" under the prohibited personnel practice and whistleblower retaliation protection provisions of Title 5.

OSC's 2302(c) Certification Program allows federal agencies to meet the statutory obligation to inform their workforces about the rights and remedies available to them under the Whistleblower Protection Act (WPA) and related civil service laws. Under the 2302(c) Certification Program, OSC will certify an agency's compliance with 5 U.S.C. §2302(c) if the agency meets the following five requirements:

1. Placing informational posters at agency facilities;
2. Providing information about PPPs and the WPA to new employees as part of the orientation process;
3. Providing information to current employees about PPP's and the WPA;
4. Training supervisors on PPPs and the WPA; and
5. Creation of a computer link from the agency's web site to OSC's web site.[23]

On December 31, 2002, the United States Office of Special Counsel certified the DoD Office of Inspector General as the first federal Office of Inspector General that had formally complied with 5

U.S.C. §2302(c). The official "Certificate of Compliance" read that it was "in recognition of meeting 5 U.S.C. §2302(c)'s obligation to inform the DODIG work force of their rights under the prohibited personnel practice and whistleblower protection provisions of chapters 12 and 23 of Title 5."

Office Special Counsel whistleblower protection certification is for a set period of time, and remains in effect provided that the agency meets its ongoing information obligations under the Office of Special Counsel's Certification Program. As of the writing of this handbook, 24 federal agencies, including the DoD OIG and four other Offices of Inspector General, were certified as compliant under the Office of Special Counsel's Certification Program.[24]

CASE STUDY: TOMBSTONES AT ARLINGTON
NATIONAL CEMETERY

The following are selected excerpts from 27-page Department of Defense Office of Inspector General Report, "Whistleblower Reprisal Investigation: Arlington National Cemetery," Report Number CRI-HL109655, June 29, 2010.[25]

Report No. CRI-HL109655 June 29, 2010

Inspector General
United States
Department *of* Defense

Whistleblower Reprisal Investigation

Arlington National Cemetery

MEMORANDUM FOR THE ASSISTANT SECRETARY OF THE ARMY
(CIVIL WORKS)

SUBJECT: Investigation under 5 U.S.C. § 2302(b)(8)

We recently completed an investigation into allegations that Arlington
National Cemetery (ANC) officials terminated Ms. Jennifer "Gina" Gray from her
public affairs position in June 2008 in reprisal for making protected disclosures.

We did not substantiate Ms. Gray's allegation of reprisal. Although
Ms. Gray was a whistleblower, we conclude that her protected disclosures were not
contributing factors in the personnel action taken against her because responsible
ANC management officials lacked knowledge of the disclosures.

However, we determined that, with respect to the employment and
termination of Ms. Gray, ANC management demonstrated an obvious failure to
exercise sound personnel management. Contrary to Agency regulations and
practice, ANC management elected to terminate Ms. Gray, rather than make a
reasonable effort to address public affairs policy issues that she raised, provide her
suitable guidance, or document performance deficiencies that ANC management
later claimed formed the basis for the termination.

Our report of investigation is attached. We recommend that you consider
corrective action with respect to responsible ANC officials and an appropriate
remedy for Ms. Gray. A response within 60 days would be appreciated. If you
have any questions, please contact me or Mr. Dan Meyer, Director, Civilian
Reprisal Investigations, at ███████████

Donald M. Horstman
Deputy Inspector General for
Administrative Investigations

Attachment:
As stated

WHISTLEBLOWER REPRISAL INVESTIGATION
Arlington National Cemetery

Introduction And Summary

We initiated this investigation in response to a Defense Hotline complaint on October 10, 2008, from Ms. Gina Gray, a former GS-12, Public Affairs (PA) Specialist, U.S. Army, Arlington National Cemetery (ANC), Arlington, VA. Ms. Gray was referred to the Office of the Inspector General, U.S. Department of Defense (OIG DoD), Civilian Reprisal Investigations Directorate (CRI), by the Project on Government Oversight.

Ms. Gray alleged that she suffered 12 acts of reprisal for making protected disclosures.

Ms. Gray's disclosures pertained to the restriction of media access to service personnel funeral ceremonies, and in particular, the funeral of Lieutenant Colonel (LtCol) William G. Hall, U.S. Marine Corps (hereinafter referred to as the Hall funeral), and other matters at ANC.

We concluded that Ms. Gray was a whistleblower as she made four communications that qualified as protected under Title 5, United States Code, Section 2302. However, none of those protected disclosures were contributing factors in the personnel action taken against her, because responsible ANC management officials were not aware of those disclosures at the time they made adverse decisions concerning Ms. Gray. We therefore did not substantiate Ms. Gray's allegation of reprisal.[26]

However, we determined that with respect to the employment and termination of Ms. Gray, ANC management demonstrated an obvious failure to exercise sound personnel management. That is, based on public affairs policy issues that Ms. Gray raised during her first weeks of employment, ANC management elected to terminate her, rather than make a reasonable effort to address those policy issues, provide suitable guidance to Ms. Gray, or document performance deficiencies that ANC management later claimed formed the basis for Ms. Gray's termination.

Accordingly, we recommend that the Assistant Secretary of the Army for Civil Works consider corrective action with respect to responsible ANC officials and an appropriate remedy for Ms. Gray.

This report sets forth our findings and conclusions based on applicable evidentiary standards.

Background

Since 1864, ANC has been a fully operational national cemetery, drawing more than four million visitors annually. ANC is an American shrine and hallowed ground: it is a place of immense importance to the United States, to the military community, and to the families whose loved ones are buried there. Today, ANC is actively involved with the funerals of military casualties from the Iraqi and Afghanistan war fronts, as well as aging World War II veterans.

Funerals average about 27 each workday. At the family's request, many of these military funeral ceremonies receive media coverage.

Ms. Gray's primary duties and responsibilities as a PA Specialist from April 14 to June 27, 2008, included, but were not limited to, promoting the understanding of the mission, programs, and activities of ANC; serving as the principal PA staff advisor to ANC staff on all matters involving PA; serving as the official spokesperson and primary contact for local and national media; responding to media queries; preparing and reviewing information material for public dissemination; and coordinating PA activities for official visits funerals with media interest, and special events.[27] Ms. Gray reported to her [REDACTED] ANC.

Scope And Authority

Under the Inspector General Act of 1978, as amended, the OIG DoD is responsible for improving the economy, efficiency, and effectiveness of the Department's operations through prevention and detection of fraud, waste, and mismanagement. To fulfill those responsibilities, Congress granted the OIG DoD broad powers to conduct and supervise investigations relating to the Department's programs and operations. The OIG DoD achieves this goal, in part, by acting upon information provided by federal employee(s) in investigations conducted under Sections 7(a) and 8(c)(2) of the Inspector General Act. The OIG DoD protects the confidentiality of sources providing information under the authority of Section 7(b) of the Inspector General Act.

DoD Directive 5106.01 mandates that the Inspector General "[m]aintain a whistleblower protection program in the Department of Defense that encourages personnel to report waste, fraud, and abuse to appropriate authorities; provides mechanisms for addressing complaints of reprisal; and recommends remedies for whistleblowers who encounter reprisal, consistent with applicable laws, regulations, and policies."[28] One component of this whistleblower protection program is to "[r]eceive and investigate... complaints of reprisal made by civilian appropriated fund employees" consistent with Title 5, United States Code, Section 2302 (5 U.S.C. Section 2302).[29]

Employees of the DoD are required to report "waste, fraud, abuse, and corruption to appropriate authorities.[30] Title 5 U.S.C. Section 2302 (b)(8) provides protection to DoD employees who make or prepare to make a "protected disclosure." A protected disclosure is a disclosure of information the employee reasonably believes evidences a violation of any law, rule, or regulation, or gross mismanagement, a gross waste of funds, an abuse of authority, or a substantial and specific danger to public health or safety, if such disclosure is not specifically prohibited by law and if such information is not specifically required by executive order to be kept secret in the interest of national defense or the conduct of foreign affairs.[31]

Title 5 U.S.C., Section 2302 (a)(2)(A)(i) through (xi) lists personnel actions which, if taken, withheld, or threatened in reprisal for a protected disclosure, constitute "prohibited personnel practices." These personnel actions include disciplinary or corrective action; a detail, transfer or reassignment; a performance evaluation; a decision to order psychiatric testing or examination; a decision concerning pay, benefits, or award; or any other significant change in duties, responsibilities, or working conditions.

We employ a two-stage process in conducting whistleblower reprisal investigations. The first stage focuses on the alleged protected disclosure, personnel actions, and acting official's knowledge. The second stage focuses on whether or not the Agency would have taken, withheld, or threatened the personnel action(s) absent the protected disclosure. The first stage of the whistleblower reprisal analysis is held to a preponderance of the evidence.[32] "Preponderance" of the evidence is that degree of relevant evidence that a reasonable person, considering the record as a whole, would accept as sufficient to find that a contested fact is more likely to be true than untrue.[33]

In order to progress to the second stage of the investigative process, there must be sufficient evidence based on proof by a preponderance of the evidence to make three findings:

1   the complainant made a protected disclosure;

2   the complainant was the subject of a personnel action; and

3   the disclosure was a contributing factor in the personnel action.[34]

If a preponderance of the evidence supports the three findings above, the investigation will proceed to the second stage of the analysis. At that point, the Agency is afforded the opportunity to provide evidence regarding the allegations and specifically, evidence that would establish the Agency would have taken, withheld, or threatened the personnel action against the complainant absent the protected disclosure. The second stage of analysis is held to a clear and convincing evidence standard. "Clear and convincing" evidence is that measure or degree of proof that produces in the mind of the trier of fact a firm belief as to the allegations sought to be established. It is a higher standard than preponderance of the evidence, but lower than beyond a reasonable doubt.[35]

To address the fourth element, we consider the following three factors for presence of "clear and convincing" evidence:[36]

1   the strength of the Agency's evidence in support of its personnel action;

2   the existence and strength of any motive to retaliate on the part of the Agency officials who were involved in the decision; and

3   any evidence that the Agency takes similar actions against employees who are not whistleblowers but who are otherwise similarly situated.

We interviewed 10 witnesses, including the complainant, Ms. Gray, and the responsible management officials (RMOs), [REDACTED] [REDACTED] and Mr. John Metzler (Senior Executive Service), Superintendent, ANC. We also reviewed documentation provided by Ms. Gray, the Agency, and other independent sources.

Ms. Gray had standing to file a Section 7 Complaint[37] with the Defense Hotline because she was a full-time civilian employee of the DoD and her position was financed with appropriated funds. We reviewed this complaint consistent with 5 U.S.C. Section 2302 (b)(8). Ms. Gray alleged that she was reprised against for disclosing information that she reasonably believed evidenced a violation of rule.

Chronology

On April 14, 2008, Ms. Gray was hired at ANC as a PA Specialist in probationary status for one year.[38]

On April 17, 2008, [REDACTED] expressed "her wishes for civilian media to cover the funeral ceremony" of her husband, LtCol Hall. LtCol Hall was a Marine killed by an improvised explosive device in Iraq on March 29, 2008.[39]

On April 23, 2008, [REDACTED] set the ropes where the media was to be designated for the Hall funeral.[40] When Ms. Gray escorted the media to the funeral site, she testified that the original designated location had been moved and the media became upset over the distance from and their obstructed view of the funeral site. [REDACTED] testified that Ms. Gray requested her to see if the media "could get closer" to the funeral site. [REDACTED] asked [REDACTED] if he would "speak with the media because they [the media] were complaining about the distance that they were from the gravesite" and that "they could not see [the funeral site]." [REDACTED] did so, however, because the family was approaching "it was just too late to do anything."[41] Both [REDACTED] and [REDACTED] testified that there were "larger monuments" and "[head]stones" that obstructed the media's view of the funeral at the location where the media was placed.[42] That morning, LtCol Hall was laid to rest at ANC. He was the most senior officer casualty of the Iraq war at the time.[43]

On April 24, 2008, the *Washington Post* reported on the funeral ceremony of LtCol Hall. Specifically, the *Post* wrote,

> Journalists were held 50 yards from the service, separated from the mourning party by six or seven rows of graves, and staring into the sun and penned in by a yellow rope. Photographers and reporters pleaded with Arlington officials ... 'We're not going to be able to hear a thing,' a reporter argued. 'Mm-hmm,' an Arlington official answered. The distance made it impossible to hear the words of Chaplain Ron Nordan ... Nor does the blocking of funeral coverage seem to be the work of overzealous bureaucrats. Gina Gray, Arlington's new public affairs director, pushed vigorously to allow the journalists more access to the service yesterday but she was apparently shot down by other cemetery officials.[44]

Ms. Gray testified that she was not a source for *Washington Post* reporter Mr. Dana Milbank's article.[45]

On or about April 24, 2008, Ms. Gray asked [REDACTED], "Who says where the media goes?[46] [REDACTED] testified that Ms. Gray's "biggest complaint was that the media could not see and were not close enough"[47] and that "she (Ms. Gray) just thought that the policy was not right and what we were doing was not right (in reference to the Hall funeral)."[48]

On April 24, 2008, Ms. Gray sent an e-mail to [REDACTED] U.S. Army Office of the Chief of Public Affairs OCPA; [REDACTED] OCPA; and [REDACTED] U.S. Army; regarding media access restriction. Citing a legal review of proposed regulations for media at the cemetery, Ms. Gray wrote, "there is some very strong language in favor of allowing media coverage (within reason) and directly contradicts what ihave been verbally directed to do..." She continued,

> Memorandum published on 18 Mar 2004 and distributed by MG Jackman [MG Galen Jackman, former Military District of Washington (MDW) Commanding General] clearly establishes ground rules ... memorandum further states that 'media will be allowed in an area designated by the U.S. Army MDW and placed by the Superintendent

of ANC. The distance will be between 75 to 100 feet from the ceremony or gravesite. The U.S. Army MDW PAO (Public Affairs Office) may allow slight media movement to the left and right to ensure the media have an unobstructed view of the service.' ... While it sets a good standard, ɪbelieve some improvements could and should be made as soon as possible.

Further, with regard to the Jackman Memo, Ms. Gray stated, "ɪknow that this was prior to the breakaway of the public affairs from MDW and putting it in ANC's hands, but I think there are some guidelines and precedents that have been put out."[49]

On April 25, 2008, Ms. Gray sent an e-mail to Mr. Ryan McCarthy, Special Assistant to the Secretary of Defense; [REDACTED] [REDACTED], whereby Ms. Gray attached several documents "outlining the rules of media coverage at the cemetery." In this e-mail, Ms. Gray wrote that [REDACTED] briefed her that ANC used media guidance in the current Code of Federal Regulations (CFR), and that he handed her the proposed revision to the applicable section of the CFR and told Ms. Gray to "use [it] as a guideline for the future until it becomes policy." Ms. Gray continued,

> [REDACTED] told me this afternoon that he would contact legal to see if we could publish this [proposed CFR 553] and issue this as firm guidance until the proposed changes have been codified... with regards to the events of LtCol Hall's funeral, I have attached a timeline of events from my perspective.[50]

Approximately one to two days following the Hall funeral and as a consequence of the April 24, 2008, *Washington Post* article, [REDACTED] testified that "the Secretary of the Army or the Secretary of Defense called Mr. Metzler and asked us to explain what occurred at the Hall service."[51] Additionally, sometime in this time frame, Ms. Gray communicated orally to [REDACTED] Joint Force Headquarters - National Capital Region, MDW PA Office, her concerns regarding media access during the Hall funeral. Specifically, [REDACTED] testified that Ms. Gray discussed the events surrounding the Hall funeral and that "was concerned because she felt that the media were being blocked... she basically stood up and said we need to move folks (the media attending the Hall funeral)."[52]

On April 28, 2008, [REDACTED] sent an e-mail to Mr. Metzler, whereby the Office of Secretary of Defense (OSD) requested an executive summary of the events surrounding the Hall funeral.[53]28 Later on this day, Ms. Gray sent an e-mail to [REDACTED] whereby she wrote, "They have not given me a copy of the exsum (executive summary)... there are variations of the truth being written up... the answers coming out of here are not my answers, against my advice, not based on facts, and I will not be part of it. Very anti-media sentiment coming from deputy [REDACTED].[54] 29

On April 28, 2008 [REDACTED] sent an e-mail to Mr. Metzler, [REDACTED], and other U.S. Army officials requesting "a summary of the policy about media access. We want to send SD (Secretary of Defense) as a back-up to your EXSUM (Executive Summary)... control of the media during the ceremonies... distances that are allowed... if family not available, who makes that decisions for media access"[55]30

On April 29, 2008, ANC issued a media release stating,

> In light of heightened interest surrounding the recent events regarding USMC LtCol William Hall's funeral services, ANC is reviewing its current procedures on media coverage and will publish standard guidelines that will provide transparency in the expectation for members of the press, not interfere with military funeral protocol, and respect the family's right to mourn privately. A media roundtable with ANC officials will be held on Wednesday 30 April 2008 in Room lE462 of the Pentagon to discuss current and future media practices.[56] 31

On April 30, 2008, a media roundtable was held with representatives from the media, MDW, Army PA, and ANC officials to discuss media practices at ANC as a result of media coverage of the Hall funeral.[57]

In early May 2008, [REDACTED] Fort Myer, testified that he met with [REDACTED] to discuss issues she was having with Ms. Gray. [REDACTED] further reported that at this meeting "She was considering terminating her based on that fact. She asked me basically if we could do it. Can we terminate her because they did not think she was working out." At this point, [REDACTED] advised [REDACTED] to document these reported incidents.[58]33 Mr. Metzler also testified that in the first part of May" [REDACTED] asked him if she could terminate Ms. Gray. At which point, Mr. Metzler advised [REDACTED] that "[Ms. Gray] needed more time.[59] 34

On May 7, 2008, the *Stars and Stripes* newspaper reported on the media issues surrounding ANC. Specifically, *Stars and Stripes* reported,

> It seems that Hall's family was asked, as all families are in these circumstances, whether the media could be present. They said, 'yes.' Reporters and cameramen were indeed present, but were only allowed to observe the pre-funeral procession. They were held far away from the graveside service and the family, so far away that they could not hear the chaplain's words or take close-up photographs... even the Public Affairs Director at Arlington, Gina Gray, sought to have the media moved closer, but was over-ruled... I found the man in the know: Thurman Higginbotham, Deputy Superintendent of the cemetery. He made no apologies for keeping the press at a distance.[60] 35

In approximately mid-May 2008, Mr. Metzler recalled that there was a meeting between [REDACTED] [REDACTED] and himself to discuss the events surrounding the Hall funeral And Ms. Gray's involvement. In reference to what was discussed with respect to Ms. Gray, Mr. Metzler testified,

> I think her [Ms. Gray's] lack of following his [REDACTED] instructions and/or [REDACTED] instructions. Again, she's [Ms. Gray] only on board two weeks and she's just too new here to understand what's going on here and we probably needed to explain to her in more detail or we needed to explain to her again the sensitivity of the funerals.[61] 36

On May 20, 2008, Ms. Gray sent an e-mail to [REDACTED] whereby she detailed ANC personnel regarding Memorial Day public affair assignments and provided her opinion of PA practices. Specifically, Ms. Gray wrote,

If you feel that you want ANC non-public affairs people involved beyond running the visitors center then I would strongly object... GOOD public affairs is what you don't see, and PAO's are trained to compartmentalize information and react quickly. An admin officer in a press box is not a PAO - it's an admin officer in a press pit. MDW has offered their trained personnel and institutional knowledge, and that is something we can't afford to lose on the one day of the year that we get the most coverage ... In the end, we all work for the Army, and my decision making process is based on one thing: 'Is it good for the Army?'... I would be remiss in my duties as a PAO if I didn't advise that we use PA trained folks for a PA mission and we have more than enough.

The following morning, May 21, 2008, [REDACTED] responded to Ms. Gray and informed her that she forwarded "your info to [REDACTED]"[62]

On May 21, 2008, [REDACTED] sent an e-mail to [REDACTED] whereby in referencing the May 20, 2008, e-mail from Ms. Gray to [REDACTED], *above,* asked to "Please review to see if this is insubordination."[63] [REDACTED] testified that his office told [REDACTED] the e-mail "was not insubordination."[64]

On May 22, 2008, [REDACTED] sent an e-mail to [REDACTED] and Mr. Metzler, whereby in referencing the May 20, 2008, e-mail from Ms. Gray to [REDACTED] wrote,

Her [Ms. Gray's] e-mail to [REDACTED] is characterized in several ways; disrespectful for a supervisor; insubordination and probably other charges... We can't let this go without formal action my suggestions are; 1. If she is probationary, remove her now, 2... disciplinary taken and advise her she is probationary, 3. Pull the PAO responsibility from her and give it to [REDACTED] for Memorial Day to show her we can and have done this without her and removal or disciplinary action ... We need to let her go now; I'd hate to see what kind of attitude she will have after doing one of these ceremonies. We can't let this go.[65]

On May 27,2008, [REDACTED] sent an e-mail to [REDACTED] whereby she wrote, "[REDACTED] I have more information in reference to the removal of Gina Gray."[66]

On June 2, 2008, [REDACTED] sent an e-mail to [REDACTED] requesting "the status of the removal letter?" Later that day, [REDACTED] replied, "If you want to terminate Gina (Ms. Gray) now, I'll send the letter for [REDACTED] to review."[67]

On June 3, 2008, [REDACTED] provided Ms. Gray with her civilian evaluation report form (DA Form 7222-1). This form should be provided to an employee by a supervisor within 30 days of reporting for duty in order to outline and clarify their significant duties, responsibilities, expectations, and performance objectives for the upcoming year.[68]

On June 3, 2008, Ms. Gray sent an e-mail to [REDACTED] where she questioned the "increasingly hostile and contentious" work environment and [REDACTED] refusal to address her "face-to-face" since "outlining my suggestions for Memorial Day." Ms. Gray also wrote, "What I am asking for is an environment of professionalism... where I don't feel like I am being punished for knowing the standards of my job as prescribed by the Army and the DoD."[69]

On June 6, 2008, Ms. Gray sent a letter to Senator John W. Warner communicating her belief that "there is a serious public relations problem at ANC adversely affecting our mission and reflecting poorly upon the care we give our men and women in uniform." Ms. Gray further wrote,

> Shortly after arriving, problems began to occur with cemetery administration officials after I questioned the existence and legitimacy of public affairs policies that didn't seem to exist the blatant disregard of established regulations is disappointing I refused to tell reporters who were calling about our media policies that it is regulations that prevent them from getting a good shot. There were no such regulations in place and I would not lie.[70]

On June 17 2008, [REDACTED] a reporter for Voice of America News, sent an e-mail to [REDACTED] [REDACTED] and Ms. Gray asking if there were "any updates on coverage procedures for funerals at Arlington?"[71]

On June 24, 2008, Senator Warner sent a letter to Mr. Geoff Morrell, Press Secretary, U.S. Department of Defense, to request "a summary of the guidelines that shape ANC's media coverage policy, along with the regulations and procedures for their implementation."[72]

On June 24, 2008, [REDACTED] sent an e-mail [REDACTED]. The e-mail contained an attachment with a one-page chronology of events from June 17-23, 2008, entitled "Removal Information for Gina Gray." Specifically, [REDACTED] wrote,

> Ms. Gray was not in on June 17, 2008, so I stayed to escort the media. Not knowing Ms. Gray's illness, I called to ask her who I was to meet at the gate... Ms. Gray provided me no detail information (regarding her illness)... On June 19th media from the Discovery Channel was at the gate (ANC gate) it was scheduled with Gina... I had no knowledge of such media request... On June 23rd I was notified... that Gina approved media for the 3:00 service... I was not able to accommodate the media... since I had no knowledge of the request... Ms. Gray withholds detailed information from me. I only receive a portion of what is going on.[73]

On June 25, 2008, Ms. Gray met with Major General (MG) Richard J. Rowe, Commander, MDW. She gave MG Rowe a binder of information and reported "major problems" at ANC to include allegations of failure to follow Army regulations, contract fraud, and budget mismanagement.[74]

On June 27, 2008, [REDACTED] sent an e-mail [REDACTED]. The e-mail contained an attachment with a chronology of events used to provide "supporting documentation for termination of Ms. Gray." In addition to the details provided to [REDACTED] in the June 24 chronology of events, *above,* this chronology also included events beginning on April 30, 2008, as follows:

> On April 30, 2008... there was a round table meeting held at the Pentagon... she [Ms. Gray]... left the office with a Navy Officer and did not return... she [did not] tell us she was leaving. Ms. Gray showed inappropriate and disrespectful behavior... Ms. Gray's e-mail (May 20, 2008, e-

mail, *above)* to me was disrespectful and inappropriate as her supervisor. She failed to follow instructions, by setting up the meeting with the ANC staff to make assignments... Ms. Gray notified several people of her situation [in regards to Ms. Gray being ill], but when I e-mailed her to ask about work and followed up with a phone call she said I was causing her stress... recommend immediate removal.[75]

On June 27, 2008, [REDACTED] issued Ms. Gray a letter of termination during probationary period effective immediately. [REDACTED] cited as grounds for probationary termination failure "to follow my instructions... to effectively communicate with me and Deputy Superintendent... to provide me with complete details for your work assignments, been disrespectful to me as your supervisor and failed to act in an in appropriate manner."[76] 51

On July 9, 2008, Mr. Metzler sent a letter to Senator Warner in response to his June 24, 2008, letter, *above.* Mr. Metzler wrote,

I assure you that there is not a deliberate effort to exclude the media from the funeral ... Based on the terrain or military formations required, we make every reasonable effort to accommodate the press without infringing on ceremonial protocol or the families' right to grieve... It is difficult to apply one set of standards and rules when handling something as sensitive as the death of a loved one. While one family may allow a reporter to stand next to them, another family may not want to see the media at all... I am sure that you appreciate... our responsibility to accommodate the families' wishes.[77] 52

On October 10, 2008, Ms. Gray filed a whistleblower reprisal complaint with the Defense Hotline.

Findings And Analysis

1. Did Ms. Gray make a protected disclosure? Yes.

To determine whether a disclosure qualifies as protected, we employ a two-step process based on statute and case law. First, we determine whether the disclosure fits within the definition of 5 U.S.C. Section 2302 (b)(8). Next, we determine whether the disclosure fits within the categories of protected disclosures recognized by the U.S. Court of Appeals for the Federal Circuit in *Huffman* v. *Office of Personnel Management,* 263 F.3d 1341,1353 (Fed. Cir. 2001).

Title 5 U.S.C. Section 2302 prohibits an Agency from taking, failing to take, or threatening to take a personnel action against a civilian employee, organized under Title 5 (appropriated fund), for making a protected disclosure. Section 2302 defines a protected communication as any disclosure of information which the employee reasonably believes evidences:[78]

1 a violation of any law, rule, or regulation; or

2 gross mismanagement, a gross waste of funds, an abuse of authority, or a substantial and specific danger to public health or safety.

In *Huffman,* the U.S. Circuit Court of Appeals for the Federal Circuit outlined the following three categories into which a disclosure may fall. Only the latter two constitute disclosures that are protected under the Whistleblower Protection Act:

1 disclosures made as part of normal duties through normal channels;

2 disclosures made as part of normal duties outside of normal channels; and

3 disclosures outside of assigned duties.

We identified five communications made by Ms. Gray, from April 23 to June 6, 2008, for analysis to determine whether they are protected disclosures under 5 U.S.C. Section 2302 and *Huffman:*

1. On April 23, 2008, during the Hall funeral, Ms. Gray asked if the media "could get closer" to the funeral site.[79]54 [REDACTED] asked if he would "speak with the media because they" (the media) were complaining about the distance that they were from the gravesite" and that "they could not see [the funeral site]."[80] 55 [REDACTED] did so, and according to Ms. Gray, her supervisors "exchanged words" with media representatives.[81] 56 [REDACTED] recalled telling Ms. Gray that the family was approaching and that "it was just too late to do anything."[82] 57

On April 24, 2008, the *Washington Post* reported on the Hall funeral, noting,

> Nor does the blocking of funeral coverage seem to be the work of overzealous bureaucrats. Gina Gray, Arlington's new public affairs director, pushed vigorously to allow the journalists more access to the service yesterday but she was apparently shot down by other cemetery officials.[83] 58

According to Ms. Gray, the *Washington Post* article generated numerous media inquiries regarding policy concerning media involvement in ANC channels. As a result, Ms. Gray sought guidance in her response to those media inquires.

Approximately one day after the Hall funeral, on April 24, 2008, Ms. Gray asked [REDACTED] "Who says where the media goes?"[84]59 In response to media inquiries following the *Washington Post* article, Ms. Gray also asked [REDACTED] what standard to cite for media placement.[85] [REDACTED] testified that Ms. Gray's "biggest complaint was that the media could not see an were not close enough"[86] and that "she [Ms. Gray] just thought that the policy was not right and what we were doing was not right (in reference to the Hall funeral). That was her opinion."[87]62

Within approximately two weeks of the *Washington Post* article being published, [REDACTED] reported that Ms. Gray cited the Jackman Memo as a possible governing regulation on media access during funerals. Specifically, [REDACTED] reported that, "... since April 2008, Ms. Gray did decide to use the MDW rules (the Jackman Memo). She [Ms. Gray] did state that she would use the rules she had since the CFR [32001] rules were not published. That was her decision, not mine. I did not try to sway her one way or the other."[88]63

2. On April 24, 2008, Ms. Gray sent an e-mail to [REDACTED] [REDACTED] and [REDACTED] regarding media access restriction during the Hall funeral. Specifically, Ms. Gray wrote,

> I have just found some documentation that started on 2 December 2003 with a memorandum... regarding a legal review for media guidelines for ANC. There is some very

strong language in favor of allowing media coverage (within reason) and directly contradicts what I have been verbally directed to do... Memorandum published on 18 Mar. 2004 and distributed by MG Jackman clearly establishes ground rules. Memorandum further states that 'media will be allowed in an area designated by the U.S. Army MDW and placed by the Superintendent of ANC. The distance will be between 75 to 100 feet from the ceremony or gravesite. The U.S. Army MDW PAO may allow slight media movement to the left and right to ensure the media have an unobstructed view of the service.'[89]

3. Ms. Gray orally communicated her concerns approximately April 24 or April 25, to [REDACTED] regarding media access during the funeral. Specifically, [REDACTED] testified that "she [Ms. Gray] was extremely concerned because she communicated that (the events surrounding the Hall funeral) back with our office. I know that she talked with me and she was concerned because she felt that the media were being blocked." [REDACTED] continued,

> She communicated that placement of the media was a continuing concern for her. As far as I know, that particular ceremony was the one that caused the largest stress for her because the movement of the media line was done in front of the media. Although she tried to talk to the official there about why they needed to see, it apparently fell on deaf ears. She was very upset about that ... Gina (Ms. Gray) expressed to me and a couple of people that they were really not happy with her because she basically stood up and said we need to move folks (the media attending the Hall funeral).[90]

Ms. Gray reported that she told [REDACTED] the events surround [sic] the Hall funeral and she "believed what [REDACTED] and [REDACTED] did (with respect to media access during the Hall funeral) was wrong, unethical, and mean-spirited."[91]

4. On June 6, 2008, Ms. Gray sent a letter to Senator John W. Warner communicating her belief that there is a serious public relations problem at ANC adversely affecting our mission and reflecting poorly upon the care we give our men and women in uniform ... Shortly after arriving, problems began to occur with cemetery administration officials after I questioned the existence and legitimacy of public affairs policies that didn't seem to exist the blatant disregard of established regulations is disappointing I refused to tell reporters who were calling about our media policies that it is regulations that prevent them from getting a good shot. There were no such regulations in place (restricting the media from getting a 'good shot') and I would not lie.[92]67

5. On June 25, 2008, Ms. Gray orally communicated to MG Rowe during his open office hours, "major problems" at ANC to include allegations of failures to follow Army regulations, contract fraud, and budget mismanagement.

With respect to Ms. Gray's first communication above, the evidence established that her activity at the April 23, 2008, funeral failed to qualify as a protected disclosure both under 5 U.S.C. Section 2302 and the rule in *Huffman* and its progeny. Specifically, the evidence established that during the Hall funeral, Ms. Gray's only communication of interest consisted of asking supervisors whether the press could be moved closer to the grave site. This was prompted by media complaints that they were too far away and couldn't hear the funeral procession. In short, Ms. Gray simply conveyed a media complaint to her supervisors. She did not communicate any potential violation of law, rule, or regulation at the time. Additionally, this communication was part of her normal duties and addressed through normal channels.

Interacting with the media and raising media concerns to her supervisors fell within her duties as a public affairs specialist, and the normal and logical channel for Ms. Gray to address media concerns was with her supervisors.[93]

Ms. Gray's own testimony further supports a conclusion that her comments at the funeral were a routine subordinate-supervisor exchange in the course of her duties: "And I honestly didn't realize that it was going to be that much of an issue until the following day (when the *Washington Post* published their article)... "[94] Ms. Gray's question to her supervisors was not a disclosure of information that a disinterested observer would reasonably believe evidenced a violation of law, rule, or regulation. Furthermore, to qualify as a protected disclosure under *Huffman,* the allegation of wrongdoing must be made to someone other than the wrongdoer.[95] At the Hall funeral, Ms. Gray's interaction and communication was with [REDACTED] and [REDACTED] the two people she considered to be the wrongdoers and responsible or media placement that day.[96] Therefore, Ms. Gray's communication conveying a question from the media to her supervisors does not qualify as a protected disclosure and does not satisfy *Huffman.*

We determined that Ms. Gray's second communication, her e-mail to [REDACTED] [REDACTED] and [REDACTED] qualified as a protected disclosure. Specifically, approximately one day after the Hall funeral, on April 24, 2008, Ms. Gray asked [REDACTED] what law to cite for restricting media access.[97] Ms. Gray acknowledged that [REDACTED] told her, "It's the law" and that he cited to 32 CFR as guidance.[98] Ms. Gray reported that after she learned of and reviewed potentially applicable guidance, including the Jackman Memo, she reported her concerns about the adequacy of that guidance and ANC's handling of media to [REDACTED] and [REDACTED].[99] Ms. Gray reported that she "believed that by reaching out to OCPA officials ([REDACTED and [REDACTED]), that they would intervene and some resolution some resolution could be reached with ANC officials on how to properly handle the media."[100]

We noted that the Jackman Memo may have been technically inapplicable because of an ANC organizational realignment. However, it retained some standing as a source of guidance. That is, ANC was removed from certain aspects of MDW management on October 29, 2004.

The responsibility for ANC public affairs policy was assigned to the Army Chief of Public Affairs.[101] However, no substitution or similar policy was issued regarding media placement, leaving the reasonable assumption the Jackman Memo represented guidance. Indeed, [REDACTED] acknowledged so in his testimony ("I do remember having the [Jackman] memo and saying that this is our policy until Army decides there will be something different.").[102]

We also determined that Ms. Gray's second communication fell outside of her chain of command, therefore meeting 5 U.S.C. Section 2302's application under *Huffman.*

With respect to Ms. Gray's third communication, her oral conversation with [REDACTED] in order for this communication to be protected, it must be sufficiently specific and not constitute mere vague allegations of wrongdoing regarding broad and imprecise matters.[103] We determined that Ms. Gray's communication with [REDACTED] constituted a protected disclosure. Ms. Gray's communication with [REDACTED] relayed concerns similar to those of [REDACTED] [REDACTED] and [REDACTED] *above,* and noted that during the Hall funeral, the "media were being blocked" by an "official." Ms. Gray communicated that she "stood up and said we (ANC) need[ed] to move folks (the media attending the Hall funeral)." We therefore determined that Ms. Gray clearly expressed her concerns that the media was blocked access to the Hall funeral to someone other than the wrongdoer in seeking remedial action. We also concluded that Ms. Gray's oral communication with [REDACTED] met the requirements of a bona fide protected disclosure as defined under 5 U.S.C. Section 2302 and *Huffman.* These requirements were met as Ms. Gray's communication to [REDACTED] fell outside of her chain of command and was not made as part of her normal duties.

With respect to Ms. Gray's fourth communication, we determined that Ms. Gray's complaint to Senator Warner was a protected disclosure under 5 U.S.C. Section 2302. Under Section 2302, no personnel action may be taken against an employee who discloses information to the Congress which they reasonably believe evidences a violation of any law, rule, or regulation, or gross mismanagement, a gross waste of funds, an abuse of authority, or a substantial and specific danger to public health or safety.[104] This communication also satisfies *Huffman* because it fell outside of Ms. Gray's chain of command and filing a congressional complaint was not part of her normal job duties.

With respect to Ms. Gray's fifth and final communication, we determined that Ms. Gray's complaint to MG Rowe was a protected disclosure. Specifically, the requirements of 5 U.S.C. Section 2302 were met as Ms. Gray reasonably believed that there were "major problems" at ANC to include allegations of failures to follow Army regulations, contract fraud, and budget mismanagement. This belief is evident in that Ms. Gray provided MG Rowe a notebook of information evidencing her claim.[105] We also determined that Ms. Gray's fifth communication fell outside of her chain of command and was not made as part of her normal duties, therefore meeting 5 U.S.C. Section 2302's application under *Huffman*.

Consequently, Ms. Gray made four communications that constitute protected disclosures as defined under 5 U.S.C. Section 2302 and *Huffman*. However Ms. Gray's disclosures to MG Rowe and to Senator Warner occurred subsequent to [REDACTED] initial action to terminate Ms. Gray, and therefore could not have been contributing factors in [REDACTED] decision to take the personnel action. As such, for the purposes of this investigation, we did not analyze these disclosures any further.

2. Was Ms. Gray the subject of a personnel action? Yes.

Ms. Gray alleged that she suffered a total of 12 personnel actions in reprisal for making protected disclosures. Specifically, Ms. Gray alleged:

1   April 29, 2008, [REDACTED] removed Ms. Gray's job responsibility to respond to media queries;

2   April 30, 2008, [REDACTED] required Ms. Gray to report every time she left her desk;

3   May 1, 2008, [REDACTED removed Ms. Gray's job responsibility to approve media requests;

4   May 14 and 27, 2008, [REDACTED] refused Ms. Gray's request to be provided copies of timecards;

5   May 22,2008, [REDACTED] questioned Ms. Gray's work hours;

6   May 27, 2008, [REDACTED] changed Ms. Gray's proposed supervisor of Mr. Metzler to [REDACTED];

7   May 27, 2008, [REDACTED] directed Ms. Gray not to work beyond 4:30 p.m. unless given approval by both [REDACTED] and Mr. Metzler;

8   June 3, 2008, [REDACTED] refused to backdate Ms. Gray's initial Department of Army (DA) Form 7222-1 or "Evaluation Support Form," which is a refined formal description of job duties and expectations;

9 June 9, 2008, [REDACTED] changed Ms. Gray's job title from Director of PA to PA Specialist;

10 June 9, 2008, [REDACTED] terminated Ms. Gray's Black-Berry phone service;

11 June 24,2008, [REDACTED] changed Ms. Gray's office voicemail password and refused to provide the new password for several hours; and

12 June 27, 2008, [REDACTED] issued Ms. Gray a Letter of Probationary Termination.

After completing our review of documentary and testimonial evidence, we determined that 11 of the actions did not qualify as personnel actions. Actions number one,[106] two, four, five, six, seven, eight, nine, ten, and eleven, *above,* did not meet the definition of a prohibited personnel action under 5 U.S.C. Section 2302 (a)(2)(A) because they constituted neither a decision concerning pay, benefits, or award; nor a significant change in duties, responsibilities, or working conditions.

We also determined that action number three did not warrant further investigation as this was never a duty of Ms. Gray's and therefore could not constitute a personnel action. To corroborate the allegation, Ms. Gray provided the OIG DoD with three e-mails. The first one is dated June 3, 2008, more than a month after Ms. Gray alleged that [REDACTED] orally removed this duty. ANC RMOs also denied that they removed the responsibility.[107] Therefore, we could not determine if and when the duty change happened, but proceeded on with our analysis on the evidence provided.

Ms. Gray's position description lists the responsibility of "approves or denies media requests."[108] The media request duty is also listed in her civilian evaluation report form (DA Form 7222-1) under major performance objectives and standards as "responsible for evaluating, coordinating, and scheduling all media requests."[109] This form is provided to an employee by a supervisor within 30 days of reporting for duty in order to outline and clarify the employee's significant duties, responsibilities, and performance objectives for the upcoming year. This form "takes precedence over the position description."[110] Because the DA Form 7222-1 supplants the position description, Ms. Gray would not be "approving or denying," but rather "evaluating, coordinating, and scheduling" media requests.

Ms. Gray indicated her recognition of this clarification in duty when she signed the DA Form 7222-1 on June 3, 2008. On the same day, Ms. Gray sent an e-mail to [REDACTED] clarifying the 'media request' duty.'"86 Ms. Gray provided two e-mails, both dated June 12, 2008, to corroborate her allegation that this was a removed duty.'"87 These e-mails are subsequent to Ms. Gray's June 3, 2008, clarification of duty. Based on the facts presented: 1) RMOs denied that they removed the responsibility, 2) the absence of evidence that the duty was performed before June 3, 2008, 3) the precedence of the DA Form 7222-1 over the position description, and 4) Ms. Gray's June 3, 2008, knowledge of the clarification in duty, we concluded by a preponderance of the evidence that her responsibility with media requests was never a duty to remove. Therefore, allegation of reprisal number three did not warrant further investigation because it was not a personnel action.

We therefore determined that Ms. Gray was subject to one personnel action by [REDACTED] June 27, 2008, Letter of Probationary Termination as it met the definition of a prohibited personnel action under 5 U.S.C. Section 2302 (a)(2)(A).

3. Did the acting official have knowledge, actual or constructive, of the complainant's protected disclosure and did the personnel action take place within a period of time subsequent to the disclosure, such that a reasonable person could conclude that the disclosure was a contributing factor in the decision to take the personnel action? No.

We determined by a preponderance of the evidence that [REDACTED] did not have knowledge of Ms. Gray's second and third disclosure, *above*. Specifically, there was no evidence to suggest that Ms. Gray or the recipients of Ms. Gray's protected disclosures took action to alert [REDACTED] [REDACTED] or any other RMO of the protected disclosures made.'"88 Because [REDACTED] did not have knowledge of the protected disclosures, Ms. Gray's whistleblowing could not have been a contributing factor in [REDACTED] termination decision.

While this investigation did not progress to the clear and convincing evidence analysis in the absence of a disclosure showing causation, the Inspector General is not limited by *Huffman* in reviewing the actions of DoD managers and supervisors.[114] We therefore reviewed the personnel action in the case, namely, the supervision and termination of Ms. Gray.

4. Related Issue: ANC failed to exhibit adequate performance and management in the supervision and termination of Ms. Gray:

We determined that with respect to the supervision and termination of Ms. Gray, ANC management demonstrated an obvious failure to exercise sound personnel management. That is, based on public affairs policy issues that Ms. Gray raised during her first weeks of employment, ANC management elected to terminate her rather than make a reasonable effort to address those policy issues, provide suitable guidance to Ms. Gray, or document performance deficiencies that ANC management later claimed formed the basis for Ms. Gray's termination.

We recognize the distinction between federal employees serving their probationary period and those who have completed their probation, as well as the distinction in termination requirements between the two groups. An employee in probationary status is afforded a "trial period" that provides them an opportunity to demonstrate suitability for continued employment.

Conversely, the Agency has an opportunity to assess the employee's full potential, competencies and capabilities, and has the responsibility to assess whether or not they possess satisfactory qualifications and suitability for regular full-time employment.

In determining whether the Agency adequately and appropriately performed and managed the termination of Ms. Gray, we reviewed U.S. Army Regulation (AR) 600-100, Army Leadership and AR 690-400, Total Army Performance Evaluation System.

AR 600-100 establishes Army leadership policy and sets forth the attitude and responsibilities for all aspects of leadership. Specifically, the regulation identifies several core leader competencies that are applicable in assessing the performance execution of Ms. Gray's termination. We identified several core leader competencies including effectively communicating by expressing ideas and actively listening to others, creating a positive organizational climate and fostering the setting for positive attitudes and effective work behaviors, and developing others by encouraging and supporting the growth of individuals."[115]

AR 690-400 establishes Army policy for civilian personnel performance management programs. In short, it is the direct application of performance management. Applicable to Ms. Gray's termination is section 2.6(a), which states that "although formal PIPs (Performance Improvement Plan) are not required for ratees who are serving probationary appointments, raters normally should provide ratees who are not meeting expectations with enough information to help them understand how they are failing and how they might improve."[116] A reasonable supervisor under the AR 690-400 would provide a probationary employee a formal document (e.g., letter of counseling or PIP) that would, at the very least, put the employee on notice that they are not meeting the expectations of performance and/or conduct suitable for regular full-time employment.

With respect to Ms. Gray's termination, as an application of Army leadership competencies established by AR 600-100 and in the practice of performance management as established by AR 690-400, we determined that the Agency, and specifically [REDACTED], failed to meet adequate application or performance of those standards. The following factors contributed to our determination:

* [REDACTED] did not provide Ms. Gray a single counseling document such as a letter of counseling or memorandum for record (MFR). While it may be argued that the Agency was not required to document justification to terminate Ms. Gray, it was prudent to document to provide evidence justifying their action.

* There was a lack of corroborating evidence that [REDACTED] orally counseled Ms. Gray for the reasons cited in her termination letter. [REDACTED] testified that the reasons cited for Ms. Gray's termination were "based on [her] observations."[117]92 The OIG DoD viewed the testimony of [REDACTED] as particularly important because he was Ms. Gray's second-line supervisor. For this

reason, he would have logically been privy to the issues surrounding Ms. Gray's cited performance and conduct deficiencies and any action taken to correct them. However, [REDACTED] denied direct knowledge of Ms. Gray being counseled for conduct and performance deficiencies and attributed his knowledge to only what [REDACTED] told him.[118] [REDACTED] also testified that although he had knowledge of the chronological summary of events that [REDACTED] "turned over to Human Resources," he did not have copies of the documents and never personally reviewed them.[119]

* By providing counseling to Ms. Gray, either verbal and or in writing, [REDACTED] would have demonstrated the standards set forth in AR 600-100 and 690-400, namely effectively communicating to Ms. Gray that she was not meeting performance and/or conduct standards. This communication would have provided Ms. Gray the guidance required to develop as a suitable ANC employee. As Ms. Gray's manager, [REDACTED] was responsible for facilitating Ms. Gray's development "through *counseling, coaching,* and *mentoring.*"[120]

* There was a lack of corroboration with the reasons cited in Ms. Gray's termination letter. Specifically, while the general reasons cited by [REDACTED] as grounds for probationary termination were individually questioned (*e.g.,* failure "to follow my instructions... to effectively communicate with me and [REDACTED] ... to provide me with complete details for your work assignments, been disrespectful to me as your supervisor and failed to act in an in [sic] appropriate manner"), [REDACTED] Ms. Gray's second-line supervisor, testified that he had "no direct knowledge" on all the reasons except the failure to provide complete details of Ms. Gray's work and being "disrespectful" to [REDACTED] as a supervisor.

* With respect to complete details of Ms. Gray's work, [REDACTED] cited incidents that he had personal

knowledge of including "the Kennedy gravesite" and "when [Ms. Gray] was out with her illness." However, [REDACTED] did not cite "the Kennedy gravesite (whereby allegedly Ms. Gray gave permission to close the grave for a filming)" incident in her two chronological summaries of events. Regarding Ms. Gray being "disrespectful" to [REDACTED] as a supervisor, [REDACTED] stated personal knowledge of Ms. Gray's May 20 2008, e-mail in reference to Memorial Day, *above,* out of the cited reasons in [REDACTED] two chronological summaries of events, as well as Ms. Gray "snapping" at [REDACTED] at the Memorial Day walkthrough."[121] Our review and testimony established that the e-mail was not insubordinate.[122]

✳ Notwithstanding Ms. Gray's probationary status and [REDACTED] failure to put Ms. Gray on notice for "not meeting expectations," [REDACTED] failed to provide adequate documentation justifying the decision to terminate Ms. Gray. Specifically, we found little contemporaneous documentation leading up to termination. [REDACTED] did not document any concerns regarding Ms. Gray's conduct or performance until she wrote a MFR on May 26, 2008, recording her concerns regarding ANC's 2008 Memorial Day event. The MFR, however, was unclear in what conduct or performance deficiencies Ms. Gray displayed during the Memorial Day event.[123] The only documentation provided to the OIG DoD justifying Ms. Gray's termination were two separate, one and three-page MFR chronological summaries of events described in the above chronology. Each was separately sent via e-mail to [REDACTED] on June 24 and 27, 2008, *above.* In those documents, [REDACTED] described and documented events that were used to support her recommend for Ms. Gray's termination. However, these summaries are dated over *six weeks* after [REDACTED considered terminating Ms. Gray in early May 2008, according to testimony from Mr. Metzler and [REDACTED] [REDACTED] produced this documentation to satisfy [REDACTED] request to provide him with termination documentation.[124]

* The time of Ms. Gray's termination, roughly two and a half months into probationary employment, is in accordance with AR 690-400. But the termination does not meet the regulation's intent for leaders "to develop those junior to them to the fullest extent possible."[125] The regulation also states that "decisions to remove probationary employees may be made at any time during the probationary period." This alone, however, does not excuse [REDACTED] or the Agency from properly informing Ms. Gray that she was "not meeting expectations." Nor does it justify denying Ms. Gray an opportunity to take corrective action and ameliorate cited deficiencies. Even though [REDACTED] and the Agency may not be aware of the specific language of AR 690-400, a previous probationary termination clearly demonstrates their clear grasp of its intent. In that termination, the employee was administered a mid-point counseling where "your standards were discussed and you were also informed on areas that need improvement." Additionally, the counseling included specific events or examples that prompted termination. [REDACTED] and the Agency provided Ms. Gray with neither. Moreover, the previous employee's termination took place after ten and a half months on the job; enough time for corrective action. Ms. Gray, on the other hand, received her notice of termination within approximately two and a half months of employment, without prior notice, and without the opportunity to take corrective action. [REDACTED] and the Agency may have operated within the letter of AR 690-400, but they failed to meet its intent by terminating Ms. Gray without proper development through counseling and corrective action.

Additionally, we found that ANC management viewed Ms. Gray's activities surrounding the Hall funeral as disruptive because they resulted in high-level and public focus on ANC operations. This contributed to the contentious relationship that developed between Ms.

Gray and her supervisors and their decision to terminate her without attempting reconciliation. The following factors contributed to that determination:

* Approximately one week following the Hall funeral, the Assistant Secretary of the Army for Manpower and Reserve Affairs requested ANC provide an executive summary of the events. An executive summary was also requested by the OSD;[126]

* On April 30, 2008, OCPA held a "media roundtable" where Ms. Gray, [REDACTED] [REDACTED] OCPA officials, and selected members of the media attended. The purpose of the meeting was "convened... to discuss the issue" of the "critical column by Dana Milbank of media coverage of military funeral at ANC;"[127]

* Mr. Metzler testified that subsequent to the Hall funeral, ANC had several additional meetings with OCPA to clarify media procedures. Specifically, he testified, "[OCPA] was not engaged very much and the Hall funeral caused that office to start to get engaged;"[128]

* When asked if [REDACTED] was upset that she had to attend the April 30, 2008, OCPA roundtable, she testified, "Oh yeah, I definitely did not want to do that... just with my experience with the media that it was going to be something else that we would have to do. When all parties get involved you know there is going to be something else that *you are going to have to do;"*[129]

* Subsequent funerals received increased media attention as witnessed on May 1, 2008, when ANC buried [REDACTED] U.S. Army, Operation Iraqi Freedom. The family requested media access and prior to the funeral ceremony, "ANC... received approximately forty phone calls inquiring about the next media authorized funeral;"[130] and

*   [REDACTED] consequently acknowledged that Ms. Gray was blamed for the increased media attention at ANC.[131]

Conclusion

We determined that Ms. Gray was a whistleblower. She was not, however, the subject of reprisal as [REDACTED] lacked knowledge of the qualifying protected disclosures. However, with respect to the supervision and termination of Ms. Gray, we determined that [REDACTED] and ANC management failed to exercise sound personnel management.

Recommendation

We recommend that the Assistant Secretary of the Army for Civil Works consider corrective action with respect to ANC officials responsible for handling Ms. Gray's supervision and termination and an appropriate remedy for Ms. Gray.

Chapter Review Questions:

1 By what authority and for what purpose did the Inspector General of the Department of Defense investigate Ms. Gray's allegations of whistleblower reprisal by her U.S. Army supervisors at Arlington National Cemetery, instead of referring the allegations to the Army Inspector General for a reprisal investigation?

2 What are the four elements that must be established in order for an Inspector General to substantiate any reprisal allegation?

3 Who bears the burden of establishing in each of the four elements of a reprisal allegation, and what is the respective standard of proof for each element? What justifies a higher standard of proof for one of those elements as compared to the other three, as applied in the Inspector General of the Department of Defense's Report of Investigation, "Whistleblower Reprisal Allegation: Arlington National Cemetery," Report No. CRI-HL109655, pp. 3-4 (June 29, 2010):

> The first stage of the whistleblower reprisal analysis is held to a preponderance of the evidence. "Preponderance" of the evidence is that degree of relevant evidence that a reasonable person, considering the record as a whole, would accept as sufficient to find that a contested fact is more likely to be true than untrue. . . . The second stage of analysis is held to a clear and convincing evidence standard. "Clear and convincing" evidence is that measure or degree of proof that produces in the mind of the trier of fact a firm belief as to the allegations sought to be established. It is a higher standard than preponderance of the evidence, but lower than beyond a reasonable doubt.

4 By what authority and for what purpose did the Inspector General of the Department of Defense "non-substantiate" reprisal in the Arlington National Cemetery "Whistleblower

Reprisal Investigation," yet in the same report of investigation substantiate a failure "to exhibit adequate performance and management in the supervision and termination of Ms. Gray"?

5 By what authority and for what purpose might the Inspector General of the Department of Defense have referred his findings of fact (as opposed to the fully investigated and unsubstantiated reprisal allegations) in the Arlington National Cemetery "Whistleblower Reprisal Investigation" to the Army Inspector General for an investigation into whether or not the findings of facts amounted to a violation of the Army Leadership Regulation (AR 600-100)?

6 Is the Exemplary Conduct leadership standard enacted by Congress in 1997 for, "All commanding officers and others in authority in the Army" (10 U.S.C. §3583) applicable to the Army civilian "officials responsible for handling Ms. Gray's supervision and termination," *e.g.*, the Arlington National Cemetery Superintendent, a member of the Senior Executive Service (SES)? Is this statutory leadership standard applicable to the Assistant Secretary of the Army for Civil Works, a Senate-confirmed Presidential appointee, to whom the Inspector General of the Department of Defense recommended, "consider[ation of] corrective action with respect to ANC officials responsible for handling Ms. Gray's supervision and termination"? *Compare* AR 600-100, Army Leadership, "Command," p. 17 (2007):

Command includes the leadership, authority, responsibility, and accountability for effectively using available resources and planning the employment of, organizing, directing, coordinating, and controlling military forces to accomplish assigned missions. It includes responsibility for unit readiness, health, welfare, morale, and discipline of assigned personnel. Title 10, Section 3583, requires exemplary conduct by all commanding officers and others in authority in the Army. All commanders are required to—

a. Present themselves as examples of virtue, honor, patriotism, and subordination;

b. Be vigilant in inspecting the conduct of all persons who are placed under their command;

c. Guard against and suppress all dissolute and immoral practices and to correct, according to the laws and regulations of the Army, all persons who are guilty of them; and

d. Take all necessary and proper measures under the laws, regulations, and customs of the Army to promote and safeguard the morale, physical well being, and the general welfare of officers and enlisted personnel under their command or charge.

with id., "Civilian Creed":

The Civilian Creed refers to the professional attitudes and beliefs that characterize the Department of Army Civilian (DAC). At its core, the Civilian Creed requires unrelenting and consistent determination to do what is right and to do it with pride, both in war and peace. No matter the conditions, it is the DA civilians selfless commitment to the Nation, the Army, and fellow civilians and Soldiers that keeps them going. It is the professional attitude that inspires every Department of Army Civilian.

7 How can any leader who has been "elected or appointed to an office of honor or profit in the civil service or uniformed services" (5 U.S.C. §3331, "Oath of office"), and therefore must take the same statutory oath of office to "support and defend the Constitution of the United States against all enemies, foreign and domestic," hold a subordinate officer, whether "in the civil service or uniformed services," to a leadership standard to which the senior leader is not willing to hold himself or herself?

---

¹ *See* 5 U.S.C. §2302(c) ("The head of each agency shall be responsible for the prevention of prohibited personnel practices, for the compliance with and enforcement of applicable civil service laws, rules, and regulations, and other aspects of personnel management, and for ensuring (in consultation with the Office of Special Counsel) that agency employees are informed of the rights and remedies available to them under this chapter and chapter 12 of this title. Any individual to whom the head of an agency delegates authority for personnel management, or for any aspect thereof, shall be similarly responsible within the limits of the delegation.").

² DoD Directive 6490.1, ¶5.2.

³ *See* 5 U.S.C. §2302(a)(2)(A)(x).

⁴ *See* United States Office of Special Counsel, Form 11 ("Legal Elements of a Violation[:] By law, certain elements must be present before OSC can establish that a legal violation of law has occurred. Two of the required elements that must be established are: (1) that a whistleblower disclosure was made; and (2) that an agency took, failed to take, or threatened to take or fail to take a personnel action because of the whistleblower disclosure. Your description of these elements will help OSC's investigation of your allegation(s).") (http://www.osc.gov/documents/forms/osc11.htm); Inspector General of the Department of Defense, Inspector General Guide 7050.6, "Guide to Investigating Reprisal and Improper Referrals for Mental Health Evaluation," ¶¶2.3-2.4, February 6, 1996 (http://web.archive.org/web/20120422181015/http://www.dodig.mil/INV/MRI/pdfs/IGDG7050_6.pdf).

⁵ See Inspector General Guide 7050.6, ¶2.5.

⁶ 5 C.F.R. §1209.4(d) ("Clear and convincing evidence is that measure or degree of proof that produces in the mind of the trier of fact a firm belief

as to the allegations sought to be established. It is a higher standard than 'preponderance of the evidence' as defined in 5 CFR 1201.56(c)(2)."); see Inspector General of the Department of Defense, "Whistleblower Reprisal Investigation: Arlington National Cemetery," Report No. CRI-HL109655, p. 4, June 29, 2010 (linked and excerpted below as the chapter case study).

[7] *See* Inspector General Guide 7050.6, ¶2.6; 5 C.F.R. §1209.7 ("Burden and degree of proof").

[8] 5 U.S.C. §2302(b)(1).

[9] *See* United States Office of Special Counsel, Form 11 ("Protected Disclosures[:] A disclosure of information is a protected whistleblower disclosure if a Federal employee, former employee, or applicant for Federal employment discloses information which he or she reasonably believes evidences: (a) a violation of any law, rule, or regulation; (b) gross mismanagement; (c) a gross waste of funds; (d) abuse of authority; or (e) a substantial and specific danger to public health or safety.").

[10] 10 U.S.C. §1034(b)(1)(b).

[11] United States Department of Defense, Office of the Inspector General, "History of the Military Whistleblower Protection Act and Statute Prohibiting the Use of Mental Health Evaluations in Reprisal"). (http://web.archive.org/web/20120609183916/http://www.dodig.mil/INV/ mri /pdfs/Timeline.pdf).

[12] 10 U.S.C. §1034(c)(4).

[13] 10 U.S.C. §1587(a)(1).

[14] Id., §1587(b).

[15] Department of Defense Directive 1401.03, "DoD Nonappropriated Fund Instrumentality (NAFI) Employee Whistleblower Protection," ¶5.1, April 23, 2008 (http://www.dtic.mil/whs/directives/corres/pdf/140103p.pdf).

[16] *Id.*, ¶¶5.3.1 & 5.3.3.

[17] 10 U.S.C. §2409.

[18] Department of Defense Directive 5106.01, "Inspector General of the Department of Defense," ¶5.19.2, April 13, 2006 (http://www.dtic.mil/whs/directives/corres/pdf/510601p.pdf).

[19] Department of Defense Directive 6490.1, "Mental Health Evaluations of Members of the Armed Forces," October 1, 1997 (certified Current as of November 24, 2003) http://www.dtic.mil/whs/directives/corres/pdf/649001p.pdf

[20] *Id.,* ¶2.3.

[21] Inspector General Act of 1978, as amended, §7(c).

[22] United States Office of Special Counsel. Form 11 (the completion of which requires the complainant to, "certify that all of the statements made in this complaint (including any continuation pages) are true, complete, and correct to the best of my knowledge and belief. I understand that a false statement or concealment of a material fact is a criminal offense punishable by a fine of up to $250,000, imprisonment for up to five years, or both. 18 U.S.C. § 1001.") (http://www.osc.gov/documents/forms/osc11.htm); see 18 U.S.C. § 1001 ("Statements or entries generally[:] **(a)** Except as otherwise provided in this section, whoever, in any matter within the jurisdiction of the executive, legislative, or judicial branch of the Government of the United States, knowingly and willfully— **(1)** falsifies, conceals, or covers up by any trick, scheme, or device a material fact; **(2)** makes any materially false, fictitious, or fraudulent statement or representation; or **(3)** makes or uses any false writing or document knowing the same to contain any materially false, fictitious, or fraudulent statement or entry; shall be fined under this title, imprisoned not more than 5 years or, if the offense involves international or domestic terrorism (as defined in section 2331), imprisoned not more than 8 years, or both. If the matter relates to an offense under chapter 109A, 109B, 110, or 117, or section 1591, then the term of imprisonment imposed under this section shall be not more than 8 years.").

[23] United States Office of Special Counsel, "Overview of 2302(c) Certification Program" (http://www.osc.gov/outreachCertificationProgram.htm#).

[24] *See* United States Office of Special Counsel, "Agencies That Have Completed The 2302(C) Certification Program" http://www.osc.gov/outreachAgenciesCertified.htm

[25] "Whistleblower Reprisal Investigation: Arlington National Cemetery," Report Number CRI-HL109655, June 29, 2010 http://s3.documentcloud.org/documents/5199/redacted-dodig-report-ongina-gray.pdf

[26] We acknowledge that Ms. Gray's whistleblowing activities continued after her termination and we understand that she contributed relevant information during a recently concluded investigation by the Army Inspector General into ANC operations. Because those later whistleblowing activities are not germane to the matter of her termination, we do not discuss them further in this report.

[27] U.S. Army PA Specialist (OS-1035-12) Position Description.

[28] DoD Directive 5106.01, (Apr. 13, 2006) at 5.19.

[29] DoD Directive 5106.01, (Apr. 13, 2006) at 5.19.1.

[30] Executive Order 12731 (October 17, 1990).

[31] 5 U.S.C. Section 2302 (b)(8)(A)(i-ii).

[32] 5 C.F.R. Section 1209.7.

[33] 5 C.F.R. Section 1201.56(c)(2).

[34] This third finding may be established where the acting official had knowledge, actual or imputed, of the complainant's disclosure and the personnel action took place within a period of time subsequent to the disclosure, such that a reasonable person could conclude that the disclosure was a contributing factor in the decision to take the action. *Redschlag v. Department of the Army, 89 MS.P.R. 589,635 (2001), review dismissed, 32 Fed. Appx. 543 (Fed. Cir. 2002)* In deciding whether a personnel action occurred within a period of time sufficient to conclude the disclosure was a contributing factor, the probative value of the evidence may be affected by the passage of

time. Weak but substantiating evidence may be sufficient to prove reprisal after a short time frame; stronger evidence may be required to prove reprisal over relatively longer time frames.

[35] 5 C.F.R. Section 1209.4(d).

[36] *Carr* v. *Social Security Admin.*, 185 F.3d 1318, 1323 (Fed. Cir. 1999) (stating it is appropriate to consider the strength of the Agency's evidence in support of its personnel action when determining whether the Agency has shown by clear and convincing evidence that it would have taken that action in the absence of the employee's protected disclosure).

[37] 5 U.S.C. Appendix, Section 7(A)(2008) (provisions by which a DoD employee may file complaints with the Inspector General).

[38] Standard Form 50-B - Notification of Personnel Action (Apr. 14, 2008).

[39] Memorandum from [REDACTED], Marine Barracks Washington, D.C., to OIG DoD, *Media Coverage concerning the funeral of [REDACTED] at ANC* (Apr. 8, 2009).

[40] OIG DoD Interview of [REDACTED] (Apr. 29, 2009) at 31. [REDACTED] testified that the original location was changed "because the Marine Corps, and the Air Force, and the Navy put their escorts at the foot of the grave" and "we [ANC] just can't put you [the media] in the middle of the funeral."

[41] OIG DoD Interview o A r. 28, 2009) at 26 and 28.

[42] OIG DoD Interview o (Apr. 29,2009) at 31 and OIG DoD Interview o-

(Apr. 28, 2009) at 26.

[43] *William Gregory Hall,* ANC,
http://www.pdfonfly.com/pdfs/http___www.arlingtoncemetery.net_wghall.h tm.pdf

[44] Dana Milbank, *What the Family Would Let You See, the Pentagon Obstructs,* Washington Post (Apr. 24, 2008) at A3.

[45] OIG DoD Interview of Ms. Gray (Jan. 15, 2009) at 22.

[46] OIG DoD Interview of [REDACTED] (Apr. 28, 2009) at 39.

[47] *Id.* at 40.

[48] *Id.* at 36.

[49] E-mail from Ms. Gray to[REDACTED] [REDACTED] and [REDACTED] *More Documentation* (Apr. 24, 2008, 9:10 p.m.).

[50] E-mail from Ms. Gray to [REDACTED] [REDACTED] and [REDACTED] ANC Documents (Apr. 25, 2008,7:19 p.m.).

[51] OIG DoD Interview of [REDACTED] (Apr. 28, 2009) at 24-25.

[52] OIG DoD Interview of [REDACTED] (Apr. 15, 2009) at 10 and 12-13.

[53] E-mail from [REDACTED] to Mr. Metzler and other Army officials, *EXSUM* (April. 28, 2008, 10:08 a.m.).

[54] E-mail from Ms. Gray to [REDACTED] *FW: EXSUM Additional Info* (Apr. 28, 2008, 12:34 p.m.).

[55] E-mail from [REDACTED] to Mr. Metzler, [REDACTED] and other U.S. Army officials, *EXSUM additional info* (Apr. 28, 2008, 11:42 a.m.).

[56] ANC Media Release (Apr. 29, 2008).

[57] OIG DoD Interview of Ms. Gray (Jan. 15, 2009) at 55. *See also* OIG DoD Interview of [REDACTED] (Apr. 29, 2009) at 35-36, 42, and 63 and OIG DoD Interview [REDACTED] (Apr. 28, 2009) at 61-63.

[58] OIG DoD Interview of [REDACTED] (Apr. 16, 2009) at 23-24.

[59] *Id.* at 54-55.

[60] Dave Mazzarella, *Agendas collide at Arlington National Cemetery,* Stars and Stripes (May 7, 2008).

[61] OIG DoD Interview of Mr. Metzler (Apr. 17, 2009) at 34-35 and 37-38.

[62] E-mail from Ms. Gray to [REDACTED] and Mr. Metzler, *Memorial Day PAO Assignments* (May 20, 2008, 6:44 p.m.) and E-mail from [REDACTED] to Ms. Gray, *RE: Memorial Day PAO Assignments* (May 21, 2008, 7:48 a.m.).

[63] E-mail from to *FW: Memorial Day PAG Assignments* (May 21, 2008, 1:39 p.m.).

[64] OIG DoD Interview of [REDACTED] (Apr. 16, 2009) at 36.

[65] E-mail from [REDACTED] to [REDACTED] and Mr. Metzler, *Gina Gray* (May 22, 2008, 8:21 a.m.).

[66] E-mail from [REDACTED] to [REDACTED] *Gina Gray* (May 27, 2008, 8:13 a.m.).

[67] E-mail from [REDACTED to [REDACTED] *Status* (June 2, 2008, 11:03 a.m.) and E-mail from [REDACTED] to [REDACTED] *RE: Status* (June 2, 2008, 11:17 a.m.).

[68] AR 690-400 (Oct. 16, 1998) Chapter 4302, Total Army Performance Evaluation System, Section 1-5(a).

[69] E-mail from Ms. Gray to [REDACTED] *RE: PAO* (June 3, 2008, 10:44 a.m.).

[70] Letter from Ms. Gray to Senator Warner (June 6, 2008). We determined the last line is in reference to Ms. Gray stating that there were no regulations allowing ANC to restrict the media from getting a 'good shot.' *See also* OIG DoD Interview of Ms. Gray (Jan. 15, 2009) at 31 whereby Ms. Gray testified that she was directed by [REDACTED] to lie to the media.

[71] E-mail from Mr. Pessin to [REDACTED] [REDACTED] and Ms. Gray, *RE: Reminder – Access Follow-up*

(June 19, 2008, 11:33 a.m.).

[72] Letter from Senator Warner to Mr. Morrell (June 24, 2008).

[73] E-mail from [REDACTED] to [REDACTED] *Removal Information for Gina Gray* (June 24, 2008, 1:41 p.m.).

[74] OIG DoD Interview of Ms. Gray (January 15, 2009) at 114-117 and Memorandum for Record from Ms. Gray to OIG DoD (Apr. 3, 2009).

[75] E-mail from [REDACTED] to [REDACTED] *Termination Info - Gray* (June 27, 2008, 11:18 a.m.).

[76] Memorandum from [REDACTED] to Ms. Gray, *Termination During Probationary Period* (June 27, 2008).

[77] Letter from Mr. Metzler to Senator Warner (July 9, 2008).

[78] To satisfy this element the complainant is not required to disclose information that actually evidences one of those conditions. Rather, the complainant is only required to make a non-frivolous allegation that the matters disclosed were ones that a reasonable person in his or her position would believe evidenced one of those conditions. *See Rusin v. Dep't of the Treasury,* 92 M.S.P.R. 298, 318 (2002). *See also Garst v. Dep't of the Army,* 60 M.S.P.R. 514, 518 (1994). Reasonable belief is an objective standard. That is, a disinterested observer with knowledge of essential facts known to and readily ascertainable by the employee could reasonably conclude that the actions evidence a violation of a law, rule, or regulation. *See Lachance v. White,* 174 F.3d 1378, 1381 (Fed. Cir. 1999); accord *Russin, id.*

[79] OIG DoD Interview of [REDACTED] (Apr. 28, 2009) at 39.

[80] *Id.* at 26 and 28.

[81] OIG DoD Interview of Ms. Gray (Jan. 15, 2009) at 11.

[82] OIG DoD Interview of [REDACTED] (Apr. 28, 2009) at 26.

[83] Dana Milbank, *What the Family Would Let You See, the Pentagon Obstructs,* Washington Post (Apr. 24, 2008) at A3.

[84] OIG DoD Interview of [REDACTED] (Apr. 28, 2009) at 39.

[85] OIG DoD Interview of Ms. Gray (Jan. 15, 2009) 27-28.

[86] OIG DoD Interview of [REDACTED] (Apr. 28, 2009) at 40.

[87] *Id.* at 36.

88 E-mail from [REDACTED] to OIG DoD, *FW: ANC Documents* (Dec. 17, 2009,3:57 p.m.). *See also* e-mail from [REDACTED] to OIG DoD, *Follow-up Information* (Dec. 18, 2009, 9:33 a.m.).

89 E-mail from Ms. Gray to [REDACTED] [REDACTED] and [REDACTED] *More Documentation* (Apr. 24, 2008, 9:10 p.m.).

90 OIG DoD Interview of [REDACTED] (Apr. 15, 2009) at 10 and 12-13.

91 Memorandum for Record from Ms. Gray to OIG DoD (Jan. 22, 2010).

92 Memorandum from Ms. Gray to Senator Warner (June 6, 2008) and e-mail string back and forth confirming receipt of letter and inquiring into the "status of my [Ms. Gray's] complaint from Ms. Gray to [REDACTED], Senator Warner Staffer, *RE: From Senator Warner's Office* (June 22, 2008, 7:40 p.m.). *See also* OIG DoD Interview of Ms. Gray (Jan. 15, 2009) at 31 whereby Ms. Gray testified that she was told to lie to the media.

93 Ms. Gray's position description states the following applicable responsibilities: "Assists media representatives in obtaining information... Serves as... primary contact for local and national media, which requires immediate responsiveness. Responds to media queries."

94 OIG DoD Interview of Ms. Gray (Jan. 15,2009) at 19-2l.

95 *Willis* v. *Dep't of Agriculture,* 141 F.3d 1l39, 1143 (Fed. Cir. 1998).

96 OIG DoD Interview of Ms. Gray (Jan. 15, 2009) at 19-20.

97 *Id.* at 27-28.

98 *Id.* at 8.

99 E-mail from [REDACTED] to OIG DoD, *FW: ANC Documents* (Dec. 17,2009,3:57 p.m.) ("*... since April 2008, Ms. Gray did decide to use the MDW rules (the Jackman Memo)*. She [Ms. Gray] did state that she would use the rules she had since the CFR [3200l] rules were not published. That was her decision, not mine. I did not try to sway her one way or the other.").

[100] Memorandum from Ms. Gray to OIG DoD, *Memorandum for Record; ANC Media Policies* (Apr. 9, 2009) ("This [Jackman] memorandum was a factor in my determination that there had been a violation of an established regulation and prompted me to go to OCPA for guidance.").

[101] Department of the Arm_General Order 13, *Army National Cemeteries* (Oct. 29, 2004).

[102] OIG DoD Interview of [REDACTED] (Apr. 29, 2009) at 56.

[103] *Special Counsel* v. *Costello*, 75 MSPR 562, 580, 585-86 (1997) (disclosures must be "specific and detailed, not vague allegations of wrongdoing regarding broad or imprecise matters."). *See also Padilla* v. *Department of Air Force*, 55 MSPR 540, 543-44 (1992).

[104] 5 U.S.C. Section 2302.

[105] OIG DoD Interview of Ms. Gray (Jan. 15, 2009) 116-117.

[106] Allegation of reprisal number one was not supported by sufficient evidence to conclude that the action occurred. Additionally, ANC RMOs denied they removed the responsibility. *See* OIG DoD Interview of Mr. Metzler (Apr. 17, 2009) at 18 and OIG DoD Interview [REDACTED] (Apr. 29, 2009) at 95-96; and OIG DoD Interview of [REDACTED] (Apr. 28, 2009) at 104 and 106-108.

[107] *Id.*

[108] U.S. Army PA Specialist (GS-1035-12) Position Description at 2.

[109] DA Form 7222-1 - Senior System Civilian Evaluation Report Support Form (June 3, 2008). [REDCATED] testified that this meant all media requests were to go to Mr. Metzler for approval. *See* OIG DoD Interview of [REDACTED] (Apr. 28, 2009) at 76.

[110] E-mail from [REDACTED] Fort Meyer to OIG *DoD, RE: DoD IG Investigation* (Apr. 29, 2009, 11:27 a.m.).

[111] E-mail from Ms. Gray to [REDACTED] *RE: PAO* (June 3, 2008,10:44 a.m.) ("Am I correct in understanding that you want to approve every request that comes in.").

[112] E-mail from Ms. Gray to [REDACTED] *Monday Morning* (June 12, 2008, 2:36 p.m.) (Whereby Ms. Gray asked [REDACTED] permission for the Virginia Department of Tourism to shoot a "tomb guard... walking the mat on Monday morning at sunrise."). *See also* E-mail from Ms. Gray to [REDACTED] *German film crew follow-up* (June 12, 2008, 2:12 p.m.).

[113] OIG Memorandum of Record *Conversations with [REDACTED] and [REDACTED]* (Oct. 27, 2009). *See also* OIG DoD Interview of [REDACTED] (Apr. 15, 2009) at 23 and 36-37, whereby [REDACTED] did not discuss her conversation with Ms. Gray to [REDACTED] and only interacted with [REDACTED] in preparing for Memorial Day 2008.

[114] Inspector General Act of 1978, as amended, sections 7(a) and 8(c)(2). The evidence gathered in this investigation warranted our review and comments.

[115] AR 600-100, Army Leadership (March 8, 2007) at 1-6, (4), (5), and (7). Further, section 1-8. Leader development, sub-section C. states, "All leaders have a responsibility to develop those junior to them to the fullest extent possible. In addition to institutional training and education, leaders can facilitate development through the knowledge and feedback they provide through *counseling, coaching,* and *mentoring.*"

[116] AR 690-400, Total Army Performance Evaluation System (Oct. 16, 1998) at section 2-6(a).

[117] OIG DoD Interview of [REDACTED] (Apr. 28, 2009) at 103.

[118] OIG DoD Interview of [REDACTED] (Apr. 29, 2009) at 29 and 49-50 ("I was getting some indication from [REDACTED] that she wasn't getting feedback from her. I didn't get involved. She would just mention to me she didn't get this, she wasn't getting that." ... "She's [Ms. Gray's] not doing this, she's not doing that. But that's still at

the first level... I don't get involved at that level."). *See also Id.* at 76.

[119] OIG DoD Interview of [REDACTED] (Apr. 29, 2009) at 80-81.

[120] AR 600-l00, Army Leadership (March 2007) at section l-8c.

[121] OIG DoD Interview of [REDACTED] (Apr. 29, 2009) at 69 and 82-85. [REDACTED] also testified that he agreed with the termination.

[122] OIG DoD Interview of [REDACTED] (Apr. 16, 2009) at 36. [REDACTED] testified that his office told [REDACTED] that "It was not insubordination."

[123] Memorandum for Record from [REDACTED] *Memorial Day* (May 26, 2008).

[124] OIG DoD Interview of [REDACTED] (Apr. 16, 2009) at 35 and 27 ("Because initially they [REDACTED] and [REDACTED] wanted to go ahead with termination right away (early May). Both myself and the attorney said give us some more stuff. Even though you can, it is not the right thing to do. If you want to terminate somebody we want to hear a summary of why you want to terminate them." ... "We tell all of our supervisors to give us documentation.").

[125] AR 600-100, Army Leadership (March 8, 2007) at 1-8.

[126] OIG DoD Interview of [REDACTED] (Apr. 14, 2009) at 13 and OIG DoD Interview of Ms. Gray (Jan. 15, 2009) at *44-45*. *See also* E-mail from to Mr. Metzler and other U.S. Army officials, *EXSUM* (Apr. 28, 2008, 10:08 a.m.) ("We just got a call from Sec Def office. They want an EXSUM by 12:00.").

[127] Executive Summary from MDW and_APR. 30, 2008).

[128] OIG DoD Interview of Mr. Metzler (Apr. 17, 2009) at 42. *See also* E-mail from [REDACTED] to

Ms. Hoehne, Principal Deputy Chief OCPA, [REDACTED] and Ms. Gray, *Media Guidelines Review* (May 12, 2008, 1:50 p.m.), whereby [REDACTED] states, "This follows our meeting concerning the media guidelines currently being used at ANC and the suggested changes discussed."

[129] OIG DoD Interview of [REDACTED] (Apr. 28, 2009) at 64-65.

[130] Executive Summary from Mr. Metzler (May 1, 2008).

[131] OIG DoD Interview of [REDACTED] (Apr. 28, 2009) at 57-58 ([OIG Investigator]: "Do you believe Ms. Gray was blamed for the increased media attention at ANC?" [REDACTED]: "Yes.").

PART C.

LESSONS LEARNED

CHAPTER 12. FIRST AND LASTING IG THINGS:

Enemies Foreign and Domestic

I, AB, do solemnly swear (or affirm) that I will support and defend the Constitution of the United States against all enemies, foreign and domestic; that I will bear true faith and allegiance to the same; that I take this obligation freely, without any mental reservation or purpose of evasion; and that I will well and faithfully discharge the duties of the office on which I am about to enter. So help me God.

Title 5, United States Code, Section 3331.

In *Marbury v. Madison*, the bedrock United States Supreme Court case establishing the principle of judicial review, Chief Justice John Marshall wrote, "The government of the United States has been emphatically termed a government of laws, and not of men." [1] In a society based upon the rule of law, of course, laws must first be both prescribed and promulgated before they can be enforced. [2] This final chapter summarizes some of the most significant lessons learned in the course of helping military commanders throughout the world better to promulgate and to enforce laws against human trafficking.

The Congressional request for a joint and global inspection of sex slavery, discussed in detail in Chapter 5, serves an apt background for summarizing and giving context to some more general and profound lessons learned, foremost of which are that:

1   Among the root causes of the recent resurgence of human trafficking, aside from the obvious profit motive of organized

criminals, is a general reluctance of leaders at all levels to promulgate and to enforce principle-based standards for subordinates who create the demand for prostitution generally, and for sex slavery specifically;

2   Whenever leaders, especially those of us who swear to "support and defend the Constitution of the United States,"[3] become aware of humans being referred to as "just" something else (*e.g.*, "they're just prostitutes," as discussed below), we ought never to turn a blind eye; and

3   In addition to "fraud, waste, and abuse" being domestic enemies of the United States Constitution, moral relativism itself, more fundamentally, is a domestic enemy of that same Constitution.[4]

Domestic Enemy #1: Moral Relativism

Following a ceremony at the Pentagon on the first anniversary of 9-11 honoring "America's Heroes Lost September 11, 2001," the author escorted Dr. Henry Kissinger to his waiting car. As we walked, I mentioned that I had recently queried one of Dr. Kissinger's mentors, Dr. Fritz G. A. Kraemer[5] -- who also happened to be one of my mentors -- about what Dr. Kraemer thought was the most dangerous "domestic enemy to the United States Constitution." Dr. Kraemer, who for nearly thirty years had served as a senior Pentagon advisor, unhesitatingly answered with the single word, "Relativism." Upon hearing this, Dr. Kissinger unhesitatingly replied, "I agree."

Moral relativism rejects absolute, principle-based moral values.[6] As such, moral relativism is inconsistent with foundational principles and enduring core values of the United States of America. Both moral relativism and its practical manifestations in the form of human trafficking are antithetical to foundational principles and enduring shared values of the ever-expanding Western Alliance.[7]

Our forefathers were well-schooled in Blackstone's Commentaries, the most definitive English language legal treatise at the time of the American Revolution. In his Commentaries, Blackstone explained the "Nature of Law" in terms antithetical to moral relativism:

438

Man, considered as a creature, must necessarily be subject to the laws of his creator, [who] has laid down only such laws as were founded in those relations of justice that existed in the nature of things antecedent to any positive precept. These are the eternal, *immutable laws of good and evil*, to which the creator himself in all his dispensations conforms; and which he has enabled human reason to discover, so far as they are necessary for the conduct of human actions. Such among others are these principles: that we should live honestly, should hurt nobody, and should render to every one it's due; to which three general precepts Justinian has reduced the whole doctrine of law.[8]

Even before the Declaration of Independence, John Adams embedded within our country's earliest laws the aspirational standard that no American leader should ever turn a blind eye to human practices inconsistent with these "immutable laws of good and evil,"[9] notwithstanding the fog of moral relativism that typically surrounds human practices that are objectively immoral.

Article 1 of the 1775 "Rules for the Regulation of the Navy of the United Colonies of North America," drafted by John Adams and enacted by the Continental Congress, reads in its entirety: "The Commanders of all ships and vessels belonging to the THIRTEEN UNITED COLONIES, are strictly required to shew in themselves a good example of honor and virtue to their officers and men, and to be very vigilant in inspecting the behaviour of all such as are under them, and to discountenance and suppress all dissolute, immoral and disorderly practices; and also, such as are contrary to the rules of discipline and obedience, and to correct those who are guilty of the same according to the usage of the sea."[10]

In 1798, the same founding father who had drafted the 1775 Naval leadership standard admonished American military officers that "Oaths in this country are as yet universally considered as sacred obligations,"[11] warning that "Our Constitution was made only for a moral and religious people. It is wholly inadequate to the government of any other."[12]

A century later, shortly after the Civil War, the United States Supreme Court sustained the court martial of an Army Captain "related to the incurring by the accused of debts" when "the circumstances under which the debts were contracted and not paid were such as to render the claimant amenable to the charge" of "conduct unbecoming an officer and a gentleman."[13] In the same case, the Court of Claims had explained, "We learnt as law students in Blackstone that there are things which are *malum in se* [*i.e.*, wrong in itself] and, in addition to them, things which are merely *malum prohibitum* [*i.e.*, wrong because prohibited]; but unhappily in the affairs of real life we find that there are many things which are *malum in se* without likewise being *malum prohibitum*. In military life there is a higher code termed honor, which holds its society to stricter accountability; and it is not desirable that the standard of the Army shall come down to the requirements of a criminal code."[14]

In the following century, during the Vietnam War, the United States Supreme Court upheld the constitutionality of the "general articles" of the Uniform Code of Military Justice (UCMJ), which proscribe, *inter alia*, "all disorders and neglects to the prejudice of the good order and discipline in the armed forces."[15] The Supreme Court reviewed the history of the UCMJ's general articles, tracing them back to 17th Century "British antecedents of our military law"[16] and through the United States Supreme Court's own precedent of the 19th Century.[17]

In a 1974 concurring opinion, the Supreme Court described "[r]elativistic notions of right and wrong" (*i.e.*, moral relativism) as antithetical to the principle of military necessity:

> Fundamental concepts of right and wrong are the same now as they were under the Articles of the Earl of Essex (1642), or the British Articles of War of 1765, or the American Articles of War of 1775, or during the long line of precedents of this and other courts upholding the general articles. And, however unfortunate it may be, it is still necessary to maintain a disciplined and obedient fighting force. . . . The general articles are essential not only to punish patently criminal conduct, but also to foster an orderly and dutiful fighting force. . . . Relativistic notions of right and wrong, or situation ethics, as some call it, have achieved in recent times a disturbingly high level of prominence in this country, both in the guise of law reform, and as a justification of conduct that persons would normally

eschew as immoral and even illegal. The truth is that the moral horizons of the American people are not foot-loose...[18]

Subsequently, in the midst of the Cold War between the Western Alliance and the Soviet Union, the Commander-in-Chief of the United States shared with Members of the British House of Commons his vision for leaving "Marxism-Leninism on the ash heap of history" -- based on underlying assumptions antithetical to *moral relativism*: "given strong leadership, time, and a little bit of hope, the forces of good ultimately rally and triumph over evil . . . . Here is the enduring greatness of the British contribution to mankind, the great civilized ideas: individual liberty, representative government, and the rule of law under God."[19]

Shortly after the Cold War concluded in Europe, the Polish-born Roman Pontiff, speaking in Baltimore, Maryland, likewise urged every generation of Americans to acknowledge "the moral truths which make freedom possible," starting with those "truths" acknowledged in our Declaration of Independence and reiterated in the Gettysburg Address.[20] This enduring American and profoundly Western concept of "moral truths" simply cannot be squared with moral (or ethical) models that reject immutable "concepts of right and wrong."[21]

More recently, in the aftermath of various U.S. military sexual misconduct scandals of the 1990's, the United States Congress reenacted for leaders of all three military departments (Army, Navy, and Air Force) the same "exemplary conduct" leadership standard enacted by our Continental Congress as Article I of the 1775 Navy Regulations,[22] thereby reaffirming "a very clear standard by which Congress and the nation can measure officers of our military services."[23] Title 10 of the United States Code thus still incorporates the principle-based substance of John Adams' 1775 leadership standard: "All commanding officers and others in authority . . . are required to show in themselves a good example of virtue, honor, patriotism, and subordination; . . . to guard against and suppress all dissolute and immoral practices, and to correct . . . all persons who are guilty of them."[24]

These long-standing and principle-based moral pronounce-
ments by Congress exemplify the reality that duly-enacted laws in our
republic are the societal analog to an individual's conscience.[25]

In the Anglo-American tradition, our national legislatures prescribe the national conscience through public laws, legislating what is
right and what is wrong for the nation, *i.e.*, what choices we ought and
ought not to make.[26] Of course, as with any individual conscience formation process, there is always the possibility that this societal conscience be mis-formed, *i.e.*, inconsistent with a higher law.[27] For this
reason, our first President in his first Annual Address encouraged our
representatives in Congress *"to discriminate the spirit of liberty from that of*
licentiousness, cherishing the first, avoiding the last, and uniting a speedy,
but temperate vigilance against encroachments, with an inviolable respect to the laws."[28] In this regard, as with the relationship between
individual conscience and individual behavior, societal conscience formation process is distinct from, yet integrally related to, both the
promulgation and the enforcement processes.

Lessons Learned By Inspecting Sex Slavery through
the Fog of Moral Relativism

Although volumes could be written about the reprehensible
nature of sex slavery and other forms of human trafficking, and how
moral relativism contributes to the challenges of inspecting and meeting related leadership challenges, at least five points warrant emphasis:

1   Moral relativism is an enemy of the United States Constitution;

2   The President of the United States has identified 21st Century
sex slavery as "a special evil" under "a moral law that stands
above men and nations"[29];

3   Military leaders at all levels need robustly to promulgate and
to enforce principle-based standards for subordinates who create the demand for sex slavery;

4   American and other "Western" leaders ought "to be vigilant
inspecting the conduct of all persons who are placed under

their command; to guard against and suppress all dissolute and immoral practices, and to correct . . . all persons who are guilty of them"[30] -- in this regard, ostensible consent by the parties to immoral practices such as sex slavery ought never to be an excuse for turning a blind eye; and

5 Even as we confront the new asymmetric enemies of the 21st Century, those of us who take an oath to defend the Constitution of the United States (and similar principle-based legal authorities) should recognize, confront, and suppress sexual slavery and other "dissolute and immoral practices" whenever and wherever they raise their ugly heads through the fog of moral relativism -- "so help [us] God."[31]

American First Things

In August 2005, at the request of the U.S Department of State, I addressed an international audience composed of representatives of friendly foreign nations, all interested in learning about the United States generally, on the subject (as determined by the State Department sponsors) of, "U.S. Experience with Promoting Transparency and Government Accountability."

I started my comments on "U.S. Experience with Promoting Transparency and Government Accountability" with an obscure quote from a primer on U.S. Government. It was written in 1890 by a Harvard professor named John Fiske. In his book titled "Civil Government in the United States," Professor Fiske pointed out:

> The most essential feature of a government, or at any rate, the feature with which it is important for us to become familiar at the start is the power of taxation. The government is that which taxes. If individuals take away some of your property for purposes of their own, it is robbery. You lose your money and you get nothing in return. But if the government takes away some of your property in the shape of taxes, it is supposed to render to you an equivalent in the shape of good government – something without which our lives and property would not be safe. Herein

seems to lie the difference between taxation and robbery. When the highway man points his pistol at me, and I hand him over my purse and watch, I am robbed. But when I pay the tax collector, who can seize my watch or sell my house over my head if I refuse, I am simply paying what is fairly due from me towards supporting the government.[32]

Even before our Declaration of Independence, we had a robust English common law, which forms the foundation of our system of government. A significant number of people around the world today continue to rely on the English common law. It is somewhat of a misnomer that we broke from England in 1776. When our forefathers wrote the Declaration of Independence, they were defending their rights as Englishmen to live under a free system of government based upon the rule of law.

About ten years before our Declaration, Sir William Blackstone wrote the definitive treatise on English common law, which was used by our forefathers to establish the United States Constitution. Blackstone wrote in his 1765 treatise that there are four essential attributes of all civil laws. Essentially, he was defining a system of transparent government, which forms the basis of our American system today. He mentions four essential attributes of all man-made laws:

1   A law must be a rule, as opposed to a judgment;

2   It must be of general applicability, as opposed to a bill of attainder, which would be directed at one person;

3   It must be prescribed; and

4   It must be prescribed by the sovereign, not by somebody without authority.[33]

These are the four essential elements of the Anglo-American tradition in transparent government.

According to Blackstone, rules need to be prescribed in advance. In describing this principle, Blackstone wrote that it is important the government not only prescribe, but also promulgate the laws in the most perspicuous manner available, "not like [Emperor] Caligula, who . . . wrote his laws in very small character, and hung them up upon high pillars, the more effectually to ensnare the people."[34]

This principle, citing the historical despot as the antithesis of transparent government, has found its way into, among other things, the *ex post facto* clauses of the U.S. Constitution. There are two *ex post facto* clauses: one in Article 1, Section 9, which generally proscribes retroactive lawmaking. Keep in mind that at the time the framers wrote the Constitution, Blackstone had just deemed *ex post facto* laws as even more unreasonable than the law methodology of Emperor Caligula.[35] There is a second *ex post facto* clause in Article 1, Section 10, which applies the proscription against *ex post facto* laws to the States.

That principle is one that every Office of Inspector General ought to apply. What the author of this book told his investigators is this: "If it takes our lawyers more than a week to tell [the Inspector General] what the legal standard is, we will not hold anybody else accountable to that standard -- because that would be a Caligula-esque method of enforcing laws. We're just not going to do that. It's not part of the American system of transparent and accountable government."

There is another provision of our U.S. Constitution which is called the Accountability Clause. It is also Article 1, Section 9, which reads, "a regular Statement and Account of the Receipts and Expenditures of all public Money shall be published from time to time." In effect, we have a constitutional right to a public accounting of how our money is spent by our government. This constitutional principle is what ultimately took form in the Inspector General Act of 1978,[36] a 1982 amendment to which created the DoD Office of Inspector General.[37]

The design and purpose of the Inspector General Act was to create independent and objective units in each of the government departments in the Executive Branch that would be able, in effect, to carry out that constitutional duty of public accountability. Each of the offices, each of the cabinet-level departments in the U.S. Government, has a Senate-confirmed, presidentially-appointed inspector general.

In October 2003, the President invited all members of what at the time was called the President's Council on Integrity & Efficiency (PCIE) to come to the White House to celebrate the 25th anniversary of the Inspector General Act of 1978. The President thanked all of the Inspectors General present for their service and he explained his perspective of government transparency and accountability. He said,

"Every time an inspector general roots out fraud, waste or abuse in the government, the inspector general increases the confidence of the American people in our government." That is an important American principle – the notion of it being *our* government. The first three words of the Constitution are, "We the People."

"We the People" – the principle of popular sovereignty – is also one of those foundational principles that define who we are as Americans. The principles of transparency and government accountability, along with integrity and popular sovereignty, are so foundational that they literally define who we as Americans are. Those principles are shared by most of our allies today in the Global War on Terrorism, and by many other friendly nations that rely upon the notion of the rule of law, which is so foundational to who we are as Americans.

IG Principles

During my first one-on-one meeting as Inspector General with the Secretary of Defense, I reiterated my vision to the Secretary that the DoD Inspector General ought not only to carry out the statutory duties enumerated in the Inspector General Act, but also that the DoD Inspector General ought to serve in the traditional military inspector general role as "an extension of the eyes, ears, and conscience of the Commander."[38]

Turning to his Special Assistant (who was observing the one-on-one meeting), Secretary Rumsfeld replied, "In that case, Larry, the IG needs a copy of my Principles." After the meeting, Larry DiRita handed me a two-page list of Secretary Rumsfeld's "Principles for the Department of Defense."[39]

Within weeks, I had incorporated each of Secretary Rumsfeld's principles that related in any way to either the statutory duties of the DoD Inspector General or the traditional duties of military inspectors general into a separate list of "DoD Inspector General Principles," which evolved over the three and a half years of the Inspector General's tenure.

The following is an abridged list of DoD IG Principles as of 2005:

1 An IG in the Department of Defense serves as an independent 'extension of the eyes, ears, and conscience of the Commander"; as such an IG is always a paradigm of military leadership – the only issue is whether he or she is a good paradigm.

2 Integrity is synonymous with truth.

3 Accountability is a sacred duty for all who swear (or affirm) the statutory Oath of Office; Article I of the Constitution mandates that "a Regular Statement and Account of the Receipts and Expenditures of all public Money shall be published from time to time."

4 IG reports should include, whenever possible, both a front-loaded recitation of any allegation, quoting the prescribed standards at issue, and a summary of constructive proposals.

5 Every Member of Congress deserves IG respect.

6 Whenever a federal IG contemplates the exercise of a "police power," he or she should ask and, whenever possible, insist upon a written answer to the question, "By what authority?"

* * *

15 The professional reputation of senior officials is protected by the due process clause, which requires, among other things, that legal standards to which officials may be held accountable be prescribed, widely-promulgated, and understandable by the average senior official.

* * * *

Most of these IG Principles are self explanatory, at least to professional IGs. Suffice to say, they reflect important general principles that warrant repetition within an organization of professionals that includes both experienced auditors, inspectors, and investigators, but also less experienced professionals, including some freshly graduated from college.

These IG principles, for the most part, simply adapted the Secretary of Defense's more general principles to either IG tradition or statutory guidance for the Office of Inspector General. This was a deliberate attempt to inculcate a sense of "tethered independence."

Hence, Principle #1 was, "An IG in the Department of Defense serves as an independent 'extension of the eyes, ears, and conscience of the Commander." This principle melded traditional Army IG doctrine with the "independence" mandate within the Inspector General Act of 1978, as amended.[40]

IG Principle #15 was a deliberate attempt to inculcate within the small cadre of investigators whose daily jobs placed into the balance the careers of officials who by virtue of their seniority had sacrificed substantially more privacy rights than the vast majority of soldiers, sailors, airmen, marines, and civilians serving throughout the Department of Defense.

As an example of the disparate treatment afforded senior officials, privacy restrictions in the Department of Defense prevent the web posting of most names of civilian employees on an organizational chart, including the organizational chart for an Office of Inspector General. Not so for flag officers and members of the Senior Executive Service. By virtue of their seniority these individuals sacrifice that modicum of privacy. Their names and their job descriptions can be and are published, while the names of all others are entitled to privacy protection.

The United States Supreme Court had also explained that senior officials, also known as "public officials," need to be treated differently than the average citizen in various contexts, including defamation and slander as well as the due process of law protected by the United States Constitution. Hence, IG Principle #15 formalized the Supreme Court's guidance that, "The professional reputation of senior officials is protected by the due process clause, which requires, among other things, that legal standards to which officials may be held accountable be prescribed, widely-promulgated, and understandable by the average senior official."

In August 2004, IG principle #15 found itself re-promulgated in a separate IG Policy Memo addressing the United States Supreme Court's decision in *Hamdi v. Rumsfeld*. In that case, the Supreme Court found that the Department of Defense had violated the due process rights of an American-born man who had moved as a child to Saudi Arabia with his family, and who was later detained in Afghanistan after the terrorist attacks of September 11, 2001, allegedly for having taken up arms with the Taliban.

In particular, according to the Supreme Court opinion, Yaser Esam Hamdi by 2001 "resided in Afghanistan. At some point that year, he was seized by members of the Northern Alliance, a coalition of military groups opposed to the Taliban government, and eventually was turned over to the United States military. The Government assert[ed] that it initially detained and interrogated Hamdi in Afghanistan before transferring him to the United States Naval Base in Guantanamo Bay in January 2002. In April 2002, upon learning that Hamdi is an American citizen, authorities transferred him to a naval brig in Norfolk, Virginia, ... The Government contend[ed] that Hamdi [was] an 'enemy combatant,' and that this status justifies holding him in the United States indefinitely without formal charges or proceedings unless and until it makes the determination that access to counsel or further process is warranted."[41] The Court disagreed.

While others within the Department of Defense were lamenting this legal "defeat," the Inspector General issued a policy memo,[42] reaffirming and applying to the daily challenges within the Office of Inspector General the same long-standing due process guidance reaffirmed by the Court:

> For more than a century the central meaning of procedural due process has been clear: Parties whose rights are to be affected are entitled to be heard; and in order that they may enjoy that right they must first be notified. It is equally fundamental that the right to notice and an opportunity to be heard must be granted at a meaningful time and in a meaningful manner. These essential constitutional promises may not be eroded. *Hamdi v. Rumsfeld*, 124 S. Ct. 2633, 2649 (2004) (internal citations and quotation marks omitted).

"These essential constitutional promises" are American and Inspector General "first things." During the course of every IG audit, inspection, or investigation, Inspectors General have the privilege -- as well as an oath-bound duty -- to "support and defend" these and other American "first things" against fraud, waste, abuse, and other "enemies" of the United States Constitution, "foreign and domestic . . . . So help me God."[43]

Chapter 12 Endnotes

---

[1] 5 U.S. (1 Cranch) 137, 163 (1803).

[2] *See* William Blackstone, I COMMENTARIES ON THE LAWS OF ENGLAND, pp. 44-46 (1765) (All "municipal or civil law . . . is likewise 'a rule *prescribed.*' Because a bare resolution, confined to the breast of the legislator, without manifesting itself by some external sign, can never be properly a law. It is requisite that this resolution be notified to the people who are to obey it... [W]hatever what is made use of, it is incumbent upon the promulgators to do it in the most public and perspicuous manner; not like Caligula, who (according to Dio Cassius) wrote his laws in very small character, and hung them up upon high pillars, the more effectually to ensnare the people.").

[3] 5 U.S.C. § 3331 ("An individual . . . elected or appointed to an office of honor or profit in the civil service or uniformed services, shall take the following oath: 'I, AB, do solemnly swear (or affirm) that I will support and defend the Constitution of the United States against all enemies, foreign and domestic; that I will bear true faith and allegiance to the same; that I take this obligation freely, without any mental reservation or purpose of evasion; and that I will well and faithfully discharge the duties of the office on which I am about to enter. So help me God.'").

[4] *See* Sun Tzu, THE ART OF WAR ("If you know the enemy and know yourself, you need not fear the result of a hundred battles. If you know yourself but not the enemy, for every victory gained you will also suffer a defeat. If you know neither the enemy nor yourself, you will succumb in every battle.") (http://classics.mit.edu/Tzu/artwar.html).

[5] At the October 8, 2003, Arlington National Cemetery funeral of Fritz Kraemer, Dr. Kissinger was one of three eulogists. *See* Hodgson, "Fritz Kraemer: Brilliant geopolitical strategist who launched Henry Kissinger's

rise to power," The Guardian, November 12, 2003. (http://www.guardian.co.uk/usa/story/0,12271,1083074,00.html).

[6] *See* THE CAMBRIDGE DICTIONARY OF PHILOSOPHY, p. 690 (Robert Audi, General Editor, 1995) ("relativism, the denial that there are certain kinds of universal truths"); Kreeft, A REFUTATION OF MORAL RELATIVISM, *supra*, at 28-29 ("Relativism is the philosophy that denies absolutes. Any absolutes. Everyone believes there are many relativities, that some things are relative; but relativism claims that all things are relative. . . . [M]oral relativism says, 'Perhaps there are absolutes in nonmoral knowledge, like 'two plus two makes four', but not in moral knowledge: we know no moral absolutes'.").

[7] For example, eleven republics and/or satellite states of the former Soviet Union have recently become members of the North Atlantic Treaty Organization (NATO): The German Democratic Republic (East Germany), Hungary, Poland, the Czech Republic; Bulgaria, Estonia, Latvia, Lithuania, Romania, Slovakia, and Slovenia.

[8] Blackstone's Commentaries, *supra*, pp. 39-40 (emphasis added; footnote citation omitted).

[9] *Id.*

[10] Continental Congress, "Rules for the Regulation of the Navy of the United Colonies of North America" (1775), Article 1 http://www.pdfonfly.com/pdfs/http__www.navyhistory.org_rules-for-the-regulation-of-the-navy-of-the-united-colonies-of-north-amer.pdf

[11] J. Adams, Oct. 11, 1798, Letter "to the Officers of the First Brigade of the Third Division of the Militia of Massachusetts," in THE WORKS OF JOHN ADAMS -- SECOND PRESIDENT OF THE UNITED STATES, Vol. IX, p. 229 (C.F. Adams, ed. 1854).

[12] *Id.*; *cf. Church of the Holy Trinity v. United States*, 143 U.S. 457, 468 (1892) ("Every constitution of every one of the forty-four States contains language which either directly or by clear implication recognizes a profound rever-

ence for religion and an assumption that its influence in all human affairs is essential to the well being of the community."); James H. Hutson, RELIGION AND THE FOUNDING OF THE AMERICAN REPUBLIC, pp. 57-58 (Library of Congress 1998) (At the time immediately after the American Revolution, "It appears that both the politicians and the public held an unarticulated conviction that it was the duty of the national government to support religion, that it had an inherent power to do so, as long as it acted in a nonsectarian way without appropriating public money. . . . This conviction – that holiness was a prerequisite for secular happiness, that religion was, in the words of the Northwest Ordinance, 'necessary to good government and the happiness of mankind,' was not the least of the Confederation's legacies to the new republican era that began with Washington's inauguration in 1789."); Peter Kreeft, A REFUTATION OF MORAL RELATIVISM, *supra*, p. 162 ("[E]ven in a secular society like America it's still true that religion is the firmest support for morality. There has never been a popular secular morality that's lasted and worked in holding a society together. Society has always needed morality, and morality has always needed religion. Destroy religion, you destroy morality; destroy morality, you destroy society. That's history's bottom line.").

[13] *United States v. Fletcher*, 148 U.S. 84, 91-92 (1893).

[14] *Fletcher v. United States*, 26 Ct. Cl. 541, 562-63 (1891), quoted with approbation in *Parker v. Levy*, 417 U.S. 733, 765 (1974) (Blackmun, J., joined by Burger, C.J., concurring).

[15] *Parker v. Levy*, 417 U.S. at 738 (quoting and citing Article 134 of the UCMJ, 10 U.S.C. § 934).

[16] *Id.* at 745.

[17] *Id.* at 745-49.

[18] *Id.* at 765 (Blackmun, J., joined by Burger, C.J., concurring).

[19] Ronald Reagan, "Speech to the House of Commons," June 18, 1982 (www.fordham.edu/halsall/mod/1982reagan1.html).

[20] John Paul II, "Homily in Orioles Park at Camden Yards," ¶7 (October 8, 1995) (http://www.catholic-forum.com/saints/pope0264is.htm).

[21] *Parker v. Levy, supra,* 417 U.S. at 765; *see* John Paul II, *Veritatis Splendor,* ¶¶1&101 (1993) (http://www.vatican.va/holy_father/john_paul_ii/encyclicals/documents/hf_j p-ii_enc_06081993_veritatis-splendor_en.html) ("As a result of that mysterious original sin, . . giving himself over to relativism and skepticism, [man] goes off in search of an illusory freedom apart from truth itself. . . . Indeed, 'if there is no ultimate truth to guide and direct political activity, then ideas and convictions can easily be manipulated for reasons of power. As history demonstrates, a democracy without values easily turns into open or thinly disguised totalitarianism'." (footnote and citation omitted)).

[22] *See* 10 U.S.C. §§ 3583, 5947, & 8583 (same "exemplary conduct" leadership standard for all "commanding officers and others in authority" in the Army, Naval Services and Air Force respectively).

[23] Senate Armed Services Committee, "National Defense Authorization Act for Fiscal Year 1998" (Report to Accompany S. 924), p. 277, quoted in the Introduction, "The Declaration of Independence and the Constitution of the United States of America" http://www.pdfonfly.com/pdfs/http___www.csce.gov_index.cfm_FuseActio n=ContentRecords.ViewWitness&ContentRecord_id=546&ContentType. pdf

[24] 10 U.S.C. § 5947; *see* 10 U.S.C. § 3583 (Army) and § 8583 (Air Force); *see also* 10 U.S.C. § 933 ("Conduct unbecoming an officer and a gentleman").

[25] *Cf. Church of the Holy Trinity v. United States, supra,* 143 U.S. at 467-70 ("[T]he Declaration of Independence[,] the constitutions of the various States[, and] the Constitution of the United States . . . affirm and reaffirm that this is a religious nation. These are not individual sayings, declarations

of private persons; they are organic utterances; they speak the voice of the entire people.").

[26] *See generally* Blackstone, *supra*, at 42-44 (describing "human law" as: (a) subordinate to "the law of nature and of revelation"; and (b) "properly defined to be 'a rule of civil conduct prescribed by the supreme power in a state, commanding what is right and prohibiting what is wrong'").

[27] *See id.*

[28] George Washington, First Annual Address, January 8, 1790 (emphasis added).

[29] *Id.*

[30] 10 U.S.C. § 5947, *supra.*

[31] 5 U.S.C. § 3331 (statutory Oath of Office).

[32] John Fiske, *Civil Government In The United States Considered With Some Reference To Its Origins*, p. 8 (1890).

[33] William Blackstone, COMMENTARIES ON THE LAW OF ENGLAND, p. 44-46 (1765-1769), ("[M]unicipal or civil law [is] the rule by which particular districts, communities, and nations are governed; . . . Let us endeavour to explain it's several properties, . . . first, it is a rule; not a transient sudden order from a superior to or concerning a particular person; but something permanent, uniform, and universal. . . . It is likewise 'a rule prescribed.' But farther: municipal law is 'a rule of civil conduct prescribed by the supreme power in a state'. Wherefore it is requisite to the very essence of a law, that it be made by the supreme power. Sovereignty and legislature are indeed convertible terms; one cannot subsist without the other.").

[34] *Ibid.* at p. 46.

[35] *Ibid.* ("yet, whatever way is made use of [to notify the people], it is incumbent on the promulgation to do it in the most public and perspicuous manner; not like Caligula, who (according to *Dio Cassius*) wrote his laws in very small characters, and hung them up upon high pillars, the more effectually to ensure the people. There is still a more unreasonable method that this which is called making of laws *ex post facto*.").

[36] Inspector General Act of 1978, Public Law 95-452, October 12, 1978.

[37] National Defense Authorization Act for Fiscal Year 1983, Public Law 97-252, Section 1117, September 8, 1982.

[38] Army Regulation 20-1, Inspector General Activities and Procedures 5 (Department of the Army, 2002).

[39] "SUBJECT: Principles for the Department of Defense

> "1. Do nothing that could raise questions about the credibility of DoD. DoD must tell the truth and must be believed to be telling the truth or our important work is undermined.

> "2. Do nothing that is or could be seen as partisan. The work of this Department is non-partisan. We have to continuously earn the support of all the people of the country and in the Congress. To do so we must serve all elements of our society without favor.

> "3. Nothing is more important than the men and women who work in this Department - they are its heart and soul and its future. Our country's success depends on them. We must all treat them with respect, show our concern for them and for their lives and their futures, and find opportunities to express our full appreciation for all they do for our country.

> "4. The public needs and has a right to know about the unclassified activities of DoD. It is our obligation to provide that information professionally, fully and in good spirit.

"5. Help to create an environment in DoD that is hospitable to risk-taking, innovation, and creativity. This institution must encourage people of all types if we are to transform and be successful.

"6. Work vigorously to root out any wrongdoing or corruption in DoD. Waste undermines support for the Department, and robs DoD activities of the resources they need.

"7. Consistently demonstrate vigilance against waste. It is the tax-payers' money, earned by people who work hard all across this land. We owe it to them to treat their dollars respectfully, and we owe it to the importance of our responsibilities to see that every dollar is spent wisely.

"8. Reflect the compassion we all feel when innocent lives are lost, whether U.S. service people or innocents killed by collateral damage.

"9. Demonstrate our appreciation for the cooperation we receive from other nations and for the valuable contributions coalition forces bring to our efforts - whether in peacetime by way of strengthening the deterrent, or in wartime by securing victory.

"10. Because of the complexity of our tasks, DoD must work with other departments and agencies of the federal government in a professional manner, respectful of others' views but willing to raise issues to the next higher level up the chain of command, as necessary.

"11. DoD personnel-civilian and military-must not compromise classified information. It is a violation of federal criminal law, and those who do so are criminals. They are also individuals who have lost their moorings and are willing to put the lives of the men and women in uniform at risk. They must be rooted out, stopped and punished.

"12. The Legislative Branch is in Article I of the Constitution; the Executive Branch is Article II. That is not an accident. We must respect the Constitutional role of Congress, learn from those who have knowledge that can be helpful and work constructively, with revolving coalitions, to achieve the important goals of the Department and the country.

"13. Finally, the President of the United States is our Commander-in-Chief.

Those of us in DoD - military and civilian - believe in civilian control, are respectful of it and must be vigilant to see that our actions reflect that important Constitutional obligation.

"Donald Rumsfeld."

[40] *See, e.g.*, Inspector General Act of 1978, as amended, § 2 ("Purpose and establishment of Offices of Inspector General; departments and agencies involved[:] In order to create independent and objective units...").

[41] *Hamdi v. Rumsfeld*, 542 U.S. 507, 510-11 (2004).

[42] Inspector General Policy Memo, "Due Process in the Activities of the Office of Inspector General," August 20, 2004
http://web.archive.org/web/20050612185319/http://www.dodig.osd.mil/IGInformation/IGPolicy/dueprocess0804.pdf

[43] 5 U.S.C. § 3331 ("Oath of Office").

CONCLUSION

An enemy of the United States Constitution gnaws at the good order and discipline of the American Armed Forces and, by extension, of the entire Western Alliance. This enemy answers to the name *moral relativism*, feeding on the side of human nature that would turn a blind eye to moral truths, as in "We hold these truths to be self-evident, ..."[1] In the midst of a Global War on Terrorism, our Commander-in-Chief admonished us all, "when we forget these truths, we risk sliding into a dictatorship of relativism."[2]

One such would-be "dictatorship of relativism" manifested itself during the course of an inspection requested by Congress into human trafficking -- also known as "Trafficking in Persons," "TIP," or in its most common form, "sex slavery,"[3] the subject matter of another chapter of this book. Even as this joint and global sex slavery inspection was being launched, the President of the United States devoted almost one fifth of his speech to the United Nations General Assembly to the subject of human trafficking.

You might ask why, in the midst of the Global War on Terrorism, our national leader would focus so much on human trafficking. One answer might be the nexus between human traffickers and the arms traffickers supporting the terrorists.[4] A more fundamental answer might be that the challenges of modern-day human slavery force us to focus on "first things," *i.e.*, the principles worth fighting for, in order that we might better focus on important "second things," which include survival.

The principle of "first and second things," as explained by the late British author C.S. Lewis, maintains that, "You can't get second things by putting them first; you can get second things only by putting first things first. . . . The first and most practical [thing is] to have something to live for and to die for, lest we die."[5] A contemporary C.S. Lewis expert explains the principle more bluntly: "the society that believes in nothing worth surviving for beyond mere survival will not survive."[6]

Although C.S. Lewis may have coined the term, the principle of first and second things is much older than the United States of America. It appears to have been recorded by Plato in the year 360 BC, in his explanation of "Just Laws."[7] In any event, for Americans in the 21st Century, the combination of our Declaration of Independence, Constitution, and Bill of Rights comes as close to a written embodiment of the core principles that define who we are. C.S. Lewis, and perhaps Plato, would have called these defining principles American "First Things."

For an American Inspector General, "First Things" include integrity, efficiency, independence, and transparent accountability. Three and a half years at the helm of the most expansive Office of Inspector General in the world taught the author of this book that humility, too, is another necessary Inspector General "First Thing."

While serving as Inspector General, the author found himself constantly asking not only his staff but also himself two core questions, "By what authority and for what purpose"? These two questions routinely guided how this Inspector General carried out his constitutional and statutory duties. The same two questions can help prevent any Inspector General from misconstruing his statutory authority or otherwise abusing power.[8]

---

[1] Declaration of Independence (July 4, 1776) ("We hold these truths to be self-evident, that all men are created equal, that they are endowed by their Creator with certain unalienable Rights, that among these are Life, Liberty and the pursuit of Happiness. . . .").

[2] George W. Bush, "President Attends National Catholic Prayer Breakfast," May 20, 2005 (describing Pope Benedict XVI's warning about "the dictatorship of relativism" as tied to "the American Model of liberty rooted in moral conviction.").

[3] *See* George W. Bush, "President Bush Addresses United Nations General Assembly," September 23, 2003 ("an estimated 800,000 to 900,000 human beings are bought, sold or forced across the world's borders . . . generat[ing] billions of dollars each year -- much of which is used to finance organized crime"); *see also* "Findings," Victims of Trafficking and Violence Protection Act of 2000, Section 102(b)(1) ("Approximately 50,000 women and children are trafficked into the United States each year."); Trafficking Victims Protection Reauthorization Act of 2003; George W. Bush, "President Bush Addresses United Nations General Assembly," September 21, 2004 ("Because we believe in human dignity, America and many nations have joined together to confront the evil of trafficking in human beings. We're supporting organizations that rescue the victims, passing stronger anti-trafficking laws, and warning travelers that they will be held to account for supporting this modern form of slavery. Women and children should never be exploited for pleasure or greed, anywhere on Earth.").

[4] *See* United States Department of State, "Trafficking in Persons Report," p. 14 (June 2004) ("Trafficking Fuels Organized Crime . . . . According to the UN, human trafficking is the third largest criminal enterprise worldwide, generating an estimated 9.5 billion USD in annual revenue according

to the U.S. intelligence community. . . . There have also been documented ties to terrorism.").

⁵ C.S. Lewis, "Time and Tide," reprinted in *God in the Dock* (1942).

⁶ Peter Kreeft, *A Refutation Of Moral Relativism: Interviews With An Absolut-ists*, p. 133 (1999).

⁷ Plato, *The Laws* 361b-d (360BC) ("[Just laws] serve the right end, that of effecting the happiness of those who enjoy them. They, in fact, secure them all good things. But there are two different kinds of good things, the merely human and the divine; the former are consequential on the latter. Hence a city which accepts the greater goods acquires the lesser along with them, but one which refuses them misses both. The lesser are those among which health holds the first place, comeliness the second, strength for the race and all other bodily exercises the third, while the fourth place belongs to a wealth which is not blind, but clear-sighted, because attendant on wis-dom. Of divine goods, the first and chiefest is this same wisdom, and next after it sobriety of spirit; a third, resulting from the blending of both of these with valor is righteousness, and valor itself is fourth. All of these naturally rank before the former class, and, of course, a lawgiver must ob-serve that order. Next, he should impress it upon his citizens that all his other injunctions have a view to these ends, and that among the ends, the human look to the divine, and all the divine to their leader, wisdom.").

⁸ *See generally* U.S. Const., Preamble to the Bill of Rights ("THE Conven-tions of a number of the States, having at the time of their adopting the Constitution, expressed a desire, in order to prevent misconstructions or abuse of its powers, that further declaratory and restrictive clauses be add-ed: And as extending the ground of public confidence in the Government, will best ensure the beneficent ends of its institution. . . .")

INDEX

COMPENDIUM OF INSPECTOR GENERAL

LEGAL AUTHORITIES

APPENDIX 1.

Inspector General Act of 1978,

as amended

§ 1. SHORT TITLE

This Act may be cited as the "Inspector General Act of 1978".

§ 2. PURPOSE AND ESTABLISHMENT OF OFFICES OF INSPECTOR GENERAL; DEPARTMENTS AND AGENCIES INVOLVED

In order to create independent and objective units--

(1) to conduct and supervise audits and investigations relating to the programs and operations of the establishments listed in section 12(2);

(2) to provide leadership and coordination and recommend policies for activities designed (A) to promote economy, efficiency, and effectiveness in the administration of, and (B) to prevent and detect fraud and abuse in, such programs and operations; and

(3) to provide a means for keeping the head of the establishment and the Congress fully and currently informed about problems and deficiencies relating to the administration of such programs and operations and the necessity for and progress of corrective action;

there is established--

(A) in each of such establishments an office of Inspector General, subject to subparagraph (B); and

(B) in the establishment of the Department of the Treasury--

(i) an Office of Inspector General of the Department of the Treasury; and

(ii) an Office of Treasury Inspector General for Tax Administration.

§ 3. APPOINTMENT OF INSPECTOR GENERAL; SUPERVISION; REMOVAL; POLITICAL ACTIVITIES; APPOINTMENT OF ASSISTANT INSPECTOR GENERAL FOR AUDITING AND ASSISTANT INSPECTOR GENERAL FOR INVESTIGATIONS

(a) There shall be at the head of each Office an Inspector General who shall be appointed by the President, by and with the advice and consent of the Senate, without regard to political affiliation and solely on the basis of integrity and demonstrated ability in accounting, auditing, financial analysis, law, management analysis, public administration, or investigations. Each Inspector General shall report to and be under the general supervision of the head of the establishment involved or, to the extent such authority is delegated, the officer next in rank below such head, but shall not report to, or be subject to supervision by, any other officer of such establishment. Neither the head of the establishment nor the officer next in rank below such head shall prevent or prohibit the Inspector General from initiating, carrying out, or completing any audit or investigation, or from issuing any subpoena during the course of any audit or investigation.

(b) An Inspector General may be removed from office by the President. If an Inspector General is removed from office or is transferred to another position or location within an establishment, the President shall communicate in writing the reasons for any such removal or transfer to both Houses of Congress, not later than 30 days before the removal or transfer. Nothing in this subsection shall prohibit a personnel action otherwise authorized by law, other than transfer or removal.

(c) For the purposes of section 7324 of Title 5, United States Code, no Inspector General shall be considered to be an employee who determines policies to be pursued by the United States in the nationwide administration of Federal laws.

(d) Each Inspector General shall, in accordance with applicable laws and regulations governing the civil service—

(1) appoint an Assistant Inspector General for Auditing who shall have the responsibility for supervising the performance of auditing activities relating to programs and operations of the establishment, and

(2) appoint an Assistant Inspector General for Investigations who shall have the responsibility for supervising the performance of investigative activities relating to such programs and operations.

(e) The annual rate of basic pay for an Inspector General (as defined under section 12(3)) shall be the rate payable for level III of the Executive Schedule under section 5314 of title 5, United States Code, plus 3 percent.

(f) An Inspector General (as defined under section 8G(a)(6) or 12(3)) may not receive any cash award or cash bonus, including any cash award under chapter 45 of title 5, United States Code.

(g) Each Inspector General shall, in accordance with applicable laws and regulations governing the civil service, obtain legal advice from a counsel either reporting directly to the Inspector General or another Inspector General.

§ 4. DUTIES AND RESPONSIBILITIES; REPORT OF CRIMINAL VIOLATIONS TO ATTORNEY GENERAL

(a) It shall be the duty and responsibility of each Inspector General, with respect to the establishment within which his Office is established--

(1) to provide policy direction for and to conduct, supervise, and coordinate audits and investigations relating to the programs and operations of such establishment;

(2) to review existing and proposed legislation and regulations relating to programs and operations of such establishment and to make recommendations in the semiannual reports required by section 5(a) concerning the impact of such legislation or regulations on the economy and efficiency in the administration of programs and operations administered or financed by such establishment or the prevention and detection of fraud and abuse in such programs and operations;

(3) to recommend policies for, and to conduct, supervise, or coordinate other activities carried out or financed by such establishment for the purpose of promoting economy and efficiency in the administration of, or

preventing and detecting fraud and abuse in, its programs and operations;

(4) to recommend policies for, and to conduct, supervise, or coordinate relationships between such establishment and other Federal agencies, State and local governmental agencies, and nongovernmental entities with respect to (A) all matters relating to the promotion of economy and efficiency in the administration of, or the prevention and detection of fraud and abuse in, programs and operations administered or financed by such establishment, or (B) the identification and prosecution of participants in such fraud or abuse; and

(5) to keep the head of such establishment and the Congress fully and currently informed, by means of the reports required by section 5 and otherwise, concerning fraud and other serious problems, abuses, and deficiencies relating to the administration of programs and operations administered or financed by such establishment, to recommend corrective action concerning such problems, abuses, and deficiencies, and to report on the progress made in implementing such corrective action.

(b)(1) In carrying out the responsibilities specified in subsection (a)(1), each Inspector General shall—

(A) comply with standards established by the Comptroller General of the United States for audits of Federal establishments, organizations, programs, activities, and functions;

(B) establish guidelines for determining when it shall be appropriate to use non-Federal auditors; and

(C) take appropriate steps to assure that any work performed by non-Federal auditors complies with the standards established by the Comptroller General as described in paragraph (1).

(2) For purposes of determining compliance with paragraph (1)(A) with respect to whether internal quality controls are in place and operating and whether established audit standards, policies, and procedures are being followed by Offices of Inspector General of establishments defined under section 12(2), Offices of Inspector General of designated Federal entities defined under section 8F(a)(2), and any audit office established within a Federal entity defined under section

8F(a)(1), reviews shall be performed exclusively by an audit entity in the Federal Government, including the Government Accountability Office or the Office of Inspector General of each establishment defined under section 12(2), or the Office of Inspector General of each designated Federal entity defined under section 8F(a)(2).

(c) In carrying out the duties and responsibilities established under this Act, each Inspector General shall give particular regard to the activities of the Comptroller General of the United States with a view toward avoiding duplication and insuring effective coordination and cooperation.

(d) In carrying out the duties and responsibilities established under this Act, each Inspector General shall report expeditiously to the Attorney General whenever the Inspector General has reasonable grounds to believe there has been a violation of Federal criminal law.

§ 5. SEMIANNUAL REPORTS; TRANSMITTAL TO CONGRESS; AVAILABILITY TO PUBLIC; IMMEDIATE REPORT ON SERIOUS OR FLAGRANT PROBLEMS; DISCLOSURE OF INFORMATION; DEFINITIONS.

(a) Each Inspector General shall, not later than April 30 and October 31 of each year, prepare semiannual reports summarizing the activities of the Office during the immediately preceding six-month periods ending March 31 and September 30. Such reports shall include, but need not be limited to--

(1) a description of significant problems, abuses, and deficiencies relating to the administration of programs and operations of such establishment disclosed by such activities during the reporting period;

(2) a description of the recommendations for corrective action made by the Office during the reporting period with respect to significant problems, abuses, or deficiencies identified pursuant to paragraph (1);

(3) an identification of each significant recommendation described in previous semiannual reports on which corrective action has not been completed;

(4) a summary of matters referred to prosecutive authorities and the prosecutions and convictions which have resulted;

(5) a summary of each report made to the head of the establishment under section 6(b)(2) during the reporting period;

(6) a listing, subdivided according to subject matter, of each audit report issued by the Office during the reporting period and for each report, where applicable, the total dollar value of questioned costs (including a separate category for the dollar value of unsupported costs) and the dollar value of recommendations that funds be put to better use;

(7) a summary of each particularly significant report;

(8) statistical tables showing the total number of audit reports, inspection reports, and evaluation reports and the total dollar value of questioned costs (including a separate category for the dollar value of unsupported costs), for reports—

> (a) for which no management decision had been made by the commencement of the reporting period;
>
> (b) which were issued during the reporting period;
>
> (c) for which a management decision was made during the reporting period, including—
>
> > (i) the dollar value of disallowed costs; and
> >
> > (ii) the dollar value of costs not disallowed; and
>
> (d) for which no management decision has been made by the end of the reporting period;

(9) statistical tables showing the total number of audit reports, inspection reports, and evaluation reports and the dollar value of recommendations that funds be put to better use by management, for reports—

> (a) for which no management decision had been made by the commencement of the reporting period;
>
> (b) which were issued during the reporting period;

(c) for which a management decision was made during the reporting period, including—

(i) the dollar value of recommendations that were agreed to by management; and

(ii) the dollar value of recommendations that were not agreed to by management; and

(d) for which no management decision has been made by the end of the reporting period;

(10) summary of each audit report issued before the commencement of the reporting period for which no management decision has been made by the end of the reporting period (including the date and title of each such report), an explanation of the reasons such management decision has not been made, and a statement concerning the desired timetable for achieving a management decision on each such report;

(11) a description and explanation of the reasons for any significant revised management decision made during the reporting period;

(12) information concerning any significant management decision with which the Inspector General is in disagreement;

(13) the information described under section 05(b) of the Federal Financial Management Improvement Act of 1996;

(14)(A) an appendix containing the results of any peer review conducted by another Office of Inspector General during the reporting period; or (B) if no peer review was conducted within that reporting period, a statement identifying the date of the last peer review conducted by another Office of Inspector General;

(15) a list of any outstanding recommendations from any peer review conducted by another Office of Inspector General that have not been fully implemented, including a statement describing the

status of the implementation and why implementation is not complete; and

(16) a list of any peer reviews conducted by the Inspector General of another Office of the Inspector General during the reporting period, including a list of any outstanding recommendations made from any previous peer review (including any peer review conducted before the reporting period) that remain outstanding or have not been fully implemented.

(a) Semiannual reports of each Inspector General shall be furnished to the head of the establishment involved not later than April 30 and October 31 of each year and shall be transmitted by such head to the appropriate committees or subcommittees of the Congress within thirty days after receipt of the report, together with a report by the head of the establishment containing—

(1) any comments such head determines appropriate;

(2) statistical tables showing the total number of audit reports, inspection reports, and evaluation reports and the dollar value of disallowed costs, for reports—

(A) for which final action had not been taken by the commencement of the reporting period;

(B) on which management decisions were made during the reporting period;

(C) for which final action was taken during the reporting period, including—

(i) the dollar value of disallowed costs that were recovered by management through collection, offset, property in lieu of cash, or otherwise; and

(ii) the dollar value of disallowed costs that were written off by management; and

(D) for which no final action has been taken by the end of the reporting period;

(3) statistical tables showing the total number of audit reports, inspection reports, and evaluation reports and the dollar value of recommendations that funds be put to better use by management agreed to in a management decision, for reports—

(A) for which final action had not been taken by the commencement of the reporting period;

(B) on which management decisions were made during the reporting period;

(C) for which final action was taken during the reporting period, including—

(i) the dollar value of recommendations that were actually completed; and

(ii) the dollar value of recommendations that management has subsequently concluded should not or could not be implemented or completed; and

(D) for which no final action has been taken by the end of the reporting period; and

(4) a statement with respect to audit reports on which management decisions have been made but final action has not been taken, other than audit reports on which a management decision was made within the preceding year, containing—

(A) a list of such audit reports and the date each such report was issued;

(B) the dollar value of disallowed costs for each report;

(C) the dollar value of recommendations that funds be put to better use agreed to by management for each report; and

(D) an explanation of the reasons final action has not been taken with respect to each such audit report, except that such statement may exclude such audit reports that are under formal administrative or judicial appeal or upon which management of an establishment has agreed to pursue a legislative solution, but shall identify the number of reports in each category so excluded.

(c) Within sixty days of the transmission of the semiannual reports of each Inspector General to the Congress, the head of each establishment shall make copies of such report available to the public upon request and at a reasonable cost. Within 60 days after the transmission of the semiannual reports of each establishment head to the Congress, the head of each establishment shall make copies of such report available to the public upon request and at a reasonable cost.

(d) Each Inspector General shall report immediately to the head of the establishment involved whenever the Inspector General becomes aware of particularly serious or flagrant problems, abuses, or deficiencies relating to the administration of programs and operations of such establishment. The head of the establishment shall transmit any such report to the appropriate committees or subcommittees of Congress within seven calendar days, together with a report by the head of the establishment containing any comments such head deems appropriate.

(e)(1) Nothing in this section shall be construed to authorize the public disclosure of information which is—

(a) specifically prohibited from disclosure by any other provision of law;

(b) specifically required by Executive order to be protected from disclosure in the interest of national defense or national security or in the conduct of foreign affairs; or

(c) a part of an ongoing criminal investigation.

(2) Notwithstanding paragraph (1)(C), any report under this section may be disclosed to the public in a form which includes information with respect to a part of an ongoing criminal investigation if such information has been included in a public record.

(3) Except to the extent and in the manner provided under section 6103(f) of the Internal Revenue Code of 1986 [26 U.S.C. § 6103(f)], nothing in this section or in any other provision of this Act shall be construed to authorize or permit the withholding of information from the Congress, or from any committee or subcommittee thereof.

(f) As used in this section—

(1) the term "questioned cost" means a cost that is questioned by the Office because of—

(A) an alleged violation of a provision of a law, regulation, contract, grant, cooperative agreement, or other agreement or document governing the expenditure of funds;

(B) a finding that, at the time of the audit, such cost is not supported by adequate documentation; or

(C) a finding that the expenditure of funds for the intended purpose is unnecessary or unreasonable;

(2) the term "unsupported cost" means a cost that is questioned by the Office because the Office found that, at the time of the audit, such cost is not supported by adequate documentation;

(3) the term "disallowed cost" means a questioned cost that management, in a management decision, has sustained or agreed should not be charged to the Government;

(4) the term "recommendation that funds be put to better use" means a recommendation by the Office that funds could be used more efficiently if management of an establishment took actions to implement and complete the recommendation, including—

    (A) reductions in outlays;

    (B) deobligation of funds from programs or operations;

    (C) withdrawal of interest subsidy costs on loans or loan guarantees, insurance, or bonds;

    (D) costs not incurred by implementing recommended improvements related to the operations of the establishment, a contractor or grantee;

    (E) avoidance of unnecessary expenditures noted in preaward reviews of contract or grant agreements; or

    (F) any other savings which are specifically identified;

(5) the term "management decision" means the evaluation by the management of an establishment of the findings and recommendations included in an audit report and the issuance of a final decision by management concerning its response to such findings and recommendations, including actions concluded to be necessary; and

(6) gthe term "final action" means—

(A) the completion of all actions that the management of an establishment has concluded, in its management decision, are necessary with respect to the findings and recommendations included in an audit report; and

(B) in the event that the management of an establishment concludes no action is necessary, final action occurs when a management decision has been made.

§ 6. AUTHORITY OF INSPECTOR GENERAL; INFORMATION AND ASSISTANCE FROM FEDERAL AGENCIES; UNREASONABLE REFUSAL; OFFICE SPACE AND EQUIPMENT

(a) In addition to the authority otherwise provided by this Act, each Inspector General, in carrying out the provisions of this Act, is authorized--

(1) to have access to all records, reports, audits, reviews, documents, papers, recommendations, or other material available to the applicable establishment which relate to programs and operations with respect to which that Inspector General has responsibilities under this Act;

(2) to make such investigations and reports relating to the administration of the programs and operations of the applicable establishment as are, in the judgment of the Inspector General, necessary or desirable;

(3) to request such information or assistance as may be necessary for carrying out the duties and responsibilities provided by this Act from any Federal, State, or local governmental agency or unit thereof;

(4) to require by subpoena the production of all information, documents, reports, answers, records, accounts, papers, and other data in any medium (including electronically stored information, as well as any tangible thing) and documentary evidence necessary in the performance of the functions assigned by this Act, which subpoena, in the case of contumacy or refusal to obey, shall be enforceable by order of any appropriate United States district court: *Provided*, That procedures other than subpenas shall be used by the Inspector General to obtain documents and information from Federal agencies;

(5) to administer to or take from any person an oath, affirmation, or affidavit, whenever necessary in the performance of the functions assigned by this Act, which oath, affirmation, or affidavit when administered or taken by or before an employee of an Office of Inspector General designated by the Inspector General shall have the same force and effect as if administered or taken by or before an officer having a seal;

(6) to have direct and prompt access to the head of the establishment involved when necessary for any purpose pertaining to the performance of functions and responsibilities under this Act;

(7) to select, appoint, and employ such officers and employees as may be necessary for carrying out the functions, powers, and duties of the Office subject to the provisions of Title 5, United States Code, governing appointments in the competitive service, and the provisions of chapter 51 and subchapter III of chapter 53 of such title relating to classification and General Schedule pay rates;

(8) to obtain services as authorized by section 3109 of Title 5, United States Code, at daily rates not to exceed the equivalent rate prescribed for grade GS-18 of the General Schedule by section 5332 of Title 5, United States Code; and

(9) to the extent and in such amounts as may be provided in advance by appropriations Acts, to enter into contracts and other arrangements for audits, studies, analyses, and other services with public agencies and with private persons, and to make such payments as may be necessary to carry out the provisions of this Act.

(b)(1) Upon request of an Inspector General for information or assistance under subsection (a)(3), the head of any Federal agency involved shall, insofar as is practicable and not in contravention of any existing statutory restriction or regulation of the Federal agency from which the information is requested, furnish to such Inspector General, or to an authorized designee, such information or assistance.

(2) Whenever information or assistance requested under subsection (a)(1) or (a)(3) is, in the judgment of an Inspector General, unreasonably refused or not provided, the Inspector General shall report the circumstances to the head of the establishment involved without delay.

(c) Each head of an establishment shall provide the Office within such establishment with appropriate and adequate office space at central and field office locations of such establishment, together with such equipment, office supplies, and communications facilities and services as may be necessary for the operation of such offices, and shall provide necessary maintenance services for such offices and the equipment and facilities located therein.

(d)(1)(A) For purposes of applying the provisions of law identified in subparagraph (B)—

(i) each Office of Inspector General shall be considered to be a separate agency; and

(ii) the Inspector General who is the head of an office referred to in clause (i) shall, with respect to such office, have the functions, powers, and duties of an agency head or appointing authority under such provisions.

(B) This paragraph applies with respect to the following provisions of title 5, United States Code:

(i) Subchapter II of chapter 35.

(ii) Sections 8335(b), 8336, 8344, 8414, 8468, and 8425(b).

(iii) All provisions relating to the Senior Executive Service (as determined by the Office of Personnel Management), subject to paragraph (2).

(2) For purposes of applying section 4507(b) of title 5, United States Code, paragraph (1)(A)(ii) shall be applied by substituting "the Council of the Inspectors General on Integrity and Efficiency (established by section 11 of the Inspector General Act) shall" for "the Inspector General who is the head of an office referred to in clause (i) shall, with respect to such office,".

(e)(1) In addition to the authority otherwise provided by this Act, each Inspector General, any Assistant Inspector General for Investigations under such an Inspector General, and any special agent supervised by such an Assistant Inspector General may be authorized by the Attorney General to—

(A) carry a firearm while engaged in official duties as authorized under this Act or other statute, or as expressly authorized by the Attorney General;

(B) make an arrest without a warrant while engaged in official duties as authorized under this Act or other statute, or as expressly authorized by the Attorney General, for any offense against the United States committed in the presence of such Inspector General, Assistant Inspector General, or agent, or for any felony cognizable under the laws of the United States if such Inspector General, Assistant Inspector General, or agent has reasonable grounds to believe that the person to be arrested has committed or is committing such felony; and

(C) seek and execute warrants for arrest, search of a premises, or seizure of evidence issued under the authority of the United

States upon probable cause to believe that a violation has been committed.

(2) The Attorney General may authorize exercise of the powers under this subsection only upon an initial determination that—

(A) the affected Office of Inspector General is significantly hampered in the performance of responsibilities established by this Act as a result of the lack of such powers;

(B) available assistance from other law enforcement agencies is insufficient to meet the need for such powers; and

(C) adequate internal safeguards and management procedures exist to ensure proper exercise of such powers.

(3) The Inspector General offices of the Department of Commerce, Department of Education, Department of Energy, Department of Health and Human Services, Department of Homeland Security, Department of Housing and Urban Development, Department of the Interior, Department of Justice, Department of Labor, Department of State, Department of Transportation, Department of the Treasury, Department of Veterans Affairs, Agency for International Development, Environmental Protection Agency, Federal Deposit Insurance Corporation, Federal Emergency Management Agency, General Services Administration, National Aeronautics and Space Administration, Nuclear Regulatory Commission, Office of Personnel Management, Railroad Retirement Board, Small Business Administration, Social Security Administration, and the Tennessee Valley Authority are exempt from the requirement of paragraph (2) of an initial determination of eligibility by the Attorney General.

(4) The Attorney General shall promulgate, and revise as appropriate, guidelines which shall govern the exercise of the law enforcement powers established under paragraph (1).

(5)(A) Powers authorized for an Office of Inspector General under paragraph (1) may be rescinded or suspended upon a determination by the Attorney General that any of the requirements under paragraph (2) is no longer satisfied or that the exercise of authorized powers by that Office of Inspector General has not complied with the guidelines promulgated by the Attorney General under paragraph (4).

(B) Powers authorized to be exercised by any individual under paragraph (1) may be rescinded or suspended with respect to that individual upon a determination by the Attorney General that such individual has not complied with guidelines promulgated by the Attorney General under paragraph (4).

(6) A determination by the Attorney General under paragraph (2) or (5) shall not be reviewable in or by any court.

(7) To ensure the proper exercise of the law enforcement powers authorized by this subsection, the Offices of Inspector General described under paragraph (3) shall, not later than 180 days after the date of enactment of this subsection, collectively enter into a memorandum of understanding to establish an external review process for ensuring that adequate internal safeguards and management procedures continue to exist within each Office and within any Office that later receives an authorization under paragraph (2). The review process shall be established in consultation with the Attorney General, who shall be provided with a copy of the memorandum of understanding that establishes the review process. Under the review process, the exercise of the law enforcement powers by each Office of Inspector General shall be reviewed periodically by another Office of Inspector General or by a committee of Inspectors General. The results of each review shall be communicated in writing to the applicable Inspector General and to the Attorney General.

(8) No provision of this subsection shall limit the exercise of law enforcement powers established under any other statutory authority, including United States Marshals Service special deputation.

(9) In this subsection, the term "Inspector General" means an Inspector General appointed under section 3 or an Inspector General appointed under section 8G.

(f)(1) For each fiscal year, an Inspector General shall transmit a budget estimate and request to the head of the establishment or designated Federal entity to which the Inspector General reports. The budget request shall specify the aggregate amount of funds requested for such fiscal year for the operations of that Inspector General and shall specify the amount requested for all training needs, including a certification from the Inspector General that the amount requested satisfies all training requirements for the Inspector General's office for that fiscal year, and any resources necessary to support the Council of the Inspectors General on Integrity and Efficiency. Resources necessary to support the Council of the Inspectors General on Integrity and Efficiency shall be specifically identified and justified in the budget request.

(2) In transmitting a proposed budget to the President for approval, the head of each establishment or designated Federal entity shall include—

> > (A) an aggregate request for the Inspector General;
> >
> > (B) amounts for Inspector General training;
> >
> > (C) amounts for support of the Council of the Inspectors General on Integrity and Efficiency; and
> >
> > (D) any comments of the affected Inspector General with respect to the proposal.
>
> (3) The President shall include in each budget of the United States Government submitted to Congress—
>
> > (A) a separate statement of the budget estimate prepared in accordance with paragraph (1);
> >
> > (B) the amount requested by the President for each Inspector General;
> >
> > (C) the amount requested by the President for training of Inspectors General;
> >
> > (D) the amount requested by the President for support for the Council of the Inspectors General on Integrity and Efficiency; and
> >
> > (E) any comments of the affected Inspector General with respect to the proposal if the Inspector General concludes that the budget submitted by the President would substantially inhibit the Inspector General from performing the duties of the office.

§ 7. COMPLAINTS BY EMPLOYEES; DISCLOSURE OF IDENTITY; REPRISALS

(a) The Inspector General may receive and investigate complaints or information from an employee of the establishment concerning the possible existence of an activity constituting a violation of law, rules, or regulations, or mismanagement, gross waste of funds, abuse of authority or a substantial and specific danger to the public health and safety.

(b) The Inspector General shall not, after receipt of a complaint or information from an employee, disclose the identity of the employee without the consent of the employee, unless the Inspector General determines such disclosure is unavoidable during the course of the investigation.

(c) Any employee who has authority to take, direct others to take, recommend, or approve any personnel action, shall not, with respect to such authority, take or threaten to take any action against any employee as a reprisal for making a complaint or disclosing information to an Inspector General, unless the complaint was made or the information disclosed with the knowledge that it was false or with willful disregard for its truth or falsity.

§ 8. ADDITIONAL PROVISIONS WITH RESPECT TO THE INSPECTOR GENERAL OF THE DEPARTMENT OF DEFENSE

(a) No member of the Armed Forces, active or reserve, shall be appointed Inspector General of the Department of Defense.
(b)   (1) Notwithstanding the last two sentences of section 3(a), the Inspector General shall be under the authority, direction, and control of the Secretary of Defense with respect to audits or investigations, or the issuance of subpoenas, which require access to information concerning--

(A) sensitive operational plans;

(B) intelligence matters;

(C) counterintelligence matters;

(D) ongoing criminal investigations by other administrative units of the Department of Defense related to national security; or

(E) other matters the disclosure of which would constitute a serious threat to national security.

(2) With respect to the information described in paragraph (1) the Secretary of Defense may prohibit the Inspector General from initiating, carrying out, or completing any audit or investigation, or from issuing any subpoena, after the Inspector General has decided to initiate, carry out or complete such audit or investigation or to issue such subpoena, if the Secretary determines that such prohibition is necessary to preserve the national security interests of the United States.

(3) If the Secretary of Defense exercises any power under paragraph (1) or (2), the Inspector General shall submit a statement concerning such exercise within thirty days to the Committees on Armed Services and Governmental Affairs of the Senate and the Committee on Armed Services and the Committee on Government Reform and Oversight of the House of Representatives and to other appropriate committees or subcommittees of the Congress.

(4) The Secretary shall, within thirty days after submission of a statement under paragraph (3), transmit a statement of the reasons for the exercise of power under paragraph (1) or (2) to the congressional committees specified in paragraph (3) and to other appropriate committees or subcommittees.

(c) In addition to the other duties and responsibilities specified in this Act, the Inspector General of the Department of Defense shall—

(1) be the principal adviser to the Secretary of Defense for matters relating to the prevention and detection of fraud, waste, and abuse in the programs and operations of the Department;

(2) initiate, conduct, and supervise such audits and investigations in the Department of Defense (including the military departments) as the Inspector General considers appropriate;

(3) provide policy direction for audits and investigations relating to fraud, waste, and abuse and program effectiveness;

(4) investigate fraud, waste, and abuse uncovered as a result of other contract and internal audits, as the Inspector General considers appropriate;

(5) develop policy, monitor and evaluate program performance, and provide guidance with respect to all Department activities relating to criminal investigation programs;

(6) monitor and evaluate the adherence of Department auditors to internal audit, contract audit, and internal review principles, policies, and procedures;

(7) develop policy, evaluate program performance, and monitor actions taken by all components of the Department in response to contract audits, internal audits, internal review reports, and audits conducted by the Comptroller General of the United States;

(8) request assistance as needed from other audit, inspection, and investigative units of the Department of Defense (including military departments); and

(9) give particular regard to the activities of the internal audit, inspection, and investigative units of the military departments with a view toward avoiding duplication and insuring effective coordination and cooperation.

(d) Notwithstanding section 4(d), the Inspector General of the Department of Defense shall expeditiously report suspected or alleged violations of chapter 47 of title 10, United States Code (Uniform Code of Military Justice), to the Secretary of the military department concerned or the Secretary of Defense.

(e) For the purposes of section 7, a member of the Armed Forces shall be deemed to be an employee of the Department of Defense, except that, when the Coast Guard operates as a service of another department or agency of the Federal Government, a member of the Coast Guard shall be deemed to be an employee of such department or agency.

(f)(1) Each semiannual report prepared by the Inspector General of the Department of Defense under section 5(a) shall include information concerning the numbers and types of contract audits conducted by the Department during the reporting period. Each such report shall be transmitted by the Secretary of Defense to the Committees on Armed Services and Governmental Affairs of the Senate and the Committee on Armed Services and the Committee on Government Reform and Oversight of the House of Representatives and to other appropriate committees or subcommittees of the Congress.

(2) Any report required to be transmitted by the Secretary of Defense to the appropriate committees or subcommittees of the Congress under section 5(d) shall also be transmitted, within the seven-day period specified in such section, to the congressional committees specified in paragraph (1).

(g) The provisions of section 1385 of title 18, United States Code, shall not apply to audits and investigations conducted by, under the direction of, or at the request of the Inspector General of the Department of Defense to carry out the purposes of this Act.

(h)(1) There is a General Counsel to the Inspector General of the Department of Defense, who shall be appointed by the Inspector General of the Department of Defense.

(2)(A) Notwithstanding section 140(b) of Title 10, the General Counsel is the chief legal officer of the Office of the Inspector General.

(B) The Inspector General is the exclusive legal client of the General Counsel.

(C) The General Counsel shall perform such functions as the Inspector General may prescribe.

(D) The General Counsel shall serve at the discretion of the Inspector General.

(3)There is an Office of the General Counsel to the Inspector General of the Department of Defense. The Inspector General may appoint to the Office to serve as staff of the

General Counsel such legal counsel as the Inspector General considers appropriate.

(i)(1) The Inspector General of the Department of Defense is authorized to require by subpoena the attendance and testimony of witnesses as necessary in the performance of functions assigned to the Inspector General by this Act, except that the Inspector General shall use procedures other than subpoenas to obtain attendance and testimony from Federal employees.

(2) A subpoena issued under this subsection, in the case of contumacy or refusal to obey, shall be enforceable by order of any appropriate United States district court.

(3) The Inspector General shall notify the Attorney General 7 days before issuing any subpoena under this section.

§ 8A. SPECIAL PROVISIONS RELATING TO THE AGENCY FOR INTERNATIONAL DEVELOPMENT

(a) In addition to the other duties and responsibilities specified in this Act, the Inspector General of the Agency for International Development shall supervise, direct, and control all security activities relating to the programs and operations of that Agency, subject to the supervision of the Administrator of that Agency.

(b) In addition to the Assistant Inspector Generals provided for in section 3(d) of this Act, the Inspector General of the Agency for International Development shall, in accordance with applicable laws and regulations governing the civil service, appoint an Assistant Inspector General for Security who shall have the responsibility for supervising the performance of security activities relating to programs and operations of the Agency for International Development.

(c) In addition to the officers and employees provided for in section 6(a)(6) of this Act, members of the Foreign Service may, at the request of the Inspector General of the Agency for International Development, be assigned as employees of the Inspector General. Members of the Foreign Service so assigned shall be responsible solely to the Inspector General, and the Inspector General (or his or her designee) shall prepare the performance evaluation reports for such members.

(d) In establishing and staffing field offices pursuant to section 6(c) of this Act, the Administrator of the Agency for International Development shall not be bound by overseas personnel ceilings established under the Monitoring Overseas Direct Employment policy.

(e) The Inspector General of the Agency for International Development shall be in addition to the officers provided for in section 624(a) of the Foreign Assistance Act of 1961 [22 U.S.C. § 2384(a)].

(f) As used in this Act, the term "Agency for International Development" includes any successor agency primarily responsible for administering part I of the Foreign Assistance Act of 1961 [22 U.S.C. § 2151 et seq.], an employee of the Inter-American Foundation, and an employee of the African Development Foundation.

§ 8B. SPECIAL PROVISIONS CONCERNING THE NUCLEAR REGULATORY COMMISSION

(a) The Chairman of the Commission may delegate the authority specified in the second sentence of section 3(a) to another member of the Nuclear Regulatory Commission, but shall not delegate such authority to any other officer or employee of the Commission.

(b) Notwithstanding sections 6(a)(7) and (8), the Inspector General of the Nuclear Regulatory Commission is authorized to select, appoint, and employ such officers and employees as may be necessary for carrying out the functions, powers and duties of the Office of Inspector General and to obtain the temporary or intermittent services of experts or consultants or an organization thereof, subject to the applicable laws and regulations that govern such selections, appointments and employment, and the obtaining of such services, within the Nuclear Regulatory Commission.

§ 8C. SPECIAL PROVISIONS CONCERNING THE FEDERAL DEPOSIT INSURANCE CORPORATION

(a) Delegation.--The Chairperson of the Federal Deposit Insurance Corporation may delegate the authority specified in the second sentence of section 3(a) to the Vice Chairperson of the Board of Directors of the Federal Deposit Insurance Corporation, but may not delegate such authority to any other officer or employee of the Corporation.

(b) Personnel.--Notwithstanding paragraphs (7) and (8) of section 6(a), the Inspector General of the Federal Deposit Insurance Corporation may select, appoint, and employ such officers and employees as may be necessary for carrying out the functions, powers, and duties of the Office of Inspector General and to obtain the temporary or intermittent services of experts or consultants or an organization of experts or consultants, subject to the applicable laws and regulations that govern such selections, appointments, and employment, and the obtaining of such services, within the Federal Deposit Insurance Corporation.

§ 8D. SPECIAL PROVISIONS CONCERNING THE DEPARTMENT OF THE TREASURY

(a)(1) Notwithstanding the last two sentences of section 3(a), the Inspector General of the Department of the Treasury shall be under the authority, direction, and control of the Secretary of the Treasury with respect to audits or investigations, or the issuance of subpenas, which require access to sensitive information concerning—

    (A) ongoing criminal investigations or proceedings;

    (B) undercover operations;

    (C) the identity of confidential sources, including protected witnesses;

    (D) deliberations and decisions on policy matters, including documented information used as a basis for making policy decisions, the disclosure of which could reasonably be expected to have a significant influence on the economy or market behavior;

    (E) intelligence or counterintelligence matters; or

    (F) other matters the disclosure of which would constitute a serious threat to national security or to the protection of any person or property authorized protection by section 3056 of title 18, United States Code, section 3056A of title 18, United States Code, or any provision of the Presidential Protection Assistance Act of 1976 (18 U.S.C. 3056 note; Public Law 94-524).

(2) With respect to the information described under paragraph (1), the Secretary of the Treasury may prohibit the Inspector General of the Department of the Treasury from carrying out or completing any audit or investigation, or from issuing any subpena, after such Inspector General has decided to initiate, carry out, or complete such audit or investigation or to issue such subpena, if the Secretary determines that such prohibition is necessary to prevent the disclosure of any information described under paragraph (1) or to prevent significant impairment to the national interests of the United States.

(3) If the Secretary of the Treasury exercises any power under paragraph (1) or (2), the Secretary of the Treasury shall notify the Inspector General of the Department of the Treasury in writing stating the reasons for such exercise.

Within 30 days after receipt of any such notice, the Inspector General of the Department of the Treasury shall transmit a copy of such notice to the Committees on Governmental Affairs and Finance of the Senate and the Committees on Government Operations and Ways and Means of the House of Representatives, and to other appropriate committees or subcommittees of the Congress.

(4) The Secretary of the Treasury may not exercise any power under paragraph (1) or (2) with respect to the Treasury Inspector General for Tax Administration.

(b)(1) In carrying out the duties and responsibilities specified in this Act, the Inspector General of the Department of the Treasury shall have oversight responsibility for the internal investigations performed by the Office of Internal Affairs of the Tax and Trade Bureau. The head of such office shall promptly report to the Inspector General of the Department of the Treasury the significant activities being carried out by such office.

(2) The Inspector General of the Department of the Treasury shall exercise all duties and responsibilities of an Inspector General for the Department of the Treasury other than the duties and responsibilities exercised by the Treasury Inspector General for Tax Administration.

(3) The Secretary of the Treasury shall establish procedures under which the Inspector General of the Department of the Treasury and the Treasury Inspector General for Tax Administration will—

(A) determine how audits and investigations are allocated in cases of overlapping jurisdiction; and

(B) provide for coordination, cooperation, and efficiency in the conduct of such audits and investigations.

(c) Notwithstanding subsection (b), the Inspector General of the Department of the Treasury may initiate, conduct and supervise such audits and investigations in the Department of the Treasury (including the bureau referred to in subsection (b)) as the Inspector General of the Department of the Treasury considers appropriate.

(d) If the Inspector General of the Department of the Treasury initiates an audit or investigation under subsection (c) concerning the bureau referred to in subsection (b), the Inspector General of the Department of the Treasury may provide the head of the office of such bureau referred to in subsection (b) with written notice that the Inspector General of the Department of the Treasury has initiated such an audit or investigation. If the Inspector General of the

Department of the Treasury issues a notice under the preceding sentence, no other audit or investigation shall be initiated into the matter under audit or investigation by the Inspector General of the Department of the Treasury and any other audit or investigation of such matter shall cease.

(e)(1) The Treasury Inspector General for Tax Administration shall have access to returns and return information, as defined in section 6103(b) of the Internal Revenue Code of 1986 [26 U.S.C. § 6103(b)], only in accordance with the provisions of section 6103 of such Code [26 U.S.C. § 6103] and this Act.

(2) The Internal Revenue Service shall maintain the same system of standardized records or accountings of all requests from the Treasury Inspector General for Tax Administration for inspection or disclosure of returns and return information (including the reasons for and dates of such requests), and of returns and return information inspected or disclosed pursuant to such requests, as described under section 6103(p)(3)(A) of the Internal Revenue Code of 1986 [26 U.S.C. § 6103(p)(3)(A)]. Such system of standardized records or accountings shall also be available for examination in the same manner as provided under section 6103(p)(3) of the Internal Revenue Code of 1986 [26 U.S.C. § 6103(p)(3)].

(3) The Treasury Inspector General for Tax Administration shall be subject to the same safeguards and conditions for receiving returns and return information as are described under section 6103(p)(4) of the Internal Revenue Code of 1986 [26 U.S.C. § 6103(p)(4)].

(f) An audit or investigation conducted by the Inspector General of the Department of the Treasury or the Treasury Inspector General for Tax Administration shall not affect a final decision of the Secretary of the Treasury or his delegate under section 6406 of the Internal Revenue Code of 1986 [26 U.S.C. § 6406].

(g)(1) Any report required to be transmitted by the Secretary of the Treasury to the appropriate committees or subcommittees of the Congress under section 5(d) shall also be transmitted, within the seven-day period specified under such section, to the Committees on Governmental Affairs and Finance of the Senate and the Committees on Government Reform and Oversight and Ways and Means of the House of Representatives.

(2) Any report made by the Treasury Inspector General for Tax Administration that is required to be transmitted by the Secretary of the Treasury to the appropriate committees or subcommittees of Congress under section 5(d) shall also be transmitted, within

the 7-day period specified under such subsection, to the Internal Revenue Service Oversight Board and the Commissioner of Internal Revenue.

(h) The Treasury Inspector General for Tax Administration shall exercise all duties and responsibilities of an Inspector General of an establishment with respect to the Department of the Treasury and the Secretary of the Treasury on all matters relating to the Internal Revenue Service. The Treasury Inspector General for Tax Administration shall have sole authority under this Act to conduct an audit or investigation of the Internal Revenue Service Oversight Board and the Chief Counsel for the Internal Revenue Service.

(i) In addition to the requirements of the first sentence of section 3(a), the Treasury Inspector General for Tax Administration should have demonstrated ability to lead a large and complex organization.

(j) An individual appointed to the position of Treasury Inspector General for Tax Administration, the Assistant Inspector General for Auditing of the Office of the Treasury Inspector General for Tax Administration under section 3(d)(1), the Assistant Inspector General for Investigations of the Office of the Treasury Inspector General for Tax Administration under section 3(d)(2), or any position of Deputy Inspector General of the Office of the Treasury Inspector General for Tax Administration may not be an employee of the Internal Revenue Service—

(1) during the 2-year period preceding the date of appointment to such position; or

(2) during the 5-year period following the date such individual ends service in such position.

(k)(1) In addition to the duties and responsibilities exercised by an inspector general of an establishment, the Treasury Inspector General for Tax Administration—

(A) shall have the duty to enforce criminal provisions under section 7608(b) of the Internal Revenue Code of 1986 [26 U.S.C. § 7608(b)];

(B) in addition to the functions authorized under section 7608(b)(2) of such Code [26 U.S.C. § 7608(b)(2)], may carry firearms;

(C) shall be responsible for protecting the Internal Revenue Service against external attempts to corrupt or threaten employees of the Internal Revenue Service, but shall not be responsible for the conducting of background checks and the providing of protection to the Commissioner of Internal Revenue; and

(D) may designate any employee in the Office of the Treasury Inspector General for Tax Administration to enforce such laws and perform such functions referred to under subparagraphs (A), (B), and (C).

(2)(A) In performing a law enforcement function under paragraph (1), the Treasury Inspector General for Tax Administration shall report any reasonable grounds to believe there has been a violation of Federal criminal law to the Attorney General at an appropriate time as determined by the Treasury Inspector General for Tax Administration, notwithstanding section 4(d).

(B) In the administration of section 5(d) and subsection (g)(2) of this section, the Secretary of the Treasury may transmit the required report with respect to the Treasury Inspector General for Tax Administration at an appropriate time as determined by the Secretary, if the problem, abuse, or deficiency relates to—

(i) the performance of a law enforcement function under paragraph (1); and

(ii) sensitive information concerning matters under subsection (a)(1)(A) through (F).

(3) Nothing in this subsection shall be construed to affect the authority of any other person to carry out or enforce any provision specified in paragraph (1).

(l)(1) The Commissioner of Internal Revenue or the Internal Revenue Service Oversight Board may request, in writing, the Treasury Inspector General for Tax Administration to conduct an audit or investigation relating to the Internal Revenue Service. If the Treasury Inspector General for Tax Administration determines not to conduct such audit or investigation, the Inspector General shall timely provide a written explanation for such determination to the person making the request.

(2)(A) Any final report of an audit conducted by the Treasury Inspector General for Tax Administration shall be timely submitted by the Inspector General to the Commissioner of Internal Revenue and the Internal Revenue Service Oversight Board.

(B) The Treasury Inspector General for Tax Administration shall periodically submit to the Commissioner and Board a list of investigations for which a final report has been completed by the Inspector General and shall provide a copy of any such report upon request of the Commissioner or Board.

(C) This paragraph applies regardless of whether the applicable audit or investigation is requested under paragraph (1).

§ 8E. SPECIAL PROVISIONS CONCERNING THE DEPARTMENT OF JUSTICE

(a)(1) Notwithstanding the last two sentences of section 3(a), the Inspector General shall be under the authority, direction, and control of the Attorney General with respect to audits or investigations, or the issuance of subpenas, which require access to sensitive information concerning—

(A) ongoing civil or criminal investigations or proceedings;

(B) undercover operations;

(C) the identity of confidential sources, including protected witnesses;

(D) intelligence or counterintelligence matters; or

(E) other matters the disclosure of which would constitute a serious threat to national security.

(2) With respect to the information described under paragraph (1), the Attorney General may prohibit the Inspector General from carrying out or completing any audit or investigation, or from issuing any subpena, after such Inspector General has decided to initiate, carry out, or complete such audit or investigation or to issue such subpena, if the Attorney General determines that such prohibition is necessary to prevent the disclosure of any information described under paragraph (1) or to prevent the significant impairment to the national interests of the United States.

(3) If the Attorney General exercises any power under paragraph (1) or (2), the Attorney General shall notify the Inspector General in writing stating the reasons for such exercise. Within 30 days after receipt of any such notice, the Inspector General shall transmit a copy of such notice to the Committees on Governmental Affairs and Judiciary of the Senate and the Committees on Government Operations and Judiciary of the House of Representatives, and to other appropriate committees or subcommittees of the Congress.

(b) In carrying out the duties and responsibilities specified in this Act, the Inspector General of the Department of Justice—

(1) may initiate, conduct and supervise such audits and investigations in the Department of Justice as the Inspector General considers appropriate;

(2) except as specified in subsection (a) and paragraph (3), may investigate allegations of criminal wrongdoing or administrative misconduct by an employee of the Department of Justice, or may, in the discretion of the Inspector General, refer such allegations to the Office of Professional Responsibility or the internal affairs office of the appropriate component of the Department of Justice;

(3) shall refer to the Counsel, Office of Professional Responsibility of the Department of Justice, allegations of misconduct involving Department attorneys, investigators, or law enforcement personnel, where the allegations relate to the exercise of the authority of an attorney to investigate, litigate, or provide legal advice, except that no such referral shall be made if the attorney is employed in the Office of Professional Responsibility;

(4) may investigate allegations of criminal wrongdoing or administrative misconduct by a person who is the head of any agency or component of the Department of Justice; and

(5) shall forward the results of any investigation conducted under paragraph (4), along with any appropriate recommendation for disciplinary action, to the Attorney General.

(c) Any report required to be transmitted by the Attorney General to the appropriate committees or subcommittees of the Congress under section 5(d) shall also be transmitted, within the seven-day period specified under such section, to the Committees on the Judiciary and Governmental Affairs of the Senate and the Committees on the Judiciary and Government Operations of the House of Representatives.

(d) The Attorney General shall ensure by regulation that any component of the Department of Justice receiving a nonfrivolous allegation of criminal wrongdoing or administrative misconduct by an employee of the Department of Justice, except with respect to allegations described in subsection (b)(3), shall report that information to the Inspector General.

§ 8F. SPECIAL PROVISIONS CONCERNING THE CORPORATION FOR NATIONAL AND COMMUNITY SERVICE

(a) Notwithstanding the provisions of paragraphs (7) and (8) of section 6(a), it is within the exclusive jurisdiction of the Inspector General of the Corporation for National and Community Service to--

(1) appoint and determine the compensation of such officers and employees in accordance with section 195(b) of the National and Community Service Act of 1990; and

(2) procure the temporary and intermittent services of and compensate such experts and consultants, in accordance with section 3109(b) of title 5, United States Code, as may be necessary to carry out the functions, powers, and duties of the Inspector General.

(b) No later than the date on which the Chief Executive Officer of the Corporation for National and Community Service transmits any report to the Congress under subsection (a) or (b) of section 5, the Chief Executive Officer shall transmit such report to the Board of Directors of such Corporation.

(c) No later than the date on which the Chief Executive Officer of the Corporation for National and Community Service transmits a report described under section 5(b) to the Board of Directors as provided under subsection (b) of this section, the Chief Executive Officer shall also transmit any audit report which is described in the statement required under section 5(b)(4) to the Board of Directors. All such audit reports shall be placed on the agenda for review at the next scheduled meeting of the Board of Directors following such transmittal. The Chief Executive Officer of the Corporation shall be present at such meeting to provide any information relating to such audit reports.

(d) No later than the date on which the Inspector General of the Corporation for National and Community Service reports a problem, abuse, or deficiency under section 5(d) to the Chief Executive Officer of the Corporation, the Chief Executive Officer shall report such problem, abuse, or deficiency to the Board of Directors.

§ 8G. REQUIREMENTS FOR FEDERAL ENTITIES AND DESIGNATED FEDERAL ENTITIES

(a) Notwithstanding section 12 of this Act, as used in this section—

(1) the term "Federal entity" means any Government corporation (within the meaning of section 103(1) of title 5, United States Code), any Government controlled corporation (within the meaning of section 103(2) of such title), or any other entity in the Executive branch of the Government, or any independent regulatory agency, but does not include--

(A) an establishment (as defined under section 12(2) of this Act) or part of an establishment;

(B) a designated Federal entity (as defined under paragraph (2) of this subsection) or part of a designated Federal entity;

(C) the Executive Office of the President;

(D) the Central Intelligence Agency;

(E) the Government Accountability Office; or

(F) any entity in the judicial or legislative branches of the Government, including the Administrative Office of the United States Courts and the Architect of the Capitol and any activities under the direction of the Architect of the Capitol;

(2) the term "designated Federal entity" means Amtrak, the Appalachian Regional Commission, the Board of Governors of the Federal Reserve System and the Bureau of Consumer Financial Protection, the Board for International Broadcasting, the Commodity Futures Trading Commission, the Consumer Product Safety Commission, the Corporation for Public Broadcasting, the Defense Intelligence Agency, the Denali Commission, the Equal Employment Opportunity Commission, the Farm Credit Administration, the Federal Communications Commission, the Federal Election Commission, the Election Assistance Commission, the Federal Housing Finance Board, the Federal Labor Relations Authority, the Federal Maritime Commission, the Federal Trade Commission, the Legal Services Corporation, the National Archives and Records Administration, the National Credit Union Administration, the National Endowment for the Arts, the National Endowment for the Humanities, the National Geospatial-Intelligence Agency, the National Labor Relations Board, the National Reconnaissance Office, the National Security Agency, the National Science Foundation, the Panama Canal Commission, the Peace Corps, the Pension Benefit Guaranty Corporation, the Securities and Exchange Commission, the Smithsonian Institution, the United States International Trade Commission, the Postal Regulatory Commission, and the United States Postal Service;

(3) the term "head of the Federal entity" means any person or persons designated by statute as the head of a Federal entity, and if no such designation exists, the chief policy-making officer or board of a Federal entity as identified in

the list published pursuant to subsection (h)(1) of this section;

(4) the term "head of the designated Federal entity" means the board or commission of the designated Federal entity, or in the event the designated Federal entity does not have a board or commission, any person or persons designated by statute as the head of a designated Federal entity and if no such designation exists, the chief policymaking officer or board of a designated Federal entity as identified in the list published pursuant to subsection (h)(1) of this section, except that—

(A) with respect to the National Science Foundation, such term means the National Science Board;

(B) with respect to the United States Postal Service, such term means the Governors (within the meaning of section 102(3) of title 39, United States Code);

(C) with respect to the Federal Labor Relations Authority, such term means the members of the Authority (described under section 7104 of title 5, United States Code);

(D) with respect to the National Archives and Records Administration, such term means the Archivist of the United States;

(E) with respect to the National Credit Union Administration, such term means the National Credit Union Administration Board (described under section 102 of the Federal Credit Union Act (12 U.S.C. 1752a);

(F) with respect to the National Endowment of the Arts, such term means the National Council on the Arts;

(G) with respect to the National Endowment for the Humanities, such term means the National Council on the Humanities; and

(H) with respect to the Peace Corps, such term means the Director of the Peace Corps;

(5) the term "Office of Inspector General" means an Office of Inspector General of a designated Federal entity; and

(6) the term "Inspector General" means an Inspector General of a designated Federal entity.

(b) No later than 180 days after the date of the enactment of this section [Oct. 18, 1988], there shall be established and maintained in each designated Federal entity an Office of Inspector General. The head of the designated Federal entity shall transfer to such office the offices, units, or other components, and the functions, powers, or duties thereof, that such head determines are properly related to the functions of the Office of Inspector General and would, if so transferred, further the purposes of this section. There shall not be transferred to such office any program operating responsibilities.

(c) Except as provided under subsection (f) of this section, the Inspector General shall be appointed by the head of the designated Federal entity in accordance with the applicable laws and regulations governing appointments within the designated Federal entity. Each Inspector General shall be appointed without regard to political affiliation and solely on the basis of integrity and demonstrated ability in accounting, auditing, financial analysis, law, management analysis, public administration, or investigations. For purposes of implementing this section, the Chairman of the Board of Governors of the Federal Reserve System shall appoint the Inspector General of the Board of Governors of the Federal Reserve System and the Bureau of Consumer Financial Protection. The Inspector General of the Board of Governors of the Federal Reserve System and the Bureau of Consumer Financial Protection shall have all of the authorities and responsibilities provided by this Act with respect to the Bureau of Consumer Financial Protection, as if the Bureau were part of the Board of Governors of the Federal Reserve System.

(d)(1) Each Inspector General shall report to and be under the general supervision of the head of the designated Federal entity, but shall not report to, or be subject to supervision by, any other officer or employee of such designated Federal entity. Except as provided in paragraph (2), the head of the designated Federal entity shall not prevent or prohibit the Inspector General from initiating, carrying out, or completing any audit or investigation, or from issuing any subpena during the course of any audit or investigation.

(2)(A) The Secretary of Defense, in consultation with the Director of National Intelligence, may prohibit the inspector general of an element of the intelligence community specified in subparagraph (D) from initiating, carrying out, or completing any audit or investigation if the Secretary determines that the prohibition is necessary to protect vital national security interests of the United States.

(B) If the Secretary exercises the authority under subparagraph (A), the Secretary shall submit to the committees of Congress specified in subparagraph (E) an appropriately classified statement of the reasons for the exercise of such authority not later than 7 days after the exercise of such authority.

(C) At the same time the Secretary submits under subparagraph (B) a statement on the exercise of the authority in subparagraph (A) to the committees of Congress specified in subparagraph (E), the Secretary shall notify the inspector general of such element of the submittal of such statement and, to the extent consistent with the protection of intelligence sources and methods, provide such inspector general with a copy of such statement. Such inspector general may submit to such committees of Congress any comments on a notice or statement received by the inspector general under this subparagraph that the inspector general considers appropriate.

(D) The elements of the intelligence community specified in this subparagraph are as follows:

(i) The Defense Intelligence Agency.

(ii) The National Geospatial-Intelligence Agency.

(iii) The National Reconnaissance Office.

(iv) The National Security Agency.

(E) The committees of Congress specified in this subparagraph are—

(i) the Committee on Armed Services and the Select Committee on Intelligence of the Senate; and

(ii) the Committee on Armed Services and the Permanent Select Committee on Intelligence of the House of Representatives.

(e)(1) In the case of a designated Federal entity for which a board or commission is the head of the designated Federal entity, a removal under this subsection may only be made upon the written concurrence of a 2/3 majority of the board or commission.

(2) If an Inspector General is removed from office or is transferred to another position or location within a designated Federal entity, the head of the designated Federal entity shall communicate in writing the reasons for any such removal or transfer to both Houses of Congress, not later than 30 days before the removal or transfer. Nothing in this subsection shall prohibit a personnel action otherwise authorized by law, other than transfer or removal.

(e)(1) For purposes of carrying out subsection (c) with respect to the United States Postal Service, the appointment provisions of section 202(e) of title 39, United States Code, shall be applied.

(2) In carrying out the duties and responsibilities specified in this Act, the Inspector General of the United States Postal Service (hereinafter in this subsection referred to as the "Inspector General") shall have oversight responsibility for all activities of the Postal Inspection Service, including any internal investigation performed by the Postal Inspection Service. The Chief Postal Inspector shall promptly report the significant activities being carried out by the Postal Inspection Service to such Inspector General.

(3)(A)(i) Notwithstanding subsection (d), the Inspector General shall be under the authority, direction, and control of the Governors with respect to audits or investigations, or the issuance of subpoenas, which require access to sensitive information concerning—

> (I) ongoing civil or criminal investigations or proceedings;
>
> (II) undercover operations;
>
> (III) the identity of confidential sources, including protected witnesses;
>
> (IV) intelligence or counterintelligence matters; or
>
> (V) other matters the disclosure of which would constitute a serious threat to national security.
>
> (ii) With respect to the information described under clause (i), the Governors may prohibit the Inspector General from carrying out or completing any audit or investigation, or from issuing any subpoena, after such Inspector General has decided to initiate, carry out, or complete such audit or investigation or to issue such subpoena, if the Governors determine that such prohibition is necessary to prevent the disclosure of any information described under clause (i) or to prevent the significant impairment to the national interests of the United States.
>
> (iii) If the Governors exercise any power under clause (i) or (ii), the Governors shall notify the Inspector General in writing stating the reasons for such exercise. Within 30 days after receipt of any such notice, the Inspector General shall transmit a copy of such notice to the Committee on Governmental Affairs of the Senate and the

Committee on Government Reform and Oversight of the House of Representatives, and to other appropriate committees or subcommittees of the Congress.

(B) In carrying out the duties and responsibilities specified in this Act, the Inspector General—

(i) may initiate, conduct and supervise such audits and investigations in the United States Postal Service as the Inspector General considers appropriate; and

(ii) shall give particular regard to the activities of the Postal Inspection Service with a view toward avoiding duplication and insuring effective coordination and cooperation.

(C) Any report required to be transmitted by the Governors to the appropriate committees or subcommittees of the Congress under section 5(d) shall also be transmitted, within the seven-day period specified under such section, to the Committee on Governmental Affairs of the Senate and the Committee on Government Reform and Oversight of the House of Representatives.

(4) Nothing in this Act shall restrict, eliminate, or otherwise adversely affect any of the rights, privileges, or benefits of either employees of the United States Postal Service, or labor organizations representing employees of the United States Postal Service, under chapter 12 of title 39, United States Code, the National Labor Relations Act, any handbook or manual affecting employee labor relations with the United States Postal Service, or any collective bargaining agreement.

(5) As used in this subsection, the term "Governors" has the meaning given such term by section 102(3) of title 39, United States Code.

(6) There are authorized to be appropriated, out of the Postal Service Fund, such sums as may be necessary for the Office of Inspector General of the United States Postal Service.

(g)(1) Sections 4, 5, 6 (other than subsections (a)(7) and (a)(8) thereof), and 7 of this Act shall apply to each Inspector General and Office of Inspector General of a designated Federal entity and such sections shall be applied to each designated Federal entity and head of the designated Federal entity (as defined under subsection (a)) by substituting—

(A) "designated Federal entity" for "establishment"; and

(B) "head of the designated Federal entity" for "head of the establishment".

(2) In addition to the other authorities specified in this Act, an Inspector General is authorized to select, appoint, and employ such officers and employees as may be necessary for carrying out the functions, powers, and duties of the Office of Inspector General and to obtain the temporary or intermittent services of experts or consultants or an organization thereof, subject to the applicable laws and regulations that govern such selections, appointments, and employment, and the obtaining of such services, within the designated Federal entity.

(3) Notwithstanding the last sentence of subsection (d) of this section, the provisions of subsection (a) of section 8C (other than the provisions of subparagraphs (A), (B), (C), and (E) of subsection (a)(1)) shall apply to the Inspector General of the Board of Governors of the Federal Reserve System and the Bureau of Consumer Financial Protection and the Chairman of the Board of Governors of the Federal Reserve System in the same manner as such provisions apply to the Inspector General of the Department of the Treasury and the Secretary of the Treasury, respectively.

(4) Each Inspector General shall—

(A) in accordance with applicable laws and regulations governing appointments within the designated Federal entity, appoint a Counsel to the Inspector General who shall report to the Inspector General;

(B) obtain the services of a counsel appointed by and directly reporting to another Inspector General on a reimbursable basis; or

(C) obtain the services of appropriate staff of the Council of the Inspectors General on Integrity and Efficiency on a reimbursable basis.

(h)(1) No later than April 30, 1989, and annually thereafter, the Director of the Office of Management and Budget, after consultation with the Comptroller General of the United States, shall publish in the Federal Register a list of the Federal entities and designated Federal entities and if the designated Federal entity is not a board or commission, include the head of each such entity (as defined under subsection (a) of this section).

(2) Beginning on October 31, 1989, and on October 31 of each succeeding calendar year, the head of each Federal entity (as

defined under subsection (a) of this section) shall prepare and transmit to the Director of the Office of Management and Budget and to each House of the Congress a report which—

    (A) states whether there has been established in the Federal entity an office that meets the requirements of this section;

    (B) specifies the actions taken by the Federal entity otherwise to ensure that audits are conducted of its programs and operations in accordance with the standards for audit of governmental organizations, programs, activities, and functions issued by the Comptroller General of the United States, and includes a list of each audit report completed by a Federal or non-Federal auditor during the reporting period and a summary of any particularly significant findings; and

    (C) summarizes any matters relating to the personnel, programs, and operations of the Federal entity referred to prosecutive authorities, including a summary description of any preliminary investigation conducted by or at the request of the Federal entity concerning these matters, and the prosecutions and convictions which have resulted.

§ 8H. ADDITIONAL PROVISIONS WITH RESPECT TO INSPECTORS GENERAL OF THE INTELLIGENCE COMMUNITY--

(a)(1)(A) An employee of the Defense Intelligence Agency, the National Geospatial-Intelligence Agency, the National Reconnaissance Office, or the National Security Agency, or of a contractor of any of those Agencies, who intends to report to Congress a complaint or information with respect to an urgent concern may report the complaint or information to the Inspector General of the Department of Defense (or designee).

    (B) An employee of the Federal Bureau of Investigation, or of a contractor of the Bureau, who intends to report to Congress a complaint or information with respect to an urgent concern may report the complaint or information to the Inspector General of the Department of Justice (or designee).

    (C) Any other employee of, or contractor to, an executive agency, or element or unit thereof, determined by the President under section 2302(a)(2)(C)(ii) of title 5, United States Code, to have as its principal function the conduct of foreign intelligence or counterintelligence activities, who intends to report to Congress a complaint or information with respect to an urgent concern may report the complaint or information to the appropriate Inspector General (or designee) under this Act or section 17 of the Central Intelligence Agency Act of 1949 [50 U.S.C. § 403a et seq.].

(2) If a designee of an Inspector General under this section receives a complaint or information of an employee with respect to an urgent concern, that designee shall report the complaint or information to the Inspector General within 7 calendar days of receipt.

(3) The Inspectors General of the Defense Intelligence Agency, the National Geospatial-Intelligence Agency, the National Reconnaissance Office, and the National Security Agency shall be designees of the Inspector General of the Department of Defense for purposes of this section.

(b) Not later than the end of the 14-calendar day period beginning on the date of receipt of an employee complaint or information under subsection (a), the Inspector General shall determine whether the complaint or information appears credible. Upon making such a determination, the Inspector General shall transmit to the head of the establishment notice of that determination, together with the complaint or information.

(c) Upon receipt of a transmittal from the Inspector General under subsection (b), the head of the establishment shall, within 7 calendar days of such receipt, forward such transmittal to the intelligence committees, together with any comments the head of the establishment considers appropriate.

(d)(1) If the Inspector General does not find credible under subsection (b) a complaint or information submitted to the Inspector General under subsection (a), or does not transmit the complaint or information to the head of the establishment in accurate form under subsection (b), the employee (subject to paragraph (2)) may submit the complaint or information to Congress by contacting either or both of the intelligence committees directly.

(2) The employee may contact the intelligence committees directly as described in paragraph (1) only if the employee—

(A) before making such a contact, furnishes to the head of the establishment, through the Inspector General, a statement of the employee's complaint or information and notice of the employee's intent to contact the intelligence committees directly; and

(B) obtains and follows from the head of the establishment, through the Inspector General, direction on how to contact the intelligence committees in accordance with appropriate security practices.

(3) A member or employee of one of the intelligence committees who receives a complaint or information under paragraph (1) does so in that member or employee's official capacity as a member or employee of that committee.

(e) The Inspector General shall notify an employee who reports a complaint or information under this section of each action taken under this section with respect to the complaint or information. Such notice shall be provided not later than 3 days after any such action is taken.

(f) An action taken by the head of an establishment or an Inspector General under subsections (a) through (e) shall not be subject to judicial review.

(g)(1) The Inspector General of the Defense Intelligence Agency, the National Geospatial-Intelligence Agency, the National Reconnaissance Office, and the National Security Agency shall each submit to the congressional intelligence committees each year a report that sets forth the following:

(A) The personnel and funds requested by such Inspector General for the fiscal year beginning in such year for the activities of the office of such Inspector General in such fiscal year.

(B) The plan of such Inspector General for such activities, including the programs and activities scheduled for review by the office of such Inspector General during such fiscal year.

(C) An assessment of the current ability of such Inspector General to hire and retain qualified personnel for the office of such Inspector General.

(D) Any matters that such Inspector General considers appropriate regarding the independence and effectiveness of the office of such Inspector General.

(2) The submittal date for a report under paragraph (1) each year shall be the date provided in section 507 of the National Security Act of 1947.

(3) In this subsection, the term "congressional intelligence committees" shall have the meaning given that term in section 3 of the National Security Act of 1947 (50 U.S.C. 401a).

(h) In this section:

(1) The term "urgent concern" means any of the following:

(A) A serious or flagrant problem, abuse, violation of law or Executive order, or deficiency relating to the funding, administration, or operations of an intelligence activity involving classified information, but does not include differences of opinions concerning public policy matters.

(B) A false statement to Congress, or a willful withholding from Congress, on an issue of material fact relating to the funding, administration, or operation of an intelligence activity.

(C) An action, including a personnel action described in section 2302(a)(2)(A) of Title 5, constituting reprisal or threat of reprisal prohibited under section 7(c) in response to an employee's reporting an urgent concern in accordance with this section.

(2) The term "intelligence committees" means the Permanent Select Committee on Intelligence of the House of Representatives and the Select Committee on Intelligence of the Senate.

§ 8I. SPECIAL PROVISIONS CONCERNING THE DEPARTMENT OF HOMELAND SECURITY

(a)(1) Notwithstanding the last two sentences of section 3(a), the Inspector General of the Department of Homeland Security shall be under the authority, direction, and control of the Secretary of Homeland Security with respect to audits or investigations, or the issuance of subpoenas, that require access to sensitive information concerning—

(A) intelligence, counterintelligence, or counterterrorism matters;

(B) ongoing criminal investigations or proceedings;

(C) undercover operations;

(D) the identity of confidential sources, including protected witnesses;

(E) other matters the disclosure of which would, in the Secretary's judgment, constitute a serious threat to the protection of any person or property authorized protection by section 3056 of Title 18, section 3056A of title 18, or any provision of the Presidential Protection Assistance Act of 1976 (18 U.S.C. 3056 note); or

(F) other matters the disclosure of which would constitute a serious threat to national security.

(2) With respect to the information described in paragraph (1), the Secretary of Homeland Security may prohibit the Inspector General of the Department of Homeland Security from carrying out or completing any audit or investigation, or from issuing any subpoena, after such Inspector General has decided to initiate, carry out, or complete such audit or investigation or to issue such subpoena, if the Secretary determines that such prohibition is necessary to prevent the disclosure of any information described in paragraph (1), to preserve the national security, or to prevent a significant impairment to the interests of the United States.

(3) If the Secretary of Homeland Security exercises any power under paragraph (1) or (2), the Secretary shall notify the Inspector General of the Department of Homeland Security in writing within seven days stating the reasons for such exercise. Within 30 days after receipt of any such notice, the Inspector General shall transmit to the President of the Senate, the Speaker of the House of Representatives, and appropriate committees and subcommittees of Congress the following:

(A) A copy of such notice.

(B) A written response to such notice that includes a statement regarding whether the Inspector General agrees or disagrees with such exercise, and the reasons for any disagreement.

(b) The exercise of authority by the Secretary described in paragraph (2) should not be construed as limiting the right of Congress or any committee of Congress to access any information it seeks.

(c) Subject to the conditions established in subsections (a) and (b) above, in carrying out the duties and responsibilities specified in this Act, the Inspector General of the Department of Homeland Security may initiate, conduct, and supervise such audits and investigations in the Department of Homeland Security as the Inspector General considers appropriate.

(d) Any report required to be transmitted by the Secretary of Homeland Security to the appropriate committees or subcommittees of Congress under section 5(d) shall be transmitted, within the seven-day period specified under such section, to the President of the Senate, the Speaker of the House of Representatives, and appropriate committees and subcommittees of Congress.

(e) Notwithstanding any other provision of law, in carrying out the duties and responsibilities specified in this Act, the Inspector General of the Department of Homeland Security shall have oversight responsibility for the internal investigations performed by the Office of Internal Affairs of the United States Customs Service, the Office of Inspections of the United States Secret Service, the Bureau of Border Security, and the Bureau of Citizenship and Immigration Services. The head of each such office or bureau shall promptly report to the Inspector General the significant activities being carried out by such office or bureau.

(f)(1) The Inspector General of the Department of Homeland Security shall designate a senior official within the Office of Inspector General, who shall be a career member of the civil service at the equivalent to the GS-15 level or a career member of the Senior Executive Service, to perform the functions described in paragraph (2).

(2) The senior official designated under paragraph (1) shall—

(A) coordinate the activities of the Office of Inspector General with respect to investigations of abuses of civil rights or civil liberties;

(B) receive and review complaints and information from any source alleging abuses of civil rights and civil liberties by employees or officials of the Department and employees or officials of independent contractors or grantees of the Department;

(C) initiate investigations of alleged abuses of civil rights or civil liberties by employees or officials of the Department and employees or officials of independent contractors or grantees of the Department;

(D) ensure that personnel within the Office of Inspector General receive sufficient training to conduct effective civil rights and civil liberties investigations;

(E) consult with the Officer for Civil Rights and Civil Liberties regarding—

(i) alleged abuses of civil rights or civil liberties; and

(ii) any policy recommendations regarding civil rights and civil liberties that may be founded upon an investigation by the Office of Inspector General;

(F) provide the Officer for Civil Rights and Civil Liberties with information regarding the outcome of investigations of alleged abuses of civil rights and civil liberties;

(G) refer civil rights and civil liberties matters that the Inspector General decides not to investigate to the Officer for Civil Rights and Civil Liberties;

(H) ensure that the Office of the Inspector General publicizes and provides convenient public access to information regarding—

(i) the procedure to file complaints or comments concerning civil rights and civil liberties matters; and

(ii) the status of corrective actions taken by the Department in response to Office of the Inspector General reports; and

(I) inform the Officer for Civil Rights and Civil Liberties of any weaknesses, problems, and deficiencies within the Department relating to civil rights or civil liberties.

§ 8J. RULE OF CONSTRUCTION OF SPECIAL PROVISIONS

The special provisions under section 8, 8A, 8B, 8C, 8D, 8E, 8F, or 8H of this Act relate only to the establishment named in such section and no inference shall be drawn from the presence or absence of a provision in any such section with respect to an establishment not named in such section or with respect to a designated Federal entity as defined under section 8G(a).

§ 8K. AUTHORITY TO ESTABLISH INSPECTOR GENERAL OF THE OFFICE OF THE DIRECTOR OF NATIONAL INTELLIGENCE

If the Director of National Intelligence determines that an Office of Inspector General would be beneficial to improving the operations and effectiveness of the Office of the Director of National Intelligence, the Director of National Intelligence is authorized to establish, with any of the duties, responsibilities, and authorities set forth in this Act, an Office of Inspector General.

§ 8L. Information on Websites of Offices of Inspectors General

(a) Direct links to Inspectors General offices.--

(1) **In general.**--Each agency shall establish and maintain on the homepage of the website of that agency, a direct link to the website of the Office of the Inspector General of that agency.

(2) **Accessibility.**--The direct link under paragraph (1) shall be obvious and facilitate accessibility to the website of the Office of the Inspector General.

(b) **Requirements for Inspectors General websites.—**

(1) **Posting of reports and audits.**--The Inspector General of each agency shall—

(A) not later than 3 days after any report or audit (or portion of any report or audit) is made publicly available, post that report or audit (or portion of that report or audit) on the website of the Office of Inspector General; and

(B) ensure that any posted report or audit (or portion of that report or audit) described under subparagraph (A)—

(i) is easily accessible from a direct link on the homepage of the website of the Office of the Inspector General;

(ii) includes a summary of the findings of the Inspector General; and

(iii) is in a format that—

(I) is searchable and downloadable; and

(II) facilitates printing by individuals of the public accessing the website.

(2) **Reporting of fraud, waste, and abuse.—**

(A) **In general.**--The Inspector General of each agency shall establish and maintain a direct link on the homepage of the website of the Office of the Inspector General for individuals to report fraud, waste, and abuse. Individuals reporting fraud, waste, or abuse using the direct link established under this paragraph shall not be required to provide personally identifying information relating to that individual.

(B) **nonymity.**--The Inspector General of each agency shall not disclose the identity of any individual making a report under this paragraph without the consent of the individual unless the Inspector General determines that such a disclosure is unavoidable during the course of the investigation.

§ 9. TRANSFER OF FUNCTIONS

(a) There shall be transferred—

    (1) to the Office of Inspector General—

        (A) of the Department of Agriculture, the offices of that department referred to as the "Office of Investigation" and the "Office of Audit";

        (B) of the Department of Commerce, the offices of that department referred to as the "Office of Audits" and the "Investigations and Inspections Staff" and that portion of the office referred to as the "Office of Investigations and Security" which has responsibility for investigation of alleged criminal violations and program abuse;

        (C) of the Department of Defense, the offices of that department referred to as the "Defense Audit Service" and the "Office of Inspector General, Defense Logistics Agency", and that portion of the office of that department referred to as the "Defense Investigative Service" which has responsibility for the investigation of alleged criminal violations;

        (D) of the Department of Education, all functions of the Inspector General of Health, Education, and Welfare or of the Office of Inspector General of Health, Education, and Welfare relating to functions transferred by section 301 of the Department of Education Organization Act [20 U.S.C. § 3441];

        (E) of the Department of Energy, the Office of Inspector General (as established by section 208 of the Department of Energy Organization Act);

        (F) of the Department of Health and Human Services, the Office of Inspector General (as established by title II of Public Law 94-505);

        (G) of the Department of Housing and Urban Development, the office of that department referred to as the "Office of Inspector General";

(H) of the Department of the Interior, the office of that department referred to as the "Office of Audit and Investigation";

(I) of the Department of Justice, the offices of that Department referred to as (i) the "Audit Staff, Justice Management Division", (ii) the "Policy and Procedures Branch, Office of the Comptroller, Immigration and Naturalization Service", the "Office of Professional Responsibility, Immigration and Naturalization Service", and the "Office of Program Inspections, Immigration and Naturalization Service", (iii) the "Office of Internal Inspection, United States Marshals Service", (iv) the "Financial Audit Section, Office of Financial Management, Bureau of Prisons" and the "Office of Inspections, Bureau of Prisons", and (v) from the Drug Enforcement Administration, that portion of the "Office of Inspections" which is engaged in internal audit activities, and that portion of the "Office of Planning and Evaluation" which is engaged in program review activities;

(J) of the Department of Labor, the office of that department referred to as the "Office of Special Investigations";

(K) of the Department of Transportation, the offices of that department referred to as the "Office of Investigations and Security" and the "Office of Audit" of the Department, the "Offices of Investigations and Security, Federal Aviation Administration", and "External Audit Divisions, Federal Aviation Administration", the "Investigations Division and the External Audit Division of the Office of Program Review and Investigation, Federal Highway Administration", and the "Office of Program Audits, Urban Mass Transportation Administration";

(L)(i) of the Department of the Treasury, the office of that department referred to as the "Office of Inspector General", and, notwithstanding any other provision of law, that portion of each of the offices of that department referred to as the "Office of Internal Affairs, Tax and Trade Bureau", the "Office of Internal Affairs, United States Customs Service", and the "Office of Inspections, United States Secret Service" which is engaged in internal audit activities; and

    (ii) of the Treasury Inspector General for Tax Administration, effective 180 days after the date of the enactment of the Internal Revenue Service Restructuring and Reform Act of 1998, the Office of Chief Inspector of the Internal Revenue Service;

    (M) of the Environmental Protection Agency, the offices of that agency referred to as the "Office of Audit" and the "Security and Inspection Division";

    (N) of the Federal Emergency Management Agency, the office of that agency referred to as the "Office of Inspector General";

    (O) of the General Services Administration, the offices of that agency referred to as the "Office of Audits" and the "Office of Investigations";

    (P) of the National Aeronautics and Space Administration, the offices of that agency referred to as the "Management Audit Office" and the "Office of Inspections and Security";

    (Q) of the Nuclear Regulatory Commission, the office of that commission referred to as the "Office of Inspector and Auditor";

    (R) of the Office of Personnel Management, the offices of that agency referred to as the "Office of Inspector General", the "Insurance Audits Division, Retirement and Insurance Group", and the "Analysis and Evaluation Division, Administration Group";

    (S) of the Railroad Retirement Board, the Office of Inspector General (as established by section 23 of the Railroad Retirement Act of 1974);

    (T) of the Small Business Administration, the office of that agency referred to as the "Office of Audits and Investigations";

    (U) of the Veterans' Administration, the offices of that agency referred to as the "Office of Audits" and the "Office of Investigations"; and

(V) of the Corporation for National and Community Service, the Office of Inspector General of ACTION;

(W) of the Social Security Administration, the functions of the Inspector General of the Department of Health and Human Services which are transferred to the Social Security Administration by the Social Security Independence and Program Improvements Act of 1994 (other than functions performed pursuant to section 105(a)(2) of such Act), except that such transfers shall be made in accordance with the provisions of such Act and shall not be subject to subsections (b) through (d) of this section; and

(2) to the Office of the Inspector General, such other offices or agencies, or functions, powers, or duties thereof, as the head of the establishment involved may determine are properly related to the functions of the Office and would, if so transferred, further the purposes of this Act, except that there shall not be transferred to an Inspector General under paragraph (2) program operating responsibilities.

(b) The personnel, assets, liabilities, contracts, property, records, and unexpended balances of appropriations, authorizations, allocations, and other funds employed, held, used, arising from, available or to be made available, of any office or agency the functions, powers, and duties of which are transferred under subsection (a) are hereby transferred to the applicable Office of Inspector General.

(c) Personnel transferred pursuant to subsection (b) shall be transferred in accordance with applicable laws and regulations relating to the transfer of functions except that the classification and compensation of such personnel shall not be reduced for one year after such transfer.

(d) In any case where all the functions, powers, and duties of any office or agency are transferred pursuant to this subsection, such office or agency shall lapse. Any person who, on the effective date of this Act [Oct. 1, 1978], held a position compensated in accordance with the General Schedule, and who, without a break in service, is appointed in an Office of Inspector General to a position having duties comparable to those performed immediately preceding such appointment shall continue to be compensated in the new position at not less than the rate provided for the previous position, for the duration of service in the new position.

§ 10. CONFORMING AND TECHNICAL AMENDMENTS

[Section amended sections 5315 and 5316 of Title 5, Government Organization and Employees, and section 3522 of Title 42, The Public Health and Welfare, which amendments have been executed to text.]

§ 11. ESTABLISHMENT OF COUNCIL OF THE INSPECTORS GENERAL ON INTEGRITY AND EFFICIENCY

(a) Establishment and mission.—

(1) **Establishment.**--There is established as an independent entity within the executive branch the Council of the Inspectors General on Integrity and Efficiency (in this section referred to as the "Council").

(2) **Mission.**--The mission of the Council shall be to—

(A) address integrity, economy, and effectiveness issues that transcend individual Government agencies; and

(B) increase the professionalism and effectiveness of personnel by developing policies, standards, and approaches to aid in the establishment of a well-trained and highly skilled workforce in the offices of the Inspectors General.

(b) **Membership.**—

(1) **In general.**--The Council shall consist of the following members:

(A) All Inspectors General whose offices are established under—

(i) section 2; or

(ii) section 8G.

(B) The Inspectors General of the Office of the Director of National Intelligence and the Central Intelligence Agency.

(C) The Controller of the Office of Federal Financial Management.

(D) A senior level official of the Federal Bureau of Investigation designated by the Director of the Federal Bureau of Investigation.

(E) The Director of the Office of Government Ethics.

(F) The Special Counsel of the Office of Special Counsel.

(G) The Deputy Director of the Office of Personnel Management.

(H) The Deputy Director for Management of the Office of Management and Budget.

(I) The Inspectors General of the Library of Congress, Capitol Police, Government Printing Office, Government Accountability Office, and the Architect of the Capitol.

(2) **Chairperson and Executive Chairperson.**—

(A) **Executive Chairperson.**--The Deputy Director for Management of the Office of Management and Budget shall be the Executive Chairperson of the Council.

(B) **Chairperson.**--The Council shall elect 1 of the Inspectors General referred to in paragraph (1)(A) or (B) to act as Chairperson of the Council. The term of office of the Chairperson shall be 2 years.

(3) **Functions of Chairperson and Executive Chairperson.**—

(A) **Executive Chairperson.**--The Executive Chairperson shall—

(i) preside over meetings of the Council;

(ii) provide to the heads of agencies and entities represented on the Council summary reports of the activities of the Council; and

(iii) provide to the Council such information relating to the agencies and entities represented on the Council as assists the Council in performing its functions.

(B) **Chairperson.**--The Chairperson shall—

(i) convene meetings of the Council—

(I) at least 6 times each year;

(II) monthly to the extent possible; and

(III) more frequently at the discretion of the Chairperson;

(ii) carry out the functions and duties of the Council under subsection (c);

(iv) appoint a Vice Chairperson to assist in carrying out the functions of the Council and act in the absence of the Chairperson, from a category of Inspectors General described in subparagraph (A)(i), (A)(ii), or (B) of paragraph (1), other than the category from which the Chairperson was elected;

(v) make such payments from funds otherwise available to the Council as may be necessary to carry out the functions of the Council;

(vi) select, appoint, and employ personnel as needed to carry out the functions of the Council subject to the provisions of title 5, United States Code, governing appointments in the competitive service, and the provisions of chapter 51 and subchapter III of chapter 53 of such title, relating to classification and General Schedule pay rates;

(vii) to the extent and in such amounts as may be provided in advance by appropriations Acts, made available from the revolving fund established under subsection (c)(3)(B), or as otherwise provided by law, enter into contracts and other arrangements with public agencies and private persons to carry out the functions and duties of the Council;

(viii) establish, in consultation with the members of the Council, such committees as determined by the Chairperson to be necessary and appropriate for the efficient conduct of Council functions; and

(c) prepare and transmit a report annually on behalf of the Council to the President on the activities of the Council. Functions and duties of Council.--

(1) In general.--The Council shall—

(A) continually identify, review, and discuss areas of weakness and vulnerability in Federal programs and operations with respect to fraud, waste, and abuse;

(B) develop plans for coordinated, Governmentwide activities that address these problems and promote economy and efficiency in Federal programs and operations, including interagency and interentity audit, investigation, inspection, and evaluation programs and projects to deal efficiently and effectively with those problems concerning fraud and waste that exceed the capability or jurisdiction of an individual agency or entity;

(C) develop policies that will aid in the maintenance of a corps of well-trained and highly skilled Office of Inspector General personnel;

(D) maintain an Internet website and other electronic systems for the benefit of all Inspectors General, as the Council determines are necessary or desirable;

(E) maintain 1 or more academies as the Council considers desirable for the professional training of auditors, investigators, inspectors, evaluators, and other personnel of the various offices of Inspector General;

(F) submit recommendations of individuals to the appropriate appointing authority for any appointment to an office of Inspector General described under subsection (b)(1)(A) or (B);

(G) make such reports to Congress as the Chairperson determines are necessary or appropriate; and

(H) perform other duties within the authority and jurisdiction of the Council, as appropriate.

(2) **Adherence and participation by members.**--To the extent permitted under law, and to the extent not inconsistent with standards established by the Comptroller General of the United States for audits of Federal establishments, organizations, programs, activities, and functions, each member of the Council, as appropriate, shall—

(A) adhere to professional standards developed by the Council; and

(B) participate in the plans, programs, and projects of the Council, except that in the case of a member described under subsection (b)(1)(I), the member shall participate only to the extent requested by the member and approved by the Executive Chairperson and Chairperson.

(3) **Additional administrative authorities.**—

(A) **Interagency funding.**--Notwithstanding section 1532 of title 31, United States Code, or any other provision of law prohibiting the interagency funding of activities described under subclause (I), (II), or (III) of clause (i), in the performance of the responsibilities, authorities, and duties of the Council—

(i) the Executive Chairperson may authorize the use of interagency funding for—

(I) Governmentwide training of employees of the Offices of the Inspectors General;

(II) the functions of the Integrity Committee of the Council; and

(III) any other authorized purpose determined by the Council; and

(ii) upon the authorization of the Executive Chairperson, any department, agency, or entity of the executive branch which has a member on the Council shall fund or participate in the funding of such activities.

(B) **Revolving fund.**—

(i) **In general.**--The Council may—

(I) establish in the Treasury of the United States a revolving fund to be called the Inspectors General Council Fund; or

(II) enter into an arrangement with a department or agency to use an existing revolving fund.

(ii) **Amounts in revolving fund.**—

(I) **In general.**--Amounts transferred to the Council under this subsection shall be deposited in the revolving fund described under clause (i)(I) or (II).

(II) **Training.**--Any remaining unexpended balances appropriated for or otherwise available to the Inspectors General Criminal Investigator Academy and the Inspectors General Auditor Training Institute shall be transferred to the revolving fund described under clause (i)(I) or (II).

(iii) **Use of revolving fund.**—

(I) **In general.**--Except as provided under subclause (II), amounts in the revolving fund described under clause (i)(I) or (II) may be used to carry out the functions and duties of the Council under this subsection.

(II) **Training.**--Amounts transferred into the revolving fund described under clause (i)(I) or (II) may be used for the purpose of maintaining any training academy as determined by the Council.

(iv) **Availability of funds.**--Amounts in the revolving fund described under clause (i)(I) or (II) shall remain available to the Council without fiscal year limitation.

(C) **Superseding provisions.**--No provision of law enacted after the date of enactment of this subsection shall be construed to limit or supersede any authority under subparagraph (A) or (B), unless such provision makes specific reference to the authority in that paragraph.

(4) **Existing authorities and responsibilities.**--The establishment and operation of the Council shall not affect—

(A) the role of the Department of Justice in law enforcement and litigation;

(B) the authority or responsibilities of any Government agency or entity; and

(C) the authority or responsibilities of individual members of the Council.

(d) **Integrity Committee.**—

(1) **Establishment.**--The Council shall have an Integrity Committee, which shall receive, review, and refer for investigation allegations of wrongdoing that are made against Inspectors General and staff members of the various Offices of Inspector General described under paragraph (4)(C).

(2) **Membership.**--The Integrity Committee shall consist of the following members:

(A) The official of the Federal Bureau of Investigation serving on the Council, who shall serve as Chairperson of the Integrity Committee, and maintain the records of the Committee.

(B) Four Inspectors General described in subparagraph (A) or (B) of subsection (b)(1) appointed by the Chairperson of the Council, representing both establishments and designated Federal entities (as that term is defined in section 8G(a)).

(C) The Special Counsel of the Office of Special Counsel.

(D) The Director of the Office of Government Ethics.

(3) **Legal advisor.**--The Chief of the Public Integrity Section of the Criminal Division of the Department of Justice, or his designee, shall serve as a legal advisor to the Integrity Committee.

(4) **Referral of allegations.**—

(A) **Requirement.**--An Inspector General shall refer to the Integrity Committee any allegation of wrongdoing against a staff member of the office of that Inspector General, if—

(i) review of the substance of the allegation cannot be assigned to an agency of the executive branch with appropriate jurisdiction over the matter; and

(ii) the Inspector General determines that—

(I) an objective internal investigation of the allegation is not feasible; or

(II) an internal investigation of the allegation may appear not to be objective.

(B) **Definition.**--In this paragraph the term "staff member" means any employee of an Office of Inspector General who—

(i) reports directly to an Inspector General; or

(ii) is designated by an Inspector General under subparagraph (C).

(C) **Designation of staff members.**--Each Inspector General shall annually submit to the Chairperson of the Integrity Committee a designation of positions whose holders are staff members for purposes of subparagraph (B).

(5) **Review of allegations.**--The Integrity Committee shall—

(A) review all allegations of wrongdoing the Integrity Committee receives against an Inspector General, or against a staff member of an Office of Inspector General described under paragraph (4)(C);

(B) refer any allegation of wrongdoing to the agency of the executive branch with appropriate jurisdiction over the matter; and

(C) refer to the Chairperson of the Integrity Committee any allegation of wrongdoing determined by the Integrity Committee under subparagraph (A) to be potentially meritorious that cannot be referred to an agency under subparagraph (B).

(6) **Authority to investigate allegations.**—

(A) **Requirement.**--The Chairperson of the Integrity Committee shall cause a thorough and timely investigation of each allegation referred under paragraph (5)(C) to be conducted in accordance with this paragraph.

(B) **Resources.**--At the request of the Chairperson of the Integrity Committee, the head of each agency or entity represented on the Council—

(i) may provide resources necessary to the Integrity Committee; and

(ii) may detail employees from that agency or entity to the Integrity Committee, subject to the control and direction of the Chairperson, to conduct an investigation under this subsection.

(7) **Procedures for investigations.**—

(A) **Standards applicable.**-- Investigations initiated under this subsection shall be conducted in accordance with the most current Quality Standards for Investigations issued by the Council or by its predecessors (the President's Council on Integrity and Efficiency and the Executive Council on Integrity and Efficiency).

(B) **Additional policies and procedures.**—

(i) **Establishment.**--The Integrity Committee, in conjunction with the Chairperson of the Council, shall establish additional policies and procedures necessary to ensure fairness and consistency in—

(I) determining whether to initiate an investigation;

(II) conducting investigations;

(III) reporting the results of an investigation; and

(IV) providing the person who is the subject of an investigation with an opportunity to respond to any Integrity Committee report.

(ii) **Submission to Congress.**-- The Council shall submit a copy of the policies and procedures established under clause (i) to the congressional committees of jurisdiction.

(C) **Reports.**—

(i) **Potentially meritorious allegations.**--For allegations described under paragraph (5)(C), the Chairperson of the Integrity Committee shall make a report containing the results of the investigation of the Chairperson and shall provide such report to members of the Integrity Committee.

(ii) **llegations of wrongdoing.**--For allegations referred to an agency under paragraph (5)(B), the head of that agency shall make a report containing the results of the investigation and shall provide such report to members of the Integrity Committee.

(8) **Assessment and final disposition.**—

(A) **In general.**--With respect to any report received under paragraph (7)(C), the Integrity Committee shall—

(i) assess the report;

(ii) forward the report, with the recommendations of the Integrity Committee, including those on disciplinary action, within 30 days (to the maximum extent practicable) after the completion of the investigation, to the Executive Chairperson of the Council and to the President (in the case of a report relating to an Inspector General of an establishment or any employee of that Inspector General) or the head of a designated Federal entity (in the case of a report relating to an Inspector General of such an entity or any employee of that Inspector General) for resolution; and

(iii) submit to the Committee on Government Oversight and Reform of the House of Representatives, the Committee on Homeland Security and Governmental Affairs of the Senate, and other congressional committees of jurisdiction an executive summary of such report and recommendations within 30 days after the submission of such report to the Executive Chairperson under clause (ii).

(B) **Disposition.**--The Executive Chairperson of the Council shall report to the Integrity Committee the final disposition of the matter, including what action was taken by the President or agency head.

(9) **Annual report.**--The Council shall submit to Congress and the President by December 31 of each year a report on the activities of the Integrity Committee during the preceding fiscal year, which shall include the following:

(A) The number of allegations received.

(B) The number of allegations referred to other agencies, including the number of allegations referred for criminal investigation.

(C) The number of allegations referred to the Chairperson of the Integrity Committee for investigation.

(D) The number of allegations closed without referral.

(E) The date each allegation was received and the date each allegation was finally disposed of.

(F) In the case of allegations referred to the Chairperson of the Integrity Committee, a summary of the status of the investigation of the allegations and, in the case of investigations completed during the preceding fiscal year, a summary of the findings of the investigations.

(G) Other matters that the Council considers appropriate.

(10) **Requests for more information.**--With respect to paragraphs (8) and (9), the Council shall provide more detailed information about specific allegations upon request from any of the following:

(A) The chairperson or ranking member of the Committee on Homeland Security and Governmental Affairs of the Senate.

(B) The chairperson or ranking member of the Committee on Oversight and Government Reform of the House of Representatives.

(C) The chairperson or ranking member of the congressional committees of jurisdiction.

(11) **No right or benefit.**--This subsection is not intended to create any right or benefit, substantive or procedural, enforceable at law by a person against the United States, its agencies, its officers, or any person.

§ 12. DEFINITIONS

As used in this Act—

(1) the term "head of the establishment" means the Secretary of Agriculture, Commerce, Defense, Education, Energy, Health and Human Services, Housing and Urban Development, the Interior, Labor, State, Transportation, Homeland Security, or the Treasury;

the Attorney General; the Administrator of the Agency for International Development, Environmental Protection, General Services, National Aeronautics and Space, Small Business, or Veterans' Affairs; the Administrator of the Federal Emergency Management Agency, or the Office of Personnel Management; the Chairman of the Nuclear Regulatory Commission or the Railroad Retirement Board; the Chairperson of the Thrift Depositor Protection Oversight Board; the Chief Executive Officer of the Corporation for National and Community Service; the Administrator of the Community Development Financial Institutions Fund; the chief executive officer of the Resolution Trust Corporation; the Chairperson of the Federal Deposit Insurance Corporation; the Commissioner of Social Security, Social Security Administration; the Director of the Federal Housing Finance Agency; the Board of Directors of the Tennessee Valley Authority; the President of the Export-Import Bank; or the Federal Cochairpersons of the Commissions established under section 15301 of title 40, United States Code; as the case may be;

(2) the term "establishment" means the Department of Agriculture, Commerce, Defense, Education, Energy, Health and Human Services, Housing and Urban Development, the Interior, Justice, Labor, State, Transportation, Homeland Security, or the Treasury; the Agency for International Development, the Community Development Financial Institutions Fund, the Environmental Protection Agency, the Federal Emergency Management Agency, the General Services Administration, the National Aeronautics and Space Administration, the Nuclear Regulatory Commission, the Office of Personnel Management, the Railroad Retirement Board, the Resolution Trust Corporation, the Federal Deposit Insurance Corporation, the Small Business Administration, the Corporation for National and Community Service, the Veterans' Administration, the Social Security Administration, the Federal Housing Finance Agency, the Tennessee Valley Authority, the Export-Import Bank, or the Commissions established under section 15301 of title 40, United States Code, as the case may be;

(3) the term "Inspector General" means the Inspector General of an establishment;

(4) the term "Office" means the Office of Inspector General of an establishment; and

(5) the term "Federal agency" means an agency as defined in section 552(f) of Title 5 (including an establishment as defined in paragraph

(2)), United States Code, but shall not be construed to include the Government Accountability Office.

§ 13. EFFECTIVE DATE

The provisions of this Act and the amendments made by this Act [see section 10 of this Act] shall take effect October 1, 1978.

The

Declaration of Independence

and the

Constitution

of the

United States of America

**including selected appendices of historical
documents relating to the duty of all who
serve within the Department of Defense to
honor and to uphold the law**

IN HONOR OF LIBERTY DAY

James Madison, the fourth President of the United States and the "Father of our Constitution," was born on March 16, 1751. It is therefore fitting and proper that Congress has proclaimed that each year, on the 16th of March, we should pause and recognize "Liberty Day" as a "celebration of the Declaration of Independence and the United States Constitution, where our unalienable rights and liberties are enumerated."

I encourage all to examine the words of the Declaration of Independence and of the Constitution, which together form the basis for our freedom and prosperity. These documents serve as a constant reminder of the oath that Congress has ordained for every "individual elected or appointed to an office of honor or profit in the civil service or uniformed services":

> that I will support and defend the Constitution of the United States against all enemies, foreign and domestic; that I will bear true faith and allegiance to the same; that I take this obligation freely, without any mental reservation or purpose of evasion; and that I will well and faithfully discharge the duties of the office on which I am about to enter. So help me God.

Donald H. Rumsfeld

INTRODUCTION

Two centuries and two years before the 106th Congress established "Liberty Day" as an annual "celebration of the Declaration of Independence and the United States Constitution, where our unalienable rights and liberties are enumerated," President John Adams admonished American military officers that "Oaths in this country are as yet universally considered as sacred obligations." For all of us who have sworn to support and defend this Constitution, therefore, it behooves us to familiarize ourselves with its text and historical content.

It might appear to some that Congress requiring ever "individual elected or appointed to an office of honor or profit in the civil service or uniformed services" to take an office concluding with "So help me Go" (5 U.S.C. § 3331) would violate the First Amendment's prohibition against "an establishment of religion." In his 1796 Farewell Address, President George Washington described the fundamentally religious nature of oaths: "Of all the dispositions and habits which lead to national prosperity, Religion and morality are indispensible supports... [W]here is the security for property, for reputation, for life, if the sense of religious obligation desert the Oaths, which are instruments of investigation in Courts of Justice?"

The Constitution itself requires that "a regular Statement and Account of the Reciepts and Expenditure of all public Money shall be published from time to time" Moreover, as explained in the 1789 Preamble to the Bill of Rights (reproduced in this booklet), the first ten Amendments were designed "to prevent misconstructions or abuse of its power," i.e., to prevent abuses of "powers... delegated to the United States by the Constitution," U.S. Const., amend X.

The financial accountability of federal officers and the prevention of fraud, waste, and abuse of authority by those officers are thus core constitutional functions. When the Secretary of Defense "declared war" on bureaucratic waste within the Pentagon—the day before the September 11, 2001, terrorist attacks—he anchored his remarks in a constitutionally-based notion of accountability: "Every dollar squandered on waste is one denied to the warfighter.... Every dollar we spend was entrusted to us by a taxpayer who earned it...."

According to 1998 congressional testimony by retired Admiral Thomas H. Moorer, former Chief of Naval Operations and Chairman of the Joint Chiefs of Staff, "Responsibility without accountability 'according to law' undermines the core foundation of the Constitution, the principle known as the Rule of Law (as opposed to the rule of men), without which our Constitution is no more than a piece of paper."

All those who serve within this Department can be proud of our military's historical commitment to the principles underlying our Constitution, which require above all a firm commitment to personal integrity and leadership. Former Secretary of the Navy and then President Theodore Roosevelt reminded us of the profound role of personal integrity and leadership in the American republic:

> The stream will no permanently rise higher than the main source; and the main source of national power and national greatness is found in the average citizenship of the nation. Therefore it behooves us to do our best to see that the standard of the average citizen is kept high; and the average cannot be kept high unless the standard of the leaders is very much higher.

The first Article of the 1775 "Rules for the Regulation of the Navy of the United Colonies of North-America"... mandated exemplary conduct by Naval leaders:

> The Commanders of all ships and vessels belonging to the THIRTEEN UNITED COLONIES, are strictly required to shew in themselves a good example of honor and virtue to their officers and men, to be very vigilant in inspecting the behaviour of all such as are under them, and to discountenance and suppress all dissolute, immoral and disorderly practices;...

Likewise, the current statutory mandate that officers of all services comport to a higher standard of personal behavior—both on and off duty (10 U.S.C § 993)—traces to the 1775 "American Aticles of War... Article XLVII of the Articles of War forbade officers from "behaving in a scandalous, infamous manner." A November 1995 Amendment required not only that an officer found guilty of fraud "be *ipso facto* cashiered, and deemed unfit for further service as an officer," but also that "it be added in the punishment, that the crime, name, place of abode, and of that colony from which the offender came, or usually resides: after which it shall be deemed scandalous in any officer to associate with him."

These 1775 first principles were recodified by Congress in 1956, almost vermatim, into federal statutory law for the Navy and Marine Corps: "All commanding officers and others in authority in the naval service are required to show in themselves a good example of virtue, honor, patriotism, and subordination; to be vigilant inspecting the conduct of all persons who are placed under their command; to guard against and suppress all dissolute and immoral practices, and to correct, according to the laws and regulations of the Navy, all persons who are guilty of them;...." 10 U.S.C. § 5947. In 1997, when Congress adapted and legislated these same first principles for the Army and Air Force (10 U.S.C. §§ 3583 & 8583), the accompanying Senate Report "note[d] that these standards have applied to Naval and Marine Corps officers since they were first drafted by John Adams and approved by the Continental Congress in 1775." The Senate Armed Services Committee explained the purpose of the 1997 legislation:

> This provision will not prevent an officer from shunning responsibility or accountability for an action or event. It does, however, establish a very clear standard by which Congress and the nation can measure officers of our military services. The committee holds military officers to a higher standard than other members of society. The nation entrusts its greatest resource, our young men and women, to our military officers. In return, the nation deserves complete integrity, moral courage, and the highest moral and ethical conduct.

All who serve within this Department should familiarize themselves with the Declaration of Independence and the Constitution, as well as with the historical documents reproduced in the appendices.*

---

* The Secretary of Defense would like to express his gratitude to the Historian of the Navy, Dr. William S. Dudley, and to his staff, for proofreading and verifying the historical accuracy of documents produced in this compilation.

The Declaration of Independence

IN CONGRESS, July 4, 1776.

The unanimous Declaration of the thirteen united States of America,

When in the Course of human events, it becomes necessary for one people to dissolve the political bands which have connected them with another, and to assume among the powers of the earth, the separate and equal station to which the Laws of Nature and of Nature's God entitle them, a decent respect to the opinions of mankind requires that they should declare the causes which impel them to the separation.

We hold these truths to be self-evident, that all men are created equal, that they are endowed by their Creator with certain unalienable Rights, that among these are Life, Liberty and the pursuit of Happiness.--That to secure these rights, Governments are instituted among Men, deriving their just powers from the consent of the governed, --That whenever any Form of Government becomes destructive of these ends, it is the Right of the People to alter or to abolish it, and to institute new Government, laying its foundation on such principles and organizing its powers in such form, as to them shall seem most likely to effect their Safety and Happiness. Prudence, indeed, will dictate that Governments long established should not be changed for light and transient causes; and accordingly all experience hath shewn, that mankind are more disposed to suffer, while evils are sufferable, than to right themselves by abolishing the forms to which they are accustomed. But when a long train of abuses and usurpations, pursuing invariably the same Object evinces a design to reduce them under absolute Despotism, it is their right, it is their duty, to throw off such Government, and to provide new Guards for their future security.--Such has been the patient sufferance of these Colonies; and such is now the necessity which constrains them to alter their former Systems of Government. The history of the present King of Great Britain is a history of repeated injuries and usurpations, all having in direct object the establishment of an absolute Tyranny over these States. To prove this, let Facts be submitted to a candid world.

He has refused his Assent to Laws, the most wholesome and necessary for the public good.

He has forbidden his Governors to pass Laws of immediate and pressing importance, unless suspended in their operation till his Assent should be obtained; and when so suspended, he has utterly neglected to attend to them.

He has refused to pass other Laws for the accommodation of large districts of people, unless those people would relinquish the right of Representation in the Legislature, a right inestimable to them and formidable to tyrants only.

He has called together legislative bodies at places unusual, uncomfortable, and distant from the depository of their public Records, for the sole purpose of fatiguing them into compliance with his measures.

He has dissolved Representative Houses repeatedly, for opposing with manly firmness his invasions on the rights of the people.

He has refused for a long time, after such dissolutions, to cause others to be elected; whereby the Legislative powers, incapable of Annihilation, have returned to the People at large for their exercise; the State remaining in the mean time exposed to all the dangers of invasion from without, and convulsions within.

He has endeavoured to prevent the population of these States; for that purpose obstructing the Laws for Naturalization of Foreigners; refusing to pass others to encourage their migrations hither, and raising the conditions of new Appropriations of Lands.

He has obstructed the Administration of Justice, by refusing his Assent to Laws for establishing Judiciary powers.

He has made Judges dependent on his Will alone, for the tenure of their offices, and the amount and payment of their salaries.

He has erected a multitude of New Offices, and sent hither swarms of Officers to harrass our people, and eat out their substance.

He has kept among us, in times of peace, Standing Armies without the Consent of our legislatures.

He has affected to render the Military independent of and superior to the Civil power.

He has combined with others to subject us to a jurisdiction foreign to our constitution, and unacknowledged by our laws; giving his Assent to their Acts of pretended Legislation:

For Quartering large bodies of armed troops among us:

For protecting them, by a mock Trial, from punishment for any Murders which they should commit on the Inhabitants of these States:

For cutting off our Trade with all parts of the world:

For imposing Taxes on us without our Consent:

For depriving us in many cases, of the benefits of Trial by Jury:

For transporting us beyond Seas to be tried for pretended offences

For abolishing the free System of English Laws in a neighbouring Province, establishing therein an Arbitrary government, and enlarging its Boundaries so as to render it at once an example and fit instrument for introducing the same absolute rule into these Colonies:

For taking away our Charters, abolishing our most valuable Laws, and altering fundamentally the Forms of our Governments:

For suspending our own Legislatures, and declaring themselves invested with power to legislate for us in all cases whatsoever.

He has abdicated Government here, by declaring us out of his Protection and waging War against us.

He has plundered our seas, ravaged our Coasts, burnt our towns, and destroyed the lives of our people.

He is at this time transporting large Armies of foreign Mercenaries to compleat the works of death, desolation and tyranny, already begun with circumstances of Cruelty & perfidy scarcely paralleled in the most barbarous ages, and totally unworthy the Head of a civilized nation.

He has constrained our fellow Citizens taken Captive on the high Seas to bear Arms against their Country, to become the executioners of their friends and Brethren, or to fall themselves by their Hands.

He has excited domestic insurrections amongst us, and has endeavoured to bring on the inhabitants of our frontiers, the merciless Indian Savages, whose known rule of warfare, is an undistinguished destruction of all ages, sexes and conditions.

In every stage of these Oppressions We have Petitioned for Redress in the most humble terms: Our repeated Petitions have been answered only by repeated injury. A Prince whose character is thus marked by every act which may define a Tyrant, is unfit to be the ruler of a free people.

Nor have We been wanting in attentions to our British brethren. We have warned them from time to time of attempts by their legislature to extend an unwarrantable jurisdiction over us. We have reminded them of the circumstances of our emigration and settlement here. We have appealed to their native justice and magnanimity, and we have conjured them by the ties of our common kindred to disavow these usurpations, which, would inevitably interrupt our connections and correspondence. They too have been deaf to the voice of justice and of consanguinity. We must, therefore, acquiesce in the necessity, which denounces our Separation, and hold them, as we hold the rest of mankind, Enemies in War, in Peace Friends.

We, therefore, the Representatives of the united States of America, in General Congress, Assembled, appealing to the Supreme Judge of the world for the rectitude of our intentions, do, in the Name, and by Authority of the good People of these Colonies, solemnly publish and declare, That these United Colonies are, and of Right ought to be Free and Independent States; that they are Absolved from all Allegiance to the British Crown, and that all political connection between them and the State of Great Britain, is and ought to be totally dissolved; and that as Free and Independent States, they have full Power to levy War, conclude Peace, contract Alliances, establish Commerce, and to do all other Acts and Things which Independent States may of right do. And for the support of this Declaration, with a firm reliance on the protection of divine Providence, we mutually pledge to each other our Lives, our Fortunes and our sacred Honor.

We the People of the United States, in Order to form a more perfect Union, establish Justice, insure domestic Tranquility, provide for the common defence, promote the general Welfare, and secure the Blessings of Liberty to ourselves and our Posterity, do ordain and establish this Constitution for the United States of America.

Article. I.

Section. 1.

All legislative Powers herein granted shall be vested in a Congress of the United States, which shall consist of a Senate and House of Representatives.

Section. 2.

The House of Representatives shall be composed of Members chosen every second Year by the People of the several States, and the Electors in each State shall have the Qualifications requisite for Electors of the most numerous Branch of the State Legislature.

No Person shall be a Representative who shall not have attained to the Age of twenty five Years, and been seven Years a Citizen of the United States, and who shall not, when elected, be an Inhabitant of that State in which he shall be chosen.

Representatives and direct Taxes shall be apportioned among the several States which may be included within this Union, according to their respective Numbers, which shall be determined by adding to the whole Number of free Persons, including those bound to Service for a Term of Years, and excluding Indians not taxed, three fifths of all other Persons. The actual Enumeration shall be made within three Years after the first Meeting of the Congress of the United States, and within every subsequent Term of ten Years, in such Manner as they shall by Law direct. The Number of Representatives shall not exceed one for every thirty Thousand, but each State shall have at Least one Representative; and until such enumeration shall be made, the State of

New Hampshire shall be entitled to chuse three, Massachusetts eight, Rhode-Island and Providence Plantations one, Connecticut five, New-York six, New Jersey four, Pennsylvania eight, Delaware one, Maryland six, Virginia ten, North Carolina five, South Carolina five, and Georgia three.

When vacancies happen in the Representation from any State, the Executive Authority thereof shall issue Writs of Election to fill such Vacancies.

The House of Representatives shall chuse their Speaker and other Officers; and shall have the sole Power of Impeachment.

Section. 3.

The Senate of the United States shall be composed of two Senators from each State, chosen by the Legislature thereof for six Years; and each Senator shall have one Vote.

Immediately after they shall be assembled in Consequence of the first Election, they shall be divided as equally as may be into three Classes. The Seats of the Senators of the first Class shall be vacated at the Expiration of the second Year, of the second Class at the Expiration of the fourth Year, and of the third Class at the Expiration of the sixth Year, so that one third may be chosen every second Year; and if Vacancies happen by Resignation, or otherwise, during the Recess of the Legislature of any State, the Executive thereof may make temporary Appointments until the next Meeting of the Legislature, which shall then fill such Vacancies.

No Person shall be a Senator who shall not have attained to the Age of thirty Years, and been nine Years a Citizen of the United States, and who shall not, when elected, be an Inhabitant of that State for which he shall be chosen.

The Vice President of the United States shall be President of the Senate, but shall have no Vote, unless they be equally divided.

The Senate shall chuse their other Officers, and also a President pro tempore, in the Absence of the Vice President, or when he shall exercise the Office of President of the United States.

The Senate shall have the sole Power to try all Impeachments. When sitting for that Purpose, they shall be on Oath or Affirmation. When the President of the United States is tried, the Chief Justice shall preside: And no Person shall be convicted without the Concurrence of two thirds of the Members present.

Judgment in Cases of Impeachment shall not extend further than to removal from Office, and disqualification to hold and enjoy any Office of honor, Trust or Profit under the United States: but the Party convicted shall nevertheless be liable and subject to Indictment, Trial, Judgment and Punishment, according to Law.

Section. 4.

The Times, Places and Manner of holding Elections for Senators and Representatives, shall be prescribed in each State by the Legislature thereof; but the Congress may at any time by Law make or alter such Regulations, except as to the Places of chusing Senators.

The Congress shall assemble at least once in every Year, and such Meeting shall be on the first Monday in December, unless they shall by Law appoint a different Day.

Section. 5.

Each House shall be the Judge of the Elections, Returns and Qualifications of its own Members, and a Majority of each shall constitute a Quorum to do Business; but a smaller Number may adjourn from day to day, and may be authorized to compel the Attendance of absent Members, in such Manner, and under such Penalties as each House may provide.

Each House may determine the Rules of its Proceedings, punish its Members for disorderly Behaviour, and, with the Concurrence of two thirds, expel a Member.

Each House shall keep a Journal of its Proceedings, and from time to time publish the same, excepting such Parts as may in their Judgment require Secrecy; and the Yeas and Nays of the Members of either House on any question shall, at the Desire of one fifth of those Present, be entered on the Journal.

Neither House, during the Session of Congress, shall, without the Consent of the other, adjourn for more than three days, nor to any other Place than that in which the two Houses shall be sitting.

Section. 6.

The Senators and Representatives shall receive a Compensation for their Services, to be ascertained by Law, and paid out of the Treasury of the United States. They shall in all Cases, except Treason, Felony and Breach of the Peace, be privileged from Arrest during their Attendance at the Session of their respective Houses, and in going to and returning from the same; and for any Speech or Debate in either House, they shall not be questioned in any other Place.

No Senator or Representative shall, during the Time for which he was elected, be appointed to any civil Office under the Authority of the United States, which shall have been created, or the Emoluments whereof shall have been encreased during such time; and no Person holding any Office under the United States, shall be a Member of either House during his Continuance in Office.

Section. 7.

All Bills for raising Revenue shall originate in the House of Representatives; but the Senate may propose or concur with Amendments as on other Bills.

Every Bill which shall have passed the House of Representatives and the Senate, shall, before it become a Law, be presented to the President of the United States: If he approve he shall sign it, but if not he shall return it, with his Objections to that House in which it shall have originated, who shall enter the Objections at large on their Journal, and proceed to reconsider it. If after such Reconsideration two thirds of that House shall agree to pass the Bill, it shall be sent, together with the Objections, to the other House, by which it shall likewise be reconsidered, and if approved by two thirds of that House, it shall become a Law. But in all such Cases the Votes of both Houses shall be determined by yeas and Nays, and the Names of the Persons voting for and against the Bill shall be entered on the Journal of each House respectively. If any Bill shall not be returned by the President within ten Days (Sundays excepted) after it shall have been presented to him, the Same shall be a Law, in like Manner as if he had signed it, unless the Congress by their Adjournment prevent its Return, in which Case it shall not be a Law.

Every Order, Resolution, or Vote to which the Concurrence of the Senate and House of Representatives may be necessary (except on a question of Adjournment) shall be presented to the President of the United States; and before the Same shall take Effect, shall be approved by him, or being disapproved by him, shall be repassed by two thirds of the Senate and House of Representatives, according to the Rules and Limitations prescribed in the Case of a Bill.

Section. 8.

The Congress shall have Power To lay and collect Taxes, Duties, Imposts and Excises, to pay the Debts and provide for the common Defence and general Welfare of the United States; but all Duties, Imposts and Excises shall be uniform throughout the United States;

To borrow Money on the credit of the United States;

To regulate Commerce with foreign Nations, and among the several States, and with the Indian Tribes;

To establish an uniform Rule of Naturalization, and uniform Laws on the subject of Bankruptcies throughout the United States;

To coin Money, regulate the Value thereof, and of foreign Coin, and fix the Standard of Weights and Measures;

To provide for the Punishment of counterfeiting the Securities and current Coin of the United States;

To establish Post Offices and post Roads;

To promote the Progress of Science and useful Arts, by securing for limited Times to Authors and Inventors the exclusive Right to their respective Writings and Discoveries;

To constitute Tribunals inferior to the supreme Court;

To define and punish Piracies and Felonies committed on the high Seas, and Offences against the Law of Nations;

To declare War, grant Letters of Marque and Reprisal, and make Rules concerning Captures on Land and Water;

To raise and support Armies, but no Appropriation of Money to that Use shall be for a longer Term than two Years;

To provide and maintain a Navy;

To make Rules for the Government and Regulation of the land and naval Forces;

To provide for calling forth the Militia to execute the Laws of the Union, suppress Insurrections and repel Invasions;

To provide for organizing, arming, and disciplining, the Militia, and for governing such Part of them as may be employed in the Service of the United States, reserving to the States respectively, the Appointment of the Officers, and the Authority of training the Militia according to the discipline prescribed by Congress;

To exercise exclusive Legislation in all Cases whatsoever, over such District (not exceeding ten Miles square) as may, by Cession of particular States, and the Acceptance of Congress, become the Seat of the Government of the United States, and to exercise like Authority over all Places purchased by the Consent of the Legislature of the State in which the Same shall be, for the Erection of Forts, Magazines, Arsenals, dock-Yards, and other needful Buildings;--And

To make all Laws which shall be necessary and proper for carrying into Execution the foregoing Powers, and all other Powers vested by this Constitution in the Government of the United States, or in any Department or Officer thereof.

Section. 9.

The Migration or Importation of such Persons as any of the States now existing shall think proper to admit, shall not be prohibited by the Congress prior to the Year one thousand eight hundred and eight, but a Tax or duty may be imposed on such Importation, not exceeding ten dollars for each Person.

The Privilege of the Writ of Habeas Corpus shall not be suspended, unless when in Cases of Rebellion or Invasion the public Safety may require it.

No Bill of Attainder or ex post facto Law shall be passed.

No Capitation, or other direct, Tax shall be laid, unless in Proportion to the Census or enumeration herein before directed to be taken.

No Tax or Duty shall be laid on Articles exported from any State.

No Preference shall be given by any Regulation of Commerce or Revenue to the Ports of one State over those of another; nor shall

Vessels bound to, or from, one State, be obliged to enter, clear, or pay Duties in another.

No Money shall be drawn from the Treasury, but in Consequence of Appropriations made by Law; and a regular Statement and Account of the Receipts and Expenditures of all public Money shall be published from time to time.

No Title of Nobility shall be granted by the United States: And no Person holding any Office of Profit or Trust under them, shall, without the Consent of the Congress, accept of any present, Emolument, Office, or Title, of any kind whatever, from any King, Prince, or foreign State.

Section. 10.

No State shall enter into any Treaty, Alliance, or Confederation; grant Letters of Marque and Reprisal; coin Money; emit Bills of Credit; make any Thing but gold and silver Coin a Tender in Payment of Debts; pass any Bill of Attainder, ex post facto Law, or Law impairing the Obligation of Contracts, or grant any Title of Nobility.

No State shall, without the Consent of the Congress, lay any Imposts or Duties on Imports or Exports, except what may be absolutely necessary for executing it's inspection Laws: and the net Produce of all Duties and Imposts, laid by any State on Imports or Exports, shall be for the Use of the Treasury of the United States; and all such Laws shall be subject to the Revision and Controul of the Congress.

No State shall, without the Consent of Congress, lay any Duty of Tonnage, keep Troops, or Ships of War in time of Peace, enter into any Agreement or Compact with another State, or with a foreign Power, or engage in War, unless actually invaded, or in such imminent Danger as will not admit of delay.

Article. II.

Section. 1.

The executive Power shall be vested in a President of the United States of America. He shall hold his Office during the Term of four Years, and, together with the Vice President, chosen for the same Term, be elected, as follows:

Each State shall appoint, in such Manner as the Legislature thereof may direct, a Number of Electors, equal to the whole Number of Senators and Representatives to which the State may be entitled in the Congress: but no Senator or Representative, or Person holding an Office of Trust or Profit under the United States, shall be appointed an Elector.

The Electors shall meet in their respective States, and vote by Ballot for two Persons, of whom one at least shall not be an Inhabitant of the same State with themselves. And they shall make a List of all the Persons voted for, and of the Number of Votes for each; which List they shall sign and certify, and transmit sealed to the Seat of the Government of the United States, directed to the President of the Senate. The President of the Senate shall, in the Presence of the Senate and House of Representatives, open all the Certificates, and the Votes shall then be counted. The Person having the greatest Number of Votes shall be the President, if such Number be a Majority of the whole Number of Electors appointed; and if there be more than one who have such Majority, and have an equal Number of Votes, then the House of Representatives shall immediately chuse by Ballot one of them for President; and if no Person have a Majority, then from the five highest on the List the said House shall in like Manner chuse the President. But in chusing the President, the Votes shall be taken by States, the Representation from each State having one Vote; A quorum for this purpose shall consist of a Member or Members from two thirds of the States, and a Majority of all the States shall be necessary to a Choice. In every Case, after the Choice of the President, the Person having the greatest Number of Votes of the Electors shall be the Vice President. But if there should remain two or more who have equal Votes, the Senate shall chuse from them by Ballot the Vice President.

The Congress may determine the Time of chusing the Electors, and the Day on which they shall give their Votes; which Day shall be the same throughout the United States.

No Person except a natural born Citizen, or a Citizen of the United States, at the time of the Adoption of this Constitution, shall be eligible to the Office of President; neither shall any Person be eligible to that Office who shall not have attained to the Age of thirty five Years, and been fourteen Years a Resident within the United States.

In Case of the Removal of the President from Office, or of his Death, Resignation, or Inability to discharge the Powers and Duties of the said Office, the Same shall devolve on the Vice President, and the Congress may by Law provide for the Case of Removal, Death, Resignation or Inability, both of the President and Vice President, declaring what Officer shall then act as President, and such Officer shall act accordingly, until the Disability be removed, or a President shall be elected.

The President shall, at stated Times, receive for his Services, a Compensation, which shall neither be increased nor diminished during the Period for which he shall have been elected, and he shall not receive within that Period any other Emolument from the United States, or any of them.

Before he enter on the Execution of his Office, he shall take the following Oath or Affirmation:--"I do solemnly swear (or affirm) that I will faithfully execute the Office of President of the United States, and will to the best of my Ability, preserve, protect and defend the Constitution of the United States."

Section. 2.

The President shall be Commander in Chief of the Army and Navy of the United States, and of the Militia of the several States, when called into the actual Service of the United States; he may require the Opinion, in writing, of the principal Officer in each of the executive Departments, upon any Subject relating to the Duties of their respective Offices, and he shall have Power to grant Reprieves and Pardons for Offences against the United States, except in Cases of Impeachment.

He shall have Power, by and with the Advice and Consent of the Senate, to make Treaties, provided two thirds of the Senators present concur; and he shall nominate, and by and with the Advice and Consent of the Senate, shall appoint Ambassadors, other public Ministers and Consuls, Judges of the supreme Court, and all other Officers of the United States, whose Appointments are not herein otherwise provided for, and which shall be established by Law: but the Congress may by Law vest the Appointment of such inferior Officers, as they think proper, in the President alone, in the Courts of Law, or in the Heads of Departments.

The President shall have Power to fill up all Vacancies that may happen during the Recess of the Senate, by granting Commissions which shall expire at the End of their next Session.

Section. 3.

He shall from time to time give to the Congress Information of the State of the Union, and recommend to their Consideration such Measures as he shall judge necessary and expedient; he may, on extraordinary Occasions, convene both Houses, or either of them, and in Case of Disagreement between them, with Respect to the Time of Adjournment, he may adjourn them to such Time as he shall think proper; he shall receive Ambassadors and other public Ministers; he shall take Care that the Laws be faithfully executed, and shall Commission all the Officers of the United States.

Section. 4.

The President, Vice President and all civil Officers of the United States, shall be removed from Office on Impeachment for, and Conviction of, Treason, Bribery, or other high Crimes and Misdemeanors.

Article III.

Section. 1.

The judicial Power of the United States shall be vested in one supreme Court, and in such inferior Courts as the Congress may from time to time ordain and establish. The Judges, both of the supreme and inferior Courts, shall hold their Offices during good Behaviour, and shall, at stated Times, receive for their Services a Compensation, which shall not be diminished during their Continuance in Office.

Section. 2.

The judicial Power shall extend to all Cases, in Law and Equity, arising under this Constitution, the Laws of the United States, and Treaties made, or which shall be made, under their Authority;--to all Cases affecting Ambassadors, other public Ministers and Consuls;--to all Cases of admiralty and maritime Jurisdiction;--to Controversies to which the United States shall be a Party;--to Controversies between two or more States;-- between a State and Citizens of another State,-- between Citizens of different States,--between Citizens of the same State claiming Lands under Grants of different States, and between a State, or the Citizens thereof, and foreign States, Citizens or Subjects.

In all Cases affecting Ambassadors, other public Ministers and Consuls, and those in which a State shall be Party, the supreme Court shall have original Jurisdiction. In all the other Cases before mentioned, the supreme Court shall have appellate Jurisdiction, both as to Law and Fact, with such Exceptions, and under such Regulations as the Congress shall make.

The Trial of all Crimes, except in Cases of Impeachment, shall be by Jury; and such Trial shall be held in the State where the said Crimes shall have been committed; but when not committed within any State, the Trial shall be at such Place or Places as the Congress may by Law have directed.

Section. 3.

Treason against the United States, shall consist only in levying War against them, or in adhering to their Enemies, giving them Aid and Comfort. No Person shall be convicted of Treason unless on the Testimony of two Witnesses to the same overt Act, or on Confession in open Court.

The Congress shall have Power to declare the Punishment of Treason, but no Attainder of Treason shall work Corruption of Blood, or Forfeiture except during the Life of the Person attainted.

Article. IV.

Section. 1.

Full Faith and Credit shall be given in each State to the public Acts, Records, and judicial Proceedings of every other State. And the Congress may by general Laws prescribe the Manner in which such Acts, Records and Proceedings shall be proved, and the Effect thereof.

Section. 2.

The Citizens of each State shall be entitled to all Privileges and Immunities of Citizens in the several States.

A Person charged in any State with Treason, Felony, or other Crime, who shall flee from Justice, and be found in another State, shall on Demand of the executive Authority of the State from which he fled, be delivered up, to be removed to the State having Jurisdiction of the Crime.

No Person held to Service or Labour in one State, under the Laws thereof, escaping into another, shall, in Consequence of any Law or Regulation therein, be discharged from such Service or Labour, but shall be delivered up on Claim of the Party to whom such Service or Labour may be due.

Section. 3.

New States may be admitted by the Congress into this Union; but no new State shall be formed or erected within the Jurisdiction of any other State; nor any State be formed by the Junction of two or more States, or Parts of States, without the Consent of the Legislatures of the States concerned as well as of the Congress.

The Congress shall have Power to dispose of and make all needful Rules and Regulations respecting the Territory or other Property belonging to the United States; and nothing in this Constitution shall be so construed as to Prejudice any Claims of the United States, or of any particular State.

Section. 4.

The United States shall guarantee to every State in this Union a Republican Form of Government, and shall protect each of them against Invasion; and on Application of the Legislature, or of the Executive (when the Legislature cannot be convened), against domestic Violence.

Article. V.

The Congress, whenever two thirds of both Houses shall deem it necessary, shall propose Amendments to this Constitution, or, on the Application of the Legislatures of two thirds of the several States, shall call a Convention for proposing Amendments, which, in either Case, shall be valid to all Intents and Purposes, as Part of this Constitution, when ratified by the Legislatures of three fourths of the several States, or by Conventions in three fourths thereof, as the one or the other Mode of Ratification may be proposed by the Congress; Provided that no Amendment which may be made prior to the Year One thousand eight hundred and eight shall in any Manner affect the first and fourth Clauses in the Ninth Section of the first Article; and that no State, without its Consent, shall be deprived of its equal Suffrage in the Senate.

Article. VI.

All Debts contracted and Engagements entered into, before the Adoption of this Constitution, shall be as valid against the United States under this Constitution, as under the Confederation.

This Constitution, and the Laws of the United States which shall be made in Pursuance thereof; and all Treaties made, or which shall be made, under the Authority of the United States, shall be the supreme Law of the Land; and the Judges in every State shall be bound thereby, any Thing in the Constitution or Laws of any State to the Contrary notwithstanding.

The Senators and Representatives before mentioned, and the Members of the several State Legislatures, and all executive and judicial Officers, both of the United States and of the several States, shall be bound by Oath or Affirmation, to support this Constitution; but no religious Test shall ever be required as a Qualification to any Office or public Trust under the United States.

Article. VII.

The Ratification of the Conventions of nine States, shall be sufficient for the Establishment of this Constitution between the States so ratifying the Same.

The Word, "the," being interlined between the seventh and eighth Lines of the first Page, the Word "Thirty" being partly written on an Erazure in the fifteenth Line of the first Page, The Words "is tried" being interlined between the thirty second and thirty third Lines of the first Page and the Word "the" being interlined between the forty third and forty fourth Lines of the second Page.

AMENDMENTS TO THE CONSTITUTION

Congress OF THE United States

begun and held at the City of New-York, on Wednesday the fourth of March, one thousand seven hundred and eighty nine.

THE Conventions of a number of the States, having at the time of their adopting the Constitution, expressed a desire, in order to prevent misconstruction or abuse of its powers, that further declaratory and restrictive clauses should be added: And as extending the ground of public confidence in the Government, will best ensure the beneficent ends of its institution.

RESOLVED by the Senate and House of Representatives of the United States of America, in Congress assembled, two thirds of both Houses concurring, that the following Articles be proposed to the Legislatures of the several States, as amendments to the Constitution of the United States, all, or any of which Articles, when ratified by three fourths of the said Legislatures, to be valid to all intents and purposes, as part of the said Constitution; viz.

ARTICLES in addition to, and Amendment of the Constitution of the United States of America, proposed by Congress, and ratified by the Legislatures of the several States, pursuant to the fifth Article of the original Constitution.

Article the first. .... After the first enumeration required by the first Article of the Constitution, there shall be one Representative for every thirty thousand, until the number shall amount to one hundred, after which, the proportion shall be so regulated by Congress, that there shall be not less than one hundred Representatives, nor less than one Representative for every forty thousand persons, until the number of Representatives shall amount to two hundred, after which the proportion shall be so regulated by Congress, that there shall not be less than two hundred Representatives, nor more than one Representative for every fifty thousand persons.

Article the second. .... No law, varying the compensation for the services of the Senators and Representatives, shall take effect, until an election of Representatives shall have intervened.

Note: The following text is a transcription of the first 10 amendments to the Constitution in their original form. These amendments were ratified December 15, 1791, and form what is known as the "Bill of Rights."

Article [I]

Congress shall make no law respecting an establishment of religion, or prohibiting the free exercise thereof; or abridging the freedom of speech, or of the press; or the right of the people peaceably to assemble, and to petition the Government for a redress of grievances.

Article [II]

A well regulated Militia, being necessary to the security of a free State, the right of the people to keep and bear Arms, shall not be infringed.

Article [III]

No Soldier shall, in time of peace be quartered in any house, without the consent of the Owner, nor in time of war, but in a manner to be prescribed by law.

Article [IV]

The right of the people to be secure in their persons, houses, papers, and effects, against unreasonable searches and seizures, shall not be violated, and no Warrants shall issue, but upon probable cause, supported by Oath or affirmation, and particularly describing the place to be searched, and the persons or things to be seized.

Article [V]

No person shall be held to answer for a capital, or otherwise infamous crime, unless on a presentment or indictment of a Grand Jury, except in cases arising in the land or naval forces, or in the Militia, when in actual service in time of War or public danger; nor shall any person be subject for the same offence to be twice put in jeopardy of life or limb; nor shall be compelled in any criminal case to be a witness against himself, nor be deprived of life, liberty, or property, without due process of law; nor shall private property be taken for public use, without just compensation.

Article [VI]

In all criminal prosecutions, the accused shall enjoy the right to a speedy and public trial, by an impartial jury of the State and district wherein the crime shall have been committed, which district shall have been previously ascertained by law, and to be informed of the nature and cause of the accusation; to be confronted with the witnesses against him; to have compulsory process for obtaining witnesses in his favor, and to have the Assistance of Counsel for his defence.

Article [VII]

In Suits at common law, where the value in controversy shall exceed twenty dollars, the right of trial by jury shall be preserved, and no fact tried by a jury, shall be otherwise re-examined in any Court of the United States, than according to the rules of the common law.

Article [VIII]

Excessive bail shall not be required, nor excessive fines imposed, nor cruel and unusual punishments inflicted.

Article [IX]

The enumeration in the Constitution, of certain rights, shall not be construed to deny or disparage others retained by the people.

Article [X]

The powers not delegated to the United States by the Constitution, nor prohibited by it to the States, are reserved to the States respectively, or to the people.

[Article XI]

Passed by Congress March 4, 1794. Ratified February 7, 1795.
Note: Article III, section 2, of the Constitution was modified by amendment 11.

The Judicial power of the United States shall not be construed to extend to any suit in law or equity, commenced or prosecuted against one of the United States by Citizens of another State, or by Citizens or Subjects of any Foreign State.

[Article XII]

Passed by Congress December 9, 1803. Ratified June 15, 1804.
Note: A portion of Article II, section 1 of the Constitution was superseded by the 12th amendment.

The Electors shall meet in their respective states, and vote by ballot for President and Vice-President, one of whom, at least, shall not be an inhabitant of the same state with themselves; they shall name in their ballots the person voted for as President, and in distinct ballots the person voted for as Vice-President, and they shall make distinct lists of all persons voted for as President, and of all persons voted for as Vice-President, and of the number of votes for each, which lists they shall sign and certify, and transmit sealed to the seat of the government of the United States, directed to the President of the Senate;--The President of the Senate shall, in the presence of the Senate and House of Representatives, open all the certificates and the votes shall then be counted;--The person having the greatest number of votes for President, shall be the President, if such number be a majority of the whole number of Electors appointed; and if no person have such majority, then from the persons having the highest numbers not exceeding three on the list of those voted for as President, the House of Representatives shall choose immediately, by ballot, the President. But in choosing the President, the votes shall be taken by states, the representation from each state having one vote; a quorum for this purpose shall consist of a member or members from two-thirds of the states, and a majority of all the states shall be necessary to a choice. And if the House of Representatives shall not choose a President whenever the right of choice shall devolve upon them, before the fourth day of March next

following, then the Vice-President shall act as President, as in the case
of the death or other constitutional disability of the President.14 --
The person having the greatest number of votes as Vice-President, shall
be the Vice-President, if such number be a majority of the whole number of Electors appointed, and if no person have a majority, then from
the two highest numbers on the list, the Senate shall choose the Vice-
President; a quorum for the purpose shall consist of two-thirds of the
whole number of Senators, and a majority of the whole number shall be
necessary to a choice. But no person constitutionally ineligible to the
office of President shall be eligible to that of Vice-President of the
United States.

Article XIII

Passed by Congress January 31, 1865. Ratified December 6, 1865.
*Note: A portion of Article IV, section 2, of the Constitution was superseded by
the 13th amendment.*

   1: Neither slavery nor involuntary servitude, except as a punishment for crime whereof the party shall have been duly convicted,
shall exist within the United States, or any place subject to their jurisdiction.
   2: Congress shall have power to enforce this article by appropriate legislation.

Article XIV

Passed by Congress June 13, 1866. Ratified July 9, 1868.
*Note: Article I, section 2, of the Constitution was modified by section 2 of the
14th amendment.*

   1: All persons born or naturalized in the United States, and
subject to the jurisdiction thereof, are citizens of the United States and
of the State wherein they reside. No State shall make or enforce any
law which shall abridge the privileges or immunities of citizens of the
United States; nor shall any State deprive any person of life, liberty, or
property, without due process of law; nor deny to any person within its
jurisdiction the equal protection of the laws.

2: Representatives shall be apportioned among the several States according to their respective numbers, counting the whole number of persons in each State, excluding Indians not taxed. But when the right to vote at any election for the choice of electors for President and Vice President of the United States, Representatives in Congress, the Executive and Judicial officers of a State, or the members of the Legislature thereof, is denied to any of the male inhabitants of such State, being twenty-one years of age,15 and citizens of the United States, or in any way abridged, except for participation in rebellion, or other crime, the basis of representation therein shall be reduced in the proportion which the number of such male citizens shall bear to the whole number of male citizens twenty-one years of age in such State.

3: No person shall be a Senator or Representative in Congress, or elector of President and Vice President, or hold any office, civil or military, under the United States, or under any State, who, having previously taken an oath, as a member of Congress, or as an officer of the United States, or as a member of any State legislature, or as an executive or judicial officer of any State, to support the Constitution of the United States, shall have engaged in insurrection or rebellion against the same, or given aid or comfort to the enemies thereof. But Congress may by a vote of two-thirds of each House, remove such disability.

4: The validity of the public debt of the United States, authorized by law, including debts incurred for payment of pensions and bounties for services in suppressing insurrection or rebellion, shall not be questioned. But neither the United States nor any State shall assume or pay any debt or obligation incurred in aid of insurrection or rebellion against the United States, or any claim for the loss or emancipation of any slave; but all such debts, obligations and claims shall be held illegal and void.

5: The Congress shall have power to enforce, by appropriate legislation, the provisions of this article.

Article XV

Passed by Congress February 26, 1869. Ratified February 3, 1870.

1: The right of citizens of the United States to vote shall not be denied or abridged by the United States or by any State on account of race, color, or previous condition of servitude.

2: The Congress shall have power to enforce this article by appropriate legislation.

Article XVI

Passed by Congress July 2, 1909. Ratified February 3, 1913.
Note: Article I, section 9, of the Constitution was modified by amendment 16.

The Congress shall have power to lay and collect taxes on incomes, from whatever source derived, without apportionment among the several States, and without regard to any census or enumeration.

[Article XVII]

Passed by Congress May 13, 1912. Ratified April 8, 1913.
Note: Article I, section 3, of the Constitution was modified by the 17th amendment.

1: The Senate of the United States shall be composed of two Senators from each State, elected by the people thereof, for six years; and each Senator shall have one vote. The electors in each State shall have the qualifications requisite for electors of the most numerous branch of the State legislatures.

2: When vacancies happen in the representation of any State in the Senate, the executive authority of such State shall issue writs of election to fill such vacancies: Provided, That the legislature of any State may empower the executive thereof to make temporary appointments until the people fill the vacancies by election as the legislature may direct.
3: This amendment shall not be so construed as to affect the election or term of any Senator chosen before it becomes valid as part of the Constitution.

Article [XVIII]

Passed by Congress December 18, 1917. Ratified January 16, 1919. Repealed by the Twenty-First Amendment.

1: After one year from the ratification of this article the manufacture, sale, or transportation of intoxicating liquors within, the importation thereof into, or the exportation thereof from the United States and all territory subject to the jurisdiction thereof for beverage purposes is hereby prohibited.

2: The Congress and the several States shall have concurrent power to enforce this article by appropriate legislation.

3: This article shall be inoperative unless it shall have been ratified as an amendment to the Constitution by the legislatures of the several States, as provided in the Constitution, within seven years from the date of the submission hereof to the States by the Congress.

Article [XIX]

Passed by Congress June 4, 1919. Ratified August 18, 1920.

1: The right of citizens of the United States to vote shall not be denied or abridged by the United States or by any State on account of sex.

2: Congress shall have power to enforce this article by appropriate legislation.

Article [XX]

Passed by Congress March 2, 1932. Ratified January 23, 1933.
Note: Article I, section 4, of the Constitution was modified by section 2 of this amendment. In addition, a portion of the 12th amendment was superseded by section 3.

1: The terms of the President and Vice President shall end at noon on the 20th day of January, and the terms of Senators and Representatives at noon on the 3d day of January, of the years in which such terms would have ended if this article had not been ratified; and the terms of their successors shall then begin.

2: The Congress shall assemble at least once in every year, and such meeting shall begin at noon on the 3d day of January, unless they shall by law appoint a different day.

3: If, at the time fixed for the beginning of the term of the President, the President elect shall have died, the Vice President elect shall become President. If a President shall not have been chosen before the time fixed for the beginning of his term, or if the President elect shall have failed to qualify, then the Vice President elect shall act as President until a President shall have qualified; and the Congress may by law provide for the case wherein neither a President elect nor a Vice President elect shall have qualified, declaring who shall then act as President, or the manner in which one who is to act shall be selected, and such person shall act accordingly until a President or Vice President shall have qualified.

4: The Congress may by law provide for the case of the death of any of the persons from whom the House of Representatives may choose a President whenever the right of choice shall have devolved upon them, and for the case of the death of any of the persons from whom the Senate may choose a Vice President whenever the right of choice shall have devolved upon them.

5: Sections 1 and 2 shall take effect on the 15th day of October following the ratification of this article.

6: This article shall be inoperative unless it shall have been ratified as an amendment to the Constitution by the legislatures of three-fourths of the several States within seven years from the date of its submission.

Article [XXI]

Passed by Congress February 20, 1933. Ratified December 5, 1933.

1: The eighteenth article of amendment to the Constitution of the United States is hereby repealed.

2: The transportation or importation into any State, Territory, or possession of the United States for delivery or use therein of intoxicating liquors, in violation of the laws thereof, is hereby prohibited.

3: This article shall be inoperative unless it shall have been ratified as an amendment to the Constitution by conventions in the several States, as provided in the Constitution, within seven years from the date of the submission hereof to the States by the Congress.

Amendment XXII

Passed by Congress March 21, 1947. Ratified February 27, 1951.

1: No person shall be elected to the office of the President more than twice, and no person who has held the office of President, or acted as President, for more than two years of a term to which some other person was elected President shall be elected to the office of the President more than once. But this article shall not apply to any person holding the office of President when this article was proposed by the Congress, and shall not prevent any person who may be holding the office of President, or acting as President, during the term within which this article becomes operative from holding the office of President or acting as President during the remainder of such term.

2: This article shall be inoperative unless it shall have been ratified as an amendment to the Constitution by the legislatures of three-fourths of the several states within seven years from the date of its submission to the states by the Congress.

Amendment XXIII

Passed by Congress June 16, 1960. Ratified March 29, 1961.

1: The District constituting the seat of government of the United States shall appoint in such manner as the Congress may direct: A number of electors of President and Vice President equal to the whole number of Senators and Representatives in Congress to which the District would be entitled if it were a state, but in no event more than the least populous state; they shall be in addition to those appointed by the states, but they shall be considered, for the purposes of the election of President and Vice President, to be electors appointed by a state; and they shall meet in the District and perform such duties as provided by the twelfth article of amendment.

2: The Congress shall have power to enforce this article by appropriate legislation.

Amendment XXIV

Passed by Congress August 27, 1962. Ratified January 23, 1964.

1. The right of citizens of the United States to vote in any primary or other election for President or Vice President, for electors for President or Vice President, or for Senator or Representative in

Congress, shall not be denied or abridged by the United States or any state by reason of failure to pay any poll tax or other tax.

2. The Congress shall have power to enforce this article by appropriate legislation.

Amendment XXV

Passed by Congress July 6, 1965. Ratified February 10, 1967. Note: Article II, section 1, of the Constitution was affected by the 25th amendment.

1: In case of the removal of the President from office or of his death or resignation, the Vice President shall become President.

2: Whenever there is a vacancy in the office of the Vice President, the President shall nominate a Vice President who shall take office upon confirmation by a majority vote of both Houses of Congress.

3: Whenever the President transmits to the President pro tempore of the Senate and the Speaker of the House of Representatives his written declaration that he is unable to discharge the powers and duties of his office, and until he transmits to them a written declaration to the contrary, such powers and duties shall be discharged by the Vice President as Acting President.

4: Whenever the Vice President and a majority of either the principal officers of the executive departments or of such other body as Congress may by law provide, transmit to the President pro tempore of the Senate and the Speaker of the House of Representatives their written declaration that the President is unable to discharge the powers and duties of his office, the Vice President shall immediately assume the powers and duties of the office as Acting President.

Thereafter, when the President transmits to the President pro tempore of the Senate and the Speaker of the House of Representatives his written declaration that no inability exists, he shall resume the powers and duties of his office unless the Vice President and a majority of either the principal officers of the executive department or of such other body as Congress may by law provide, transmit within four days to the President pro tempore of the Senate and the Speaker of the House of Representatives their written declaration that the President is unable to discharge the powers and duties of his office. Thereupon

Congress shall decide the issue, assembling within forty-eight hours for that purpose if not in session. If the Congress, within twenty-one days after receipt of the latter written declaration, or, if Congress is not in session, within twenty-one days after Congress is required to assemble, determines by two-thirds vote of both Houses that the President is unable to discharge the powers and duties of his office, the Vice President shall continue to discharge the same as Acting President; otherwise, the President shall resume the powers and duties of his office.

Amendment XXVI

Passed by Congress March 23, 1971. Ratified July 1, 1971.

1: The right of citizens of the United States, who are 18 years of age or older, to vote, shall not be denied or abridged by the United States or any state on account of age.

2: The Congress shall have the power to enforce this article by appropriate legislation.

Amendment XXVII

Originally proposed September 25, 1789, as part of the twelve-articled Bill of Rights. This article was not ratified along together with the first ten Amendments, which became effective on December 15, 1791. The Twenty-Seventh Amendment was ratified on May 7, 1992, by the vote of Michigan.

No law varying the compensation for the services of the Senators and Representatives shall take effect until an election of Representatives shall have intervened.

Rules for the Regulation of the Navy of the United Colonies of North-America; 1775 (Liberty Day Booklet, Appendix A)

Established for Preserving their Rights and Defending their Liberties, and for Encouraging all those who Feel for their Country, to enter into its service in that way in which they can be most Useful.

ART. 1. The Commanders of all ships and vessels belonging to the THIRTEEN UNITED COLONIES, are strictly required to shew in themselves a good example of honor and virtue to their officers and men, and to be very vigilant in inspecting the behaviour of all such as are under them, and to discountenance and suppress all dissolute, immoral and disorderly practices; and also, such as are contrary to the rules of discipline and obedience, and to correct those who are guilty of the same according to the usage of the sea.

ART. 2. The Commanders of the ships of the Thirteen United Colonies are to take care that divine service be performed twice a day on board, and a sermon preached on Sundays, unless bad weather or other extraordinary accidents prevent it.

ART. 3. If any shall be heard to swear, curse or blaspheme the name of God, the Captain is strictly enjoined to punish them for every offence, by causing them to wear a wooden collar or some other shameful badge of distinction, for so long a time as he shall judge proper:-- If he be a commissioned officer he shall forfeit one shilling for each offence, and a warrant or inferior officer, six- pence: He who is guilty of drunkenness (if a seaman) shall be put in irons until he is sober, but if an officer, he shall forfeit two days pay.

****

SOURCE: *Rules for the Regulation of the Navy of the United Colonies of North-America...* (Philadelphia: William and Thomas Bradford, 1775; reprinted Washington, D.C.: Naval Historical Foundation, 1944). The text is abridged and reproduced here exactly as in the original, following the original use of capitalization and italics.

FRIDAY, JUNE 30, 1775 (adoption of Rules and Regulations
of the continental Army)

Article I. That every officer who shall be retained, and every soldier who shall serve in the Continental Army, shall, at the time of his acceptance of his commission or inlistment, subscribe these rules and regulations. And that the officers and soldiers, already of that army, shall also, as soon as may be, subscribe the same; from the time of which subscription every officer and soldier, shall be bound by those regulations. But if any of the officers or soldiers, now of the said army, do not subscribe these rules and regulations, then they may be retained in the said army, subject to the rules and regulations under which they entered into the service, or be discharged from the service, at the option of the Commander in chief.

Art. II. It is earnestly recommended to all officers and soldiers, diligently to attend Divine Service; and all officers and soldiers who shall behave indecently or irreverently at any place of Divine Worship, shall, if commissioned officers, be brought before a court-martial, there to be publicly and severely reprimanded by the President; if non-commissioned officers or soldiers, every person so offending, shall, for his first offence, forfeit One Sixth of a Dollar, to be deducted out of his next pay; for the second offence, he shall not only forfeit a like sum, but be confined for twenty-four hours, and for every like offence, shall suffer and pay in like manner; which money so forfeited, shall be applied to the use of the sick soldiers of the troop or company to which the offender belongs.

Art. III. Whatsoever non-commissioned officer or soldier shall use any profane oath or execration, shall incur the penalties expressed in the second article; and if a commissioned officer be thus guilty of profane cursing or swearing, he shall forfeit and pay for each and every such offence, the sum of Four Shillings, lawful money.

***

Art. XLVII. Whatsoever commissioned officer shall be convicted before a general court-martial, of behaving in a scandalous, infamous manner, such as is unbecoming the character of an officer and a gentleman, shall be discharged from the service. . . .

TUESDAY, NOVEMBER 7, 1775

Resolved, That the following additions and alterations or amendments, be made in the RULES and REGULATIONS of the continental Army, viz. . . .

All commissioned Officers found guilty by a general court-martial of any fraud or embezzlement, shall forfeit all his pay, be ipso facto cashiered, and deemed unfit for further service as an officer. . . . In all cases where a commissioned officer is cashiered for cowardice or fraud, it be added in the punishment, that the crime, name, place of abode, and punishment of the delinquent be published in the news papers, in and about the camp, and of that colony from which the offender came, or usually resides: after which it shall be deemed scandalous in any officer to associate with him. . . .

SOURCE: *Journals of the Continental Congress 1774-1789, Vol. II* Pages 111-123. Edited and abridged from the original records in the Library of Congress by Worthington Chauncey Ford; Chief, Division of Manuscripts. Washington, DC: Government Printing Office, 1905; Library of Congress, Journals of the Continental Congress, 1774-1789, Volume 3, Pages 331-34.

INSPECTOR GENERAL REFERENCE GUIDE
(AS INCLUDED IN THE LIBERTY DAY BOOKLET)

The military Inspector General in America has traditionally served as "an extension of the eyes, ears, and conscience of the Commander."

Pursuant to the Inspector General Act of 1978, as amended, "the Inspector General of the Department of Defense shall . . . be the principal adviser to the Secretary of Defense for matters relating to the prevention of fraud, waste, and abuse in the programs and operations of the Department." The law also requires the Inspector General "to keep the [Secretary of Defense] and the Congress fully and currently informed . . . concerning fraud and other serious problems, abuses, and deficiencies . . . ." The Inspector General is also obligated by law to "give particular regard to the activities of the internal audit, inspection, and investigative units of the military departments with a view towards avoiding duplication and insuring effective coordination and cooperation."

Anyone who has doubts about the conformity of his or her own conduct with ethical standards and/or with the law should not hesitate to seek advice through the chain of command. Anyone, whether uniformed or civilian, who witnesses what he or she believes to be a violation of ethical standards and/or the law, including but not limited to fraud, waste, or abuse of authority, should report such conduct through the chain of command or either directly to his or her respective service Inspector General (see links listed below) or directly to the Inspector General of the Department of Defense Hotline at 800-424-9098 (e-mail: hotline@dodig.osd.mil).

Made in the USA
Middletown, DE
06 August 2017